# STUDYING FOOTBALL

Football is the most widely played, watched and studied sport in the world. It's hard to develop a full understanding of the significance of sport in global society without understanding the significance of football. *Studying Football* is the first book designed specifically to guide and support the study of football on degree-level courses, across the full range of social-scientific perspectives.

Written by a team of leading international football experts, and considering themes of globalization, corporatization and prejudice and discrimination throughout, it introduces key topics in football studies, including:

- media and celebrity
- fandom and consumption
- identity and gender
- violence
- racism
- corruption.

Every chapter includes up-to-date case study material, a 'Research in Action' section and features to aid student understanding and bring theory to life. *Studying Football* introduces all the key themes and facets of the social-scientific study of football, and is therefore an essential text for students on football studies courses and useful reading for any undergraduates studying the sociology of sport more generally.

**Ellis Cashmore** is the author of *Making Sense of Sports*, *Celebrity Culture* and *Beckham*. He is Visiting Professor of Sociology at Aston University, UK and tweets @elliscashmore.

**Kevin Dixon** is the author of *Consuming Football in Late Modern Life* and 'A woman's place recurring: structuration, football fandom and sub-cultural subservience' (in *Sport in Society*), and the co-editor of *The Impact of the London 2012 Olympic and Paralympic Games: Diminishing Contrasts, Increasing Varieties*. He is Senior Lecturer in Sports Studies at Teesside University, UK and tweets @KevinDixon20.

# STUDYING FOOTBALL

*Edited by Ellis Cashmore and Kevin Dixon*

Routledge
Taylor & Francis Group

LONDON AND NEW YORK

First published 2016
by Routledge
2 Park Square, Milton Park, Abingdon, Oxon OX14 4RN

and by Routledge
711 Third Avenue, New York, NY 10017

*Routledge is an imprint of the Taylor & Francis Group, an informa business*

*British Library Cataloguing-in-Publication Data*
A catalogue record for this book is available from the British Library

*Library of Congress Cataloging in Publication Data*
Names: Cashmore, Ellis, editor. | Dixon, Kevin, editor.Title: Studying football / edited by Ellis Cashmore & Kevin Dixon.Description: Abingdon, Oxon ; New York, NY : Routledge is an imprint of the Taylor & Francis Group, an Informa Business, [2016] | Includes bibliographical references and index.Identifiers: LCCN 2015036970| ISBN 9781138830721 (hardback) | ISBN 9781138830738 (pbk.) | ISBN 9781315737072 (ebook)Subjects: LCSH: Soccer--Study and teaching. | Soccer--Social aspects.Classification: LCC GV943 .S7575 2016 | DDC 796.33407--dc23LC record available at http://lccn.loc.gov/2015036970

ISBN: 978-1-138-83072-1 (hbk)
ISBN: 978-1-138-83073-8 (pbk)
ISBN: 978-1-315-73707-2 (ebk)

Typeset in Bembo
by Fakenham Prepress Solutions, Fakenham, Norfolk NR21 8NN

Printed and bound in Great Britain by Ashford Colour Press Ltd, Gosport, Hampshire

# CONTENTS

# NOTES ON CONTRIBUTORS

## Editors

**Ellis Cashmore** is the author of *Making Sense of Sports*, *Celebrity Culture* and *Beckham*. He is Visiting Professor of Sociology at Aston University, UK and tweets @elliscashmore.

**Kevin Dixon** is the author of *Consuming Football in Late Modern Life* and 'A woman's place recurring: structuration, football fandom and sub-cultural subservience', and the co-editor *of The Impact of the London 2012 Olympic and Paralympic Games: Diminishing Contrasts, Increasing Varieties*. He is Senior Lecturer in Sports Studies at Teesside University, UK and tweets @KevinDixon20.

## Contributors

**Chris Bolsmann** is the co-editor of *Africa's World Cup: Critical Reflections on Play, Patriotism, Spectatorship, and Space* and *South Africa and the Global Game: Football, Apartheid and Beyond*. He is an Associate Professor at California State University Northridge in Los Angeles, USA and tweets @chrisbolsmann.

**Jamie Cleland** is the author of *A Sociology of Football in a Global Context* and co-author of *Football's Dark Side: Corruption, Homophobia, Violence and Racism in the Beautiful Game*. He is Lecturer in the Department of Social Sciences at Loughborough University, UK and tweets @drjamiecleland.

**Gerald Gems** is the author of *The Athletic Crusade: Sport and American Cultural Imperialism*. He is Professor of Health and Physical Education at North Central College, Illinois, USA.

**Richard Haynes** is the author of *BBC Sport in Black and White* and has published extensively on sport and the media. He is Professor of Communications, Media and Culture at the University of Stirling, UK and tweets @rhaynes66.

**Stefan Lawrence** is the co-author of 'Reading Ronaldo: contingent whiteness in the football media'. He is Senior Lecturer in Football Studies at Southampton Solent University, UK and tweets @StefanoLawrence.

**Andrew Manley** is the co-author of 'Disciplinary power, the oligopticon and rhizomatic surveillance in elite sports academies'. He is Lecturer in Sociology at the University of Bath, UK and tweets @ATManley.

**Andrew Parker** is the co-editor of *Sport and Social Identities* and several other books. He is Professor of Sport and Christian Outreach at the University of Gloucestershire, UK.

**Gertrud Pfister** is the co-editor of *Gender and Sport: Changes and Challenges* and several articles on female fans and women's football. She was a member of the FREE project (Football Research in an Enlarged Europe) and is now Professor Emeritus of Sport Sociology at the University of Copenhagen, Denmark.

**Magdalini Pipini** is researching cyber hooliganism. She is Lecturer in Criminology and Cybercrime at Southampton Solent University, UK and tweets @Dr_Pipini.

**Andy Ruddock** is the author of *Investigating Audiences* and *Youth and Media*. He is Senior Lecturer in Communications and Media Studies at Monash University, Australia and tweets @Andyruddock1.

# 1

# INTRODUCTION

*Ellis Cashmore and Kevin Dixon*

---

**Chapter highlights**

- The media's growth has led to an explosive rise in football's global popularity.
- The Neil Franklin case shows how much football has changed since the mid-twentieth century.
- Football is as integral to contemporary society as politics, crime, religion and the family – and, as such, must be studied.
- Studies of violence and racism established an analytical template for football studies.

---

## Cultural rebranding

If you stepped back, you might see football for what it is: 11 grown men kicking a ball in one direction, while another 11 grown men try to move the same ball in the opposite direction. Ridiculous, isn't it? Utterly without purpose or logic. Football's trick is to stop you stepping back. Once inside the football world, you are surrounded by multiple sensations: excitement, suspense, interest, fright, exultation and many more besides. You cheer teams but are not sure exactly why. You buy merchandise that displays your affinity, though the source of that affinity escapes you. You travel distances to watch games that will make no material impact on your life. That's how immersive football is: no one notices how pointless and nonsensical it is. Nothing stands still long enough to study it. In fact, why should we study it at all? Why should we care enough to enquire, examine, analyze, interpret and evaluate a phenomenon that has kept us agreeably captivated for at least 150 years?

The answer can be another question: how can we ignore it? After all, football is inescapable; practically everywhere in the world, populations play and watch the sport. The media carry coverage of games and analysis to all four corners. England's Premier League alone is taken to 212 territories by over 80 different broadcasters, giving it a potential combined audience of 4.7 billion, over 64 per cent of the world's population. Fifa (Fédération Internationale de Football Association), the organization responsible for international football, was founded in 1904. Today it has a capital reserve of $1.52 billion (about £1 billion). Its annual profits vary, but can reach $338 million (£217 million), as they did in 2014, the year of the Brazil World Cup, dropping slightly to $337 million in the following year (Associated Press, 2015). Whichever way you look at it, Fifa is an extremely rich organization, governing the world's most popular and most lucrative sport.

The sport's sharp ascent is directly related to the globalization of the media. Up until the 1990s, the sport was, if the reader will excuse the seeming tautology, a sport. Since then, the actual 90 minutes of competitive activity has become just one feature in a deliriously dramatic narrative. It's also become very bankable. Consider that, in 1992, the pay-per-view broadcaster Sky (then BSkyB) paid a then unheard of £191 million for the rights to screen Premier League matches for five years. 24 years later, the value of a three-year deal was £5.14 billion – itself more than double the value of the previous contract, agreed in 2011.

Is it a coincidence that football's popularity has risen with the increased media coverage, or a case of cause and effect – and if the latter, which is the cause? Some might argue that this is as fruitless as trying to determine whether the chicken preceded the egg, so we should resist over-analyzing what is after all dazzling entertainment. A hungry intellect isn't satisfied with this. There are too many compelling questions. 'Modern football and the modern media are locked together,' wrote Roger Domeneghetti in 2014 (p. xiv). 'I doubt they could live without each other.' Could they?

Take football out of television schedules and there would be gaping holes. Newspapers and magazines would also be deprived of one of their mainstays. And just key 'football' into your search engine and see how many billion hits you get. The media would survive without football, but it would not be so well nourished. It's pointless contemplating whether football could survive without the media because, in a genuine sense, the media is now part of football. Football is just not the same sport that it was in the middle of the twentieth century. We can illustrate this with the case of Neil Franklin.

In 1949, Franklin, who played for Stoke City and the England national team, earned £12 per week, the maximum wage permitted by England's Football Association rules (the maximum wage was an imposed ceiling that remained in place until 1961). Franklin and his teammate George Mountford had their heads turned by the offer of £60 per week plus win bonuses, but the offer came from abroad. Independiente Santa Fe of Bogotá in Colombia proposed the transfer and, seduced by the wages and a handsome signing-on bonus, the players made their way to South America via New York. Colombia was then outside the jurisdiction of Fifa and was effectively a rebel football nation. When Franklin and Mountford returned, they were ostracized, slated as 'greedy traitors', according to Franklin's obituarist Ivan Ponting (1996). 'Suspended for four months by the football authorities and his club, shunned by some of his erstwhile colleagues', Franklin played out the rest of his career carrying a stigma.

This was the middle of the twentieth century. Improbable as it is today, try to imagine if one of England's top players were transferred to a South American club that promised to increase his wages five-fold. The build-up to the move would keep the media busy for weeks, the transfer itself would be monitored minute by minute and the physical move across continents would be screened around the world. Far from being cold-shouldered, the player would be lionized, honoured and celebrated. His adventures in Colombia – today the headquarters of many powerful drug cartels – would be conveyed around the world like a rake's progress, though without the implied decline and fall. Franklin and Mountford's stay in Latin America was ill-starred and short-lived; they returned no better off than when they had set out, and faced ignominy on their return. Had they set forth in 1992, the year Paul Gascoigne left England for Italy, they would have had a very different experience.

There was only one broadcasting organization in Britain at the time of the Franklin–Mountford case. The BBC had been established in 1927 and held a monopoly. Radio was the dominant medium even after 1936, when BBC television began transmitting to a few hundred viewers; even in the early 1950s, few people had TV sets. Commercial television started in 1955 with the launch of ITV. In fact, ITV screened the first live football game, in 1960. The groundbreaking deal to show 26 games live was worth £150,000. Even indexed to inflation, this would be worth only £1.2 million today – compared to the £11 million *per game* that broadcasters paid in the deal struck in 2015. Today's media contracts are reflected in players' earnings. Cristiano Ronaldo earns £47 million ($73 million) in salary, bonuses and endorsements per year, while Lionel Messi limps by on only £42 million (Settimi, 2014). Franklin slipped out and back into the country with no broadcast media to chronicle his move and probably no public interest in the exploits of a self-interested sportsman in pursuit of money.

We repeat: nothing stands still in football. One of the most astonishing instances of cultural rebranding in history has taken place. Once sneered at as an unscrupulous pursuit fit only for the industrial working class, its practitioners disparaged for their money-grabbing and its club owners for being vulgar and *nouveau riche*, association football is now universally recognized as 'the global game', 'the beautiful game' or 'the people's game'. Its players enjoy the same kind of status as movie stars, pop singers or supermodels. It's barely believable that Franklin and Mountford were practically expunged from history for being ahead of their time.

It's simply impossible to analyze any aspect of football in perspective without understanding how the media became a major constituent of the sport. The media will recur in every chapter, sometimes in passing, but mostly as a dominating presence. Practically everything that happens in football is linked to its association with the media. Some instances are obvious. Manchester United's deals with adidas and Chevrolet, worth £75 million and £53 million per year respectively, would be incomprehensible without considering how, once on screen, the club's players become moving advertisements for brands. Up to 24 international broadcasters are present at a Manchester United game, potentially taking the human ads to 650 million outlets in 175 countries. This prompts a thought: are the millions of viewers just watching a game of football, or are they gaping at a two-hour advertisement for sports goods, cars, airlines and the many other products displayed on their screens?

If you're drawn towards the latter interpretation, ask who or what football's governing organizations serve: fans, clubs, nations or global corporations? Today, football's regulating bodies do deals worth millions, sometimes billions, with broadcasters and global corporations that have no interest in the sport itself but value the access that it provides to arguably the biggest and most demographically attractive market the world has ever known. The likes of adidas, Budweiser and Coca-Cola spend prodigiously on football-related advertising. The yearly advertising spend for adidas, for example, is typically worth 13–14 percent of its sales; in 2015, it spent £159 million, much of it on football advertising, according to Julia Kollewe (2015). Fifa's major 'partners' (including Emirates, Sony and Visa) pay world football's governing organization $25–50 million per year to associate their brands with football, reports *Forbes*' Chris Smith (2014). Looked at from this perspective, football's ruling organizations are pimping fans to advertisers (and we return to this in Chapter 10).

This is not as cynical as it sounds; it's merely a reminder that football is a social and cultural institution as well as a 90-minute competition. It might have begun as a straightforward activity pursued by industrial workers on their day off, but it's grown organically, developing new characteristics as it's passed through the generations. Today football is a behemoth, so large and powerful that it can command the attention not just of fans and journalists, but also of students.

We don't think twice about studying politics, crime, religion, the family or any of the other institutions than affect us. Football, it could be argued, affects us as much and, in some cases, more than these. Even those who have no interest in or even hate football can't avoid it: football is inescapable. Every time the football-phobic citizen switches on the radio, watches TV, glances at a newspaper, walks around a supermarket or sees an ad on a hoarding or the side of a bus, he or she is involved. The sport is ubiquitous. It takes up too much of our time, money and emotion to be ignored.

## Solving the puzzles

Football was an activity created to be enjoyed. Participants in the nineteenth century took delight in either playing or watching the spectacle of men demonstrating their physical prowess. What started as a recreational pastime became an occupation, paid labour for industrial workers who were inclined to swap a few years in the factory for a sportsman's life. Not that football was regarded as a sport. Association football resembled a sport, but money perverted the principle of fair play that was so central to 'pure' sports such as cricket, rugby or athletics. Football was more like an industrial enterprise. Like boxing, which was also professional from the nineteenth century, football was never ennobled as a proper sport.

But football inspired engagement rather than respect: it drew greater crowds than any other sport in history, instilled its followers with the kind of passion typically associated with religious assemblies and, with the rise of television from the early 1950s, mutated into what it is in the present. The unintended consequences of the mutation were sometimes repellent. When, in the 1960s, the pitch invasions that concluded practically every game started to become fractious, there were suggestions that football had become a kind of crucible for sectarian conflict. In Glasgow and Liverpool, Protestants and Roman Catholics had formed their own clubs. Hostile behaviour was commonplace in football in the late nineteenth and early twentieth centuries, but hooliganism, as it was called, starting in the 1960s, appeared puzzling. The pattern of violence presented a topic for study. For the first time, academic enquirers flexed their intellectual muscles and started to consider the reason why football fans had, in a relatively short period of time, morphed in marauding hordes of barbarians – at least, that's how the media depicted them.

Violence – or, more specifically, hooliganism – was the first topic to engage serious researchers in a systematic way and, in a sense, it established a presence for the sport academically. Criminologists, psychologists, anthropologists, geographers and sociologists were among the academic specialists who turned their attention to hooliganism. It would be satisfying to report that they identified the root causes and rendered the seemingly senseless aggression comprehensible. However, over five decades later, erudite collections of research papers, such as that edited by Matt Hopkins and James Treadwell (2014), serve as reminders that even if the questions are obvious, the answers are not so straightforward.

At least football's next problem worthy of attention was comprehensible. When black players started to emerge in the late 1970s, crowds reacted as if they were uninvited guests to an all-white party. Racist slurs, chants and pelting were weekly occurrences. It was abhorrent but intelligible; by this, we mean that, when set against a background of rising far-right political sentiment and the racist behaviour that was commonplace at the time, it seemed to chime with the times.

Football had been conceived by white men, played by white men, run by white men and watched by white men since the nineteenth century. Occasionally, black players would distinguish themselves – for example, Walter Tull (1888–1918), Lloyd Delapenha (1927–), Albert Johanneson (1940–1995) and, in the 1960s and 1970s, Clyde Best (1951–). As the sons of Britain's post-war migrants from the Caribbean matured, they broke into football in numbers. The barracking was consistent with the wider social milieu; Britain was not a hospitable place for black people, as riots in all major cities between 1980 and 1985 indicated.

Unlike the collective violence and vandalism, which had no recognizable counterpart in everyday life, racism in football reflected a pattern that was prevalent in wider society and so didn't give rise to an academic tradition comparable to that focused on hooliganism. The UK's Economic and Social Research Council (ESRC) commissioned one of us (EC) to conduct the first study of what was, in the early 1980s, a new and unwelcome phenomenon.

Studies of violence and racism established a kind of analytical template: football, when scrutinized, could be educative as well as enjoyable. It was possible to learn about matters outside the sport. Who knows what we might have learned had scholars decided to ask why there were so few women in football in the 1980s? England's Football Association (FA) had lifted the ban on women's football in 1971. It's barely believable today, but women had been prevented from playing football by the FA in 1921. 'The game of football is quite unsuitable for females and ought not to be encouraged,' declared football's governing body (Football Association quoted in Croydon, 2013). So it's hardly surprising that, 50 years later, when the ban was lifted, there was little interest among women. In 1975, the UK's Sex Discrimination Act made it easier for women to train to become professional referees, but what little women's football was being played went unnoticed.

Jane Couch was a provocateur in women's sport. In 1996, after being refused a licence by the British Boxing Board of Control (BBBofC), she claimed this was a contravention of the sex discrimination legislation. She won her case in 1998 and became a professional boxer. The media interest in the case embarrassed boxing's governing organization and this, no doubt, weighed on the collective mind of the FA, which, in 1997, announced plans for the development of women's football. Remember: this was a sport that, like boxing, was originally created by and for men; women were expected to be at home preparing dinner and taking care of the children, not testing their physical prowess.

Fifa staged the first World Cup for women in China in 1991, though the 1999 tournament, held in the US, is acknowledged as the breakthrough: the final game was the most-attended women's sports event in history. In the 1990s, all sports were stung by the spirit of Billie-Jean King (1943–), the tennis player who campaigned for equal pay for women. Women had competed at Wimbledon since 1880, when the tournament was in its third year – though they didn't receive equal prize money until 2007. Today's women footballers earn nowhere near the same amount of money as male players, but considering that they were not allowed to play until the 1970s, the progress they've made is giddying.

Later in this book, we'll refer to football's *inflection point*, meaning a time when there was a significant change. In football's case, the blisteringly rapid growth of global communications media and the corresponding elevation of players to the status of celebrities in the 1990s marked a dramatic change. Football mutated from a white working-class man's sport played in the spirit of fair play and honest endeavour into a global, multi-ethnic, polylingual extravaganza that was available to all – or at least all who were willing to pay; we don't just watch or play football, we consume it.

Football's media-generated globalization demonstrated a laudable philosophy to unify nations, ethnicities and genders through a common sport. The governing organization Fifa referred to football's 'family', as if a common enthusiasm for the sport was comparable to blood ties. But the old animosities and inequalities didn't just dissolve: as we will see in chapters to follow, the violence persisted and the racism took on new forms. Women's football is undeniably far stronger and better regarded than it was 25 years ago and it has produced celebrity athletes like Mia Hamm, Christine Sinclair and Marta. And yet, as we will discover later in the book, football is still a steadfast symbol of masculine triumph.

How about the study of football? This too has been dominated by an interest in men. Understandably so: for most of football's history, it has been played and governed by men and this is reflected in the way it has been studied – as a man's sport. Study, whether scientific or humanistic, doesn't take place in a vacuum; like everything else, it's affected by cultural priorities, values and mores (these being the customs of a particular culture; pronounced 'mor-ayz'). By the end of the twentieth century, football had attracted a respectable body of academic researchers as well as journalists who were writing thoughtfully about football as a kind of microcosm, or miniature version, of society, or as a source of new social issues worthy of analysis. The launch of a scholarly peer-reviewed journal published by Routledge (publishers of this volume too, in case you haven't noticed) in the year 2000 titled *Soccer & Society* effectively confirmed football's arrival as an academically respectable subject for study.

There will inevitably be doubters, who will argue that football, like other sports, is entertainment: it's supposed to be enjoyed, not analyzed. It's easy to see the point. But entertainment is never just the provision of amusement or enjoyment. What one generation finds an agreeable distraction, another will find intolerably boring; some cultures are interested in presentations that bore others stiff. Entertainment offers the opportunity to ask questions about why populations find watching and doing some things fun. If you could somehow zap the next game you see, take it back 200 years, reproduce it and ask people to watch the 90 minutes of action, do you think they'd endure it?

What's the difference between observing football and studying it? The student doesn't just watch football; he or she methodically scrutinizes the structure and substance of the subject under study, typically to explain or interpret the reasons for something. Some of the subjects covered in this book have been described in detail: racism, violence, corruption and so on. The analyst goes beyond description. This is why *studying* football is different from reporting on it, recounting memorable moments or cataloguing relevant details. We study principally to learn, not so much to appreciate or enjoy, although learning in itself brings satisfaction. Studying football means inquiring, investigating and appraising; all of these are features of the research process. To illustrate this, we provide an example of actual football research at the end of every chapter. The Research in Action features are intended to disclose the variety of topics addressed and different approaches taken by researchers and journalists in studying football. The first of these features reflects on three studies that were influential in establishing football as a field of academic study.

## Research in Action

(a) 'Soccer consciousness and soccer hooliganism' by Ian Taylor (1971)
(b) *We Hate Humans* by David Robins (1984)
(c) *Hooligans Abroad: The Behaviour and Control of English Fans in Continental Europe* by John Williams, Eric Dunning and Patrick Murphy (1984 [1989])

### What were the goals of the research?

These three projects were among the first attempts to bring scholarly discipline and theoretical insight to bear upon a phenomenon that was, in the 1970s and 1980s, a perplexing problem that had originated in football stadiums in Britain and was spreading to other parts of Europe. All three studies were conducted against the background of an economic recession, high inflation, large-scale youth unemployment, hardening racist attitudes and fears that migrants were taking jobs away from the domestic British population.

### Why was the research relevant?

Taylor's early attempt to make sense out of what appeared to be senseless violence was especially relevant because he designed a framework of analysis derived from Marxist theory and produced an ingeniously novel way of understanding what was, at the time, regarded as incomprehensible. It had the virtue of trying to explain behaviour among football fans with reference to the wider changes in society and in the structure and ownership of football. Taylor argued that fans had become progressively more alienated from a game they believed they properly owned and that their aggression was a symbolic way of trying to reclaim the sport. In effect, violence was resistance against the changes brought about by professionalism and commercialization. Taylor drew on Eric Dunning's pioneering study of rugby (1967) and a paper by Janet Lever on Brazilian football (1969). 'Masculinity (embodying a stress on toughness, stamina and autonomy) derives from the experience of industrial work,' wrote Taylor, establishing a theme that would run through football-related research for decades. The other two projects were effectively responses to Taylor's conclusions and, while they weren't published until 1984, helped to establish football as a legitimate area of study.

### What methods were used?

(a) Taylor: Marxist theory. Taylor's method was typical of its time. His emphasis on analyzing behaviour in terms of a pre-defined theoretical model meant that the voices of the fans involved weren't heard.

(b)  Robins: ethnography. Robins corrected this by listening to and recording the thoughts and conversations of fans, observing the customs and habits of youths living on vandalized council housing estates in North London. His title came from a Manchester United fans' chant after they had been called 'animals' by the media. Robins' method is called ethnography, mixing with the 'crews' that were then emerging. Unlike Taylor, he didn't attempt to construct a theory; the study is largely Robins' subjective impressions.

(c)  Williams *et al.*: archival research and participant observation. By contrast, Williams *et al.* used a theoretical and historical approach. Their model was based on the idea that there has been a centuries-long civilizing process, which has rendered legitimate violence almost redundant in modern society. The research team's methods involved combing through archives of old newspapers as well as travelling with and interviewing fans, a method known as participant observation. Like Robins, Williams *et al.* were engaged in empirical research, meaning research based on observation and experience rather than theory or logic, as in Taylor's case.

### *What were the main arguments?*

(a)  Taylor argued that hooliganism was a logical working-class resistance to change that was perceived to be threatening.

(b)  Robins argued that the day-to-day experience of living in run-down areas with little hope of improvement made the excitement of fighting in crews appealing and quite normal.

(c)  Williams *et al.* argued that there was nothing new about football violence and that violence had been part of football culture since the nineteenth century. The unusual feature of football in the twentieth century was the relative absence of violence immediately after the end of the Second World War in 1945.

### *And the conclusions or key findings?*

All three studies offered contrasting interpretations, though all shared a rejection of the popular understanding of violence as portrayed by the popular media, i.e. that it was mindless. None of the projects attempted to advance policy recommendations. Young men (there were no women featured in the studies) needed work, self-respect and a new conception of masculinity in a society dominated at the time by 'authoritarian populism', as some called it, meaning that there was public support for hard-line policing and the strong state promoted by Margaret Thatcher, who became Prime Minister in 1979 and remained in power until 1990. In different ways, the three projects explained the violence as the result of social conditions faced by groups of young lower-working-class men who felt dislocated from mainstream society. Their manliness depended on a willingness to fight in defence of local, parochial or tribal concerns, according to the Williams *et al.* study. The violence, which was shaped by government policies and the police's response, was amplified or exaggerated by the media.

### What were the strengths of the research?

By approaching football as an area of academic study, Taylor's study created what we have earlier called an analytical template. By the time the results of the other two projects were published (13 years later), other studies had begun to engage with football-related issues. In all cases, the research shifted focus away from the individuals and towards the underlying conditions, the cultural contexts and, in some cases, the social-psychological processes that occurred in assemblies of football fans. The strength of Robins' project was that it was the first in-depth study; the author immersed himself in the culture of his subjects. Like Williams *et al.*, he produced empirical content; both studies uncovered fresh and original information on how young people were thinking and feeling.

### Were there any weaknesses?

Taylor's work was imaginative, but didn't produce empirical material to support his thesis and, by imputing motives to fans, was at best speculative. Robins offered a rich seam of evidence but no theory that would have made it possible to understand violence in a more generic way; as such, it remained a one-off study without an explanation of the causes of football violence. For example, he quoted a youth as saying 'One week you just went to see the game, the next week you were going there to have a good kickin'', but didn't then try to interpret or generalize from this type of insight. Williams *et al.* satisfied both the empirical and theoretical demands of research, but didn't link them in a credible way; in other words, their evidence didn't always support their general theory of the civilizing process. Chapter 2 explores Taylor's and Williams *et al.*'s contributions in more detail.

# 2

# VIOLENCE

*Stefan Lawrence and Magdalini Pipini*

---

### Chapter highlights

- Violence and football violence come in a variety of forms that resist fixed definitions.
- Violent outbursts at football matches can't be explained away as a tendency of rowdy Brits, nor is the international spread of football violence copycat behaviour.
- The global nature of football violence has led to calls for scholars to explore the specific societal conditions that breed disorderly behaviour at football matches, as well as the role of social media.
- Historically, football violence has been linked to men's quest to be seen as masculine – but, as more women take up the sport, football violence involving women and girls hints at a changing relationship between football, violence and gender.

---

## Introduction

> *Violence.* Action involving the exercise of physical force to hurt, injure or disrespect another human, or property. ... In sports, as in many other areas, violence is equated with the unlawful use of force, though many sports either tacitly condone or explicitly encourage violence. ... Violence among fans is prevalent, especially in soccer's fandom.
>
> *(Cashmore, 2008, p. 474)*

Speaking after he had witnessed the chaotic events of Sunday 26 April 2015 at the Stadio Olympico, the Juventus FC manager, Massimiliano Allegri, claimed that 'only a madman' would consider taking a child to a football stadium in Italy (*Guardian*, 2015). Allegri's comments were made following the detonation of a paper bomb, which exploded in the middle of a crowded stand housing Torino fans during the Turin derby. The bomb seriously injured at least ten people and marked a new low in violence at football stadiums; a scene from the incident is shown on the cover of this book. However, the event, although especially poignant, was not an isolated incident. Only a month prior, Torino's Serie A rival AS Roma was disciplined by the Italian Football Association for failing to prevent its fans from displaying banners insulting the mother of a Napoli fan who had been killed after he had clashed with Roma Ultras. These kinds of incidents are not confined to Italian football; incidents of violence at football matches are reported right across the football world. Furthermore, despite popular beliefs to the contrary, they are not the reserve of 'the right' (a political position broadly encompassing capitalist, conservative, fascist, monarchist and neo-liberal views) nor 'the left' (the opposing political position, which includes anarchist, anti-imperialist, communist, feminist and green ideologies, amongst others) of the political spectrum. Neither does football violence discriminate on the grounds of ethnic affiliation and/or social or economic class. From right-wing fascist groups attached to clubs like Russia's FC Zenit St Petersburg and Italy's SS Lazio to the left-wing anarchist ultras of German outfit FC St Pauli and their allies such as Scotland's Glasgow Celtic FC, it is clear that where there is football, there are usually people ready to conduct violence in its name.

Violence and football have long been associated with one another. The question we might want to ask, therefore, is not so much why is there football violence but why is there not more? This might, at first, seem like a rather perverse proposition; however, given the recent growth in football fandom literature, which documents most powerfully the inextricably strong social, geographical, cultural and political links that exist between football teams and their spectator communities (Hague and Mercer, 1998; Nash, 2001; Giulianotti, 2002; Brown *et al.*, 2006; Clark, 2006; Brown, 2008; Lawrence, forthcoming), is it not surprising that violent expressions of fandom are not more common in the (late) modern game (*c.*1990 to the present)? What's more, given the physical nature of football – not to mention the 'win at *all* costs' mentality, championed in football dressing rooms across the world – might Uruguayan striker Luis Suárez's seemingly uncontrollable urge to bite opponents at the World Cup in 2014, Zinedine Zidane's headbutt on Marco Materazzi in the 2006 World Cup final, Lady Andrade's right hook to the face of Abby Wambach during the London 2012 Olympic Games, or indeed the spectator violence at the Turin derby in 2015 be understood better as the logical conclusion to a sport fraught with contradictory directives regarding the acceptability of violence? In order to answer these questions, or at least to begin to provoke debate, throughout this chapter we will explore a number of competing definitions, perspectives and theories on the existence of player and crowd football violence.

## Definitions of violence and football violence

The legal definition of violence – the most obvious way in which we might begin to think about the term – is contained in Section 8 of the UK's Public Order Act 1986 (legislation.gov.uk, n.d.). It states:

> violence means any violent conduct, so that—(a) except in the context of affray [see Section 3 of the Public Order Act 1986 for a definition], it includes violent conduct towards property as well as violent conduct towards persons, and (b) it is not restricted to conduct causing or intended to cause injury or damage but includes any other violent conduct.

In criminology, illegal acts of violence, such as the ones falling within the definition above, are of primary concern and are, in simpler terms than those used above, deemed to be 'violent … offences against [a] person officially recorded by the police' (Maguire, 2007, p. 706). These legal interpretations lead us to focus on individuals using severe violence, such as assault, rape and murder, and the causes of these actions (Hare, 2002). However, from the outset we must be clear that legal definitions are open to interpretation, meaning that scholars and legal practitioners are not always consistent in their use of the term. At first, it might be surprising to learn that something as serious as violence is not easily definable; yet, if we accept that violence takes many forms – such as domestic (e.g. often enacted in the home, often against women), media (e.g. whereby violent behaviour is normalized in cinema, video games and on the internet), youth (e.g. the use of knives and/or guns during gang warfare or as a result of drug-trafficking) and discriminatory (e.g. human rights violations, such as unfavourable treatment based on race, nationality, class, religion, language, sexual orientation, gender or age) – its complexity becomes obvious. (By 'normalize', we mean to make normal or conform to a common standard.)

To make things yet more complicated, not all violence is illegal. While murder, for instance, is illegal, the violence we see in sports is often not only legitimate but actively encouraged. Sociological studies of violence, therefore, are concerned with *any* 'actions that inflict, threaten or cause injury; are corporal [i.e. physical or embodied], written or verbal; and injuries may be corporal, psychological material or social' (Jackman, 2002, p. 405), from bullying in schools to genocide and terrorism. Willem de Haan (2008, p. 28) thus suggests that violence is challenging to define because:

- it is multifaceted, meaning that it comes in many forms;
- it is socially and historically constructed, meaning that it changes depending on the society in which it happens and when it happens; and
- it is highly ambivalent in the ways that it is socially sanctioned and legitimized (or, in other words, sometimes it's acceptable and sometimes it's not).

Paradoxically, the most consistent theme that emerges from attempts to define violence is inconsistency (Bauman, 1995). We must then begin to think about violence as 'a slippery term' (Levi *et al.*, 2002, p. 796) and an everyday phenomenon (Stanko, 2003), which affects a variety of people in both legal and illegal ways.

The question then arises: what happens when violence occurs in sport and football? To begin to answer this question, we must distinguish between the two most common forms of violence in sport: player violence and crowd violence.

## Player violence

Violence committed by sportspeople/athletes might be understood as 'the use of excessive physical force, which causes or has obvious potential to cause harm or destruction' (Coakley, 2009, p. 196). Furthermore, Michael Smith (1983) identifies four types of player violence that are helpful for us to understand violence in football:

1. *brutal body contact*, a non-punishable common practice (e.g. jostling for position at corners);
2. *borderline violence*, which is accepted and beneficial for competitive tactics (e.g. tackles that deliberately take out both the player and the ball, but make clean contact with the ball first);
3. *quasi-criminal violence*, which disrespects the formal rules of the sport (e.g. a professional foul or a two-footed tackle);
4. *criminal violence*, which includes prosecutable offences (e.g. Duncan Ferguson's headbutt on Raith Rovers defender John McStay in 1994, which resulted in a three-month prison sentence).

However, in the case of player violence, different sports treat violence in different ways (Cashmore, 2008). For example, in ice hockey, fighting on the ice is not technically legal, and players are temporarily suspended from the game for five minutes after the fight drops to the ice, but, nonetheless, throwing punches at fellow competitors is accepted as being a part of the sport (Lewinson and Palma, 2012). Conversely, in boxing, not only is fighting legal, it the very reason that competitors get in the ring. Thus, although the levels of acceptable violence across sports differ, violence outside of the regulations is always punishable according to the perceived significance of the violation, in relation to sport-specific sub-cultural norms.

## Crowd violence

Violence enacted by spectators of sport in groups or crowds has, in its most simple terms, been described as 'physically assaultive behaviour that has the potential to, or does, injure another person or persons' (Sage and Eitzen, 2013, p. 130). Thus, rather inconsistently, while much player violence is tacitly condoned, crowd violence is thought of almost exclusively as a social problem. In the most extreme of cases, an Egyptian court sentenced 11 men to death after they were convicted of taking part in a stadium riot that took place on 2 February 2012 in Port Said (BBC News, 2015c). Indeed, crowd violence takes place at the venues for a number of different sports; however, no other sport has attracted quite as much crowd violence as football or provoked quite such varied responses from the authorities.

Giovanni Carnibella and colleagues (1996) argue that there are three stages of football crowd violence:

1.  The initial stage describes violence against sports officials, coaches and players, inside the stadium (verbal assaults and missile-throwing being the most common).
2.  The second stage involves the above, including clashes amongst vicious fans, mass fights with the police, and pitch invasions.
3.  The third stage involves fights outside the stadium with fans of opposing teams at pubs and train stations.

In contrast, other approaches include descriptions of football violence as merely symbolic opposition (e.g. cheering, shouting and singing in an aggressive manner etc.), which is often misinterpreted as real (i.e. nasty and physical) violence (Marsh, 1977), or as a 'construct of the media and politicians' (Dunning, 2000, p. 42). Nevertheless, despite attempts to define football crowd violence – or, as some call it, football hooliganism – there remains no general agreement (not least because it is hard to know when violence stops being violence per se and starts being *football* violence). Of course, there are some competing accounts that define football crowd violence, but the authors themselves, sometimes unwittingly, have challenged their own definitions, in sum, because it is difficult to divorce football violence from its wider social context (Frosdick and Marsh, 2005, p. 25). Given the term's complexity, therefore, when approaching the study of football violence, it is vitally important that we consider those who produce definitions of violence, or legislation to prevent it, and ask what their motivation is for doing so. How does this person's or institution's views on violence reflect their/its background, history or vested interests? And why are certain types of violence legal while others are illegal?

## Origins, developments and responses

At the supposed height of football violence in Britain, during the 1960s, 1970s and 1980s, the weekly troubles associated with football crowds were condemned as unacceptable. For instance, perpetrators were often vilified in the media and crowd disorderliness was becoming a serious problem that politicians could not ignore. (For more on the media, see Chapter 8.) Indeed, the mainstream media – which we must remember, at the time, were largely 'top down' in the way that they made and dispensed news (i.e. a very small number of producers gave information to, but rarely received it from, myriad consumers) – were especially receptive to stories of football violence because it sold newspapers (Goode and Ben-Yehuda, 2006). Yet historical sources suggest that football violence, as well as other forms of sports-related violence, far pre-date the formation of the Football Association (FA) in 1863, and that violence was widespread in early forms of football, right up to the First World War (Dunning *et al.*, 2004). Nigel Cawthorne (2012) goes so far as to suggest that even for the earliest forms of the game, in Ancient Greece and Rome, as well as during medieval times, brutality was a prerequisite of participation. From this perspective, given that the sport has *always* been a violent pastime, far from it existing as a 'problem' (a term that implies abnormality or irregularity), the real object of enquiry might be people's reaction to the presence of football violence – not the existence of violence in and of itself.

Before the First World War (pre-1914), football violence certainly existed in Britain, but was performed mainly impulsively, often occurring as a reaction to what happened in the game. During the inter-war period (1914–1939), and for a while after the Second World War (post-1945), levels of violence notably decreased (Frosdick and Marsh, 2005). However, from the 1950s onwards, the frequency of violent episodes began to increase. The Chester Report (1968), for instance, found that football violence had doubled in the first five years of the 1960s, a development that coincided with the first broadcasts of football on British television. Football violence at this time, however, was not confined to Britain. The 1962 World Cup group match in Santiago between Chile and Italy – or, as it is more colloquially known, 'the Battle of Santiago' (bit.ly/1LqvgfE) – saw players kick and punch each other in full view of television cameras and a packed stadium. The match between Peru and Argentina in 1964, too, which later became known as the Estadio Nacional disaster, witnessed an estimated 328 people lose their lives (Edwards, 2014). Notwithstanding these international examples, however, the academic sources available to us that document football crowd violence pre-1990 are overwhelmingly related to Britain (Spaaij, 2006), pointing to a need for more international historical investigations.

What the Britcentric literature does help us to understand, however, is that the 1970s in particular was an important era for football crowd violence for a number of reasons. This is because it tells the story of how groups of young British men, who attended football matches primarily to fight, were able to become more organized, establish 'firms' and develop rivalries with opposing fans – mainly because access to away matches had improved and a more committed club culture amongst fans was emerging (Perryman, 2001). In the first half of the 1980s, the scale of football violence intensified (Dunning *et al.*, 2004) and, in 1985, fans across Europe would witness a defining event in football history. The Heysel Stadium disaster took place in Brussels prior to the 1985 European Cup final between Liverpool FC and Juventus FC, and claimed the lives of 39 people, with a further 600 reported to have been injured (Murphy *et al.*, 1990; Kech, 2015). On that infamous night, Fabio Chisari (2004) reports that Liverpool hooligans charged at Juventus non-hooligans, causing the Italians to pile up against a wall, resulting in its collapse. This event led people around the world to regard football violence as an English disease (Dunning *et al.*, 2004), and English clubs were subsequently banned from European competitions for the next five years (with Liverpool getting an extra year, until 1991). However, in a sense, the events of that night, although tragic, were not quite as extraordinary as they might appear today, given that, for the previous couple of decades, Britain had become accustomed to violence at football matches.

A few months before Heysel, clashes between fans of Luton Town FC and Millwall FC at Kenilworth Road in March 1985 had drawn responses from the then Conservative Prime Minister, Margaret Thatcher, who saw football violence quite simply as a law and order issue that legislation could help curb. Thatcher (1986, quoted in Margaret Thatcher Foundation, 2015) demanded 'stiff sentences' for those convicted of disorder and reacted by setting up a War Cabinet, which she claimed would 'eradicate [football hooligans] from our [British] society'. In reaction to public fear, the Sporting Events Act 1985 and the Public Order Act 1986 were initially used to establish restrictions on the consumption of alcohol at football matches and to make arrests for offences of rioting, violent disorder, affray and provocations of violence. However, Thatcher identified a need for football-specific legislation and, when introduced, the Football Spectators Act 1989 became the first act tasked specifically with controlling the admission of fans to football matches and preventing violence and disorder in England and Wales.

More specifically, the latter act was introduced in response to the Hillsborough disaster of 1989 – a crush against the steel-fenced terraces of the stadium, in which 96 Liverpool fans were killed and 766 were injured, during the FA Cup semi-final game between Liverpool FC and Nottingham Forest FC (Scraton, 2004). At the time, the police, politicians and parts of the media blamed the tragedy on Liverpool supporters (and continued to do so until September 2012, when the Hillsborough Independent Panel concluded that the authorities had attempted to conceal the truth to absolve themselves of blame) and a number of laws were passed with the aim of countering football crowd disorder:

- the Football Offences Act 1991, which focused on preventing missiles being thrown, indecent or racial chanting and pitch invasions;
- the Criminal Justice and Public Order Act 1994, which enhanced police powers to stop and search;
- the Football Act 1999, which improved previous laws and removed vague terms; and
- the Football Disorder Act 2000, which combined domestic and international football banning orders.

As well as legislation, the 'Policing Football' document also further constrained football crowd violence and reduced the prospect of violence in and around football stadiums. Hence, in Britain, it would seem that since the implementation of the aforementioned laws, the number of football-related arrests within stadiums has fallen (Piquero *et al.*, 2015).

However, legislation must not be taken as a sure-fire means of controlling football violence. This is because, along with a cultural, commercially-driven shift in dominant forms of fandom (which is detailed in Chapter 4), significant funding from Premier League clubs has enabled a large, organized police presence to attend 'high-risk' matches, meaning that legislation in Britain is supported by other developments. Indeed, we only need to look to other countries where legislation exists, and where football violence remains rife, to see that the historical, cultural and political context matters for successful policing. What this brief history of football violence and responses to it has, however, alluded to is that violent outbursts must not be explained away as a cultural trait of purportedly unruly Brits who simply like to fight. We expand on this argument further throughout the remainder of the chapter so that we may begin to think about football violence in more nuanced and complex ways.

## Theories: making sense of football violence

There are always a number of different ways in which football player and crowd violence can be interpreted, and how social scientists make sense of events often depends on what lens (or theoretical framework) they use in their research. Each different lens has its own distinguishing ideas or key tenets that help us to explore social phenomena in a broadly coherent manner. The following section will explore how scholars have attempted to explain football violence over the years, and the frameworks they have used.

As we discovered in Chapter 1, sociologist Ian Taylor was amongst the first scholars to consider football crowd violence to be a notable area of academic study. In his work, Taylor contrasted the reality of pre-Second World War British football with what were (at the time) modern developments, such as the rise in players' wages and the shift in club ownership from the community to wealthy businessmen. Taylor adopted a Marxist approach, a social and economic theory developed by Karl Marx and Friedrich Engels, which meant that he focused on the relations between classes and the conflicts that arise from these relations. Therefore, he believed that, given that both British football and British society more broadly were subject to a number of social and economic changes, traditional working-class values were being undermined by capitalist agendas (Taylor, 1971b, 1976). Because of the ever-widening financial divide that was opening up between fans and club representatives, especially after the abolition of the official distinction between 'amateurs' and 'professionals' in 1974 (meaning that all players of the elite game were referred to thereafter simply as 'players'), this fledgling process of commercialization meant that fans felt increasingly distant from the game they once knew. Taylor (1971b, p. 369) called this the 'bourgeoisification' of football and, as such, violent outbursts on football terraces were a reaction to this process. In other words, the sport's players and fans began to shed their working-class origins and acquire the characteristics typically associated with the middle class – whom Marx called the bourgeoisie. Materialistic values and conventional attitudes replaced the more hedonistic and rebellious spirit of early football. For Marxists such as Taylor, football violence, therefore, had emerged out of a sense of *alienation* and *exploitation* and was evidence of a disaffected working people, whose male youth were denouncing the gradual erosion of democracy in football and the creeping agendas of professionalization and commercialization. (For more on the development of consumer culture, see Chapter 10.)

Another approach to understanding football crowd violence from within a tradition sympathetic to, but emergent from Marxism, was prompted by scholars at the Centre for Contemporary Cultural Studies at the University of Birmingham. Cultural studies, as its name suggests, is a tradition in social theory that investigates the ways in which culture influences individual and collective identities, social interactions and relations of power between people and institutions. John Clarke and Stuart Hall in particular utilized this framework to argue that crowd violence was a form of subcultural resistance, a means of fighting back against those feelings of subordination articulated by Taylor above. Clarke, for instance, paid particular attention to a subcultural group known as skinheads (Clarke, 1973, 1976), whose style was visible amongst late twentieth- and early twenty-first-century 'football casuals' (read: a 'new' kind of football hooligans). These young men, with their emphasis on workmen-style fashion, self-governance, stoutness and racism, which at times verged on self-parody, were read through a cultural studies lens as men seeking to reclaim and exaggerate 'old' working-class customs. Violence at football matches, often committed in the name of a particular area, town or city, therefore, was linked to a 'magical recovery of community' (Clarke, 1976). In other words, fighting was an act that linked participants to the past, albeit an imagined one, and to some of the social rituals and activities of a bygone era.

Authors such as Steve Redhead (1997, 2008, 2014) and Richard Giulianotti (1995, 2001, 2002) are also noted for building on and departing from cultural studies traditions. Utilizing two linked but distinctive theories, postmodernism (concerned with multiple 'realities' and the fragmentary nature of society, culture and history) and poststructuralism (concerned more with how language constructs and categorizes individuals and how knowledge is created), their studies have explored the various meanings attached to being a fan of (late/post-) modern football and emphasized the roles of fashion, popular culture, and new and mass media. An important concept for those influenced by these approaches is the notion of 'post-fandom' (Redhead, 1997) – an idea that treats football violence less as a reaction to structural inequalities and more as a site wherein social, cultural and historical forces collide. These theories are marked by explorations of the contradictions and inconsistencies endemic within global football cultures and their treatment of football violence as a product of political and media attention. (For more on theories of football fandom, see Chapter 4.)

The most commonly adopted approach in the study of football violence is a theory called figurationalism. It is primarily attributed to the sociologist Norbert

Elias and is largely concerned with the connections between history, power, behaviour, emotions and knowledge. As its name suggests, figurational sociology – or process sociology, as it is otherwise known – is concerned with 'figurations' (Murphy *et al.*, 2000) or, in other words, how people are 'fundamentally oriented toward and dependent on other people' (Elias, 1978 [1939], p. 261). To use a football example to elaborate: when Paris Saint-Germain (PSG) FC striker Zlatan Ibrahimovic reportedly complained about the quality of food served in the canteen at the Camp des Loges training ground, the club sacked two chefs, replaced them with new ones and increased the catering budget per player (Richards, 2014). Figurationalists would contend that the whole team is potentially affected by this change, not to mention the chefs who have lost their jobs and the chefs' families, as well as other staff around the training ground. These changes might then have 'unintended consequences' for others who are part of the same figuration (in this case, PSG); for instance, should other key players have liked the food, they may be upset by the change, which may affect the team's performance, or, because of an increase in the catering budget, another department's finances might be impacted, thus provoking further change. Figurationists, therefore, seek to avoid blanket or singular explanations of why certain phenomena occur, such as football violence, because they believe that all experiences and actions are *interdependent*.

Another key tenet of figurationalism, and especially of its attempt to explain football crowd violence, is the concept of 'civilizing process' (Giulianotti, 2004). In short, proponents of figurational sociology have argued that there has been a general shift, over time, towards a valuing of what we know as 'good manners'. These 'civilizing spurts' have resulted in what those who dwell in twenty-first-century Western democracies would recognize as a more 'civilized' society. For example, twenty-first-century social etiquette dictates that people should refrain from engaging in 'indecent' behaviours, such as belching at the dinner table and/ or fighting to settle disputes (at least, outside of the playing of sport), because of the ways in which others might view them. Therefore, this has led some to suggest that people's 'threshold of repugnance', including witnessing and engaging in violent acts, is lower. This means that the civilizing process has affected our capacity for experiencing violence (Maguire, 2011, p. 884). (*Editors' note*: The 'threshold' – i.e. the magnitude or intensity that must be exceeded for us to be repelled or find violent behaviour disgusting – has changed, so that we can't or won't tolerate observing some deliberate attempts to hurt, damage or kill someone in some contexts, though we can or will in others. Paradoxically, our capacity for vicariously experiencing violence in film or in games seems to have expanded as our capacity in many other areas of life has contracted.)

Proponents of this theory – namely Eric Dunning, John Williams, Patrick Murphy and Joseph Maguire – form what has been termed as the Leicester School and have applied these ideas to explain football violence (Dunning *et al.*, 2014 [1988]). At the risk of oversimplification, this school of thought suggests that there has been a 'defining and redefining of the limits of "decent" spectating' (Maguire, 1986, p. 217) and that these limits are not adhered to by what Dunning and colleagues (2014 [1988]) have called the 'rougher' lower-working-class communities as readily as they are by other social groups. Like Taylor and Clarke above, figurational sociologists do see football violence in a British context, in part, as a matter of class, masculinity and identity. Indeed, Dunning has considered violence at football matches to be one of the few practices that enable lower-working-class men to engage in 'the quest for excitement' (Elias and Dunning, 1986). Importantly, however, advocates of figurationalism differ from Marxists and neo- and post-Marxists (i.e. those theorists who have adapted, built on and departed from classical Marxist principles) insofar as they do not view crowd violence at football matches as a reaction to alienation or exploitation or as resistance; rather, their understanding of football violence relies heavily on the notion that aggressive self-expression and violence is tolerated more willingly in lower-working-class communities (Murphy *et al.*, 2000).

Moving away from sociological approaches, briefly, to scientific disciplines influenced more heavily by the traditions of 'hard' science (i.e. positivism), social ethologists and psychologists have offered alternative perspectives on the existence of football violence. These approaches differ to those aforementioned in that they do not understand football violence necessarily as a social phenomenon. Both ethology (the study of animal behaviour) and psychology (the science of the mind) are disciplines that, to varying degrees, understand aggression and violence as a 'natural' feature of animal and human interaction or, in extreme instances, as a psychological or biological abnormality. Hence, given that humans have significantly greater degrees of ingenuity than animals, sport has emerged as 'a formalized, rule-bound order that licensed combative, violent, even warlike conduct but within a relatively secure framework' (Cashmore, 2008, p. 70). As the work of Peter Marsh (1977, 1982a, 1982b) asserts, for example, the 'rituals of soccer violence' must be understood as cathartic releases – an unpleasant but necessary evil that prevents more 'serious' violence from spreading to other parts of society. Unlike sociological explanations, then, which, broadly speaking, understand violence as a learned behaviour – a consequence of the interactions between societal norms and individual choice (i.e. structure and agency) – ethological and psychological studies lead researchers to explore violence and aggression as an innate and inevitable condition of humanity.

To explain further, John Kerr (1994) offered a psychological account of football crowd violence in which he claimed that collective displays of aggression lead to a heightened emotional state; therefore, for those with abnormal needs, violence is an act through which they might satisfy an inborn, atypical desire for this sort of arousal. Accordingly, ethologists have added to this line of argument, stating that during physical, tactile sport-related encounters on or off the pitch, an intense feeling of pleasure is induced, by way of release of the 'hormone of happiness', dopamine. Put simply, when an individual is emotionally invested in a sporting duel (whether as a spectator or a participant), their psychology changes and aggressive tendencies are heightened (Arms *et al.*, 1979). In the case of violence, after the first attack is completed, anxiety often decreases but the desire to attack rises, usually until the individual is physically exhausted (Couppis, 2008). To this end, given that football is known to intensify and encourage aggressive and somewhat violent acts (illustrated by such expressions as 'get stuck in' and 'be hard but fair'), aggressive behaviour is inevitable. For scholars such as Kerr, therefore, those who engage in violent behaviours, such as hooliganism or aggressive playing styles, must not be treated like criminals, given that this will do very little to deal with any perceived 'problem'. Rather, those convicted of violent acts in football, such as Luis Suárez and others, might be better thought of as over-conformers to football's subcultural norms or as football extremists who take pleasure from acting out a literal interpretation of football's social codes, directives and mantras.

During the 1990s and 2000s, a growing number of investigations into crowd violence at football matches in a European and world context emerged. Football violence has therefore been shown to occur in every country in which football is played (Frosdick and Marsh, 2005), giving rise to questions about the suitability of those theories outlined above, especially sociological theories and their focus on class-based analysis. Furthering this point, a number of studies conducted in the Netherlands (Van der Brug, 1994; Kerr and de Kock, 2002; Spaaij, 2007b, 2008), Spain (Viñas, 2005; Llopis-Goig, 2007), Italy (Roversi, 1991; Podaliri and Balestri, 1998), Argentina (Paradiso, 2009) and Germany (Pilz, 1996; Lösel and Bliesener, 2003) reveal that crowd violence at football matches is not confined to one particular nation or social or economic class. Seeking to expand some of his own ideas, Dunning (2000, p. 161) has asserted that football violence often takes place at a nation's major 'societal fault lines', meaning that people from a variety of backgrounds partake in football violence, for a variety of reasons:

> In England, that means social class and regional inequalities; in Scotland and Northern Ireland, religious sectarianism; in Spain, linguistic subnationalisms of the Catalans, Castilians, Gallegos and Basques; in Italy, city particularism and perhaps the division between North and South as expressed in the formation of the 'Northern League'; and in Germany, the relations between East and West and political groups of the left and right.

In the same way that Simon Kuper (1994) demonstrated that the fall of the Soviet Union began on football terraces, due to a rise in violent nationalist sentiment across a number of territories, Dunning's observations above illustrate how the study of football stands at the very forefront of social, economic, ethno-religious and political debates, precisely because it shines new and often first light on issues that go far beyond the sport itself.

Of further note, more recent investigations into football violence have debated the merits of popular media (Dart, 2008), cinema (Redhead, 2006; Poulton, 2007; Rehling, 2011) and the internet, especially, as spaces for future investigation. Thus, with more and more hooligan groups across the world communicating, trading insults and sharing videos of fights via social media (Zaitch and de Leeuw, 2010; Spaaij, 2011) – even moments of player and, more surprisingly, referee violence have been caught on camera and shared globally, online – social-scientific scholarship must find new ways to theorize contemporary football-related phenomena from a transnational perspective (Dunning, 2000; Bairner, 2006; Spaaij, 2007a). These studies, having cleared new trajectories for theory, invite internationally facing research into the matter of football crowd and player violence. (Chapter 8 charts the rise of social media and explores its implications for football cultures.)

## Violence, aggression and masculinities

Despite differences in emphasis, most theoretical perspectives have marked those who engage in football violence, almost exclusively, as white, able-bodied, heterosexual, youthful and male (Armstrong and Giulianotti, 2002; Frosdick and Marsh, 2005). Thus, while international research into football violence suggests that social and economic deprivation does not present itself universally as a convincing lens through which to understand football crowd or player violence, the ever-presence of men and, by association, masculinity, is worth exploring further. Emma Poulton (2012), for instance, asserts that the world of football crowd violence in particular is a 'hyper-masculine' one, saturated with extreme representations of men and masculinities. We explore this idea, amongst others, further throughout this section (see also Chapter 6), but first we turn to a brief discussion of the historical relationship between football and masculinity.

Football has long been thought of as an arena through and in which masculinity is made and/or proven. Supposedly, it is a social sphere in which 'men can be men', by acting on their most primitive of urges. For many, the physical duel between men is a way for participants to prove that they are strong, battle-hardened, tough, heterosexual and self-sufficient (Lawrence, 2014). Striving for such 'ideals', however, has at times lent itself to aggressive behaviour, which often spills over into violence. In turn, violence and aggression, to varying degrees, have become closely tied to traditional masculine approaches to playing and watching football (Hylton and Lawrence, 2015). Football has been accused, therefore, of fostering a culture through and in which hegemonic masculinity – a kind of masculinity that is defined largely as aggressive, heterosexual, white, homophobic, sexist, authoritative and physical (Connell, 2005) – has been glorified and promoted as the most normal way to 'be a man' (Messner, 1992; Bairner, 1999).

One way in which we might begin to understand football violence and its links to masculinity is offered by Anoop Nayak and Mary Jane Kehily (2013, p. 52). They point to the film *Fight Club* (1999) as a suitable medium through which to understand the behaviour of a number of young men, of all ages and income levels, and their willingness to be violent. The film, set in Los Angeles, centres around two men, both of whom are bored with their lives, their jobs and the capitalist mantras that demand that they go shopping in order to buy a masculine identity. Seeking, therefore, to re-engage their most primal male instincts, an urge that the film implies they have been asked to suppress, the two decide to form an underground society wherein like-minded men meet to fight. To this end, the film portrays men of the late twentieth and early twenty-first century to be

> living lives of wasted potential, in meaningless jobs, surrounded by the allure of consumerism and celebrity culture that appears full of promise but actually generates anger and discontent … In *Fight Club* these white collar slaves throw off the starchy rigmarole of polite bourgeois society. In so doing, they engage in the undulated bodily practice of spectacular bare-knuckle fighting.

The comparison between the film's portrayal of an organized, men-only, underground fighting society and football violence is obvious; however, it is important for our purposes for three reasons. First, the film is also able to speak to the changing nature of masculinities in late modern` societies and their relationship with new labour markets. In other terms, given that the new types of jobs done across the world are largely desk-based – meaning that an unprecedented number of men, many of whom would have done manual labour only a few generations ago, are expected to don a shirt and tie, learn delicate keyboard skills, accept flexible working hours and even develop a caring customer service-type persona – those who reject this version of manhood, or who feel the need to reclaim 'old' hegemonic forms of masculinity, can do so behind the veil of 'football fandom' in the most explicitly violent of ways. Thus, if masculinity is understood as an identity constructed around ideas of independence, competition, physicality and emotional toughness, and if popular media culture legitimizes only those forms of manhood perceived by some as effeminate (e.g. preening boy bands, perfectly groomed reality TV personalities and Hollywood film stars with impeccable teeth), violence will never be too far away.

Second, the film does well to capture the hedonistic pleasure of fighting. In other words, while it is broadly acknowledged that many people enjoy watching violence (e.g. mixed martial arts (MMA), boxing and wrestling), what is acknowledged far less frequently is that some people actually enjoy doing it. In simple terms, there is, as George Orwell (1970, p. 63) would have it, a 'sadistic pleasure' (but a pleasure nonetheless) that emerges from participation in football violence, or else watching others engage in it (Poulton, 2013, 2014).

Third, as well as identifying the psychosocial pleasures associated with violence, *Fight Club* also enables us to understand that an engagement in violence bestows on willing participants what Loïc Wacquant (2004, p. 127) calls 'bodily capital'. In simple terms, in much the same way that money is a form of capital, and thus, at the same time, a resource with an exchange value, the violent body, too, is capital. Accepting this enables us to appreciate that 'the embodiment of a violent potential' aids and abets those willing to fight to gain and maintain 'respect' amongst peers (Ilan, 2015, p. 8). We see this idea manifest in football amongst hooligans in terms like 'top lad' – a label inferring high status, which has currency both inside and outside hooligan groups and circles. Even amongst professional players and managers, this idea resonates, both on and off the pitch; those who are perceived as 'hard' (i.e. willing to be violent by word or action) can 'cash in' on such a reputation by intimidating opponents and/or other teammates. Thus, in both senses, violence is not just behaviour but resource, a form of bodily capital, which can be utilized to maintain and/or elevate an individual's position in informal social hierarchies. (See Chapter 11 for a discussion of gender and violence that draws on the theories of the media scholar George Gerbner.)

Football culture across Europe, however, has undergone a revolution of sorts since its inflection point in the early 1990s, which has gradually affected football's relationship with traditional performances of masculinity and, in turn, violence. Having been confronted *politically* by Fifa, Uefa and some national football associations, by way of anti-discrimination campaigns and changes to the laws of the game – drawing complaints from British managers and players in particular, who object to football becoming a 'non-contact sport' (Wilson, 2011); *legally* by the Bosman ruling in 1995, which allowed players to move between clubs on free transfers once their contracts had expired; and *culturally* by globalization (especially the international migration of players and managers and the sharing of off-pitch practices, such as diet, professionalism and lifestyle), the traditionally 'masculine … image' of the men's elite professional game is now disputed (Hylton and Lawrence, 2015, p. 774). Writing with reference to fans and spectators, a number of authors have observed that dominant football communities and fan groups, too, are seemingly less concerned by aggressive, hegemonic and/or violent displays of masculinity (Adams *et al.*, 2010; Adams, 2011; Anderson, 2011; Cashmore and Cleland, 2012). This body of literature, led by a theory of masculinity known as inclusive masculinity, contends that men's behaviour and moral codes have become softer. And so, although this research is still in its infancy, these claims, at best, point to a less violent type of masculine football culture or, at worst, to a willingness to turn away from aggression, violence and hostility as means to prove 'real' manhood.

Amidst these scholarly debates, reports of male violence at football matches, nevertheless, remain forthcoming – notably, the death of a volunteer assistant referee, who was kicked to death following a vicious attack at a junior football match in the Netherlands (Waterfield, 2013), and the decapitation of a referee in Brazil, after the official had reportedly stabbed a player (BBC News, 2013a). Even so, and while it is true to say male football violence is certainly better reported and researched, there have been numerous examples of football violence involving women, including the University of New Mexico's YouTube 'star' Elizabeth Lambert, who was filmed punching and kicking opponents – even viciously yanking an opponent to the ground by her ponytail (bit.ly/1QAALQA). Thus, from the US goalkeeper Hope Solo, who was arrested in 2014 after accusations of domestic violence (Luther, 2015), to reports of a female fan in Paraguay throwing scalding hot tea over a match official at a game between Olimpia and Paraguayos Unidos (Snowball, 2015), violence by women is not unheard of. Additionally, to make the point that this is not simply a twenty-first-century phenomenon, Matthew McDowell (2013, p. 297) points to a historical example from 1898, reported in the *Port Glasgow Express and Observer,* which describes how 'a general scuffle' broke out amongst female football supporters, leaving one woman hospitalized. It is important to note here, therefore, that violence is not irrevocably tied to men. As such, we might also say the same about masculinity (Mac an Ghaill and Haywood, 2007). To this end, masculinity in football might be better thought of as a part of the dominant culture, a performance, an action, a language, a state of mind, in which both men and women might engage.

To elaborate further, Carrie Dunn's work on female football fans illustrates how women and girls are keen to present themselves as 'normal' and/or 'authentic' members of the football community (2014, p. 107). Dunn argues that in order to do this, women present themselves in 'typically male' ways and refrain from disclosing too much of their femininity for fear of undermining their 'authenticity'. Not only does Dunn's work, therefore, mark mainstream football culture as 'masculine', it also reveals how women, too, might police the game's association with traditional masculinity and male interpretations of football, for instance, by way of their opposition to other women 'who are too overtly feminine in their dress at football grounds' (Dunn, 2014, p. 108). In turn, as opposed to viewing violence as a problem deeply ingrained in the male psyche, one way to respond to Dunn's call to interrogate and challenge the stereotypes associated with women in football is to document women's and girls' perceptions of and involvement in football violence. Future research might then wish to add to the literature on women in football, which rightly continues to illustrate matters of sexualization and stigmatization, by considering football's role in promoting cultures of violence amongst female participants and spectators.

## Conclusion

Football is certainly unique in the sense that no other sport generates such a strong sense of belonging. Football crowds are not merely collections of spectators and/or observers, as they are in many other sports, nor can they be categorized simply as enthusiasts or aficionados. Both football crowds and players are deeply invested in the game, owing their attachments to myriad reasons, be they historical, political, religious, cultural or geographical, to name but a few, or a mix of all of the above. In other words, given that fans invest emotionally in their team, it is logical for us to suggest that this causes them to crave a deeper engagement with football, sometimes in the most violent of ways.

That said, football violence in the early part of the twenty-first century is less visible than it was during the 1970s and 1980s – in a British context, at least. Yet, as we have argued above, football violence, both on and off the pitch, has not miraculously disappeared. Quite simply, therefore, it remains an area that deserves scholarly attention. This must not be read as a call to merely reproduce and regurgitate 'old' arguments, however, or to add more noise to, as some see it, an over-researched and over-populated area (Carnibella *et al.*, 1996; Frosdick and Marsh, 2005); quite the contrary, 'new' explanations and approaches must be sought in order to keep pace with emergent cultures of football violence. Research has revealed that violent behaviour in football is historically, culturally and geographically specific in the sense that it has some features that are specific and some that are general. Therefore, given the gaps in literature, some of which we have highlighted, future studies into the relationship between football and violence are still welcome, providing that they are innovative and genuinely enlightening.

## Research in Action

'Reading Ronaldo: contingent whiteness in the football media' by Kevin Hylton and Stefan Lawrence (2015)

(*Editors' note*: Unlike the other authors in this volume, Lawrence and Pipini have chosen a piece of research unrelated to their chapter. Their **Research in Action** is a small but unusual and innovative study on Cristiano Ronaldo and conceptions of whiteness.)

### What were the goals of the research?

The research had two main goals:

1. to name whiteness, in the same way that blackness is named, given that white practices and people in football are rarely considered to have racialized identities or behaviours (i.e. drinking pints in a pub after football is often considered 'normal', when it is actually a cultural activity associated closely with white British social rituals);
2. to explore how white men made sense of Cristiano Ronaldo's racialized and masculine identity and what this revealed about how they construct the category 'white men'. (*Editors' note*: To 'racialize' means to impose a racial interpretation on someone or something i.e. to categorize them in terms of membership of racial groups.)

### Why was the research relevant?

There has been much written about black athletes and their disadvantages; however, there has been far less written about white athletes and their privileges. The field's ignorance of the matter of whiteness has meant that some scholars have argued that the study of sport, race and racism is all too often considered to be a field concerned only with black and South Asian people's experience of sport. This research was relevant, therefore, because it sought to provide an obverse view of racism, to mark whiteness so that it is more visible and to challenge white people to think about themselves as harbouring racialized and ethnic identities.

## What methods were used?

### Sample

In order to mark whiteness as a racialized category in the same way that blackness is marked, 22 white British men were presented with a media image of Cristiano Ronaldo and were asked a series of questions during a semi-structured interview.

### Interviews

The questions that were asked challenged the men to think about who they thought Ronaldo was as a person, as a man and as a footballer. The authors of the project also utilized participant observation to support the study so as to add further weight to some of the claims made about whiteness and masculinity that emanated from interviews. Semi-structured interviews proceed with questions that allow the respondent to express their thoughts and deviate, rather than having to stick to answering a list of questions, as in a structured interview.

## What were the main arguments?

The study made two main claims:

1. The social category 'white people' is an unstable and changing concept. That is, when participants were asked to articulate how they understood Ronaldo's ethnicity, some considered him to be 'white', some 'Mediterranean' and some as 'Other' i.e. distinct and different. Hence, while there was a reluctant acceptance of Ronaldo as 'white', what kind of white man he was and/or how white he might be was more ambiguous. This speaks to society's inability to define absolutely what is and is not white and adds further support to the notion that the category 'white people' is socially, not biologically, constructed.
2. So difficult was this task that even Ronaldo's style of play, which was often interpreted as overly theatrical by the British respondents, was used as a measure of what sort of white man he was. In simple terms, how a person plays football was amongst myriad things that these white men took into account when attempting to understand a person's ethnicity! Thus, while a number of responses interpreted the question about Ronaldo's ethnicity as a question about his body and what it looks like, people also use behaviour and actions as a way to understand and ascribe meaning to footballers.

### And the conclusions or key findings?

The discussions that were summoned by readings of Ronaldo contested the notion that racism is something that 'whites do to blacks'. That is, a number of the disparaging comments made about Ronaldo by white men were attributed to his nationality and thus can be considered to be a form of racism.

White people in sport and leisure, rather than existing as one homogeneous group with the same beliefs, genetics and world-view, were recognized as a diverse collection of people, divided along ethnic, national, gendered and sporting lines. However, while white men are able to recognize that the category 'white people' is fractured and inconsistent, this privilege is rarely extended to those who are racialized as black, South Asian or Hispanic.

### What were the strengths of the research?

The strengths of this research lay in its willingness to engage in discussions about whiteness, especially when compared with the reluctance of others.

Another strength was its consideration of whiteness and masculinity together. As opposed to focusing on simply one or the other, exploring the intersection between whiteness and masculinity made for a more comprehensive and complex study of racialized masculinities.

### Were there any weaknesses?

There were few weaknesses to speak of as such; however, in order to extend the research and build on its successes, other researchers might be advised to explore how black or South Asian men, or white, black or South Asian women, interpret the images of Ronaldo. This would allow for numerous other perspectives to be added to those emanating from white men.

# 3

# GLOBALIZATION

*Chris Bolsmann*

---

**Chapter highlights**

- Globalization is the process by which the world is becoming increasingly interconnected as a result of international trade and cultural exchange.
- Football has been operating on an international scale and developing its global influence since the 1880s.
- The British Empire was instrumental in diffusing football around the world.
- Despite scandals, Fifa has been a progressive force.
- Globalization shapes the women's game as well as the men's.

---

## Introduction

> An astonishing void: official history ignores soccer. Contemporary history texts fail to mention it, even in passing, in countries where soccer has been and continues to be a primordial symbol of collective identity. I play therefore I am: a style of play is a way of being that reveals the unique profile of each community and affirms its right to be different. Tell me how you play and I'll tell you who you are.
>
> *(Galeano, 2003, pp. 204–205)*

On a cold February afternoon in Highbury in north London in 2005, history was made in the English Premier League. Arsenal FC beat fellow London rival Crystal Palace FC 5–1. What made this particular game historic was that none of the 11 Arsenal starting players nor any of the substitutes were English. Six players were French, three were Spanish, two were Dutch and the remaining players originated from Brazil, Cameroon, Germany, the Ivory Coast and Switzerland. Arsenal's French manager, Arsene Wenger, responded to criticism in the press by stating, 'I don't look at the passport of people, I look at their quality and their attitude' (BBC Sport, 2005). He also noted that England's Swedish manager Sven-Göran Eriksson was in the crowd that day. Chelsea FC was the first English team to field a starting eleven with only non-English players in December 1999; however, there were a number of English substitutes on the bench for its game against Southampton.

Since the early 1990s, English football has attracted large numbers of international footballers, managers and club owners. There has undoubtedly been a significant movement of players from all over the world to English football. At the same time, English football, and particularly its Premier League, has also become a significant export product that is consumed around the world. During the off-season, most top English football clubs embark on extensive worldwide tours. Clubs regularly visit the US, South Africa, China, Malaysia, Thailand and numerous other countries. The reasons for this are the following: clubs are able to train in different conditions and climates and play against a number of teams (not necessarily English) in preparation for the upcoming season. Tours help to generate and sustain the popularity of the football clubs that are increasingly world-famous brands. Think of the number of shirt sponsorship deals that appear on English football club shirts that are not written in English. Visit the webpage of any English football club and it is more than likely that, in addition to English, text will appear in Arabic, French, Korean, Mandarin and Japanese amongst others. The top European clubs all have significant foreign support bases around the world. This suggests that football is truly global. (For more on the evolution of football marketing, see Chapter 10.)

In this chapter, we will consider the rise of football as a global game from the 1880s onwards. The phenomenon of football as *the* global game is not a recent development due to the processes of globalization. Rather, football as a game and a cultural product was at the forefront of globalizing sport and popular culture more generally. In looking at global football, we will consider the role of the institution that regulates football at the global level. In so doing, we will consider the World Cup as the world's single largest sporting event. We will also consider the nature and governance of football at the continental level and the impact that the game has around the world.

## Britain, empire and the diffusion of football

The formation of England's Football Association (FA) in 1863 meant that the game was regulated and controlled by one body that was responsible for the oversight and development of the game in England (Mason, 1980). The FA Cup was first contested in 1872, while the first international match between Scotland and England was also played that year, in Glasgow (Walvin, 1994). A regional divide emerged within English football. In the south, the amateur ethos and elitism prevailed, while in the Midlands and the north, the middle classes, entrepreneurs and industrialists controlled professional football (Giulianotti, 1999, p. 4; Taylor, 2008; Giulianotti and Robertson, 2009).

While association football was codified and institutionalized in England, Britain more generally and a number of European powers found themselves in an 'age of empire' (Hobsbawm, 1989). This era manifested itself in the form of colonies in which 'most of the world outside of Europe and the Americas was formally portioned into territories under the formal rule or informal political domination of one or more of a handful of states' (Hobsbawm, 1989, p. 55). European powers such as Britain, France, Germany, Italy, the Netherlands and Belgium in particular scrambled for territories to conquer, exploit and control for their own purposes. Britain colonized vast stretches of the African and Asian continents. The British Empire directly and indirectly sought to control all aspects of life within these colonies for the benefit of Britain, British officials and settlers in these regions. Sport was an important pastime in the colonies, initially for recreation purposes for British subjects and the military, but was increasingly used by colonial authorities to control indigenous populations. For James Mangan, sport was an integral part of the 'civilizing mission'. He asserts that sport for

> the colonizers [carried] with it a series of moral lessons, regarding hard work and perseverance, about team loyalty and obedience to authority and indeed involving concepts of correct physical development and 'manliness'. As such it was used as a key weapon in the battle to win over local populations and indeed to begin transforming them from an 'uncivilized' and 'heathen' state to one where they might be considered 'civilized' and 'Christian'.
>
> *(Mangan, 2001, p. 41)*

Richard Giulianotti (1999, p. 6) argues that 'trade connections, rather than imperial links' were important in spreading football around the world. In particular, northern industrialists sought business opportunities abroad and one of the consequences of this quest was the popularization of football in a range of industrial settings around the world. Football clubs were established across the British Empire and beyond from the 1870s onwards. For David Goldblatt (2006, p. 76), 'football was certainly an accurate barometer of Britain's relationship with the rest of the world'. Giulianotti (1999, p. 22) asserts 'there would be no "global game" without the sporting imperialism of British workers, teachers and soldiers during the late nineteenth century'. This claim fits within the broader assumptions in Anglophone scholarship that football was a part of British formal and informal empire (Brown, 2014, p. 10). While this claim is important, Matthew Brown (2014, p. 10) observes that South American scholarship considers the role of local and indigenous actors in the development of the game within South America. He argues that a transnational history is necessary, one in which we can understand the spread of football from Britain around the world but also appreciate that local actors were able to claim football for themselves and mould it in ways that they saw appropriate.

With the establishment of football clubs, football leagues and regional associations followed. In South Africa, for example, the regional Natal Football Association was formed in 1882 and the national South African Football Association (SAFA) in 1892 (Bolsmann, 2010). In South America, Argentina, while not a British colony, nevertheless had significant British business interests and was part of what can be considered the informal empire where football became very popular. In 1891, the Argentine Association Football League was established. In 1903, the name was changed to the Argentine Football Association. In 1912, the name was changed from English to Spanish (Mason, 1995, p. 5). Football associations were founded in Chile in 1895 and Uruguay in 1900. For Christopher Gaffney (2008, p. 51), football in South America during this period (1890s–1910s) 'signified elitism, refinement, and exclusivity'. Further afield, the New Zealand Soccer Association was formed in 1891 and the Singapore Amateur Football Association in 1892. In the case of Argentina and South Africa, both national associations affiliated to the FA in London. By 1903, there were more than 20 football associations around the world (Lanfranchi *et al.*, 2004). While Britain exported the game around the world and a number of British teams toured from the 1890s onwards, this was not a unidirectional process; a number of foreign football teams toured Britain and in turn left their mark on the British game. As early as 1888, a team from Canada toured Britain and played 23 games in 61 days (Jones, 2013, p. 46), while in 1899 a black team from South Africa toured Britain (Bolsmann, 2011). Wilfred Waller became the first South African to play professional football in England in 1899. The amateur and elite English team Corinthian FC, established in 1882, undertook regular foreign football tours. The team, composed of the best public-school footballers, travelled extensively from the 1890s until the late 1930s. Corinthian first travelled to South Africa in 1897, and again in 1903 and 1907; it toured Hungary and Scandinavia in 1904 and Germany and Holland in 1906; it visited Canada and the US in 1906, 1911 and 1924 (Creek, 1933). The team also visited Brazil in 1910, and the country's largest football club, Sport Club Corinthians Paulista, is named after the English visitors (Hamilton, 1998). Not only did Corinthian help to further popularize the game around the world, it also extolled the virtues of amateurism (Bolsmann, 2010). Professional English teams toured abroad during this period too. Southampton visited Argentina and Uruguay in 1904, as did Nottingham Forest in 1905, and Everton and Tottenham Hotspur in 1909. Significantly, men's football clubs were not the only teams touring. Women's football was increasingly popular during this period, too. The FA banned women from playing football at its member grounds in 1921, with the ban only repealed in 1971. Despite this ban, Dick, Kerr's Ladies toured Canada and the US in 1922 (Newsham, 1994; Williams, 2007b). (For an in-depth discussion of women in football, see Chapter 6.)

While Britain was exporting football through its formal and informal colonial networks, European countries were establishing their own football associations and national leagues during this period. National football associations were established in Denmark and the Netherlands in 1889, in Belgium and Switzerland in 1895 and in Sweden in 1904. These football associations, along with French and

Spanish football associations, were instrumental in forming the first international FA.

## Fifa and the control of global football

Prior to the outbreak of the First World War in 1914, Britain dominated football in both the professional and the amateur games. The British Olympic football team won the 1908 and 1912 gold medals. The first steps towards creating an international football federation were taken in the late 1890s when the Belgians communicated with the English FA (Tomlinson, 2014a), with whom little progress was made. In 1904, representatives from Belgium, Denmark, France, the Netherlands, Spain, Sweden and Switzerland met in Paris and established the Fédération Internationale de Football Association (Fifa). The association was formed on the one hand due to the wish to play international football matches between European countries and on the other to standardize the laws of the game (Lanfranchi et al., 2004). The British FAs (England, Ireland, Scotland and Wales) joined Fifa in 1905. Daniel Woolfall, the first English president of Fifa (1906–1918), stated in 1909 that 'formerly football was considered the national game of some countries, now this sport had become the game of the world' (Fifa, 1909, p. 1). The British FAs left Fifa in 1920, only to briefly return between 1924 and 1928 and finally rejoin in 1946.

From its inception in 1904, Fifa was unable to establish an international tournament for member nations. Due to a lack of finances, Fifa approached the International Olympic Committee (IOC) to arrange an international football tournament. Football was included in the Stockholm Olympic Games in 1912 for the second occasion and participants had to be members of Fifa. However, with the increasing professionalization of football around the world, this development was at odds with the IOC ethos of amateurism (Rinke, 2014). In South America, football's popularity increased and intense national rivalries emerged. In 1916, the first continental football association was established. The Confederación Sudamericana de Fútbol (CONMEBOL) ushered in a South American championship, which was first contested by Argentina, Brazil, Chile and Uruguay. Uruguay won the first continental competition and won the title on a further five occasions during the 1920s. In addition, Uruguay won the gold medal at the 1924 and 1928 Olympic Games. Fittingly, the first World Cup was held in Uruguay in 1930 and won by the host nation despite European resistance to staging the event in South America. Two further World Cups were held in 1934 and 1938 in Italy and France respectively. In 1938, membership of Fifa stood at 51 (Tomlinson, 2014b). The Second World War put an end to further World Cups. The first post-war competition returned to South America, with host nation Brazil unexpectedly losing to Uruguay. Fifa membership continued to grow and by 1950 the organization was composed of 68 members; by 1975, this number had reached 139 nations. With Fifa membership nearly doubling in a 25-year period, there was a shift in the power dynamics within world football.

In the aftermath of the Second World War, numerous African and Asian states emerged from colonialism to become independent nation states that in turn sought recognition through a range of world sporting bodies, and Fifa in particular. The Confédération Africaine de Football (CAF) was formed in 1957 with Egypt, Ethiopia, South Africa and Sudan the founding members. CAF remains Fifa's largest confederation, with 54 member states. Egypt competed in the 1934 World Cup but not until 1970 did another African team (Morocco) play in the finals. For many of the newly independent African states, the distribution of World Cup places was considered discriminatory (Darby, 2002). Three continental football associations composed of 65 member states competed for one World Cup berth (Darby, 2002). Ghanaian president Kwame Nkrumah led the campaign for African and Asian states to boycott the 1966 finals in England. Englishman Stanley Rous was Fifa's president at the helm of world football during this period. In many respects, Rous was considered conservative, with an 'old-school attitude' according to which sport and politics were not meant to mix (Darby, 2002, p. 63). This stance was most evident in relation to racism in South African football. SAFA returned to Fifa in 1952 and, despite removing the 'whites-only' membership clause from its constitution, the association remained a racist body representing white South African footballers only (Bolsmann, 2010). Rous was close to officials within SAFA, and sympathetic to and supportive of their attempt to destroy the non-racial and progressive South African Soccer Federation (Alegi, 2004). (There is a wider discussion of racism in football in Chapter 5; see also Bolsmann, 2013a.)

While the issue of apartheid South Africa remained a central concern in Fifa, Rous was challenged by João Havelange, a former Brazilian Olympian and member of the IOC, for the presidency of Fifa in 1974 (Darby, 2008). Havelange defeated Rous in the election to become Fifa's eighth president and the first to hail from outside Europe. Importantly, he had sought the support of states from outside the traditional football strongholds of Europe and South America in his quest to become president (Tomlinson, 2014b). The ambitious Brazilian embarked on a process of modernizing Fifa. According to Tomlinson (2014b, p. 63), this included increasing the number of World Cup places from 16 to 24 for the tournament in Spain in 1982; the establishment of an Under-20 World Championship and an intercontinental club championship; and material, financial and personnel support to football associations across the world. Havelange needed financial support for the implementation of his ambitious modernization agenda and sought the assistance of Horst Dassler, the boss of adidas, the German sports manufacturer (Smit, 2006). Through Dassler, Havelange was introduced to Joseph 'Sepp' Blatter, who was brought into Fifa in 1975 as technical director. He was tasked with securing sponsorship from adidas and Coca-Cola. Moreover, Blatter's salary was partially paid by adidas due to the lack of funds within Fifa (Tomlinson, 2014a, p. 72). Blatter became general secretary of Fifa in 1981 and Havelange's trusted right-hand man.

The 1990s represented an important era in Fifa's history. The Women's World Cup was first contested in 1991 and, like the men's version, is held every four years. The Fifa Confederations Cup was first staged in 1992 and later became a rehearsal event for the World Cup. The men's World Cup was held in the US in 1994 and outside the Americas and Europe in 2002, when Japan and South Korea co-hosted the event. The number of tournament finalists was increased in 1998 from 24 to 32. Under Havelange's presidency, Fifa was able to attract significant television revenues from the sale of World Cup broadcasting rights, and shrewdly sold television rights to the highest bidders for forthcoming World Cups. This, in turn, meant that corporate sponsors were keen to be associated with the global game and the world's single largest sports event. The world's largest multinational corporations clamoured for the opportunity to be associated with world football. The Fifa model had become a moneyspinner. In the 1998 Fifa presidential elections, the Union of European Football Associations (Uefa) president Lennart Johansson stood against Havelange's protégé, Blatter. The Swede lost the election to the Fifa general secretary and cried foul. He exclaimed: 'I will never engage myself in such dirty business ... we must be prepared to fight against corruption and bribery and dishonest people' (quoted in Tomlinson, 2014b, p. 74).

In more recent times, Fifa has rarely been far from scandal and allegations of corruption and bribery. (This is covered in detail in Chapter 12.) Even in the 1930s, Fifa's second secretary Carl Hirschman lost Fifa money on speculative investments and embezzlement (Tomlinson, 2014b, p. 19). Important scholarly work has been published by Sugden and Tomlinson (1998, 1999, 2003), amongst others, concerned with corruption, bribery and scandal within world football, and within Fifa in particular. A number of investigative journalists have also exposed the inner wheeling and dealing of Fifa (Yallop, 1999; Jennings, 2006). In May 2015, at Fifa's 65th congress in Zürich, a number of prominent Fifa executives were arrested and indicted in relation to wire fraud, racketeering and money laundering. Despite the ensuing scandal, Blatter was re-elected president of Fifa for a fifth term, yet within days he announced he would step down as president once a suitable candidate had been found to replace him.

In light of the most recent developments, Fifa is facing its most significant challenge since the early 2000s, when the organization was dogged by numerous allegations of corruption. The Fifa agency and partner International Sport and Leisure (ISL) was established in the early 1980s to market and secure World Cups and Olympic events. ISL went bankrupt in 2001 and subsequent investigations in Swiss courts revealed Havelange and others were beneficiaries of bribes. He resigned from his position as honorary president of Fifa in 2013. Chapter 12 probes the various scandals that have beset Fifa and, indeed, world football.

## The Fifa World Cup as the global spectacle

Fifa's showcase event is the men's World Cup, held every four years. Over 200 teams entered the preliminary qualifications for the 2010 and 2014 tournaments, vying for one of the 32 places in the finals. Rinke and Schiller (2014, p. 9) argue that the World Cup 'has exerted strong influences and acted as an important indicator of political, economic, social and cultural developments'. The World Cup is the single most popular sporting event around the globe. Moreover, it 'provides a powerful lens for examining the course of globalization and global history over the last century' (Goldblatt, 2014a, p. 19). The popularity of the World Cup is heightened by the large-scale television and media coverage. It was first broadcast on television in 1954. Tomlinson (2014b, p. 103) notes that between 2007 and 2010, 65.9 per cent of Fifa's income was generated from broadcasting rights and 29.3 per cent from marketing rights. Fifa generated US$3,655 million during this period, with the majority of income derived from Europe but significant amounts from North America, too. While Fifa generates vast profits from staging World Cups (for example, the 2010 World Cup in South Africa brought in $3.7 billion in sales), host nations invest significant amounts of state funds to stage the events (Baldwin and Panja, 2011). As hosts, South Africa spent in excess of US$7 billion in preparation for the spectacle (Bond and Cottle, 2011). Cleland (2015) suggests that Fifa made profits of US$4.5 billion from Brazil in 2014. An extensive scholarly literature has emerged over the last decade that critically assesses the value of mega-events and the legacies of hosting World Cups and Olympic Games (see in particular Roche, 2000; Horne, 2007). While the emotive and unifying sentiments that World Cups generate are often tangible during the events, long-term legacies are less evident. The large-scale social protests that took place in Brazil during the Confederations Cup in 2013 attest to the concerns that broad sections of society have with the hosting of mega-events. While Fifa generates enormous profits from the World Cup, only a small percentage is reinvested into football globally. One such project is Fifa's Goal programme, started in 1999 to assist smaller football associations. Fifa claims that over 500 developmental projects costing in excess of US$200 million have been initiated (quoted in Tomlinson, 2014b). These projects include football infrastructure such as football pitches, academies, and administrative buildings and structures. While the programme ostensibly invests Fifa profits into grassroots football development, it also allows the current Fifa president to claim responsibility and kudos. This represents a patronage of sorts, which makes it difficult for any rival to challenge for the presidency. Tomlinson (2014b, p. 124) argues that the programme is 'tainted by the politics of personal ambition and institutional survival'. An additional Fifa developmental programme is Football for Hope. This programme is intended to 'develop the game, touch the world and build a better future' in poor communities (quoted in Doherty, 2013, p. 54). Fifa claims that more than 200 projects have been supported globally in the context of a broader programme of sport for development. While these projects and interventions are worthy causes in their own right, we need to contextualize them in relation to the enormous profits that Fifa generates. These profits are generated by events upon which host nations have spent significant public funds. An important component of world football is the continental confederations that represent regional interests. (For details on the 2010 World Cup in South Africa, see Bolsmann, 2013b, 2014.)

## Global football's continental confederations

Membership of Fifa currently stands at 209 football associations, of which some are non-sovereign states. Fifa membership exceeds that of the United Nations. Recognized football associations are in turn members of Fifa, although a prerequisite is membership of one of the six regional confederations. These confederations are responsible for the governance and administration of football in their respective geographical areas. The largest confederation is CAF, with a membership of 54 football associations, and its headquarters are located in Cairo, Egypt. The continental organization is headed by long-standing president Issa Hataytou of Cameroon. Despite CAF being the largest football confederation, it only receives five guaranteed World Cup places. For the 2018 World Cup in Russia, the national teams of CAF member associations were potentially obliged to progress through four qualifying rounds. While Egypt participated in the 1934 World Cup in Italy, it was not until 1970 that at least one African team played in the tournament. Despite thousands of African footballers playing in professional leagues across the world, national teams have not fared particularly well at World Cups (Lanfranchi and Taylor, 2001). Cameroon reached the quarter-finals in 1990, while Senegal and Ghana matched that achievement in 2002 and 2010 respectively (Alegi, 2010). In 2010, South Africa became the first host nation to be knocked out of the event at the group stage. As regards Women's World Cups, Nigeria has qualified for each World Cup since 1991 and reached the quarter-finals in 1999. CAF organizes the bi-annual African Cup of Nations, with Egypt the leading national team with seven continental titles. In addition, the African confederation organizes the CAF Champions League, amongst others, which was first contested in 1964.

In Europe, Uefa was established in 1954, is composed of 53 member associations and remains a powerful bloc within Fifa. Members include the Israeli FA, who joined Uefa due to ongoing political instability in the Middle East. Uefa has been allocated the largest number of World Cup berths for Russia in 2018. In addition to Russia qualifying as the host nation, 13 Uefa members will qualify for the tournament. Former French international football player Michel Platini is the president of Uefa and the headquarters of the organization are located in Nyon, Switzerland. At national level in the men's game, Uefa oversees the four-yearly European Championship and, at club level, the lucrative Champions and Europa Leagues. The Uefa Champions League is Europe's premier club completion. It was first inaugurated in 1955 as the European Champions' Club Cup and won by Real Madrid. The Spanish team has won the tournament on ten occasions. The Champions League generates significant financial rewards for competing teams. The 2012 winners, Chelsea, received £70 million for its exploits, while Uefa has television contracts with over 80 broadcasters who screen the tournament in more than 200 countries (Cleland, 2015). In addition to the large amounts of sponsorship that the Champions League generates from television, members' leagues similarly attract big media deals. In particular, the Premier League in England (PL), La Liga in Spain, the German Bundesliga and Serie A in Italy lead the way in broadcast revenue. The PL's television contract for three years from 2013 was worth £5.14 billion (Cleland, 2015).

The PL is popular throughout the world but particularly in Hong Kong, Malaysia, Thailand and Singapore, whose FAs are members of the Asian Football Confederation (AFC). AFC was formed in 1954 (Weinberg, 2015). Membership of AFC stands at 46 and includes states such as Lebanon in the Middle East, Guam further afield in the western Pacific and Australia to the south. The confederation is further divided into five geographical areas. AFC members staged the inaugural Women's World Cup in China in 1991 and the first co-hosted men's World Cup in Japan and South Korea in 2002 (Horne and Manzenreiter, 2002). The tiny Gulf state of Qatar is set to host the 2022 World Cup; however, in light of allegations of vote-rigging in allocating World Cups and ongoing labour and human rights issues, this decision was disputed. Four members of AFC qualified for the 2014 World Cup. In geopolitical terms, China and India are dominant powers globally and in the region; however, this economic and political dominance is not reflected in football terms. The Chinese Football Association was established in 1924 and the All India Football Federation in 1937. Despite a long tradition of playing the game in both countries, in men's football, the Chinese national team has only appeared in the World Cup on one occasion, in 2002. Its Indian counterpart is ranked lowly at around 140th on Fifa's world ranking chart. The Chinese women's national team has enjoyed far greater success. The team has qualified for six of the seven Women's World Cups and was runner-up in the 1999 competition, losing to the US on penalties. The Indian women's national team is ranked much higher than its male counterpart and yet still finds itself around 50th. The domestic football leagues in China and India attract large numbers of foreign players, particularly from Africa and South America.

The Oceania Football Confederation (OFC) is made up of 11 member states from the South Pacific. OFC was formed in 1968 through the efforts of New Zealand official Charles Dempsey, and the founding members included Australia, Fiji, New Zealand and Papua New Guinea. The winners of the Oceania World Cup qualifying campaign are drawn in an intercontinental play-off against a team selected from one of the other confederations, such as CONCACAF. OFC male representatives New Zealand qualified for the 1982 and 2010 World Cups, while Australia qualified in 1974 and 2006 before joining AFC.

The Americas are represented by two confederations. In the north, the Confederation of North, Central American and Caribbean Association Football (CONCACAF) represents 41 members; in the south, CONMEBOL has 10 members. CONCACAF was established in 1961 after a merger of regional organizations and is Fifa's newest confederation. Mexico and the US are important members of CONCACAF, with strong domestic leagues, and the countries have hosted the men's World Cup on three occasions between them. The US women's national team is the most successful team in the region with three World Cup titles. Major League Soccer (MLS) was established in the US in the aftermath of the World Cup held there in 1994. The MLS continues to attract high-profile European players to football clubs in Canada and the US. David Beckham was one of the first of the high-profile European or 'Designated' players to join LA Galaxy, in 2007 (Cleland, 2015). Despite the dominance of American football, baseball and basketball in the US, football is increasingly popular. During the 2010 and 2014 World Cups, American visitors were the largest group of foreigners in both countries. The premier tournament organized by CONCACAF is the Gold Cup, which is contested bi-annually for men and every four years for women.

CONMEBOL is the oldest football confederation, established in 1916. The confederation is the smallest body in Fifa but is a dominant force in world football due to the exploits of Brazil in particular, who have won five men's World Cup titles. This is followed by Argentina and Uruguay, who have both won the title on two occasions each. The Brazilian Marta Vieira da Silva (usually known as Marta) is one of the standout players in women's football, having won the Fifa World Player of the Year award on five occasions between 2006 and 2010. In men's football, CONMEBOL organizes the Copa América for national teams, first contested in 1916. At club level, the Copa Libertadores is CONMEBOL's premier competition. Argentinian and Brazilian clubs have dominated the tournament, with the Buenos Aires clubs Independiente and Boca Juniors having won the title on the most occasions.

## Conclusion

In this chapter, we have considered the diffusion of football around the globe. Britain was at the forefront of this process and was able to export the game through its formal and informal colonial networks of international trade and cultural exchange. Importantly, this process was not unidirectional and countries around the world refashioned football and the game more generally in ways that suited their needs. Significantly, British footballing authorities initially poured scorn upon the formation of a global football association. Since the early part of the last century, football has operated on a global scale and the formation of Fifa was a manifestation of this process. While Fifa has been plagued by scandal since its inception and particularly in recent times, it remains an important body in the regulation and oversight of the game globally. In an era of globalization, football remains the world's truly global game, one that is played by millions of men, women, boys and girls around the world. There are many 'countries where soccer has been and continues to be a primordial symbol of collective identity', as Eduardo Galeano (whose passage opened this chapter) puts it: 'Each … affirms its right to be different. Tell me how you play and I'll tell you who you are.' For this reason, the study of football as a process of globalization more generally remains a useful avenue of academic enquiry, shedding light on a number of political, economic and cultural processes around the world.

## Research in Action

'South African football tours at the turn of the twentieth century: amateurs, pioneers and profits' by Chris Bolsmann (2010)

### What was the goal of the research?

The goal of this research was to bring to light five groundbreaking football tours to and from South Africa between 1897 and 1907. The intention was to highlight the importance of football in the development of South African sport during the period under consideration.

### Why was the research relevant?

In the global struggle against apartheid South Africa, one of the most effective mechanisms of isolating the Pretoria regime was the sports boycott. Apartheid laws were introduced after the election victory of the National Party (NP) in 1948. While the NP never enacted legislation that specifically prohibited racially mixed sport, a range of apartheid laws made playing together impossible. In 1956, South Africa's minister of the interior, T. E. Dönges, issued the regime's first sports policy (Lapchick, 1975). He noted that sport would remain segregated and organized separately. No racially mixed sport was permitted within South Africa, nor were mixed teams allowed to represent the country abroad. The anti-apartheid movement particularly targeted the Springbok cricket and rugby teams (Hain, 2012). A number of highly successful campaigns were staged against South African tours to Britain and New Zealand in particular. While the sports boycott and the struggle against apartheid sport was one of the most effective, it resulted in a number of misconceptions of South African sport more generally. The most significant is that football is a black sport while white South Africans only play cricket and rugby. A cursory look at the male national teams in these sporting codes in South Africa today would confirm this generalization. However, this has not always been the case. As a sports-mad South African boy growing up in apartheid Pretoria, I was able to play a range of different sports, including football (Bolsmann, 2013a). As a result of this, it was clear to me that the characterization of South African sport is wrong. Through a number of research projects, I have argued that to view South African sports in these terms is theoretically weak and methodologically flawed. Moreover, South African football has important historical and contemporary roles in global football. I have considered the contribution that South African football makes to understanding the global game.

### What methods were used?

The research made use of primary and secondary documentary sources from a range of archives in South Africa and Britain. These included the official minutes and records of SAFA housed in Johannesburg and a number of British football club minutes in the UK. In addition, the research drew extensively upon the British Library's Newspaper Collections.

### What were the main arguments?

The main arguments were that South African football was at the forefront of globalizing the game in the late nineteenth century, and the country was an important destination for British football teams during this period. Corinthian FC first visited South Africa in 1897 and again in 1903 and 1907. This was its first journey outside Europe. The black South African football team from the Orange Free State toured around Britain in 1899 and played against first-class professional opposition. Despite being outplayed by British opposition, the team was groundbreaking in that most spectators had never witnessed an all-black football team play the game. South Africa sent a white football team to play in South America in 1906, which convincingly defeated opposition in Argentina, Brazil and Uruguay.

### And the conclusions or key findings?

The key findings were that South African football has a long tradition of engaging with the game globally and was at the forefront of this process. The research also suggested that we need to reconsider the role of powerful stakeholders in sport more generally who suggest that certain groups of people only play and participate in certain kinds of sports. By doing this, we highlight how meanings attached to sports can be contested.

### What were the strengths of the research?

The strengths of the project were that new evidence and data was published for the first time, requiring consideration by any serious historian or sociologist of sport in light of the myths that exist about South African sport. The research also suggested that there are a number of themes in South African sport that are under-researched and potentially offer scholars a rich vein for further enquiry.

### *Were there any weaknesses?*

A weakness of the research was that I was only able to consult archival minute books and newspaper reports from the period rather than the diaries and personal accounts of players, officials and spectators. Archival minute books and newspapers are valuable sources of information; however, they can potentially be 'censored' in that an official account can be made to represent a specific viewpoint or position more generally.

# 4

# FANDOM

*Kevin Dixon*

---

### Chapter highlights

- While football fandom is a stable part of contemporary life, social-scientific explanations of this phenomenon are often contested.
- Some scholars highlight the importance of tradition, community, convention and continuity when explaining fandom.
- Others argue that football fandom has become a reflection of a late modern age that prioritizes individualism above and beyond convention and community.
- Alternatively, some writers argue that both continuity and social change are equally important to our understanding of football fandom.

---

## Introduction

Ever since 1863, when the Football Association (FA) was formed and the conditions were set in place for mass participation, followers of football have existed. They are most frequently referred to as football 'fans'; a one-size-fits-all descriptor that draws on the fanatical nature of followers and the dominant influence that football has within the lives of individuals and groups of people. While such terminology may imply notions of a minority subculture, it is important to note that the global popularity of football is such that most people are touched by football fandom at some life intersection. For instance, despite any personal choice to follow, or not to follow football, it is likely that our social networks (i.e. family, peer groups or work colleagues) will have been infiltrated to some extent by football fans. In fact, football fans are such a common feature of contemporary life that you may think that you know everything there is to know about them, right? Why, then, is it appropriate to dedicate a book chapter to the discussion of this phenomenon? Well, as with most subject areas, it is only when we begin to look beyond the veneered surface and ask deeper questions about the substance of fandom that it is possible to reveal intricate details that are often overlooked.

So, ask yourself again: what do you really know about football fans in contemporary life? What do you know about the role that they play in the processes that maintain football cultures across time and space? What do you understand about the lived experience of fandom and those systems of power that can produce difference, exclusion and marginalization? What are the social processes relating to fandom genesis, maintenance and evolution? How can you explain variations of practice (i.e. what fans do) and the values and cultural dynamics that hold groups together for the duration of a football match and beyond?

This chapter seeks to investigate such questions by appraising social-scientific explanations of the phenomenon of football fandom across three areas. First, it briefly examines dominant categorizations of fandom as researchers have sought to compartmentalize fandom types in order to account for overt differences in fandom practice. Second, the chapter draws on conceptual studies that depict football fandom as a reflection of late modern lifestyles. Such lifestyles are thought to be influenced by accelerated changes in the evolution of technology, the realization of global interdependence (i.e. the realization that citizens of countries across the globe are mutually dependent on one another), the onset of consumer cultures (i.e. cultures whose economics are defined by the buying or spending of consumers) and an emphasis on individuality over community. Third, the chapter sets out to explore meso theories of football fandom – that is, theories that fall in the space between those that focus on accelerated social change and those that evoke notions of social structure and tradition ('meso' means 'middle' or 'intermediate'). In addition, this chapter will draw attention to the marginalization experiences of ethnic minorities and female fans as they negotiate fandom cultures. Let's start with a critique of fandom types.

## Shifting fandom cultures and fandom types

The shifting patterns of fandom cultures have proven to be problematic for sociologists of football. Indeed, over time they have led researchers to focus attention on types of fandom, and consequently arguments relating to authenticity, tradition and change have consumed the interests of scholars. One distinction that's often made exists in relation to the juxtaposition of new and traditional fans. New fans are thought to differ from the traditional variety in terms of the means, motives and underlying philosophies that they are alleged to hold (Best, 2013; Dixon, 2013). They are thought to be more affluent (sometimes described as middle class) and to hold values that personify the contemporary fascination with consumption and consumer culture. Besides, it is assumed that new fans are elusive in the sense that they are open to market influences, not only with respect to what to buy, but also what football club, or indeed what sport, to follow (Rein *et al.*, 2006). It is anticipated that conventional loyalty is not a concept that resonates with new fans, given that they are understood to be attracted towards teams based on success, rather than as a consequence of personal heritage; celebrity, rather than character; and progress, rather than the maintenance of tradition (Dixon, 2015). In other words, new fans select one club that they wish to support instead of another in much the same manner as a consumer selects a pair of Ted Baker rather than Diesel jeans.

By contrast, traditional fans are often described (within both academia and the general population of football enthusiasts) as entrenched, loyal, unmoving, convention-focused individuals who hold strong emotional connections to a football team and to like-minded others. Paradoxically, however, the unswerving nature of traditional fans to blindly follow group conventions can make them prime targets for commercial exploitation (Dixon, 2011). I state that this is paradoxical (i.e. seemingly self-contradictory) because in spite of their assumed working-class status and outward promotion of the anti-consumerist message, they are just as susceptible to advertising and marketing as other fans (Critcher, 1979; King, 1997; Best, 2013). When taken together, these views assume a dichotomy, or division, between two distinct proposed fandom types. However, such accounts run the risk of presuming a rigid distinction that is perhaps too simplistic to capture the true essence of the lived experience of contemporary fandom (Crawford, 2004) – if, indeed, there is a 'true essence'.

Recognizing that football fandom is perhaps more complex than the above dichotomy suggests, Richard Giulianotti (2002) has sought to explain football fandom with the use of a conceptual taxonomy. In this instance, 'taxonomy' refers to the classification of multiple fandom types, whereas 'dichotomy' only refers to two conceptualized types of fandom: traditional and new. Let's spend a little time trying to digest Giulianotti's typology below.

Giulianotti's conceptual model is based on an attempt to examine the impact of football's commercial enlightenment (as businessmen and businesswomen have come to recognize the commercial potential of football) on spectator identities relative to their association with football clubs. In doing so, he categorizes fans with regard to performance (e.g. emotional investment and overt fan behaviour, like singing, chanting and engaging in face-to-face contact with other fans, at the match or in the community) and consumption (the type and extent of economic expenditure on experiences and merchandise) relating to the object of fandom. He proposes that fans position themselves somewhere on a continuum between traditional or consumer (i.e. relating to the extent that supporters identify with locality, place and club history) and 'hot' or 'cold' (i.e. relating to the extent to which the team is associated with their concept of self – hot being more intense reflections of self, and cold being more distant and emotionally removed).

Consequently, the following categories – in order of most authentic (and hottest) to least authentic (and coldest) – typify, in Giulianotti's view, the range of spectators in contemporary football:

1. *Supporters* are conceptualized as agents with a topophilic connection towards a club's core spaces, such as the stadium. ('Topophilia' is a term used by John Bale (1994) to describe the affective ties of people to the material environment as he attempts to capture their distinctive love of place.) Supporting the team is thought to be a preoccupation, and attending home fixtures is a routine that structures free time. Described in this way, supporters are akin to the previously discussed traditional or authentic fandom type.

2. *Followers* align themselves to certain clubs, but are thought not to be preoccupied with the team to the extent that is attributed to supporters. Giulianotti (2002, p. 36) holds that, 'for followers, football spaces (that is, locations) may be mere practical resources with few symbolic meanings'. Moreover, television and internet communications are thought to be the main sites for identification with the club.

3. *Fans* display strength of identification with the club but this is thought to be rather more distant than that experienced by supporters and followers. Through buying merchandise or shares or contributing to fundraising initiatives, fans maintain a strong but distant connection to the team. As such, consumption activities are orientated towards enhancing collective consciousness of support together with celebrity worship. Giulianotti (2002) implies that, like fans of leading musicians, actors and media personalities, football fans enter into non-reciprocal relations of intimacy with football players. In turn, it appears that football players, managers and officials are coached to draw on 'an ever expanding reservoir of clichés and dead metaphors to confirm typified public constructions of their personality', with the aim of perpetuating unidirectional para-social relations (2002, p. 38).

4. Finally, *flâneurs* are described by Giulianotti as those who stroll around and window-shop for football clubs to support. Decisions made in this regard are thought to occur in relation to club success and global reputation. The *flâneur* is said to experience football through a set of impersonal and virtual consumer relationships, using modern forms of technology both to watch live football and to communicate with others.

While this typology enables discussion of the vast and various means by which fans can engage in practice, scholars have been critical of some details. As an example of such criticism, I and others (Gibbons and Dixon, 2010; Dixon, 2013) have argued that when Giulianotti classifies sports fandom via the internet as a virtual and passive form of communication, inauthentic *flâneurs* use to experience sport in a detached manner, he is missing a significant point in relation to the shifting nature of fandom cultures. That is, he does not account for the potentially large proportion of (what Giulianotti himself would consider as) authentic supporters who, despite attending live football games with others, continue to log on and contribute to internet forums, email chains, blogs and message boards. Some scholars have forcefully argued that the internet has become an extension of fandom communication that ought not to be conceptually downgraded as an 'inferior' fandom experience simply because it is new (Gibbons and Nuttall, 2012; Gibbons, 2014). In short, despite the relative complexity of this taxonomy (as it appears at first glance), scholars have argued that it is ultimately too simplistic to explain (with any real meaning at least) fan orientations and levels of authenticity by ranking the perceived importance of consumption practices.

Consequently, this taxonomy and others like it (e.g. Wann *et al.*, 2001) fail to acknowledge the potential fluidity of fan experiences in contemporary life and hold onto a new and yet largely deterministic view of fandom types. Besides this, they focus exclusively on those fans who have an enduring relationship with football, leaving temporary forms of fandom largely unexplored. Jones and colleagues (2012) have set out to address this issue by examining the temporary nature of fandom with an investigation of what they have termed the 'football sojourner'. In this instance, 'sojourners' refers to migrants, international students and refugees who consume and use international sports events to escape overstimulation (e.g. from work and study) and as a means of finding a sense of belonging in a foreign environment by drawing on the comradeship that mega-events (such as the Fifa World Cup) can bring (see also Armstrong and Young, 1999; Lock *et al.*, 2008).

To summarize, then, while valuable for scrutinizing what fans do, dichotomies and typologies of fandom expend too much effort attempting to compartmentalize fandom types into conceptually idealistic but ultimately unrealistic components. Furthermore, it is argued that when scholars discuss the traditional and the new form of fandom, the former is often romanticized and couched in nostalgia, while the importance of the latter is often downplayed. In this regard, Anthony King (1997) and Chris Stone (2007) make an important observation. They remind us that football fandom is not a static phenomenon and consequently it does not stand still long enough for traditional fans to have ever really existed in the way that they have been portrayed in academic research.

This challenge to popular dichotomies and typologies of football fandom has led scholars more recently to explore late modern explanations of contemporary football fan practice.

## Late modern fandom

The term 'late modern fandom' is often associated with the work of scholars who are perceived to be sceptical of so-called 'orthodox' perspectives relating to this subject. Their argument is that some theoretical approaches are no longer suited to explaining the rapid changes in social life that have been brought about by advancements in technology, communications and the diminution of solid identity groups based on, for example, social class.

Steve Redhead (1997) was perhaps the first scholar to discuss a change in football fandom culture when he coined the expression 'post-fandom' to take into account those patterns of cultural movement noted above and their effect on football fandom. For instance, taking inspiration from Paul Virilio, a theorist of accelerated culture, Redhead (2004a, 2004b, 2007) argues that the acceleration of technology and the desire of businessmen and businesswomen to exploit forms of technology for commercial reasons have set the precedent for the evolution of football fan practice in this regard. (Virilio is a French scholar whose work concerns the effects of modern technological advances on humanity, particularly on conceptions of change and speed.)

As a predominant example, Redhead explains that from the moment that Sky (the global, commercial media corporation founded by business tycoon Rupert Murdoch and formerly known as BSkyB) began to use football as the hook to persuade people on lower incomes to sign up to satellite television subscriptions, the foundations were laid for an accelerated change in the way that fans would consume live football. Symptomatic of this change was the movement of kick-off times to coincide with commercial business strategies that were set to extend the influence of the English game to a global market. (Chapters 8 and 10 provide a more detailed explanation of the rise of Sky and its implications for football cultures respectively.)

Furthermore, in addition to the influence of external business strategies, football in England in the early 1990s had been rocked by and was reacting to the 1989 Hillsborough disaster. This tragic incident bore witness to excessive overcrowding within one of the stands, eventually leading to the deaths of 96 Liverpool FC fans. (The details of the incident are covered more fully in Chapter 2.) As a consequence of this tragedy, football clubs in the top two divisions in England were held by law to adapt stadiums in line with the 1990 Hillsborough Stadium Disaster Inquiry (otherwise known as the Taylor Report, to acknowledge the role of the chief investigator, Lord Justice Taylor). The main revolutionary statute, passed by Taylor, was that stadiums should be all-seater. It is largely agreed within scholarly discourse that the implementation of the recommendations of the Taylor Report, when coupled with a more overt business strategy for English football, has altered the essence of football fan practice in a variety of ways. For example, matchday ticket prices have increased, initially to contribute towards the cost of stadium renovations and then later in relation to demand; season tickets have been introduced, largely replacing pay-at-the-turnstiles tickets; and the stands and terraces that were once the cornerstone of masculine group solidarity have disappeared or significantly altered form, attracting new audiences along the way. (Chapter 10 provides a case study of cultural change at an English football club, Newcastle United FC.)

This process has led scholars to question the notion of fandom authenticity. Indeed, with this in mind, some academics have begun to argue that concepts of tradition and authenticity are in fact malleable, changeable and fluid (King, 1998; Nash, 2000; Davis, 2014; Dixon, 2014b; Gibbons and Nuttall, 2014). Others simply suggest that authenticity is 'hyperreal'. 'Hyperreality' is a term coined by social theorist Jean Baudrillard to draw attention to the possibility that most human experiences in contemporary life are so predominantly artificial that it becomes almost impossible to accurately conceptualize authenticity at all. For instance, using the media as an example, Giulianotti (2004) explains that television coverage of live events is, to all intents and purposes, a simulation of the authentic stadium experience, but nevertheless over time this message has become lost in translation. The multiple camera angles, visual gimmicks and slow-motion replays (made possible by television) have become desired, expected and integrated into the live performance via giant screens that are installed in football stadiums as part of the authentic experience. Moreover, in my own research (Dixon, 2014d), I have argued that the wider consumer experience is replicated within the football ground, too. Borrowing the term 'Disneyization' from Alan Bryman (2004), I have suggested that many of the features of contemporary life are taking on the characteristics of the global film and entertainment company Disney. Using the theoretical components originally identified by Bryman, I have pointed out how, for example, the naming of stadiums to compliment financial sponsors and the hybrid consumption opportunities (i.e. multiple types of consumption possibilities) within the football stadium – catering facilities, alcohol and gambling establishments, the museum, the club shop – have all taken their place as components of an 'authentic' and yet ultimately simulated matchday experience.

As a side but no less important issue in the accelerated evolution of football fandom cultures, scholars have noted that the development of internet technology has made it possible for football supporters to be more active in their communications than they have ever been before (Gibbons and Dixon, 2010; Gibbons and Nuttall, 2012). To be 'active', in the sense that it is used here, is to bypass the sole consumption of official club documents and mainstream media (as predominant modes of information gathering) and instead to develop independent forms of communication. Consequently, it is argued that fans can choose to adopt a more participatory rather than passive role in their own experiences (Ruddock, 2005; Hughson and Free, 2006; Dart, 2009). Microblogging sites like Twitter (a popular online social networking service which enables users to send and read short 140-character messages called tweets) are used most predominantly as a technology of fandom, often serving as a backchannel to television or other audiovisual media and allowing users to offer their own running commentary as events unfold live (Highfield et al., 2013).

Indeed, Price and colleagues (2013) indicate that, as well as opening new opportunities for fan expression, this form of new media is being seized upon by football clubs and other commercial bodies eager to redress shifting power balances by establishing themselves on sites like Twitter in an attempt to communicate with fans directly. Likewise, Cleland (2009) points out that other traditional forms of media are responding in similar ways, with television, radio and newspapers using a more involved fan format, reaching out and making fan reactions central to media presentations. Thus, despite what seems like an emergence of conditions that are conducive to the empowerment of football fans, Pearson (2010) draws attention to the possibility that the new technology can also be empowering for commercial companies, given that the internet has become an extension of the consumer market, making fans more easily accessible. In Chapter 8, Richard Haynes explains how the innovations of social networking media have transformed the traditional dominance of mass media in football.

## Late modern football communities?

The last 50 years have brought into focus the concept of globalization. In the same period, we have witnessed the rise of consumer cultures (cultures whose economies are defined by the buying or spending of consumers) and the rise of individual materialism (the desire of individuals to acquire material goods) based in part on mass acceptance of neo-liberal philosophy (attitudes towards the accumulation of capital and material wealth), the acceleration of systems of world travel and communications technology, and the blurring of class boundaries, as people from all social backgrounds search for prosperity and reject deterministic class labels.

Accordingly, some scholars argue that communities and identity groups have altered form to take on late modern characteristics. For instance, drawing on the work of social theorist Michel Maffesoli (1996), Garry Crawford (2004) talks about the emergence of 'neo-tribes' within sport fandom. Here Crawford is referring to new group formations that tend not to hold, or desire to hold, meaningful and long-lasting bonds with one another. Consequently, while such formations are still distinguished by lifestyle and taste, they are thought not to be fixed; that is, people can and do choose to come and go as they wish. In other words, it is argued that fans in late modern life do not have the time or inclination to pursue community in what is often conceived of as a traditional sense. Traditional communities, in this instance, are thought to involve close-knit, entrenched relations based on sameness and loyalty, bound together by group conventions.

Supporting this position, and with reference to football fans at the 2006 Fifa World Cup, Tim Crabbe (2008) describes the emergence of a late modern football community that differs radically from traditional forms. Accordingly, he argues that late modern football communities are less likely to be bound by colloquial closeness and therefore fans are more likely to form what Tony Blackshaw (2008) terms 'deterritorized' groupings – that is, groupings that are short term, temporary and less intimate, characterized by intense emotional involvement, infrequent gatherings and rapid dispersals. This is perhaps best captured in an articulate description of a typical post-match scene, in which Crabbe (2008, p. 435) describes how a mass collection of football fans can quickly dissolve into 'individuals making their way home like disturbed rats scuttling for cover, eager to get ahead, separate from the crowd, in a rush to get home'.

Shaun Best (2013) adds to this discussion when he suggests that Zygmunt Bauman's concept of 'liquid modernity' may be useful in discussing the social attitudes of contemporary football fans. To explain, the concept of liquid modernity works on the premise that the landscape of social life has changed from one associated with heavy modernity (a pre-existing period that was characterized by the strict, solid and clear dimensions of social life) into another for which, Bauman (2002, p. 2) suggests, the terms 'liquidity' and 'fluidity' are the most appropriate. He uses the term 'liquidity' to explain that society cannot keep its shape. He means that it is malleable, always changing form, and in fact the only consistency in liquid-modern life tends to be the necessity and desire for individuals to consume.

With similarities to Maffesoli's concept of neo-tribes, Bauman suggests that identity groups are best conceptualized as swarms in the sense that they hold our attention and focus, but do so only temporarily. Moreover, any bonds that are made between people (and groups of people) are thought not to outlast the act that holds their attention. For instance, with reference to sport, Jon Kraszewski (2008) refers to the liquid-modern conditions of relocation and displacement (as people move freely to work and live in any town, city and nation across the globe) and suggests that fans make use of sport and sports bars (public houses) to collect temporarily and connect with other fans who also find themselves displaced from their place of origin. In this sense, he argues that sports bars fulfil an important function, by allowing displaced fans to meet for comfort and to live the false notion of community before returning to an individual existence. Liquid-modern football, therefore, becomes both a product to be sold to eager consumers and a way for people to re-invent, or re-imagine, a sense of locality or community (however superficial it may be) through their sporting ties.

## Meso approaches to football fandom

In the space between assertions of accelerated social change and those solid concepts that evoke notions of social structure and tradition, it is possible to find social theories positioned at what is known as the meso level. This means that certain theorists acknowledge that both change over time (sometimes accelerated change) and modes of structural repetition can occur simultaneously. For instance, when making comment on scholarly research relating to football fandom, John Williams (2007) argues that the search for explanations of rapid change can negate or underestimate the importance of continuity, place and community in football. Conversely, Williams is equally aware that when scholars use macro theories and simplistic dichotomies to explain fan behaviour, they tend to romanticize tradition and therefore fail to position fans in the new social context of contemporary life.

Thus, given that criticisms are cast on either side of the micro or macro spectrum, Williams suggests that a meso approach would likely offer solutions to those current theoretical problems identified above. With this in mind, the remainder of this chapter sets out to acknowledge the existence of two meso theoretical approaches that are beginning to infiltrate football fandom literature. The theoretical approaches in question, habitus and structuration theory, relate to the sociologists Pierre Bourdieu and Anthony Giddens respectively.

### Habitus and football fandom

Habitus is a theoretical construction that can be used to explain the way that individual traits, attitudes and dispositions are inevitably influenced by history, traditions and cultures. This means that any action that at first glance may seem to be the result of individuality must, in actual fact, hold cultural characteristics. What we know about the world and our position within it is learned and internalized, and in order for habitus to function smoothly we must think that the possibilities from which we choose are common sense, natural or inevitable. This is not to suggest that habitus will always determine fixed responses from people, but rather that it limits the options that individuals have to act in one way or another by providing cultural norms and historical precedents that in turn determine strategies of action.

In my own research, I have used the work of Bourdieu (1977, 1984) in an attempt to explain the origins of football fandom practice (such as indicating how fans are introduced to football and how fandom careers begin). I have used evidence derived from interviews with football fans to argue that while many perceive the way that they practise fandom to be a consequence of their own individual traits (or personality) and nothing more, this is simply an illusion. To explain how I arrived at this position, let me take you through some instances from my sample, starting with Dave, a Newcastle United FC fan who is reminiscing on his origins of practice:

> People often say, 'I was born black and white' [Newcastle's team colours], but that's not strictly true is it? You learn it at home, don't you, from your family.
>
> *(quoted in Dixon, 2012, p. 339)*

Learning to behave in a particular way insinuates that fandom cultures are largely self-perpetuating in the sense that fandom practice can be, and very often is, passed from one generation to the next (Robson, 2000). It seems reasonable to suggest, then, that as football has taken root within society (i.e. since the formation of the Football League in 1888), it has become an important aspect of family or kin tradition, which continues to thrive in this sense. However, in contemporary life, it is equally important to note that habitus can be broken. In relation to this, I was able to point out that people can opt, both into and out of, football fandom at any stage of life. For instance, in what follows, another Newcastle fan, Andy, discusses the difficulty faced when attempting to pass on a traditional desire to support the local football team, while in the second example, Darlington fan Wanda explains how she was introduced to football at a later stage of life despite parental discouragement:

> Our Matty shows no interest really, he's into other things you know? He's massively into art and stuff. That's what he wants to do. I don't know where he gets it from. It's certainly not me or his mother.

> My mother thought football was a game for hooligans, so it was never on the agenda for me … In 2005 I had just gone to college and made new friends when one girl that I was in the same class with won a competition for a free box at Darlington and she invited me to go. I didn't really know what to expect, but that was it. I haven't looked back since.
>
> *(Dixon, 2012, p. 342)*

In these circumstances, it is apparent that the actions of the agents, or fans, in question (i.e. Andy's son Matty and Wanda) have occurred in contradiction to taught norms, and, furthermore, this appears to rest outside Bourdieu's theoretical framework. So, with this in mind, I reasoned that while Bourdieu's theoretical position is reflective of the period in which he was writing, the 1970s, it does not directly translate when attempting to explain the origins of contemporary fandom or the career experiences of contemporary football fans. For instance, the 1970s have been characterized as a 'solid' era in which individuals had a more defined understanding and acceptance of social positions and hierarchies in relation to class, gender, race, masculinity and sexuality (Bauman, 2002). This no longer appears to be the case, and as such I have argued that changes to the contemporary environment (as noted in the previous section on late modern football communities) have summoned conditions in which the possession of a reflexive habitus is becoming increasingly common.

To say that habitus is reflexive draws on the idea that while values and dispositions continue to be passed on in an active and reciprocal manner between generations of people, the contemporary conditions of uncertainty and fluidity (those conditions surrounding people in contemporary life) prepare social agents to be open to change, with agents possessing greater tolerance and taste for diversity (Adkins, 2002; Sweetman, 2003). The instances presented in the examples above demonstrate the role that new interactions can play in order to change life direction and consequently to provide opportunities for people to engage with practices that are estranged from habitual forms of learning during childhood. So, while habitus is useful to explain the relevance and presence of continuity, structure and routine, it is also important to note that habitus may not simply result in a duplication of the actions and values of former generations. Thus, while it is probable that fandom will follow through genetic lines (as values, dispositions and interests are transferred between significant others), contemporary life offers no guarantees that tradition will always roll over for contemporary agents who have learned to value reflexivity.

### Habitus and marginalization: racial inequality and football fandom

Beyond explanations of the genesis of fandom and subsequent fandom careers, Bourdieu's concept of habitus has also been used to draw attention to racial inequality in football and football fandom cultures. In this context, the term 'racial inequality' is used to reflect imbalances in the distribution of power and opportunities as they are specifically related to racial groups. Furthermore, 'racial habitus' refers to thought processes (often unconscious, but derived from a history of widely held discriminatory thoughts and practices) that regulate feelings, perceptions and views on matters of race and race inequality. As an example of the process of racial habitus formation, let's take the case of English football.

In England and Great Britain as a whole, racial inequality has long been associated with rising immigration after the Second World War (due in part to workforce shortages that saw many migrants arrive in search of prosperity), reaching its climax in the 1960s and 1970s (Dorling, 2011). It is argued that in the face of immigration, overt physical and cultural differences have contributed towards racial conflict – with minority groups bearing the brunt of social tension. Moreover, just as patterns of whiteness have pervaded in British society, Jamie Cleland and Ellis Cashmore (2013) remind us that this trend of dominance has been replicated throughout the organization of football per se (from dominant white middle-class rule across Fifa (Fédération International de Football Association), Uefa (Union of European Football Associations) and the English FA, through to club owners, directors and referees) and through the attitudes and overt expressions of football fans. On the latter point, when examples of multi-cultural Britain began to emerge through football in the 1970s, with high-profile players like Viv Anderson, Garth Crooks and others integrating into a traditionally white sphere of British culture, racist abuse ensued from the terraces, with some black and ethnic players leaving the game as a consequence (Robinson, 2008). While black players had existed in the British game before the 1970s, Cleland (2014) argues that their low numbers meant that supporters felt no threat to racial dominance. Throughout the 1970s and 1980s, however, social unrest, high unemployment, the existence of right-wing political groups and a right-wing Conservative government were all thought to contribute to the increasingly hostile social position adopted by football fans towards black and ethnic players (Moran, 2000; Back *et al.*, 2001).

More recently, despite the Commission for Racial Equality launching the Let's Kick Racism Out Of Football campaign (now Kick It Out) in 1993, it is argued that the FA has maintained its white, middle-class rule, with anti-racist campaigns only acquiring attention when players express disgust at their treatment (Cashmore and Cleland, 2011; Cleland and Cashmore, 2013). Moreover, following the Bosman ruling in 1995 and the subsequent increase in the numbers of overseas football players plying their trade in Great Britain, some scholars argue that football has become colour-blind, in the sense that black and ethnic minority success on the playing field, coupled with an emergent awareness of political correctness, has led to the assumption that racism has disappeared from the game (Dixon *et al.*, 2014). Arguably, however, it has simply changed shape. (The Bosman ruling is named after Belgian player Jean-Marc Bosman, who took his club, RC Liege, to court when it denied him permission to move clubs. The European Court of Justice ruling, which turned out-of-contract professionals into free agents who were able to sign for other clubs without transfer fees, came into effect in 1995.)

Daniel Burdsey (2011) agrees and suggests that racism now operates in complex, nuanced and often covert ways, creeping under the radar of the football authorities and evading the challenge of anti-racist groups. Jamie Cleland (2014) also indicates that the advent of new social media has only added to the complexity of this situation, but nonetheless it is thought that racial habitus continues to exist within and between football fans, taking a predominant role in the perpetuation of racial inequality (Bonilla-Silva, 2006; Bonilla-Silva *et al.*, 2006; Sallaz, 2010; Perry, 2012). This discussion is continued in Chapter 5, in which Jamie Cleland explores racism and white dominance in English football.

## Structuration theory and football fans

As an alternative approach to the work of Bourdieu, scholars are now beginning to explore the potential of structuration theory to explain cultures relating to football. This theory is most notably associated with sociologist Anthony Giddens' 1984 publication *The Constitution of Society* and is based on one simple but original idea: everything in social life, from encompassing world systems to an individual's state of mind, originates through the skilful performance of conduct and interaction (Cohen, 2008, p. 324). Giddens notes that social life equates to more than random social acts (i.e. emphasizing agency or freedom of expression) but also acknowledges that it is not merely determined by social forces (i.e. recurring structures). In other words, society is not merely a mass of micro-level activity, nor can it be explained only with reference to macro-level structures.

Instead, Giddens argues that social structure and human agency are in a relationship with each other and that it is the repetition of the acts between individual agents (interactions across time) that reproduces the structure. He suggests that it is the routines of everyday existence (occurring, for example, when going to university or to work, or when talking with our friends and family) that can help to reproduce social structure. This means that there is social structure in tradition – in the values that we internalize, in customs and in many other conventions where social norms are adopted and practised. However, while this might allude to the existence of a stagnant culture that simply reproduces form, structuration theory is equally successful at explaining how cultures change or transform when people react to, for example, changes in technology and means of communication, national disasters such as the Hillsborough stadium tragedy, the implementation of legal statutes such as the Bosman ruling, ticket price rises and the involvement of Sky television, amongst other issues (Dixon, 2011).

I have previously used structuration theory to explain how the public house (otherwise known as the pub) has maintained a relationship with spectator football across time and space (Dixon, 2014a). In doing so, I have argued that it was no accident that the pub became a stable, routine space for fans to congregate in and talk about the match, and that it continues to fulfil this role in contemporary life. After all, according to Holt (1990, p. 63), the pub has 'staying power' precisely because it has been able to adapt to the demands of social change relative to football fans. This has been achievable, I have suggested, through the process of structuration as it applies to both the institution (pubs) and football fans (customers) per se.

For instance, as football has diffused into the lives of working men and women (throughout the late nineteenth and early twentieth centuries), it has taken its place as part of the everyday life associated with the pastimes of ordinary people – and for centuries past, alcohol establishments have been a crucial part of this (Walvin, 1994). Indeed, prior to the codification of football, the pub maintained its position as a stable place for working-class recreation (Collins and Vamplew, 2002), and it is worth noting that the pre-industrial idea that sport should be an occasion for drinking alcohol has been carried over into football fandom via the structuration of encounters of working men and women across time. Indeed, from the inception of organized football, pubs have offered fledgling football teams premises to use as changing rooms and surrounding fields to use as grounds on which to play (Mason, 1980; Russell, 1997). Allegiances to popular pastimes such as football have brought with them custom from players, friends of players and followers of the team. In fact, by 1890, pub football teams were the most common type of all, with establishments offering a place for teams, management and supporters to convene and embrace their communal football home (Holt, 1990).

This relationship has been maintained by both fans and publicans as they each look after their own interests. For instance, as the new media age of football began to emerge, pubs (for reasons of commercial success) adapted their strategy by embracing new technology, bringing in television sets and then later buying licences to show live Sky Sports football (Weed, 2006, 2007, 2008). Furthermore, new designs to some pubs were sought after (by fans) and delivered (by publicans) in order to create an internal layout that improved the viewing experience for both men and women alike. Moreover, in an era where drinking-related health issues are concerns for some fans, tea, coffee and food are alternative attractions to the stable diet of wine, beer and spirits (Dixon, 2013).

The point is that, as structuration theory suggests, social structure is produced, reproduced and altered across time and space because it is reinforced by day-to-day actions and communications. Continuity, after all, is important to human beings as they desire to feel connected to the past (e.g. through perceptions of tradition) because it makes them feel secure, and this is often acted out through routine behaviours, such as watching football with others in the pub. Absolute continuity, of course, can only ever be an illusion because subtle changes in behaviours and thought patterns inevitably creep into the psyche of human beings as they influence and become influenced by social and technological change. Regardless, in time, those subtle changes merge seamlessly into dominant conceptions of tradition and convention, to take up what seems like a natural position in the field.

## Structuration and marginalization: female football fans

As well as explaining the stability of social institutions (such as the pub in relation to football fans), structuration theory has also been used to explain the relative stability of sub-group marginalization within football fandom cultures, such as the marginalization of female football fans.

Despite the fact that women have always attended football matches (Birley, 1993; Coddington, 1997; Williams, 2003) and that they are growing in number (Nagle *et al.*, 2010, p. 22), there is an acceptance that inequalities on account of gender continue to exist in sport fan communities (Jones, 2008; Ben-Porat, 2009; Mewett and Toffoletti, 2011; Obel, 2012). In an attempt to explore the recurring nature of gender inequality within football fandom, I have conducted research that has set out to appraise the value of structuration theory for explaining the subordinate positioning of female football fans (Dixon, 2014c). To this end, I was particularly interested in questions of how daily routines, habits and competencies shape gender power relations.

Drawing on interviews that would reveal evidence in the form of life histories, I was able to demonstrate that while many female fans may cite positive, memorable experiences in relation to their initiation into football fandom, these are inevitably short-lived. For pre-adolescent girls, an interest in football was perceived as cute and yet those approaching their teenage years were often steered away from football by family or else discredited by other girls for continuing to participate as fans:

> Because I played football with the lads in my street and because I supported my local football team, I was looked down upon by loads of bitchy girls at school.
>
> *(Dixon, 2014c, p. 7)*

Barrie Thorne (1993) explains experiences like those expressed above as a consequence of the process of gender separation in adolescence. This is a situation in which gender expectations and behaviours are highly monitored as peers and peer groups assess one another for adherence (or otherwise) to gender-appropriate behaviour (George and Brown, 2000; Clark and Paechter, 2007). The social reward (i.e. social acceptance) that girls are known to receive when engaging in gender-appropriate activities highlights the point that gender roles are constructed through recurrent interactions and yet, because they are so deeply embedded into the public psyche, they seem to represent a natural order. In a similar manner, Stacey Pope and David Kirk (2014, p. 233) argue that '[t]he idea that heterosexual teenage girls become interested in different things to boys' is potentially damaging to the long-term involvement of many women in activities chiefly associated, historically speaking, with men.

Consequently, continuing to practise football fandom, a largely masculine pursuit, against the advice of female peers and matriarchal figures tends not to be without consequence. For instance, I was able to reveal that female fans perceived themselves to be inferiorly positioned within football fandom cultures and that this was based purely on their gender. Levels of knowledgeability, enthusiasm and consumption – factors associated with prestige for male fans (Dixon, 2013) – were not always recognized or rewarded in the same way for female fans. In fact, participants explained that encounters with others were often strained on account of involvement with football fandom. For example, the ability to talk football held little value and was disparaged by other women, and was viewed with scepticism and as gimmicky by other men.

Consequently, and in line with structuration theory, it seems that reflexivity (i.e. the awareness that female fans have about instances of gender inequality) does not always result in a coordinated campaign for cultural transformation. Rather, female fans are constrained by, and contribute to, dominant thought patterns relating to gender. Take, for instance, the following quotes from Sunderland supporter, Rachel and Middlesbrough supporter, Suzi:

I do think that some female fans do us no favours. Some of them tend to go in groups to ogle at the blokes and others stand there in sexy clothes with their tits out. That's how we get a bad press.

I just think of myself as one of the lads. I get on with everyone and can hold my own. If you can't do that as a girl, then my opinion is, just don't bother.

*(Dixon, 2014c, p. 11)*

Aligned with the comments above, Jayne Cauldwell (2011, p. 334) raises an important point when she explains that it is a mistake to think that solidarity exists between women and that they form a collective. She indicates that women, just like men, vie for dominance, and consequently that 'women are not only oppressed by men but they may also be oppressed by other women'. This illustrates the unintended consequence for women in the system of structuration, given that the repetition of social inequality is made possible through the historical and contemporary personal encounters of women, as well as of men. After all, fitting in with masculine culture and disparaging those women who choose not to embrace this (such as Rachel and Suzi, quoted above) does not necessarily result in the equality that those female football fans desire. (For more on the effects of masculine cultures in football, see Chapter 6.)

To recap, then, structuration theory argues that the gender order is sustained through the encounters of individuals and groups who are dispersed across generations and throughout football fandom careers. Within the practice of football fandom, it appears that not all actors are equal, with fans positioned according to gender and associated attitudes that impact directly on authority and depictions of authenticity.

## Conclusion

This chapter has outlined the contested terrain of football fandom research as it has evolved over the course of the last five decades. As well as highlighting the strengths of each wave of studies, it has also drawn attention to associated limitations. For instance, dichotomies of football fans as traditional or new and typologies that provide multiple categorizations are helpful for acknowledging the various means via which fans can practise, and yet when attempting to explain fan behaviour in an all-encompassing manner by segmenting fans into distinct categories, they appear too simplistic. Not only do some conceptual models lack empirical support to substantiate claims to practice, but they are also thought to be too theoretically rigid.

Thus, solid ideas of traditional versus new have been challenged by scholars who have sought to explain fandom as unconstrained, fluid and individual. From this perspective, it is argued that fandom has changed shape in line with accelerated changes that have occurred in wider society, including neo-liberal attitudes, advancements in personal communication technology, the desire to consume and the diminution of collectivism. However, while such arguments can be convincing, writers have been criticized for underestimating the importance of continuity, place and community in contemporary football.

As an alternative to both approaches described above, meso theories have been used to acknowledge the importance of both continuity and change when explaining the nature of fandom cultures. In doing so, scholars have been able to demonstrate that fandom cultures are made and remade through everyday interactions. Consequently, it is possible for football fandom to simultaneously maintain aspects of tradition and convention, uphold cultures of marginalization and contribute towards the evolution of practice.

## Research in Action

*The End of the Terraces: The Transformation of English Football in the 1990s* by Anthony King (1998)

### What were the goals of the research?

The goals of the research were, first, to analyze the responses of a particular type of male supporter to the transformation of top-flight football in England after 1992 and, second, to contribute to an emerging theoretical framework related to the sociology of consumption.

### Why was the research relevant?

This was the first substantial sociological study into supporters of professional football since the inception of the English Premier League in 1992 and the concomitant transformation of modern football. The transformation was brought about by lucrative television deals, rising ticket prices, the rise of consumer culture, Government white papers (relating to the Hillsborough disaster) and the subsequent legal obligations of all teams in the top flight of English football to create all-seater stadiums. By investigating a particular group of male supporters, King was able to pay attention to a group of fans whom he considered to be traditional (in the sense that they had attended Manchester United FC matches throughout the 1970s and 1980s) and to monitor their thoughts and behaviours in light of the transformation of English football noted above.

### What methods were used?

#### Sample

In order to examine the transformation of the consumption of football, King sought to investigate fans of Manchester United, a football club that had a predominant role in campaigning for teams in the top flight of the Football League (formerly called the First Division) to create a Premier League (breaking away from the Football League, originally founded in 1888) in order to take advantage of a lucrative television rights deal. King began to attend home games in 1993–1994 with the intention of making contacts and gathering a sample of fans who were willing to take part in his study. He gained close contact with 20 fans and made the acquaintance of 20 more. This group, whom King refers to as 'the lads', was composed predominantly of youthful men (largely 20–30 years old, with a few falling outside this bracket) associated with (i.e. contributors to) the fanzines *Red Issue* and *United We Stand*. King employed three principal methods to investigate this sample, discussed briefly below.

## Participant observation

King chose participant observation as one method because he was interested in studying changes in fandom behaviour via interpretative analysis. Moreover, he argued that because young men (the focus of his attention) are notoriously difficult to attract to surveys and focus groups, participant observation would allow academic researchers to study an important population with regard to the phenomenon of football fandom. Fieldwork began during the 1993–1994 season, when King began to attend all games home and away, travelling to away games on coaches organized by the two aforementioned fanzines. In addition to this, he wrote to both fanzine editors to ask if they required any assistance, and he too became a contributor. In September 1993, he was invited to travel to a European Cup match in Budapest. The trip involved a four-day return coach journey during which the researcher began to establish himself in the informal network of the lads.

## Interviews

Post-fieldwork, King conducted 13 interviews with a selection of fans with whom he had the best rapport. Interviews lasted up to an hour and a half and, for the convenience of the participants, were conducted in participants' homes or pubs (as requested). Interviews were largely unstructured, but based on participant observations, direct experience and sociological theory.

## What were the main arguments?

In the face of overt changes to English football, King noted contradictory findings, highlighting both resistance and compliance.

## Resistance

Prior to the Taylor Report (1990, p. 12), which recommended that stadiums should be all-seater, almost all football grounds had large terraced areas. Entry to stadiums was almost always guaranteed and involved the payment of cash at the turnstiles. By contrast, all-seater stadiums had reduced potential capacity and increased prices. Consequently, the new stadiums had transformed the spaces that were central to the lads' creation of solidarity. This had restricted their ability to congregate together as they had done in the decades past, and significantly impacted on the practice of singing, dancing, jumping and celebrating together, as one. Furthermore, many of the lads reported that they had been excluded from the stadium on the grounds of capacity alone (with demand outstripping supply). They also noted that emerging club policies (relating to global marketing of the club and the active courtship of a professional class of fans) were impacting on them in negative ways. In addition, the influx of families and the encouragement of day flights from Ireland to bring tourist supporters into the stadium were also acknowledged to be symptomatic of the commercialization of football. In connection with this, the lads had formulated judgements on the types of fans who would buy merchandise and wear replica shirts. Those fans, labelled as non-masculine consumer fans, were reported to be a threat to the continued practices associated with the lads. As a means of resistance to the commodification of football, the lads would express their views through fanzine contributions and they would distinguish themselves from the new consumer fans in every conceivable way. For example, where new fans would buy club merchandise and wear Manchester United coats, shirts and other paraphernalia to attend fixtures, the lads would continue to dress for the match in casual style, while mocking all those who were following new trends.

## Compliance

Although this sample displayed resistance to certain parts of the club's commercial strategy, King was able to highlight that the lads' fandom reflected a more complex relationship with the club than mere opposition. After all, the lads had an emotional attachment to the club (and their fellow male fans). Consequently, as long as the new environment continued to allow them to remake the jubilant solidarity that they had experienced in the past (even if it meant the loss of the company of some friends who can no longer attend), they were willing to overlook major grievances and inconveniences. For example, while the lads mocked those who buy merchandise and sport replica shirts, they were pleased that the club shop was thriving; and while they criticized the replacement of standing terraces with seating, they were proud of the new stadium. All of these new elements of fandom, while alien (and initially met with confrontation), were beginning to become integrated into the psyche of this group, over time.

### And the conclusions or key findings?

The fans' reaction to the new consumption of football was paradoxical, given that King was able to evidence elements of compliance and resistance simultaneously. Consequently, he argued that while theories of hegemony (dominance of one group over another) and resistance (resistance to dominance) are important, they overemphasize the oppositions of interest and rarely consider the potentially shared interests between dominant and subordinate groups which, he implied, texture social relations in complex ways.

### What were the strengths of the research?

The strength of King's research was that it targeted those directly implicated by the change in football cultures. Consequently, the research moved away from the abstract theoretical musings of scholars and instead championed the voice of football fans by providing an empirically grounded theoretical argument. Moreover, the research challenged established theories of resistance and hegemony that had typically informed research on fandom since the 1970s.

### Were there any weaknesses?

There were few weaknesses to speak of in relation to this project; however, if we are to be picky, we could make reference to the sample used by King. As described above, the lads were a group who shared a number of common traits. Not only did they all support Manchester United, but they were also all youthful, class-conscious men, defined by masculine practice, and active fanzine producers or contributors. The specificity of this sample was not a weakness per se (in fact, there is much to admire about this specific group of fans); however, when research samples are focused in this way, the generalization of findings can be brought into question. That is to say, how far were King's findings really representative of all fans of this period in time? While King must take on board this criticism, it must be noted that generalizability of findings was not the overall aim of this project. Moreover, many scholarly studies conceived after King's *The End of the Terraces* have used these niche findings in order to test outcomes against the experiences of fans in many different contexts.

# 5
# RACISM

*Jamie Cleland*

---

**Chapter highlights**

- For most of the twentieth century, whiteness was normalized in the culture of football.
- Second-generation black British players emerged in the 1970s and 1980s, but were met with overt hostility.
- Anti-racism organizations emerged in the 1990s to combat growing levels of overt racism and reflect an increasingly transnational playing environment.
- Racist language and intent amongst fans has diversified into online social media platforms, including fan message boards, blogs, Facebook and Twitter.
- Football reflects white sensibilities, dispositions and tastes.

---

## Introduction

In practice, association football was created by white men to be played by white men, and the organizations that ran the sport were controlled by white men. However, this does not mean that black people were deliberately excluded from football. Arthur Wharton (1865–1930) in the late nineteenth century and Walter Tull (1888–1918) in the early twentieth century were both black and distinguished themselves in English football, but they were isolated examples and the complexion of football from its formal inception has been predominantly one of whiteness. 'Whiteness' has been defined by Mary McDonald (2009, p. 9) as 'institutionalised discourses and exclusionary practices seeking social, cultural, economic and psychic advantage for those bodies racially marked as white'.

As I have argued elsewhere (Cleland, 2015), the hierarchy of contemporary football remains white – from the top, where key governance and organizational decisions are made (including those made by Fifa, continental confederations like Uefa, national associations like the FA and at individual club level), to fans at the bottom. Only in the middle, consisting of the players, could it be argued that there is a blurring of 'races', such as in England, where 20 to 25 per cent of professional footballers are black or minority ethnic (BME). Yet given the number of BME players and the transnational nature of football since the 1990s, a number of key questions have emerged about the contemporary culture of football. Why does racism remain an unwelcome feature? Why do so few black players move into managerial/administrative positions when they retire? What has been the impact of racial discrimination policy towards making the culture of football ethnically inclusive? How has the everyday practice of supporters changed with the advent of social media? What forms of social and cultural capital can be accrued by racist supporters?

Taking whiteness as its central feature, this chapter addresses these questions and starts by providing a historical account of racial closure within football. In order to take account of all developments, the chapter then outlines how anti-racism has been a feature of football culture since the 1990s to reflect concerns about growing levels of racism. Although incidents of overt racism – open and observable racist language and/or behaviour – has decreased in some countries (such as in England), this is not the case everywhere (such as in Italy, Spain and certain parts of Eastern Europe) and has led to accusations that the game's authorities and anti-racism organizations are 'colour-blind' (where whites ignore the disadvantages of not being white and thus allow the continuation of racialized practices and structures) through their failure to adequately challenge racist thoughts and behaviour. The chapter then focuses on the introduction of social media (such as fan message boards, blogs, Facebook and Twitter) and how they have allowed for the often anonymous communication of racist language and hate speech. Finally, the chapter ends by considering the unconscious racial and white habitus (I will explain this concept later in the chapter) of some supporters and the ways in which football is used as a platform for the expression of racist thoughts and beliefs.

I place 'race' in quotation marks throughout this chapter to suggest how it is a contested concept that has no objective reality and is largely a fiction, albeit an influential one, that motivates some people towards discriminatory verbal and non-verbal thoughts and behaviour based on the perception that there are natural biological differences between certain groups (i.e. 'racism' – a term that first came into popular use in the 1960s and is defined differently by various scholars and organizations). These differences are then hierarchically ordered, with some 'races' perceived as being naturally superior to others.

This has led scholars such as Daniel Burdsey (2009) and Kevin Hylton (2009) to refer to the normalization of whiteness and the marginalization of the Other as key factors in explaining the existence of racism within football since the 1970s (by 'the Other', I mean a person or group who is treated as distinct or opposite from oneself, perhaps on the grounds of being regarded as a member of a different 'race'). Therefore, without whiteness, there can be no victims of racism and so it has become central in examining social divisions and inequalities in football.

## 'Race' and football in history

Across the world at the beginning of the twentieth century, racial separation and discrimination within football was widespread. In Australia, where it competed against more native sports such as Australian Rules football, rugby league, rugby union and cricket, football was referred to as 'wogball' ('wog' was a slang word in the British and Australian idiom to refer to anyone who was not white) given its participation by migrants (Skinner *et al.*, 2008; see also King, 2004). Likewise, in Peru, the successful Alianza Lima side of the 1920s was referred to as the 'negroes' and suffered widespread racial prejudice due to the composition of black players and supporters (Wade, 2010). Similar circumstances were also found in Brazil, with Marcos Natali (2007) outlining how even the Brazilian president, Epitácio Pessoa, prohibited the inclusion of black players. However, Vasco da Gama defied this ban and became the first club to sign black players in 1923. The success of this move was immediate, with the club winning the championship, and it spurred other South American clubs into signing black players. Not only did a significant number begin representing individual clubs, but they were also selected in national teams, including Leônidas da Silva and Domingos da Guia, who represented Brazil at the 1938 World Cup held in France (Goldblatt, 2014b).

Gary Armstrong and Richard Giulianotti (2004) and Paul Darby (2002) refer to how black minorities in South Africa were historically excluded from sports such as rugby union and cricket. This continued policy of racial segregation (known as 'apartheid' – meaning 'the state of being apart') eventually led to the 1977 Gleneagles Agreement that discouraged any sporting competition with South Africa. It was only after the ending of apartheid in the 1990s that South Africa was permitted to re-enter international sporting competition (Lapchick, 1975; Bolsmann, 2013a, 2014).

Following the Second World War, mass immigration into Britain diversified the demographic of the country and eventually led to second-generation black players such as Viv Anderson, Garth Crooks, Cyrille Regis, Mark Walters and John Barnes emerging as professional footballers from the late 1970s. In 1978, Viv Anderson became the first black player to represent England, 106 years after the first international match between England and Scotland. In contextualizing the growing number of black players playing professional football in England in the 1970s and 1980s, Brian Holland (1997) states that in the 1975/1976 season, 19 black players were registered to 15 clubs (an 'exposure' level of 16 per cent), while by the 1985/1986 season, this had increased to 112 black players playing for 66 clubs (an 'exposure' level of 72 per cent).

The emergence of black players in greater numbers than before was accepted by some white supporters, but came at a time of the infiltration of far-right organizations (usually based on fascist, racist and reactionary ideas) such as the National Front, who successfully targeted working-class fears about employment and immigration. A consequence of this focus on 'race' was the existence of overt racism, irrespective of performance, but the fear of rising hooliganism meant that the government and football authorities were preoccupied with sanctions against behaviour that was violent rather than racist (Cleland, 2015). England was not the only country prone to incidents of overt racism in the 1980s, however; as Giulianotti (1999) illustrates, similar fears about 'race' and immigration led to the emergence of far-right groups on the terraces in many other European countries including Spain, Sweden, Holland, Italy and Germany. (For an analysis of Italian ultras, see Testa and Armstrong (2010), and for an analysis of Spanish ultras, see Spaaij and Viñas (2005)).

## Anti-racism policy

English and Scottish football was transformed after the Hillsborough disaster in 1989, in which 96 Liverpool fans lost their lives as a result of crushing during an FA Cup semi-final against Nottingham Forest. The Taylor Report (1990) and subsequent changes to football (most notably the new Premier League starting in 1992 and the immediate investment and coverage provided by Sky) encouraged clubs to seek a wider pool of talent from overseas through the ability to offer the best salaries. Almost immediately, this led to leading players such as Ruud Gullit and Tony Yeboah being recruited into an increasingly transnational playing environment that could truly lay claim to calling itself *the* global football league.

At the same time, attention was paid to racism through the creation of a new initiative, Let's Kick Racism Out Of Football, in 1993; later becoming Kick It Out in 1997, this was supported by the FA, the players' trade union the Professional Footballers' Association (PFA), and the Premier League. For the first time, a high-profile and targeted campaign sought to eradicate racism and racist language from football through the implementation of prescriptive written codes of conduct to which supporters had to adhere while attending matches. This was also matched by the introduction of Football Against Racism in Europe (FARE) in 1999, with a continental focus on marginalized groups to promote inclusivity and integration amongst clubs and national associations.

The improving spectacle of football and the transnational composition of many teams through the 1990s led to the impression that the culture of football had eradicated racism, most notably through the domestic and international success being achieved by black players. In France, blighted by growing racial divisions exacerbated by the rising popularity of the far right, the success of the national team (which included players of African origin such as Lilian Thuram, Marcel Desailly and Patrick Vieira) at the 1998 World Cup symbolized a sense of multi-cultural cohesion rather than a fear that the inclusion of an increasing number of black French players would fuel national tensions (Cashmore and Cleland, 2014).

Racial divisions remained present within football, however, with some notable high-profile incidents. In 2004, for example, the coach of the Spanish national team, Luis Aragonés, called French player Thierry Henry a 'black shit'. The punishment was noteworthy for the wrong reasons: a £2,000 fine and the retention of his position as head coach. Likewise, in 2015, former Italian national team manager Arrigo Sacchi was quoted as saying that there were 'too many black players' at youth level in Italy and that the nation has 'no dignity, no pride' (Ronay, 2015). Views like these are reflected in some cultures across Europe, where overt racism remains a significant matchday feature. In Italy, 'buu buu' monkey noises, overtly racist chanting and frequent booing are directed not only at African players but also at Italians such as Mario Balotelli (Doidge, 2015). In January 2013, in a friendly between AC Milan and Pro Patria, Kevin-Prince Boateng walked off the pitch after being targeted for racist abuse, while in competitive matches in Italy, referees have had to intervene and threaten to abandon matches if the racist abuse coming from the terraces continued.

Incidents like this remind us of the existence of racism and its continued unwelcome stain on football's claim to be inclusive. This claim became a focal point in English football in October 2011, where two incidents occurred in two separate Premier League matches. First, following a match between Liverpool and Manchester United at Anfield, Luis Suárez of Liverpool received an eight-match ban and a £40,000 fine from an Independent Commission established by the FA for using terms deemed to be racist towards Patrice Evra of Manchester United (Bascombe, 2011). Second, following a match between Queens Park Rangers and Chelsea at Loftus Road, John Terry of Chelsea was eventually given a four-match ban and a £220,000 fine for the use of racist language towards Anton Ferdinand of Queens Park Rangers (Kelso, 2012).

These two incidents led Ellis Cashmore and me to investigate the extent of racism in British football culture through the collection of large-scale empirical data via an online survey that was mainly disseminated via football fan message boards across the UK from November 2011 to February 2012; we also advertised the research on our own Facebook and Twitter pages. Drawing on the responses of 2,500 fans, in Cleland and Cashmore (2013, 2014) we focused on two different conceptual debates to explain the reasons behind why fans had overwhelmingly illustrated the continued existence of racism. First, in Cleland and Cashmore (2014), we analyzed the wider issue of racist language and anti-racism campaigns and how the game's governing bodies operate within a 'colour-blind' ideology (Bonilla-Silva, 2003). Second, in Cleland and Cashmore (2013), Pierre Bourdieu's (1984) conceptual framework of field and habitus helped us to illuminate why racism continues to exist in the everyday practice of some white football fans. In another article (Cleland, 2014), I analyzed over 500 posts from two prominent online message boards regarding fans' views on the extent of racism in English football. The central findings of these three articles will now be placed within the context of the wider contemporary debate about racism in world football to help to explain why it continues to exist in the twenty-first century, despite the introduction of policies aimed at eradicating it.

## Football governance as 'colour-blind'

For some scholars, such as Hylton (2005, p. 85), a critical race theory (a theory emanating in the US that analyzes 'race' and racism from a legal perspective) approach to discrimination in a sport like football is logical as it 'challenges traditional dominant ideologies around objectivity, meritocracy, colour-blindness, race neutrality and equal opportunity'. ('Meritocracy' refers to a system in which individual merit is rewarded; 'race neutrality' refers to individuals being extended equal opportunity without reference to their 'race'.) Likewise, Burdsey (2007, p. 9) argues that it 'enables us to understand that dominant claims that football is "colour-blind" or meritocratic are actually a means of sustaining white hegemony in the structures and subcultures of the professional game'. ('White hegemony' refers to the powerful dominance and control by whites over other 'racial' groups.)

Although official anti-racism initiatives have been a key part of football culture since 1993, 83 per cent of the 2,500 participants in Cleland and Cashmore's (2014) study stated that despite the inception of the Premier League in 1992 and billions of pounds' worth of investment from Sky to turn it into the world's most popular league, racism has never left British football. The extent to which fans had experienced or witnessed racism had declined from 67 per cent between 1990 and 1999, but it still remained at 50 per cent since 2010. Reflecting on his experience of the extent of change since the 1980s, a Huddersfield Town fan (white, male, aged 40–49) captured the thoughts of most participants by stating:

> Racism has always been present in football, either directly or indirectly. At my club, black or Asian support is very much a minority in the stands and reflects the institutionalized racism within the game. Although racism appeared to be effectively dealt with under the shiny banner of Sky Sports, it was actually simply seen as inappropriate and unwanted. Therefore, racism was left below the surface where it has simmered away ever since.
>
> (quoted in Cleland and Cashmore, 2014, p. 644)

Throughout the data, it was argued that despite the existence of an anti-racism message, many problems remain. Directly addressing the role and impact of Kick It Out, another fan responded:

> Initiatives like Kick It Out have slowly served to highlight racism within the game but I feel it has been undermined and become nothing more than a PR T-shirt-wearing exercise because of the governing bodies' reluctance to take any kind of stance against racism.
>
> (quoted in Cleland and Cashmore, 2014, p. 649)

79 per cent of fans supported the need for organizations like Kick It Out, but were critical of the way in which they were managing to tackle issues of racism. This criticism is also raised by Randhawa (2011, p. 245), who states how Kick It

Out 'has failed to create positive, sustained change and has simply been satisfied with the insignificant success of finite exposure' over its 20-year history. Indeed, in research conducted by Kick It Out (2014) that focused on the experiences of 200 Premier League and Football League players, 92 per cent stated that the organization had been effective in raising an awareness of racism in football, but only 71 per cent felt that it had been effective in tackling the issue. Reflecting the findings of Cleland and Cashmore (2014) raised above, over 50 per cent of Premier League and Football League players had witnessed racist abuse inside football stadiums, while 24 per cent had experienced it directly. Worryingly, 20 per cent also stated that they had witnessed racism on the training field or in the dressing room in what should be a supportive environment. Therefore, although the impression was that racism was being eradicated in the 1990s and early twenty-first century, this evidence suggests that 'race' and ethnicity continue to act as cultural markers and BME individuals remain targets for discrimination.

On this point, Colin King (2004) describes the structural obstacles that black players face and how this subsequently forces them to 'play the white man' (a term used in parts of Britain that means to be decent and trustworthy in one's actions and that, by implication, contributes towards the maintenance of negative racial stereotypes) in order to be accepted. This was also a feature of Burdsey's (2007) analysis of amateur football, in which he outlined the existence of a dominant cultural habitus whereby it was important for a BME player to be 'one of the lads' – a process that allows racism to remain unchallenged, as racist comments are reduced to the status of 'jokes' or 'banter'. In fact, black players publicly challenging the internal culture of football are rare, but in 2012 ex-Gillingham player Mark McCammon was successful in claiming that the club had racially discriminated against him. Acting against advice given by the PFA, McCammon pursued the claim himself and his account that he was dismissed from his contract because he had complained of racism against the club was supported by an independent industrial tribunal (Cleland, 2015).

This lack of support has also extended to Uefa, for which there is a catalogue of examples highlighting a reluctance to punish incidents of racism effectively. When Kevin-Prince Boateng walked off the pitch in January 2013, Uefa stated that it could not act because the match was a friendly and so it was a matter for the Italian Football Federation to investigate. Numerous failures to punish national associations effectively can be listed, but include a fine of just €40,000 (£31,000) given to the Bulgarian FA for the racist behaviour of their fans towards black England players at a Euro 2012 qualifying match in Sofia in September 2011. Likewise, following a friendly between Spain and England in Madrid in 2004, Uefa fined the Spanish Football Federation just £44,750 for the racist abuse directed at England's black players (i.e. the price of a couple of corporate sales packages). At club level, the example I have used previously to highlight a lack of effective action (see Cleland and Cashmore, 2014) is Uefa's decision to fine Manchester City £24,740 in April 2012 for returning to the field of play one minute late for the scheduled start time of the second half of a Europa Cup match against Sporting Lisbon, and yet to fine FC Porto only £16,700 for the racist behaviour of their fans towards Manchester City's black players during the same competition. The reason Uefa gave for this leniency towards FC Porto was that it was the club's first offence and the punishment appropriately reflected this. This 'colour-blindness' can also be ascribed to Fifa president Sepp Blatter, who in 2011 said that any racist language between players should end with a handshake at the end of the match (BBC Sport, 2011).

Therefore, it is not surprising that 76 per cent of fans in Cleland and Cashmore's (2014) study felt that governing bodies like Uefa and Fifa were not doing enough to tackle the problem of racism. Reflecting the views of a number of fans who highlighted structural and 'colour-blind' problems, an Arsenal fan (white, male, aged 40–49) stated:

> The head of Fifa is so blasé about racism. This shows everything which is wrong with the game. How can you punish the players and fans harshly for racism when the head of Fifa condones it?
>
> *(quoted in Cleland and Cashmore, 2014, p. 648)*

While international, continental and national associations can be accused of being 'colour-blind', in research on the lack of black managers (Cashmore and Cleland, 2011), 56 per cent of 1,000 fans from across the UK accused individual clubs of deliberate discrimination, as 'colour-blind' assumptions flourish regarding the negative stereotype that black people cannot manage effectively. Even the PFA chief executive, Gordon Taylor, was quoted in 2014 as saying that football has a 'hidden resistance' towards appointing black managers (Conway, 2014). This has led to calls for the adoption of the 'Rooney Rule' – a policy introduced by Dan Rooney, owner of the US National Football League's Pittsburgh Steelers, in 2003 to ensure the shortlisting of at least one BME candidate for any senior coaching or general management position that becomes available. When we asked fans in 2011 whether they would support the introduction of the Rooney Rule in British football, only a third indicated approval of such a policy (Cashmore and Cleland, 2011). Given the widespread debate on the adoption of an equivalent of the Rooney Rule since this time, in particular with the Football League proposing that one could be in place from the start of the 2016/2017 season, I wonder if this figure would be the same today (Van Wijk, 2015).

## Racist language and intent

To try to combat overt racial chanting, Section 3 of the 1991 Football Offences Act concentrated on racist chanting 'in concert' with fellow fans, while Section 9 of the 1999 Football (Offences and Disorder) Act concentrated on the 'individu-alization' of an offence (Gardiner and Welch, 2011). Although legislation like this has helped to reduce overt racist chanting inside stadiums, it still only applies to forms of chanting; single abusive shouts are not in breach of the act. This could be one reason why statistics released by the British government's Home Office for the 2013/2014 season revealed that only 21 out of the 2,273 football-related arrests made were for racist or indecent chanting (down from 42 during the 2012/2013 season). Despite this, overt racist chanting remains an unwelcome feature of some matches (Home Office, 2013, 2014). One notable case occurred in January 2012 during an FA Cup match between Nottingham Forest and Leicester City, when a collective chant of 'You used to be English, but not anymore' was directed towards Leicester fans in reference to the increasing ethnic population in the city (Cleland and Cashmore, 2014).

In 2013, as a deterrent for ongoing incidents of racism in English football, the FA implemented a minimum five-match suspension for any player found guilty of racism. At the same time, Uefa introduced partial and full stadium closures, while Fifa threatened to relegate or expel teams whose fans continue to engage in racist chanting. One of the first clubs punished was Legia Warsaw, which was forced to close a stand for its first home match in European competition as a result of racist chanting, while a number of clubs in Italy have also been forced to close parts of their grounds. Highlighting concerns with the level to which governing associations will go to punish repeat offenders, the Italian club Lazio successfully appealed against the decision to close its whole stadium for two Europa Cup matches as a result of persistent racist chanting, and was actually only forced to close one stand for the next domestic Serie A fixture (Cleland, 2015). Stronger punishments were implemented in Japan, where Urawa Red Diamonds was forced to close its stadium for one match as a result of the display of a racist banner. Despite this, a regular feature of modern football is that most decisions that involve players tend to result in some form of ban, whereas consistently small fines are given to individual clubs or national associations if their supporters are found to have engaged in racist behaviour inside a stadium.

There has also been an upsurge in the use of anti-Semitic symbols and language, particularly across Germany and at English club Tottenham Hotspur, which has a sizeable Jewish following. The use of the pejorative 'Yid' and collective hissing to replicate the noise of the gas chamber is a regular feature of the atmosphere at matches featuring Tottenham. Reacting to this, in 2013 the FA stated that those using the word 'Yid' would be liable for prosecution and a subsequent banning order. The problem, however, is that the club's supporters also use the term themselves as a defence mechanism, chanting phrases like 'Yid Army', and reject the suggestion that this can cause offence as it lacks deliberate intent (Poulton and Durell, 2014). Indeed, while some Tottenham fans were originally charged with an offence in 2014, this was later dropped by the Crown Prosecution Service on the grounds that the term could not be legally considered to be abusive, threatening or insulting (Davis, 2014).

It is not just fans who have been punished for anti-Semitism. In December 2013, Nicolas Anelka was fined £80,000 and banned for five matches after using the 'quenelle' gesture (a movement of the arm across the body often used to symbolize an anti-Jewish sentiment) when celebrating after scoring a goal playing in a Premier

League match for West Bromwich Albion against West Ham United. This incident had significant ramifications, as his contract was cancelled by the club and led to the club's shirt sponsor at the time, Zoopla (a property website), cancelling its contract due to one of the co-owners having Jewish connections (Cleland, 2015).

Reflecting examples like this, Teun Van Dijk (2004) outlines how racist discourse (a discriminatory social practice evident in text, talk and communication) takes two particular forms:

1. It is directed *at* ethnically different Others.
2. It is *about* ethnically different Others.

In applying this to my own research, in Cleland and Cashmore (2013, 2014) we found how racial discourse is directed *at* ethnically different Others. On the other hand, after analyzing over 500 posts about ethnicity on two prominent online football message boards, I found an essentialist view of national belonging and identity that often centred on the practice of socially negative racialization (i.e. differentiating or categorizing according to 'race') of minority groups, most notably Muslims since 9/11 (Cleland, 2014). As most posters on message boards refrain from sharing their ethnicity with the rest of the online community (although some do), the discussions concerning 'race' on such message boards are therefore *about* ethnically different Others, rather than being directed *at* them.

Of course, the intent behind any phrase is open to some interpretation, with Butler (1997) outlining the existence of a gap between the intention of the speaker and its effect on the recipient. The Suárez–Evra incident put into the spotlight the cultural issues and ambiguity with regard to the use of language. Suárez did not deny calling Evra a 'negro', but his defence was to point to the term's widespread use in his native Uruguay. Although the FA-established Independent Commission acknowledged this fact, they decided that it had been used to cause offence and issued an eight-game ban (Bascombe, 2011). Transgressions carried out by football players are discussed further in Chapters 9 and 11.

For some white supporters, a form of 'casual racism' exists, whereby there is a failure to see how their discourse (whether face to face, inside stadiums as part of the crowd or on social media) is racist. In his analysis of Millwall supporters and the social and cultural meaning of the club, Garry Robson (2000) found that fans do not see themselves as racist; instead, they argue that 'banter' is part of the culture of football and that supporters will do anything to try to help their team to win. For some scholars, such as Saeed and Kilvington (2011, p. 602), this reinforcement of whiteness is a result of the influence that the media have on society, where stories are 'commonly written and spoken about in a tone which suggests anxiety over the erosion of the perceived "indigenous" national culture'. By way of illustration, in their analysis of coverage of the 2010 World Cup by the British tabloid newspaper the *Sun*, John Vincent and John Hill (2011, p. 200) concluded that it demonstrated 'a historic yearning for a bygone authentic era when England was White, masculine, and working-class'.

According to Eduardo Bonilla-Silva (2006), inconspicuous racism across the media and amongst fans highlights a structural problem as covert and nuanced forms of language protect whites from being labelled as racist. Rather than focusing on biological difference, Tariq Modood (2007) argues that Islamophobic resentment towards Muslims is a new form of cultural racism – a shift that John Solomos and Les Back (1996) state is a process within contemporary society by which national identity is central in presenting a homogeneous host culture against any perceived threat from the BME Other. Evidence of this has occurred in football, with Peter Millward's (2008) focus on the Islamophobic taunts directed at the former Middlesbrough player Mido in a Premier League match against Newcastle United and Jack Fawbert's (2011) analysis of an anti-Muslim sentiment emerging as a result of the increasing Muslim population living in the surrounding area of West Ham United's ground, Upton Park.

This discriminatory sentiment has also expanded into social media, which have fundamentally changed the everyday practice of communication for supporters. While the majority of supporters use these platforms, such as Twitter and message boards, to debate about the club or the game in general or to talk about other matters (Cleland, 2011), for others they also allow for the mostly anonymous expression of hate speech. This was recognized in Cleland and Cashmore's (2013, 2014) studies, with 80 per cent of 2,500 fans acknowledging that social media have allowed for racist thoughts to be expressed in ways that were not available to previous generations of fans, who had to communicate such thoughts through more overt forms. As one Burnley fan (white, male, 20–29) stated: 'Off the pitch the outlet available on social media is a very 21$^{st}$ century way of unleashing old prejudices without restraint' (quoted in Cleland and Cashmore, 2013, p. 10).

Of particular concern is how Twitter allows registered users to send direct messages to more high-profile individuals such as players, coaches and media commentators. Even the company's own chief executive, Dick Costolo, had to admit in February 2015 that the small number of successful prosecutions for hate speech indicates how Twitter 'sucks at dealing with abuse and trolls' (Hern, 2015). (An internet troll is a person who deliberately posts rude, aggressive and/or inflammatory comments in an online community with the intention of provoking the recipient into an emotional response.) One of the reasons behind this admission is that the hosting of sites like Twitter and Facebook in the US presents problems for the British police, who are often refused a subpoena that would identify the personal details of an individual poster.

In 2013, in an attempt to eradicate rising levels of discrimination and hate speech, the Crown Prosecution Service and the Association of Chief Police Officers in England and Wales announced that they were going to prosecute any individual engaging in racist and homophobic discourse (BBC News, 2013b). The necessity of this became apparent in April 2015 (Conn, 2015b), when Kick It Out reported that 134,000 discriminatory messages had been sent to Premier League players and clubs between August 2014 and March 2015 via fan message boards (3 per cent of abuse), blogs (1 per cent), Facebook (8 per cent) and Twitter (88 per cent). This indicated that only a fraction of incidents are being reported to the authorities, with players, coaches and managers absorbing the abuse or simply deleting their accounts rather than notifying the police. In Chapter 8, Richard Haynes makes further reference to the rise of socially networked media and its implications for football cultures.

In 2013, Kick It Out released an app that can be downloaded onto a smart-phone to anonymously report discriminatory incidents that the authorities could monitor so they could instigate retrospective action. However, while Kick It Out claim 'we are winning the battle' (Conn, 2015a), this has barely scratched the surface of the problem, with only 184 incidents of discrimination (118 race-related) reported between August 2014 and March 2015; out of the 113 from the previous season, only one led to a prosecution. With a lack of police presence inside stadiums – the Home Office report for the 2012/2013 season indicated that 58 per cent of Premier League and Football League matches had no visible police presence (Home Office, 2013) – and fans arguing that stewards (some of whom are BME) are reluctant to act, in many cases supporters are having to regulate themselves.

## Explaining fan racism

In explaining why some fans continue to express racist thoughts and behaviours, I have illustrated that Bourdieu's (1984) conceptual framework of 'field' and 'habitus' has particular pertinence in this analysis (Cleland and Cashmore, 2013). A field has been described as 'a structured system of social positions occupied by either individuals or institutions engaged in the same activity' (Thorpe, 2010, p. 181). Although the field of football fandom is obviously varied (some fans watch matches alone, others attend casually and others consume games through television), white supporters continue to have the power to define the cultural habits, tastes and styles with which different forms of capital (economic, social and cultural) can be acquired.

For Bourdieu (1984), an individual's everyday practices and thought processes are reflected through their habitus (an embodied series of internalized dispositions, perceptions, tastes, habits, rules and expressions). According to Bourdieu, these dispositions are so ingrained in people that they are rarely conscious of them, but they are compatible with objective factors such as family and the community and social group in which the individual is engaged. It is the opportunities and constraints created by these social conditions that then inform personal taste and practice.

Recognizing a wider focus on the racialized social system (Bonilla-Silva, 2003; Bonilla-Silva et al., 2006), there has been increased attention paid to the 'racial habitus', which for Samuel Perry (2012, p. 90) is 'a matrix of tastes, perceptions, and cognitive frameworks that are often unconscious (particularly for whites), and that regulate the racial practices of actors such that they tend to reproduce the very racial distinctions and inequalities that produced them'. According to Jeffrey Sallaz

(2010, p. 294), the 'dispositions of the habitus should prove durable and may even improvise new practices that transpose old racial schemata into new settings'.

With regard to the racial habitus and internal dispositions, John Williams and colleagues (1989) outline difficulties in arguing whether wider racist views are transferred into football or whether it is actually football that provokes racist thoughts through the focus on difference. This was also the conclusion of the British Government's House of Commons Culture, Media and Sport Select Committee report into racism in football in 2012 (Home Office, 2013), which recognized the significant issues within the game but then claimed that 'football is not the source of racism' (p. 18). In Cleland and Cashmore's (2013, p. 9) study, fans such as this Tottenham Hotspur supporter (white, male, age 30–39) argue that the persistence of racism is a result of the habitus and cultural practice of some white communities and that this moves from one generation to the next:

> Ignorance is passed down through the generations. Racism will always be rife unfortunately. The histories of football clubs are embedded in local inner cities and people who live in these areas have a 'world is against us' approach to life. Anyone who is not in that 'community' is seen as an 'outsider'.

Reflections like this concur with Norbert Elias and John Scotson's (1994) use of 'established–outsider relations' to explain how less powerful groups are excluded by established ones. Given the history of football raised earlier, white supporters have traditionally been able to acquire greater levels of social and cultural capital. As stated by Sallaz (2010, p. 296), 'individuals who came of age in one racial formation will tend to generate practices that simultaneously preserve entrenched racial schemata'. Likewise, as Christine Mennesson (2010, p. 6) argues, 'the more long-lasting, the stronger, and the more concerned by emotional relations a socialization process is, the stronger the constructed dispositions will be'. For some white supporters, the 'white habitus' (Bonilla-Silva, 2003) in which they operate regulates their tastes, perceptions, feelings and views on matters of 'race' and can promote solidarity and reinforce the practice for those intent on negatively stereotyping non-whites. If this practice is approved by like-minded peers, it can lead to a reinforcement or enhancement of an individual's or group's position.

Changes to football since the inception of the Premier League (such as increasing ticket prices, satellite subscription costs and a more affluent fan base) highlight the complexities of Bourdieu's (1993) view that a sport like football should help to reveal the habitus of a particular social class. The fan demographic has changed and raises a number of cultural conflicts and differences in terms of the level of economic, cultural and social capital that each individual possesses through their participation and how particular profits and rewards are accrued. For example, a Premier League survey in 2005/2006 (2006, p. 8) indicated that 48 per cent of supporters were in the higher socio-economic grouping AB (higher/intermediate managerial, administrative or professional) compared to 24 per cent in C1 (supervisory or clerical, junior managerial, administrative or professional).

While the demographic of the matchday fan has changed, there remain many profound difficulties in attempting to change individual internalized racial disposi-tions through measures adopted by governing bodies and anti-racism organizations, as expressed by this Aston Villa fan (white, male, 40–49):

> It is difficult to challenge the minority that have racist views. These views are often present from childhood and built into the mind-set of individuals. Simply fining or even jailing them will not have much impact. And banning orders are easy to evade. Racism is like a cancerous tumour: it's going to need some pretty deep surgery to tackle it.
>
> *(quoted in Cleland and Cashmore, 2013, p. 12)*

Of course, campaigns in football can have an adverse impact by negatively labelling fans as racist. Likewise, for some supporters who openly express their racial habitus through speech and/or actions, anti-racism campaigns and legislation are likely to have no impact as covert and overt racist attitudes continue to find new forms of expression. Given people's habitus, you will never stop them from thinking about 'race', but the challenge is to seek ways of ensuring that these thoughts are not spoken or made visible through their behaviour or actions.

## Conclusion

For over 150 years since the formation of the English FA, football has been dominated by 'whiteness'. Despite an increasing number of black players, this white hegemony remains unchallenged and continues to reflect racial power relations that reproduce patterns of white privilege (Hylton, 2009). In certain countries within Europe, such as Italy and Russia, overt racism and an anti-Other narrative in national discourse remain unwelcome features of contemporary football culture. Given the examples raised in this chapter, it could be argued that this situation is unlikely to change in the immediate future. This has not been helped by the football authorities' failure to fully recognize the extent of racism, and has led to accusations of being 'colour-blind', as not only do they lack an awareness of the severity of the problem, but, when an incident occurs, the punishment also fails to act as a sufficient deterrent to prevent it from happening again in the future.

In data gathered as part of the annual British Social Attitudes survey in 2014, self-reported racial prejudice had increased since 2001, rising as high as 38 per cent in 2011 (and matching what it was in 1987). Therefore, the obvious assumption is that considering racism as a problem exclusive to football is wrong. Football has the power to influence people as the national sport across many countries, but football is also reflective of society. It does not make people racist, but it now provides a diverse platform where thoughts and behaviours can be overtly or covertly communicated in other ways than were available in the 1980s and 1990s. Of course, this has been assisted by the increased consumption of technology that enables racist views to be expressed anonymously and covertly on fan message boards as well as across more public platforms such as Twitter. As Burdsey (2011, p. 7) correctly states, racism now operates 'in complex, nuanced and often covert ways that go under the radar of football authorities and beyond the capacities of anti-racist groups'.

Although racism seemed to fade (largely, I argue, as a result of under-reporting by both players and the media) during the 1990s and early 2000s, since the Suárez–Evra and Terry–Ferdinand cases of late 2011, barely a week has gone by without some form of racism being reported by the newly sensitized media and pressure groups now challenging the game's authorities to do more to tackle this discriminatory stain on the 'beautiful game'. There have clearly been advances in raising awareness of anti-racism policies and campaigns, but football remains a symbol of social division and exclusion. If anti-racism organizations can begin to change BME stereotypes, it is likely to have a positive impact on the playing, coaching and spectating environment; however, given the evidence presented in this chapter, this remains a distant reality.

## Research in Action

*Race, Ethnicity and Football: Persisting Debates and Emergent Issues* edited by Daniel Burdsey (2011)

### What were the goals of the research?

Prior to editing this book, Burdsey had published several closely related pieces of research that collectively analyzed the experiences of British Asians in football (and sport more widely), often centring on notions of social justice and sociological intervention. The goal of this particular book was to provide an opportunity for a range of scholars, including ethnic minorities and women, to debate an area that has traditionally been the domain of white men. Hence the book was broken down into five themed sections, made up of a total of 16 chapters providing an alternative account of racial inequalities from elite football down to the grassroots.

### Why was the research relevant?

Since the turn of the twenty-first century, there has been an increasing focus placed on race and ethnicity in the world's most popular sport. The themed sections all illustrated the relevance of the research as one of the first collections to analyze professional and grassroots football. For example, 'Racialised Exclusions and "Glocal" Im/mobilities' consisted of three chapters that focused on the history and contemporary placement of 'race' in Liverpool, the recruitment of African players and parallels to slavery, and racism within Irish football. 'Contested Fields and Cultural Resistance' consisted of three chapters that focused on a local ethnic minority club in Leicester (Highfield Rangers), the historical development and shifting focus of local football in Leicester, and the experiences of British female Muslims (in particular surrounding Islam, identity and the hijab).

'"New" Ethnicities and Emergent Football Communities' included three chapters on British Asian female footballers and the arguments surrounding national identity, the social and historical contours of mixed-heritage players in British football, and the impact of football on young Pakistani Muslim masculinities. 'The Cultural Politics of Fandom' consisted of three chapters on the cosmopolitanism of English fans at Euro 2008, a case study of the Asian experience at West Ham United, and the impact and conduct of sectarianism in Scottish football (focusing on Rangers and Celtic). The final section, 'Equity, Anti-Racism and the Politics of Campaigning', contained three chapters on racial equality initiatives in English grassroots football, the legal argument, and the future of British Asian football.

## What methods were used?

Although some chapters involved desk-based research that concentrated on a review of various types of literature, other chapters explored conceptual frameworks through a range of methodological approaches that included questionnaires, fieldwork diaries, semi-structured interviews and analysis of statistical information. Most of these contributions engaged in a process of thematic analysis, drawing out the main themes of the findings and comparing and contrasting them with the specific debate on race and ethnicity with which they were engaged.

## What were the main arguments?

The central argument was that racism is structural or systemic and that football clubs and international, continental and national associations, as well as anti-racism organizations, 'simultaneously fail to acknowledge the extent to which racism actually continues to exist and the various ways in which it manifests itself' (p. 7). While recognizing that overt acts of racism had declined since the tumultuous period of the 1970s and 1980s, the book argued for the need for further anti-discrimination policies that address 'more intricate, covert and institutionalized forms of prejudice and discrimination that still exist within the game' (p. 9).

### And the conclusions or key findings?

Anti-racism organizations such as Kick It Out often champion the progress that they have made in eradicating racism in British football, but throughout the book it was highlighted how racism at all levels of the game now operates through more nuanced, covert and subtle means that often go unnoticed by the relevant anti-racism organizations and football authorities.

### What were the strengths of the research?

The array of scholars writing about various aspects of the culture of football was a real strength of the book. Through a case study approach, each key stakeholder in the game was examined – from fans, agents and players to clubs, international governing organizations and anti-racism organizations. Each chapter examined the challenges as well as the possible solutions to racism in football at all levels of the game and drew attention to historical, existing and new problems of trying to achieve racial equality throughout football. The book also signposted a number of possible routes that future research might take, which was helpful to those looking for ideas to construct a research project.

### Were there any weaknesses?

Although comparisons were made to football in Europe, it would have strengthened the book if there were accounts from authors located around the world who could have provided a more global perspective as to the extent of racism. Furthermore, while some contributors used evidence effectively to address particular topics, others did not, and subsequently engaged in some speculative arguments.

# 6

# GENDER

*Gertrud Pfister and Gerald Gems*

---

**Chapter highlights**

- Sex is biologically determined, but gender is learned, practised or performed, and felt, and is thus a cultural construct i.e. formed in practices and perceptions and so liable to change. (*Editors' note*: Gender is sometimes wrongly regarded as the same as sex, but it is typically subjective, based on what people believe and expect rather than on biological fact.)
- Women in England and Scotland started to play football in the 1880s.
- Throughout history, female players have been considered to be outsiders and intruders upon the male domain.
- Positions of power remain in the hands of men in football as elsewhere.
- Even today, football's structure and participation patterns are gendered i.e. biased towards men.

---

## Introduction: origins and early developments of women's football

Interest in association football crossed gender lines in the 1880s as women in England and Scotland took up football, much to the chagrin of men, for whom the game had become a public display of their physical prowess and masculinity as the industrial process robbed previously independent craftsmen of their independence and social capital. Critics of women's football considered it a transgression upon the male domain of sports. They questioned women footballers' femininity and their abilities as the 'weaker sex'. Clergymen assailed their morality, while medical practitioners feared damage to their reproductive capacities and physiological responses to their athletic exertions. Despite such recriminations, female football players continued to play, and by the First World War games between women's teams in the UK drew large crowds (Michallat, 2005).

French women, too, had begun to pursue sports in earnest, establishing the Femina Sport Club in 1911, which flourished under the leadership of Alice Milliat (1884–1957), who campaigned vigorously for women's sport. Milliat was instrumental in the formation of the International Women's Sport Federation and the initial Women's World Games in 1921. The Femina Sport Club did not include football among its competitive events. It did, however, boast the top female athlete of the era, Violette Morris, who won a multitude of championships in several sports and then turned to motor racing after the French Women's Sport Federation denied her participation in the 1928 Games due to what was popularly perceived as her masculine style of dress and behaviour, which obviously and publicly violated the gender norms of the era.

The first international football match between women's teams had already challenged such norms. Dick, Kerr & Co. in England had employed a large number of women in its factory, increasingly so as the First World War drained the country of male employees. As part of the welfare capitalism programmes of the period, industrial employers permitted leisure breaks for their workers and some organized sports teams, not only for a respite but also for marketing purposes. The Dick, Kerr's Ladies FC resulted from such an initiative. In the aftermath of the war, a French women's team accompanied by Milliat travelled to England to play against a team from the Dick, Kerr & Co. ammunitions factory in Preston. The match was made more palatable to the general public as the proceeds from ticket sales were donated to victims of the war, reinforcing the traditional gender roles of feminine charity, care and nurturance. Later that year, Dick, Kerr's Ladies travelled to France for further competition (Buckley, 2009).

With the return of men from the war, men's football resumed its dominance in England and the football federation prohibited men's clubs from sponsoring women's teams. Women lost their use of club pitches, and their consequent attempt to establish a football federation for women failed to reignite interest and support (Williams, 2007). Nevertheless, women's football clubs began to emerge in several European countries, such as Belgium, the Netherlands and Austria, but faced increasing resistance in Germany, as evidenced by the following quote from a German women's magazine in 1927: 'Women may be playing football in England and America, but it is to be hoped that this bad example is not followed in German sport' (quoted in Pfister et al., 2002, p. 68).

This backlash doomed some female clubs to failure. A girls' team in Frankfurt had to be disbanded due to the negative press coverage and the resistance of the players' parents in 1930 (Pfister, 2012). However, when the National Socialists came to power in 1933, women's sports were supported and exploited for the glory of the state, particularly in the Berlin Olympic Games of 1936 where the successful female athletes complemented the achievements of their male counterparts in the promotion of the doctrine of Aryan supremacy; however, women's football was not an Olympic event. It was not until 1996 that female football players were able to compete for Olympic medals. The US team has won the gold medal in four of the five Olympic tournaments to date; only in 2000 did another team, Norway, prevail.

In the post-Second World War period, men's football gained increasing prominence worldwide, adopting and expressing symbolic values such as togetherness and reconciliation. Thus, when Germany won the 1954 World Cup, dubbed 'the Miracle of Bern', it was widely perceived as the country's return to the international community. Most women's football initiatives did not survive the war years, and the hard times of the post-war period discouraged women to fight for access to a men's game. However, in Germany women played football as professionals. During the 1950s, businessmen organized women's matches between German and Dutch teams in order to attract predominantly male audiences, who expected amusing scenes and hoped for erotic displays. A much-discussed question in the media was if and how women stopped the ball with their breasts. The games proved to be commercially successful and the players demonstrated that they really could play the game. However, poor management and the continued resistance of the German Football Federation (DFB) ultimately doomed the project (Gethard, 2006; Pfister, 2012). As the federation did not allow the clubs to let the women play on their football grounds, it became increasingly difficult for women's teams to find spaces to train and to play matches.

The professionalization of male football, broadcast on radio and television in the 1960s, contributed to the increase of interest in and consumption of football. (See Chapter 10 for more on consumption.) However, the men's game was framed and considered as the norm and female players were still considered to be outsiders and intruders upon the male domain. Nevertheless, they continued to play the game, often as a leisure activity, but soon they also wanted to participate in competitions. The increasing number of female players and the organization of matches required a level of bureaucracy and a governing body. Danish women responded to this need by forming their own league and a football federation by 1968, which later merged with the DBU, the Danish Football Federation (Brus and Trangbaek, 2003).

As in many other countries in the 1960s, women in Germany demanded recognition and access to facilities, including admission to the DFB. The male members of the executive committee, however, strongly objected to this request, and maintained their adherence to the traditional, sexist belief in women's inferior physical and psychological abilities with regard to athletic exertion. Despite the committee's rejection of what was felt to be an inappropriate demand, the rising number of female players and their ability to disprove the assumptions of female debility ultimately pressured the German football authorities into acceptance. They did so grudgingly, with stipulations such as a ban on cleated shoes and an insistence on breast pads to protect the female anatomy. Such precautions were summarily breached by the players and an increasing number of girls and women simply played in the same way as boys and men (Pfister, 2012). Women's football continued to spread throughout northern and central Europe and beyond, and national leagues and international competitions ensued (Williams, 2011).

## The ascendance of the women's game

By 1991, women's football had reached such prominence as to warrant a World Cup tournament, won by the US national team. After a successful Women's World Cup in Sweden in 1995, Sepp Blatter, at this time the general secretary of Fifa, announced that 'the future of football is feminine' (quoted in Degun, 2013). However, a decade later, he proposed: 'Let the women play in more feminine clothes like they do in volleyball. They could, for example, have tighter shorts' (quoted in Christenson and Kelso, 2004). In 2015, Blatter decided not to attend the Women's World Cup in Canada. Rumours circulating at this time suggested that Blatter feared extradition to the US. There were allegations of bribery, fraud and money laundering against the background of media and marketing rights for the Copa America Centenario, a competition held to celebrate the South American Football Confederation's (CONMEBOL's) centenary, to be held in the US in 2016.

The International Olympic Committee (IOC) included women's football as an event in the 1996 Summer Games. Since then, women's football has become the most popular women's team sport in Europe. Uefa counts more than 1.2 million girls and women as registered players, and there are undoubtedly many more unregistered participants. The number of female players exceeds 100,000 in the UK, Sweden and the Netherlands, while Germany has 258,000 players on 12,900 teams, the largest contingent in Europe. It is the most popular women's team sport in that country, where 140,000 women between the ages of 19 and 26 play the game, more than all other team sports combined (Uefa, 2014, 2015). In Germany, about 9,000 women play basketball, 43,000 engage in volleyball and 51,000 play handball. While impressive, however, such numbers still account for only 7 per cent of all players on the continent. Only in Denmark, the Faroe Islands (in the North Atlantic), Iceland and Sweden do women make up more than 20 per cent of the total number of players. In Turkey, Romania, Poland and the Ukraine, women amount to only 3 per cent of the players (Uefa, 2015, p. 11). Such figures underestimate total participation, however, as women who play the game for fun or do not participate in 'official' matches are not counted in the official tallies. In Germany, for example, in addition to the 258,000 registered players, the DFB claims another 758,441 women and 336,464 girls under the age of 16 also play in football clubs (DFB, 2015).

The growth in women's football over the past decade is reflected in the increasing quality of their play and a growing acceptance. In the US, the women's national soccer team is even more successful and popular than the men's team, which has greatly spurred girls' interest in the game. Worldwide, women's football has gained greater recognition and publicity through a proliferation of local, regional, national and international tournaments, culminating in the Olympic tournament and the Women's World Cup. In Europe, continental competitions such as the Women's European Championships and the Uefa Women's Champions League have gained increasing popularity.

Women's international competitions have drawn large throngs of fans and consequently gained an increasing amount of media attention over the past decade. The Women's European Championships held in Sweden in 2013 set a record for ticket sales, and the 2015 Women's World Cup in Canada was the 'biggest and most advanced broadcast for a women's football tournament' in the history of the game, according to a Fifa press release (Fifa, 2015). Attendance totalled 1.3 million people for 52 matches and the television audiences broke records in several countries. The final match alone drew 25.4 million US viewers, the highest total ever recorded in the US for a soccer match, male or female (Pingue, 2015). The US fans flocked to outdoor urban centres, such as parks equipped with large screens, to cheer for their victorious team.

## Women – the other sex: continuing issues in football

Despite the growth in the women's game, particularly in Europe and the US, the development of elite players continues to face some significant obstacles (Williams, 2011). Some of the most predominant obstacles are discussed in this section.

### *Finances and professionalization*

Over the course of 2013 and 2014, the European Club Association (ECA) conducted a study of 22 women's teams, with particular attention given to budgets, players' salaries and the support by qualified staff (ECA, 2014). Results indicated a lack of adequate financing at most of the clubs. Only three clubs had an annual budget surpassing €1 million. Three other clubs were limited to a budget of only €50,000 or less per year. Data provided by Uefa indicate that women's teams still face budgetary constraints, with support ranging from €15 million to less than €100,000. Of the 50 reporting federations, 30 listed investments of less than €1 million, with clubs in Sweden, Norway, France, Germany and England providing between €4 million and €15 million for their women's teams.

The vast majority of female football players in Europe are unpaid amateurs. Of the 54 federations who provided such data, 22 stated that there was not a single female professional on their registered lists of players. A total of 2,645 female players in Europe earned some income as professionals, although it proved to be minimal in most cases. Some earned as little as €40 for their efforts. The average salary amounted to €545 for clubs with a budget of less than €250,000; better-financed clubs paid their players €1,515. The star player, not only with regard to her skills but also with regard to her salary, was Marta, the Brazilian star who now plays for a club in Malmö, Sweden. The rise of celebrity players, both female and male, is the focus of Chapter 9.

With regard to the staff situation, the ECA survey showed that 41 per cent of clubs had a minimal staff of fewer than five employees, while 36 per cent (i.e. eight clubs) supported their team with between five and ten employees. Such figures indicate the precarious nature of women's professional football. While male professionals earn millions of Euros, the top female players are more accurately semi-professionals who must find additional means of subsistence while they practise their sport. Lack of finances also means smaller staff sizes and, for some teams, no paid staff at all. Many teams rely on voluntary labour to fulfil necessary tasks. Such limited finances inhibit the development of the women's game. In Denmark, the country with the highest percentage of registered players, the DBU has sought to alleviate such issues. In 2012, it initiated a development plan known as Vision 2020, designed to promote greater financial support for women's clubs (DBU, n.d.). Clubs that seek to participate at the highest levels must provide adequate human resources to support their competitive endeavours. Teams lacking such necessities can petition the federation for support.

## The role of consumers, sponsors and the media

Throughout the history of modern sport, media coverage has been essential to the acceptance, growth and success of professional sports. Despite the on-field success of the women's game, the development of professional leagues has continued to face large obstacles. Media publicity is necessary to promote ticket sales, which generate income for the clubs. Players are in need of greater recognition as elite athletes in order to assume the same roles as male players, who can garner large endorsement fees for product sponsorship. Corporate sponsors base their support upon the size of the potential audiences for their advertisements. Women, the majority of any population and the primary shoppers in (Western) society, could or should be the likely consumers and a natural target demographic for businesses. However, there is a large discrepancy between the need for female teams to get media coverage and the interest of media and audiences in the women's game. The growth in the global media's interest in football has been enormously influential and is the subject of Chapter 8.

The Football Research in an Enlarged Europe (FREE) project conducted a survey on public interest in football in eight European countries (FREE, 2015). It found that 35 per cent of the female respondents and 64 per cent of the male respondents indicated that they were very interested in the sport. There were, however, large discrepancies across the countries surveyed. In Austria, 71 per cent of men but only 21 per cent of women indicated that they were very interested. In Germany, results showed a very high interest of 65 per cent of men and 46 per cent of women. Denmark registered the highest percentage of football fans, with 69 per cent of men and 49 per cent of women placing themselves in the 'very interested' category. However, only 23 per cent of the respondents from all countries professed any interest in women's football. When questioned about women's football more specifically, only 7 per cent of men and 4 per cent of women showed great interest. The UK registered the greatest interest in the women's game, with

30 per cent of women and 42 per cent of men indicating that they were very interested. Denmark reported interest among 27 per cent of men and 20 per cent of women. In Germany, 27 per cent of men and 26 per cent of women indicated that they enjoyed the women's game. At the lower end of the scale, in Poland only 8 per cent of men and 3 per cent of women reported an interest. Further research is necessary to explore the reasons and backgrounds for these large international differences in attitudes towards football in general and women's football in particular.

It could be assumed that the number of female players, the quality of the women's football leagues and the success of national teams arouse interest and produce followers and fans. However, in that case the number of fans should be higher in Germany, which has one of the best women's national teams worldwide. What prevents football followers and fans from pouring into stadiums to watch women's games? One reason may be the competition with men's football. The German men's national team won the most recent World Cup and clubs such as Bayern Munich are successful competitors in the prestigious European competitions, which may cause fans to concentrate on men and their game. In addition, there is the widespread opinion – or even conviction – that not only do women and men play football differently, but also that women lack the skills needed in modern football and that it is not exciting to watch their matches. However, the developments in women's football and extremely popular tournaments such as the most recent Women's World Cup reveal an enormous progress and a very high standard of technical ability and tactics.

The relatively low interest in women's football is mirrored in relatively low attendances and near-empty stadiums during league matches. Uefa data indicate that women's teams draw an average of 350 spectators to their games, although games in the women's Bundesliga in Germany may attract 2,500 (FREE, 2015). Some matches between the top teams have been even played in front of more than 10,000 spectators. Eight of the countries in the Uefa data reported dismal figures, with only about 50 attendees, often only friends and family members of the players, whereas men's matches can attract crowds of 80,000. As gate receipts are an important part of the budget of football teams, the lack of spectators leads to lack of funding and, as a consequence, a lack of support for the players.

Journalists, who have the opportunity to promote women's football, have also shown little interest in doing so. They, too, focus on male players and teams and report endlessly on their battles on the football pitch. Scholars have conducted a considerable amount of research on sport and media in various European countries, with similar findings; that is to say, the media tends to focus on sports played by men, reported by men and ultimately consumed by male readers or viewers (Adams *et al.*, 2014; Peeters and Elling, 2015).

The fact that women's league football matches do not attract the attention of the media has severe financial consequences, as sponsors only invest in sports that command attention and ensure visibility. As such, the number of football consumers or fans and the lack of media interest noted above show that male players and men's teams continue to dominate the public interest and, as a consequence, also glean the vast bulk of endorsements and commercial sponsorships. (*Editors' note*: The 2012 Olympics is popularly regarded as a watershed in media coverage of women's sport and, while scepticism is understandable and justifiable, the increase in broadcast, print and online media coverage of the 2015 Women's World Cup in Canada suggested a growing awareness and enthusiasm for women's football.)

It may be the case that the late and slow start of the women's game in comparison to that of men has not allowed it to create a brand, develop a clientele and claim a niche in the sports market. However, with the continuous growth of women's football in the Western world and the ascendance of top female teams in Asia, particularly in Japan and China, corporate sponsors have the opportunity to capitalize on large commercial markets; however, to date, media have focused only on irregular international mega-events rather than regular league matches. (*Editors' note*: adidas, Coca-Cola, Visa, Gazprom and Hyundai were among the corporate sponsors of the 2015 Women's World Cup.)

## Exploring backgrounds

The findings about the development and current situation of women's football presented above raise several questions that have been discussed and partly answered by recent investigations. Here, four of the many 'women's issues' in football are addressed with reference to our previous or current research projects. These four questions are as follows:

1.  Why is gender a contested issue in women's football and are sex tests a way to guarantee fairness?
2.  Do women have a voice in football clubs and federations? In other words, are there women in positions of influence and power?
3.  How do mass media present female players and what sort of messages and images do they convey?
4.  Why are girls and women under-represented as players and fans?

### 'Sex tests': are they necessary for football players?

In most sports, men and women do not compete against each other. This seems to be a demand of fairness, as women would be disadvantaged because of their biological differences. However, sport is not fair per se, as it does not and cannot ensure equal chances of victory because athletes never have exactly the same bodily and psychological qualities. Nevertheless, because the sex of an individual decisively influences his or her athletic performance, since the beginnings of modern sport, the sporting authorities have differentiated between the sexes in sporting competitions. In football, too, women have their own matches and their own leagues, but, in contrast to other sports, girls can play football in mixed leagues in 35 European countries; most of them play in the Under-10 and Under-11 categories, but in some countries Under-18 mixed leagues also exist (Uefa, 2015). After they turn 18, men and women have to play in separate teams and leagues and in particular the access of men to women's competitions is strictly prohibited. The assumption that men may masquerade as women has been a nightmare of sporting officials for decades. In 1968, the IOC introduced a 'gender verification test' as a precondition to be eligible for women's competitions. As these tests proved to be inaccurate and led to misjudgements (e.g. with regard to intersex individuals), the screening of all female athletes was discontinued and replaced by examinations of only those who arouse suspicion. One of the athletes to come under suspicion was South African 800m runner Caster Semenya because of her extraordinary performances on the track. In her case, it was hyperandrogenism (i.e. high levels of androgen) that allegedly enhanced her performance. The IOC reacted to this challenge with the decision to use the testosterone level as the criterion for the eligibility of individuals for women's competitions. This rule also applies to transgender athletes.

In women's elite football, accusations and rumours about opponent players not being women seem to be quite frequent. One of the players to have come under suspicion is Genoveva Añonma, who was accused of being a man after the 2008 African Women's Championships. According to an interview with the BBC (Sheringham, 2015), she had to strip naked in front of male officials to prove her womanhood – which she did. Another player who has fought against accusations of being a man is Park Eun-seon of South Korea. Not only did players of other Korean teams ask for proof of her sex, opponents at the 2015 Women's World Cup also doubted that she was a woman and asked for a test. Suspicions, accusations and the implementation of tests continue in women's football. In 2011, a Fifa decision to ask teams to sign a declaration that their players were of 'appropriate gender' (meaning 'appropriate sex' – biological sex rather than adopted gender) appeared to bolster such suspicions. While Fifa did not decide on the form that 'sex verification' should take, in Germany, team members had to present a certificate issued by a doctor. In 2015, the German coach Silvia Neid declared proudly in public that all members of her team were truly women. (*Editors' note*: Perhaps ironically, Germany, in 2013, became the first country in Europe to give parents the option of a third 'indeterminate' gender description for their newborn children on birth certificates, in addition to the standard choices of 'male' or 'female'.)

Exploring the coverage of the sex verification of the players in German newspapers, we found predominantly negative reactions, as journalists and the writers of letters to editors considered this procedure as not only unnecessary but also humiliating and discriminatory. There are also scholars and activists who argue that the testosterone level of athletes is not the only factor that influences performances. They demand that individuals who self-identify as women should be allowed to take part in women's competitions.

## Positions of power

The large differences between men's and women's football, such as with regard to finances or to levels of public attention and interest, are mirrored in the gender ratio in positions of power. In the context of the FREE project, not only football players and fans but also federations and their policies have been the subject of research. Worldwide and in nearly all sports, positions of influence and power are almost exclusively held by men. Excellent sources for investigating the gender ratio on the boards and among the members of sport federations are their websites. The names and often also the pictures of the officials reveal that women make up only a small minority of sport leaders. The IOC's call for gender equality has gained only minimal responses from national Olympic committees, international sports federations and the International Paralympic Committee. These organizations still struggle to meet the objective that the IOC set in 2000 that women should hold at least 20 per cent of leadership positions. The IOC has, for the first time, met its stated goal of 20 per cent female representation among its membership, with 21 per cent of the current members (22 of 106) being female. However, all of the committees are headed and dominated by men. Football is no exception; on the contrary, women are a small minority on the various committees of the national football federations and there were no women at all on the executive committees of the federations in the eight countries that were investigated in the context of the FREE project. It goes without saying that all of the presidents of the football federations are men. Fifa had never had a female representative on its executive committee until 2014. Currently, there are two women among its 27 members. Progress has been made with regard to the establishment of women's committees in most of the national football federations.

The position of coach, too, can be considered as a one of influence and power. It goes without saying that men's teams are not coached by women. There seems to be a single exception: Corrine Diacre, a former French international, who was appointed as coach of the Ligue 2 team Clermont in June 2014. She followed Helena Costa, who threw in the towel before even taking charge of a first competitive match 'after male colleagues sidelined her and left her convinced she was just a "face" to attract publicity' (Willsher and Martin, 2014). Women's teams are also coached predominantly by men. According to Uefa (2015), only 16 per cent of the coaches of female players and teams are women. However, there are large differences between countries; while in France and Croatia less than 1 per cent of the coaches are women, 60 per cent of the coaches in Bulgaria are female. Although the numbers of women in positions of administrative power seem to be increasing slightly, the men in power have to be much more proactive than they have been up to now in order to reach a 'just' gender balance in leadership positions.

## Participation in football and fandom

Football is gendered; its structure is biased in favour of the male sex. Playing the game is also gendered; participation patterns differ widely across Europe. For example, while football is the most popular sport for women in Denmark and the UK, it is hardly played at all by women in East and South European countries. This may be because girls are not encouraged to play football, because of a lack of supportive influences such as peers or coaches, or because facilities and programmes for girls are few and far between.

Stacey Pope and David Kirk (2014) investigated the role of football experiences in the development of a lifelong interest in the game via 51 qualitative semi-structured interviews with three generations of female fans in the UK. They concluded that:

> Women's experiences in physical education and sport at school played an important though mostly negative role in influencing their interest in professional male football in adulthood. For some women, the lack of encouragement they received at school to become involved in football pushed them away from playing and/or spectating.
>
> *(Pope and Kirk, 2014, p. 239)*

## Women's football in the mass media: gendering, agenda-setting and framing

Exaggerated masculinity is one of the selling points of football players who advertise various products by appearing as warriors or duellists engaged in surrogate warfare on and off the football pitch. This portrayal is especially notable in advertisements that feature male players as heroes in defence of their club's, city's or nation's honour. Female footballers, it seems, do not represent their country or defend their nation's honour to the same degree that men do. They do not feed audiences' fantasies of omnipotence and they may not fit into the marketing strategies of potential sponsors. The *Washington Post* echoed many other media in its assessment of the marketing value of the 2015 Women's World Cup when it stated that the fact that it 'attracted far fewer of the marketing blitzes or mega-deals seen in men's tournaments, and far less of the cash or corporate support, [is] a glaring loss for players and fans of the world's most popular sport' (Harwell, 2015).

Such gendered coverage of football may be explained by the power and the taste of (male) sports journalists. Referring to the theoretical concepts of agenda-setting and framing, it becomes evident that the media establish men's football as the main interest of journalists and their audiences. Moreover, the repetitive media portrayals of football in such a manner continually reinforce gender stereotyping. Journalists rationalize and justify such depictions with reference to the expectations of their readers or viewers, whom they assume to be men. They or their editors, most of whom are men, select which events are to be reported upon and the manner in which narratives of the events are described (Fenton, 2000, p. 298). Such framing of events provides meanings to consumers, presenting particular contexts and messages that explain and interpret and thereby influence their audiences (Fairhurst and Sarr, 1996).

In such explanations, gender is determined to be a social construction that is embedded in social institutions as well as identity. Sex is biological, assigned at birth, but gender is something that is learned, practised or performed, and felt. Men's football is therefore promoted and accepted as 'real' football, while women's football is considered to be different, lesser, unequal and inferior (Connell, 2002). The media, after all, have the power to set agendas and frame their accounts in ways that draw more positive correlations, which influence the tastes and consumption patterns of consumers. The ESPN media network in the US has generated legions of female fans, enhancing its corporate sponsorships and transforming US sporting culture while becoming a dominant global sports network, by screening more female sports events, employing more female sports journalists and broadcasters and portraying female athletes in a more positive way.

## Conclusion

As we have learned, association football was created and developed primarily as a man's sport. In spite of its marginalized past, women's football is thriving in many parts of Europe, North America and beyond. Compared to men's football, the women's game has fewer resources, limited professional opportunities and a lack of media coverage, which in turn leads to restricted advertising and corporate sponsorship opportunities. The media still tend to regard the sport as a predominantly masculine endeavour and to assume that the sport is incompatible with traditional conceptions of femininity. Yet there is evidence of transition: female celebrities have achieved recognition and a measure of remuneration on and off the field and have inspired other women to take to the football pitch, providing hope for the future.

### Research in Action

'The way out? African players' migration to Scandinavian women's football' by Sine Agergaard and Vera Lucia Botelho (2014)

#### What were the goals of the research?

Football players have access to a huge globalized labour market that provides opportunities to earn astronomical sums of money. This encourages many players to migrate to countries with strong domestic football leagues. Women players, like their male counterparts, change clubs and countries in search of better playing conditions and higher salaries. This study investigated the motives of female footballers who had travelled from Africa to find work in Scandinavia. It aimed to provide insights into the players' ambitions and expectations, and their positive and negative experiences. In addition, the researchers explored the opportunities available to players at the end of their playing careers.

## Why was the research relevant?

This study contributed new knowledge to the existing body of research on sports labour migration, which has up until recently focused on male athletes. Research on migrant female players is a novelty because their domestic and professional experiences differ from those of male players. The authors provided details of the backgrounds of the women who had migrated and the impact that playing football has had on their lives. A particular novelty of this work was the information about the situation of women and of women's football in two very different regions, Africa and Scandinavia. Whereas women's sport in Scandinavia has been the topic of numerous projects and studies, little is known about women's sport in Africa. The study showed that women's football in Africa is still in a developmental state, that female footballers face numerous obstacles and that there are huge differences in the situation of women and women's football between different countries.

Agergaard and Botelho summarized the findings of existing studies, which revealed in particular gender ideals, norms and roles, but also economic and logistical problems that are huge barriers for girls who wish to play football. They also drew attention to the fact that there is a great deal of intra-continental migration of female players in Africa.

## What methods were used?

The authors focused on four main motives:

1. economic gains
2. settlement
3. cultural experiences
4. football ambitions.

They surveyed ten African migrant players in the premier leagues of Sweden, Denmark and Norway. The researchers used a form of 'snowball sampling' to find interviewees (snowball sampling is a technique using participants in a study to refer friends, colleagues, peers and so on, who then become part of the expanding sample of participants). It was particularly difficult for the research team to gain access to African players, but they maintained communication via Skype, Facebook and email. These channels of communication are used widely and regularly by migrant players, and therefore they served two research functions:

1.  Most obviously, email and Facebook offered a channel of communication through which relationships (between the researchers and migrant players) could be formed and Skype interviews could be arranged.
2.  This also gave access to the social world of the participants under study, allowing the researchers to become part of their communications network.

Such methods enabled extensive information to be gathered about African players who played football in Denmark, Norway and Sweden in 2011. The ages of the mostly Nigerian participants ranged from 22 to 34.

The interviews were semi-structured (meaning that they were not constrained to a uniform format, but did take direction from an interview guide consisting of key themes to be covered), with the interviewer setting out to gain an insight into the lives of the individual players and their personal backgrounds. As such, interviews focused on the players' motives for moving abroad, life adaptations on and off the field of play and their plans for the future.

## What were the main arguments?

Through their analysis, the authors were able to dispel a few myths about player migration:

*   *It's all about the money*: While financial incentive is often thought to be a primary reason for the migration of women footballers, the authors demonstrated that in their sample this was not the case. Participants identified progression (as a football player) and the availability of key facilities (i.e. training facilities) to facilitate this goal as key factors. As one participant, Megan, stated: 'Football is the most important reason, money comes second.'
*   *Long-term emigration*: Contrary to the existing literature, the authors argued that player migration is not simply used as an opportunity to move from an impoverished country in order to ensure long-term settlement in a wealthy nation. Players are only registered on short-term contracts, after all, and in interviews most participants expressed a deep emotional attachment to their country of birth and a strong desire to return. As Ruth stated: 'Nigeria is my home country. That's where I will die.' The pull to 'go home' was managed by participants with the use of

information technologies such as Skype and Facebook, which facilitate connection to various places and people and prevent feelings of dislocation and homesickness. The participants' long-term intention, however, was always to return home.

- *Cultural experience*: The desire to play abroad in order to expose themselves to cosmopolitan experiences did not appear to be a main motive for the participants. This was seen as an added bonus by some, but not as an important reason for player migration. As Patricia stated: 'I just want to play football.'

- *Football experience and ambition*: The sample suggested that it is not the case that Nigerian players move abroad simply to become professional (after all, there are professional leagues in Nigeria). The participants were, however, motivated to play in specific leagues. Olivia explained: 'When I was a kid I knew that Sweden is the best, as I grew up I wanted to come feel this.' Others mentioned the dream of playing in the Women's Professional Soccer League (now the National Women's Soccer League) in the US. Thus, as leagues grow and shrink in stature, it is likely that player migration patterns will follow contemporary trends of excellence.

- *Dreams of social mobility*: By playing football abroad, female African athletes gain social capital within their home nations. This was a key motivational driver for the interviewed football players.

## And the conclusions or key findings?

The salaries of the players were relatively small in comparison to the large sums that men can earn. The money was used by some of the women to help their families in Africa. However, earning large sums of money was not the primary motive of many players for the move to Scandinavia. It could also have been assumed that the hope to be able to live in an affluent country would have been a strong incentive for many players. However, the women did not plan to stay in Scandinavia initially, and in fact this attitude appeared not to change over time (despite their settling happily in the host country). The researchers gave the strong impression that African players set up home in Europe, but as footballing nomads, never certain where the next contract will take them. The main goal of the participants was to gain the cultural capital that is valuable in Nigeria, through playing in respected European leagues. Ultimately, it seems, they intended to return to Africa.

## What were the strengths of the research?

The strength of this study was in providing insight into the experiences and lives of a group of women whose situations, aims and dreams were widely unknown. As women's football gains increasing amounts of attention, research into the migration of female players and their motivation for migrating provides essential knowledge. Overcoming the difficulties of gaining access to the players and conducting interviews with them was a specific asset of this study. The long duration of the research period may be considered a problem because, for instance, the situation of women's football changes rapidly; however, it also enabled the authors to gain in-depth insights into the lives of these women.

## *Were there any weaknesses?*

The authors did not make clear how the various studies were interconnected and if and how they enriched each other. The description of the methods was not clear enough and it was difficult to find out when, how and by whom contacts were made, interviews were conducted, theories were selected and findings were interpreted.

(*Editors' note*: Agergaard and Botelho have (with Nina Tiesler) developed a theoretical model based on their research – see Agergaard *et al.* (2014)).

# 7

# IDENTITY

*Andrew Parker and Andrew Manley*

---

**Chapter highlights**

- While English professional football features prominently on the landscape of the contemporary sporting world, little scientific research has been carried out into the inner workings of its organizational settings.
- Those scholars who have breached the inner sanctums of the professional game report a series of cultural norms based upon traditional working-class values, hyper-masculine 'shop-floor' relations and authoritarian managerial practices.
- Some argue that the norms and values evident inside professional football are no different to those in a range of other all-male, working-class occupational locales.
- Social theory allows us to analyze the constituent elements of footballing culture, the potential impact that this can have on identity formation, and how players negotiate and contest the cultural expectations placed upon them.

---

## Introduction

Social identity is a concept that has come to be much talked about within the orbits of social science, yet which has proved notoriously difficult to explain. Widely adopted across a range of contexts it is a term which is used to denote a variety of themes and ideas primarily regarding the relationship between the self and society, and the processes of identification that take place via everyday interaction. Of central interest to writers in the sociology of sport (and indeed beyond) has been the extent to which modern–day sports represent key sites for the formation of identities.

*(Parker and Harris, 2009, p. 1)*

Within the field of social science, the concept of identity has been explored by a range of scholars and in association with a variety of disciplinary areas (Jenkins, 2008). Drawing upon the work of the social psychologist George Herbert Mead (1863–1931), whose influential book *Mind, Self and Society* was published posthumously in 1934, it is possible to gain insight into the fundamental principles of how identities are formed and how individuals present themselves in different social settings. Equally important to any discussion of identity construction are issues of affiliation and attachment. In terms of the formation of the self, for example, we must consider how and why people identify themselves in relation to those around them. Where wider processes of interaction are concerned, we must recognize that identity is not solely about the self, but about how we construct ourselves in accordance with broader social processes through communication and negotiation. Together, all of these elements comprise the basis of identity formation (MacClancy *et al.*, 1996; Parker and Harris, 2009).

The social processes that shape our individual and collective identities are also heavily influenced by a broader range of issues relating to things such as race/ethnicity, social class, gender, sexuality and religion. Locating this within a sporting context, we can see how the practice and consumption of sport, physical activity and leisure shape our understandings of who we are and how others perceive us (Harris and Parker, 2009). According to Maguire and colleagues (2002), sport offers opportunities for the display of similarities between the identities of individuals and groups, while simultaneously providing a platform upon which notions of difference might be demonstrated. With all of these things in mind, we may pose the following questions: how might the study of sport aid our understanding of identity construction and how are individual and collective identities within sporting contexts represented and maintained?

As a site for social inquiry, professional football has been explored in relation to a plethora of issues and debates. Indeed, the global dissemination of football has given rise to a whole range of investigative studies, including those focusing upon the construction and (re)presentation of identity construction. Central here have been analyses of national identity and nationalism (Tomlinson and Young, 2006; Giulianotti and Robertson, 2009; Vincent and Harris, 2014), race and ethnicity (Burdsey, 2004; Cleland and Cashmore, 2014) and gender identity and sexuality (Caudwell, 1999, 2011; Harris, 2005; Jeanes, 2011). In this sense, football provides an avenue via which a range of identity-related questions can be explored. What, we might ask, can the professional game tell us about the formation of identities? How do individuals come to define themselves through participation in professional football? And how does football club culture shape the lives of those who frequent its occupational locales?

In order to address some of these questions, the present chapter seeks to use football as a lens through which to view identity formation in an attempt to provide an understanding of how elite players make sense of who they are and how they fit into the social world around them. Football clubs provide an ideal environment through which to explore the construction and maintenance of sporting identities, and, by drawing upon conceptual studies of professional footballing life, the chapter examines the cultural norms that shape the way in which player identities emerge. Explorations of football club culture often give rise to discussions surrounding the concept of identity and, in particular, how a 'preferred' or 'expected' sense of self prevails within this occupational environment. To this end, the chapter also examines traditional power relations within the professional game and the structural codes and mechanisms via which 'core' beliefs and values are promoted and maintained. In turn, the chapter draws upon the work of social theorists in order to analyze the constituent elements of footballing culture, the potential impact that this can have on identity formation, and how players may contest the norms and values placed upon them. To begin our discussion, we turn to an exploration of some of the core beliefs that are present within footballing culture and how these might impact the everyday lives of players and those around them.

## Football club culture: norms and values

The concept of identity is complex and multifaceted, yet it is widely acknowledged that individual identities are formed through a process of socialization whereby individuals learn to adhere to the social norms present in their cultural surroundings. Socialization is a process that provides individuals with the opportunity to learn to behave in ways that allow them to gain acceptance and status from significant others within their social group (Horne *et al.*, 2013). Central to this process is an acknowledgement of the norms and values that are attached to specific cultures, organizations and institutions.

Studies that have examined identity construction within professional football have sought to highlight how individual athletes become socialized through interacting with their peers, managers and coaches (Parker, 1995, 1996a; Roderick, 2003; Cushion and Jones, 2006). For footballers in the early stages of their careers, the recognition and adoption of a specific set of cultural norms and values is crucial to identity formation and to the attainment of professional player status. Andrew Parker's (1996a, 2001) analysis of traineeship in English professional football outlines the norms and values that encompass the life of young footballers, and the (largely implicit) behavioural codes to which they must adhere. A passion for the game, a resolute dedication to training, a forceful 'will to win', an acceptance of workplace relations (i.e. authoritarianism and subservience) and a willingness to conform to the 'official' rules and regulations of football club life are highlighted as key ingredients in the lives of young players. Collectively, these values underpin a powerful set of cultural norms, which are reinforced through interactions with peers, coaches and managers on a day-to-day basis. They also encompass the kind of 'professional attitude' that is expected of young players (Cushion and Jones, 2006; Parker, 2006; Roderick, 2006a), which, in turn, is often associated with a series of desirable 'character' traits (Parker, 1996a). The display of a good professional attitude and the formation of good character thus serves as a guideline for clubs in relation to the willingness of players to accept certain norms and values, and provides evidence of the construction of an identity that is closely aligned with the wider culture of the professional game (Roderick, 2003).

While the majority of young players within football adhere to such norms, motivation to do so may vary (Parker, 2001). Moreover, attitudes towards club culture may fluctuate over the course of a player's career (Roderick, 2003). In this sense, we must acknowledge that footballing identities are unstable, fluid and subject to change. Indeed, the construction of social identity within this context can be demonstrated through the shifting patterns of interaction between individual players and significant others (i.e. coaches, managers and fellow athletes). Cashmore and Parker (2003, p. 219) note that the formation and maintenance of stable workplace identities and the successful acquisition of a long-term career within professional football are largely established through 'heavily prescribed workplace behaviours' that, in a disciplinary sense, ensure that the required attitudes and character traits are established early on in a footballer's career. These behaviours provide the initial step to acquiring a sense of acceptance from significant others within what is, after all, a rather precarious profession (Roderick, 2006c).

## Professionalism, character and workplace identity

The subcultural environment that surrounds professional football has a strong influence upon players' social practices and processes of learning (Christensen *et al.*, 2011). The concept of a good professional attitude within the everyday lives of footballers has historically constituted an acceptance of traditional and often mundane working practices (i.e. the cleaning of boots, the preparation of kit for senior players, the servicing of training equipment) and the physical rigours of playing and performing (Parker, 2000b). To adopt a good professional attitude within elite football and to display an appropriate sense of professionalism rests predominantly upon the ability of young players to adhere to a certain set of behavioural norms underpinned by the demonstration of moral character and a strong (and unquestioning) work ethic. Of course, it is not unusual for notions of professionalism to focus as much upon the formation of attitudes and behaviours as the acquisition of specific skills (Fournier, 1999). In football, coaches and managers often define a good attitude as one that spawns a work ethic that incorporates a particular emphasis on self-improvement. By displaying 'professional' ideals, young players are often looked upon more favourably by managers and coaches, thereby giving themselves a greater chance of success within the game – providing, of course, that they also demonstrate the required levels of technical competence and expertise (Cushion and Jones, 2006).

Despite the positive behavioural traits attached to displays of professionalism, unintended consequences surrounding the demonstration of a 'good professional attitude' (specifically amongst youth footballers) have been identified. In their study of the subcultural environment surrounding elite youth Danish football, Mette Christensen and Jan Kahr Sørensen (2009) indicate that a strong adherence to the core values of professional club culture make it increasingly difficult for young players within this context to pursue any sense of educational progression. The ambition to succeed as a professional, the possibility of losing recognition within the team and the potential threat of unemployment all impact academic aspiration and attainment (Christensen and Sørensen, 2009). Other studies have similarly revealed that an interest in education or the demonstration of academic ability by young academy athletes may potentially hinder their prospects of 'making the grade' as professionals (Parker, 2000a; McGillivray *et al.*, 2005; McGillivray, 2006; Platts and Smith, 2009). Indeed, Parker (2000a, p. 73) highlights how trainees in his study who demonstrated too much interest in academic work ran the risk of being chastised and ridiculed 'by coaches and players alike, on account of their ambitious educational interests'. By seriously engaging with education, these trainees were seen by significant others to be forsaking their identity as (and commitment to becoming) dedicated professionals and, because of this, the pursuit of an education was perceived by many of those concerned as a barrier to professional player status.

While such research highlights the negative perception of educational provision within football, McGillivray and McIntosh (2006) indicate that in more recent years there has been an expansion of educational opportunities open to professional players both young and old. That said, we should exercise caution when considering the level of educational engagement amongst young players given that clubs have historically been criticized for failing to adequately cater for their post-career needs. Moreover, previous research has indicated that despite the realization by youth trainees that few players graduate to the professional ranks, the majority fail to maximize the educational opportunities made available to them (Monk, 2000). Although, as we have seen, the emphasis on educational attainment has certainly increased of late, it is clear that there remain strong implicit messages within the everyday working practices of professional clubs that perpetuate a restrictive view of the value and worth of education per se (Monk and Russell, 2000).

## Masculinity, 'banter' and 'shop-floor' culture

Intertwined with notions of professionalism are a series of heavily gendered norms, values and behaviours that are rooted in what is more widely recognized as the hegemonic (dominant and pervasive) masculine culture surrounding professional football. (Aspects of gendered norms are discussed in Chapter 4 and more extensively in Chapter 6.) Indeed, an acceptance of and adherence to these dominant patterns of masculinity is often considered a central component of youth trainee identity (Parker, 1996a, 2000b). Here, young players are expected to buy into an institutional logic based upon a series of masculine codes that are commonly propagated within working-class occupational locales through what Parker and others have called 'shop-floor' language and interaction. For example, in his in-depth analysis of football youth traineeship, Parker (2006, pp. 695–696) indicates that central to the enactment of everyday life within this context is the 'stylised adoption of a sexually explicit and often highly derogatory vocabulary which … [is] typically characterised by razor-sharp wit'. In turn, a series of 'unofficial' behavioural norms exist amongst young players which manifest themselves most clearly, Parker (2000b, p. 61) argues, in the desire to embody the hyper-masculine practices of superstar status such as 'fast cars, designer clothes, financial affluence, social indulgence and sexual promiscuity' – values that are inevitably shaped by the all-male subculture that footballers typically inhabit. The existence of a series of both official and unofficial behavioural norms demonstrates the contradictory nature of the complex cultural environment that young players must negotiate (Parker, 2001). Added to this are issues of physical and personal integrity. Roderick and colleagues (2000) suggest that players who openly admit to injury face the prospect of taunts from fellow players – a practice that commonly fuels speculative 'banter' around the sexuality of the individuals concerned. In turn, players who express anxieties around their physical fitness due to injury and/or ill health may face the social stigma of becoming labelled idle and non-committal (Roderick, 2006b).

For young players in particular, the safe negotiation of one's own masculine prowess is an integral part of assimilating oneself into football club culture (Parker, 2001). Equally important are the lines of hierarchical control, authority and status that exist between players, managers and coaches (Embrey, 1986). Although it must be acknowledged that football cannot be accurately characterized by way of a single, all-encompassing cultural climate, research that has explored notions of authority and control within this context has provided vital clues as to how the professional game exhibits a commonly held set of managerial beliefs and practices and it is to a further examination of these that we now turn.

## Managerial authoritarianism and control

Studies that have focused on identity construction amongst young professional footballers have indicated that, despite the more recent introduction of regulated and systematic approaches to player development, authoritarian workplace practices continue to feature prominently within the day-to-day routines of club life (Parker, 1995, 1996a; Cushion and Jones, 2006; Kelly and Waddington, 2006). Seamus Kelly and Ivan Waddington's (2006) research concerning managerial control within the professional game indicates that abuse, intimidation and violence are utilized by managers to enforce authority over players. Other studies have highlighted similar applications of power – and the subsequent lack of agency – experienced by young footballers in relation to issues concerning both personal and professional development (Daniel, 2004; Pitchford et al., 2004; Thorpe, 2004). Cushion and Jones' (2006) investigation into the subculture of youth football and the trainee academy setting indicates that such practices and values are 'deeply rooted in the culture of professional soccer, with harsh, authoritarian, and often belligerent coaching behavior viewed as a necessary aspect of preparing young players for the rigors of the [professional] game' (p. 148). Further work by Cushion and Jones (2014) provides insight into the way in which young footballers may be inclined to demonstrate an unquestioning acceptance of subordination as a consequence of the fact that such behaviours are often seen as crucial to the establishment of a sense of legitimacy amongst peers, managers and coaches alike.

The pervasive presence of authoritarianism within professional football is not only something that players must simply endure but also something to which they must respond in a positive manner. Although (on the face of it) young players may be accepting of verbal chastisement and physical punishment, feelings of anxiety, isolation and occupational uncertainty are commonplace within professional football (Parker, 2006). As in other workplace environments (Morrison and Milliken, 2000; Piderit and Ashford, 2003), such feelings can create a culture of silence whereby players are unwilling to voice their concerns for fear of the impact that this might have on their career progression. Indeed, the hierarchical structure and organizational characteristics that serve to promote an authoritarian/subservient culture within football clubs is built upon the assumption that young players in particular are unlikely to express their discomfort with such practices due to their lack of credibility and stature within their respective organizations.

Despite the adoption of a more standardized approach to youth development in English professional football, differences in organizational practice are evident from club to club (Relvas *et al.*, 2010). Although traditional authoritarian approaches to management still appear prevalent throughout the game, measures have been taken to ensure that abusive behaviour is eliminated. The development and implementation of codes of conduct for players and coaches, the adoption of reflective diaries for monitoring development, the introduction of Education and Welfare Officers in academy settings and the management of player conduct are all measures aimed at facilitating the holistic development of young players (Brackenridge *et al.*, 2004). Yet notwithstanding the potential advantages that these changes bring, it would appear that athletes themselves have seldom played a part in consultations concerning such changes, once again demonstrating the lack of agency afforded to young players (Pitchford *et al.*, 2004).

As we have seen, the literature surrounding youth development in English professional football provides some indication of the cultural norms and values that are present within this context and how these serve to shape and influence the working lives of young players. However, it would be naïve to assume that all players readily accept the imposition of such norms or that identity construction within this environment is devoid of resistance or contestation. Indeed, it is to these issues that the final section of our discussion turns.

## Sustaining, resisting and contesting identities

It was a wretched environment, which I compare … to an open prison, at least as far as I was concerned. And yet my years with Wolves [Wolverhampton Wanders] were the most satisfying of my career. This is no contradiction, I

> loved the club, but not the managerial dictates and petty forms of discipline imposed on us, the players.
>
> *(Dougan, 1980, p. 3)*

> A total institution may be defined as a place of residence and work where a large number of like-situated individuals, cut off from the wider society for an appreciable period of time, together lead an enclosed, formally administered round of life. Prisons serve as a clear example, providing we appreciate that what is prison-like about prisons is found in institutions whose members have broken no laws.
>
> *(Goffman, 1961, p. 11)*

Taken at face value, these two statements appear poles apart. One is a personal reflection on professional footballing experience; the other is an extract from the opening paragraph of a sociological bestseller. The only obvious similarity between the two is that both make reference to prison settings, or, more accurately, both use analogies concerning 'prison-like' conditions in order to illustrate further their descriptive aims. Closer scrutiny, however, reveals a deeper connection in that also evident here are aspects of commonality that, in terms of organizational procedure, suggest that just as the everyday features of 'total institutional' life constitute some form of personal 'restriction' and 'closure', so too do the disciplinary and managerial dictates of professional football (Parker, 1996b).

As we have seen, the presence of clear cultural values perpetuated throughout the working lives of professional footballers, alongside the 'closed' nature of the game's institutional settings, provides an environment in and through which a preferred sense of self can be defined and an 'ideal' character or identity (suitable for that cultural environment) promoted. Drawing upon the work of sociologist Erving Goffman (1922–1982), Parker (1996a, 1996b) demonstrates the 'enclosed' atmosphere that envelopes the working lives of young professional footballers by illustrating the highly routinized and somewhat segregated nature of their everyday existence (see also Gearing, 1999).

Of course, in reality, it would be misleading to suggest that Goffman's (1961) work on total institutions is directly relevant to English professional football. For one thing, his analysis relies heavily upon establishments that revolve around involuntary membership; for another, his findings make no specific reference to sporting contexts. However, in terms of the wider conceptual inferences that Goffman makes concerning the range of institutions within our society and the varying degrees of 'totality' that they exhibit, his work serves as a useful theoretical vehicle through which comparisons to working relations within English professional football might be drawn.

For Goffman (1961, p. 15), all institutions (i.e. social settings where groups of people collectively adhere to a defined set of norms and values) provide something of a 'captive world' for their members and, as such, display what he calls 'encompassing tendencies'. Depending on the official aims of each institution, Goffman

(1961, p. 15) argues, these tendencies vary and change in severity. Primarily, his concerns are with those institutions that demonstrate a high degree of totality in that they construct an obvious barrier to 'social intercourse' for their 'inmates'. What Goffman (1961, pp. 15–22) is quick to point out, however, is that the institutional features he discusses are not exclusive to total institutions, nor are they shared by every one of them. Rather, for him, the hallmark of total institutional character is the 'intense' presence of a number of items from within a common 'family of attributes' relating to issues of closure, rationalization and bureaucracy (see also Foucault, 1977; Burns, 1992).

In terms of social restriction, life in and around professional football may be considered relatively low on 'totality' in comparison to the kind of institutions upon which Goffman's work is based. Yet, in an everyday sense, football clubs are not places that people can simply walk in and out of at their own discretion. They do have some element of closure, very often displaying perimeter walls or fences, for example, which offer protection against intrusion. Indeed, despite the benefits of public appeal, many teams choose to go about their everyday business amidst an atmosphere of relative seclusion in an attempt to keep the personal lives of players, and their training activities, away from the public and media gaze (Tomlinson, 1983). Such practices inevitably mediate an air of discreteness, as do those of social restriction and residential isolation, which have often accompanied notions of 'apprenticeship' within the professional game. By adopting a restrictive approach to trainee socialization, some football clubs have come to engender their own 'encompassing tendencies' which, in resembling the operational characteristics of a host of other institutional establishments, position them in one of the five 'rough groupings' within which Goffman (1961, p. 16) suggests the total institutions of our society can be classified. While elements of this broad nomenclature deal with organizations as diverse as orphanages, hospitals, prisoner-of-war camps and monastic retreats, Goffman's (1961, p. 16) fourth category is concerned primarily with those institutions 'purportedly established the better to pursue some work-like task and justifying themselves only on these instrumental grounds'. Examples cited by Goffman here are army barracks, ships, boarding schools, work camps and colonial compounds – a group that, for the purposes of the present discussion, also accommodates the rule-bound (and often residential) confines of youth traineeship within English professional football.

Individuals within a range of occupational contexts seek to adhere closely to the values of their organizations, both for purposes of personal gain and for the collective good of the organization itself. However, all institutions contain what Goffman (1961) refers to as an 'underlife' – that is, modes of social interaction that are contrary to the dominant aims and ideals of the organization, which thus constitute a form of resistance (Manning, 2008). Literature examining resistance within sporting contexts predominantly focuses upon the power relations that exist between coach and athlete. Traditionally, scholarship within this domain has sought to exemplify the role of the athlete as a passive or docile 'other', one who identifies with, and strictly adheres to, the dominant cultural norms and authoritative behaviours of the coach (Shogan, 1999; Johns and Johns, 2000; Jones et al., 2005; Manley et al., 2012; Williams and Manley, 2014). This is not to say that athletes do not possess or demonstrate any form of agency or the capacity to appropriate a mode of power that resists occupational identities bound by authoritative/subservient structures. Resistance to dominant power relations within elite sport has taken many forms and can be displayed through subtle modes of interaction that seek to subvert, challenge or distance individual conceptions of 'self' from the overarching values in place. As we have seen, research has indicated that the use of humour or scornful cynicism has been adopted by athletes to question authority and to resist instances of domination (Parker, 2006; Purdy et al., 2008; Purdy et al., 2009; Potrac and Jones, 2011). In addition, the perceived physical capital or sporting prowess that individual athletes possess provides a sense of empowerment and capacity to challenge or reverse decisions that are imposed by organizational hierarchies (Purdy et al., 2008). In this view, coaches are made aware that an authoritative statement seeking to discipline or exclude athletes who engage in resistant behaviours can be met, in some sporting cultures, with behaviours that further disrupt the organizational hierarchies in question (Lok and de Rond, 2013).

The manifestation of resistance to dominant ideals that encapsulate notions of 'professional attitude', 'character' or 'preferred identity' within football clubs may also be expressed in verbal and physical form (Cushion and Jones, 2006). For example, evidence of such resistance amongst youth players is provided by way of their disregard for official expectations around educational attainment, often displayed through a lack of engagement and attendance at educational institutions (Parker, 2000a; McGillivray et al., 2005; McGillivray, 2006; Christensen and Sørensen, 2009; Platts and Smith, 2009). While truancy may be perceived as a mode of resistant behaviour within this occupational context, it also demonstrates a strong reaffirmation of workplace identity, adhering closely to the anti-intellectual culture that has historically been associated with professional football (Parker, 2001; Thompson et al., 2015). In addition, outward displays of resistance have been highlighted through an overt rejection of the core values attached to the 'keen' and 'hardy' work ethic often associated with a good professional attitude. This has been most commonly displayed through the adoption of a laissez-faire (i.e. carefree) approach to training and the withdrawal of 'best efforts' in an attempt to acquire a sense of control amidst a culture dominated by managerial authoritarianism (Parker, 1996a; Cushion and Jones, 2006). Further forms of resistance have been witnessed through subtle displays of dis-identification (a mechanism often administered through modes of cynicism, humour, scepticism or irony) that seek to create a sense of social distance, allowing subjects to resist occupational values and acquire a feeling of relief and empowerment from the burden of adhering to predefined roles associated with the organization's culture (Fleming and Spicer, 2003; Roderick, 2006a, 2014). This particular mode of resistance adopts an understated persona, seeking not to overturn or alter existing conditions, but to undermine organizational power relations through subtle forms of subversion or resistance (Fleming and Sewell, 2002) – practices that have been reported within various occupational cultures (Willis, 1977; Collinson, 1988, 1992, 1994; Ackroyd and Thompson, 1999; Fleming and Sewell, 2002). In addition, resistance to occupational norms and values surrounding the social lives of footballers have been displayed through more general 'rule-breaking' behaviours (e.g. excessive drinking) and social acts that run the risk of being captured and disseminated through mainstream and social media for the general public to consume (Parker, 1996a).

To suggest that professional footballers are constrained by their occupational identities to such an extent that they have little or no room to resist workplace practices and values would be an oversimplification of identity (re)presentation. As the work of Nikolas Rose (1997, p. 140) indicates, individuals are not to be considered as 'unified subjects of some coherent regime of domination', but as human agents possessing the capacity to negotiate a varying range of personas across a variety of differing practices. To draw once more upon the work of Erving Goffman (1959), we may suggest that identity (re)presentation is a carefully managed process, one that encapsulates a mode of 'performativity' whereby individuals display a multitude of differing 'fronts' (selves) to conform to a range of social (and organizational) roles. That is, within any given culture, identities are managed so as to promote the appearance that individuals are adhering to the normative practices (i.e. the accepted norms and values) of the group or organization, while simultaneously possessing the capacity to engage in behaviour contrary to the dominant norms in play. This is what Goffman (1959) aptly terms 'back stage' behaviours, which encapsulate the engagement of individuals in practices that are removed from and resistant to the 'normalizing discourses' of their host organization (Pullen and Rhodes, 2014). As we have seen, throughout the everyday working lives of professional footballers, such behaviours can manifest themselves in the form of scepticism towards (or a dis-identification with) the official and/or unofficial rules of club culture and are deployed not only to undermine dominant cultural norms but also to safeguard key aspects of players' identities from exposure to the disciplinary and regulatory measures routinely imposed by coaching and management staff (Roderick, 2014).

Despite the fact that some players routinely display elements of resistance to the dominant norms and practices of professional footballing life, the appearance of adherence to the cultural expectations enforced by clubs is necessarily in their best interests if they wish to remain in employment. As Goffman (1983) notes, when interacting within an array of institutional or social settings, individuals may become dependent upon the maintenance of order and the display of compliance to conformity. Thus, to secure favour, and to ensure longevity within the professional game, it seems that individual players must, at the very least, demonstrate an adherence to the prevailing values and normative behaviours of professional football culture, while at the same time maintaining a wider sense of self both inside and outside of their occupational milieu (Cushion and Jones, 2006; Roderick, 2006a, 2006c, 2012, 2014).

## Conclusion

It has been our intention throughout this chapter to consider issues of identity in professional football and the way in which identity formation amongst players might be impacted by the norms and values evident within football club culture. In particular, we have explored the experiences of young players and how these norms and values might manifest themselves in the kinds of behaviours that such players may exhibit and the kinds of aspirations that they may hold in terms of career trajectory, educational progression and social interaction. In so doing, we have examined a selection of theoretical perspectives concerning organizational culture and power relations and considered the extent to which identity formation may be a product of the institutional practices and social interactions that professional football clubs promote. In turn, we have argued that amidst the authoritarian confines of this organizational culture, identity remains a negotiated and contested concept and one through which resistance to dominant norms and values is evident via a range of explicit and implicit workplace practices.

Of course, we recognize that there are many additional ways in which the construction of identity might be explored within the context of professional football. For example, scholars and empirical researchers may wish to examine notions of identity formation from different theoretical and methodological perspectives. These kinds of investigations would necessarily stimulate discussion around the nuances of conceptual application and may seek to examine a series of wider social variables. Studies on identity formation amongst elite female footballers are, to date, relatively few and far between and as such represent a key area for future investigation. Likewise, in-depth analyses of identity formation within a broader range of sporting locales will inevitably help scholars to think more critically about how individual and collective identities are constructed, represented and maintained. In turn, such work has the potential to locate identity formation as a more central topic of conversation within sport studies as a whole.

### Research in Action

'Narratives of identity among former professional footballers in the United Kingdom' by Brian Gearing (1999)

#### What were the goals of the research?

The preliminary aim of this research was to understand how professional footballers in the UK coped with the challenges of establishing a new identity, or notion of self, following retirement from the game. Through the acquisition of personal accounts, the research attempted to acquire insight into the occupational experiences of former players and the core values associated with the culture of professional football. By drawing on the life-stories of these players, the research sought to illustrate the difficulties associated with transitioning into post-sport retirement and the challenges connected with the establishment of new narratives of self that are far removed from the culture of professional football.

## Why was the research relevant?

Gearing's work was one of the first sociological inquiries into issues of retirement, ageing and identity negotiation surrounding the occupational context of UK professional football. Indeed, the immediate and long-term social and psychological difficulties attached to retirement had previously received sparse attention in relation to the working lives of professional players. Gearing's research exposed the difficulties in transitioning from a position of 'stardom' to one of relative obscurity. By obtaining the life-stories of those who had experienced differing levels of success within the professional game, he acquired insights into the construction and reconstitution of identity amongst those moving from a career in football to positions of uncertainty. Moreover, the occupational lifespan of professional footballers is unusual in that retirement often comes at a relatively early age. Indeed, research examining retirement amongst those leaving a profession in their mid-thirties is relatively uncommon, and thus Gearing's work provided insight into a unique population. By highlighting the challenges associated with the forging of new identities outside the cultural milieu of professional football, Gearing's research also raised awareness of a number of broader issues concerning personal health and well-being.

## What methods were used?

### Sample

Gearing sought to acquire data from a group of 12 former players with varying levels of involvement in the professional game. Nine had pursued their professional careers at an English Third Division (now League One) club either in the 1940s, 1950s or 1960s. The remaining three participants had played for First Division (now Premier League) clubs and had enjoyed far more illustrious careers. The ages of the participants ranged from early 30s to early 70s. At the time of the research, the majority of interviewees were in their 40s and 50s and remained in employment across a range of occupations, while those who were older had entered semi- or full retirement.

*Interviews*

Gearing's research placed emphasis on acquiring knowledge surrounding players' careers and their experiences upon leaving professional football. Gearing also utilized accounts of the interviewees' lives that had featured either in published autobiographies or national newspapers to further interpret their experiences. Interviews were framed around a range of theoretical and conceptual ideas that sought to understand both the institutional structure that helped to forge the occupational identities of his participants (namely the occupational culture that encompassed the working lives of those concerned) and the practices through which narratives of self were enacted, an aspect that was captured predominantly through the biographical and autobiographical accounts provided within the interviews.

## What were the main arguments?

Gearing argued that, due to the distinctive occupational culture surrounding the world of professional football, a particular type of identity had to be adhered to and displayed throughout the everyday working lives of his participants. Retirement was framed as a significant challenge, as was the search for a 'post-football identity' – one far removed from the occupational ideals, workplace routines and cultural values prevalent within the professional game.

Gearing utilized the accounts of his interviewees to illuminate the core values attached to the culture of professional football in a bid to demonstrate how and why retirement has such a strong impact upon players' constructions of self. Such values were associated with a highly routinized and disciplined lifestyle, a restriction of autonomy and individualism, and a facilitating culture that eliminated the capacity to think for oneself. While routine was integral to the everyday footballing experiences of the interviewees, they existed within a highly unpredictable and unstable working environment, whereby they felt that every aspect of their playing performances was scrutinized by the public (fans), peers, coaches and managerial staff. Gearing further argued that the high level of intensity and the emphasis upon risk-taking and success embedded within the culture of professional football provided players with an 'otherworldly' experience, acquiring a sense of ecstasy and euphoria that was often compared to the experience of drug addiction. Coupled with traditional masculine working-class values, this particular cultural environment promoted a strong sense of camaraderie amongst players, bonding them together through their shared experiences of transition from adolescence to early adulthood.

Thus, central to Gearing's thesis was the notion that the strong cultural values and behavioural norms that his participants experienced during their time in the professional game provided a 'gravitational pull' for many players, making it difficult for them to come to terms with the loss of their identities as footballers. Many retirees voiced their concerns over relinquishing an identity that was so closely influenced by, and aligned with, their playing careers. Gearing also referred to a 'social clock' within professional football – an informal timeline that denotes the expected length of a player's career. It was anticipated by the majority of his respondents that their footballing careers would last until they reached their early 30s, yet due to the unpredictable nature of the profession, many did not attain this milestone. Whether due to injury or managerial decision, those who had retired even earlier from the game had found it increasingly difficult to fashion an identity that was disconnected from the world of football, and in some instances some were unwilling to do so.

Despite the difficulties associated with forming a sense of self detached from the game, Gearing argued that those who successfully established 'post-playing identities' sought to do so through relating to less well-defined aspects of their self-image, such as the 'family man' or a 'good work colleague' within their new/chosen profession. Regardless of success, having had a career in professional football was deemed by interviewees as the pinnacle of their lives. Drawing upon past experiences and reflecting upon previous memories provided recently retired respondents with a sense of pragmatism concerning life after football and an acceptance that an important aspect of their lives was now over.

## And the conclusions or key findings?

Reminiscing about the past became a positive experience for ageing retirees once they had been able to successfully negotiate a new identity post-retirement, and provided evidence to support the notion that narrative is important in the processes of identity construction and reconstruction. Gearing argued that recalling past experiences allowed his respondents to give meaning to their current lives and to strengthen their individual identities. However, it became increasingly difficult for the former players whose careers had ended abruptly to renounce their identities as professional footballers and to renegotiate differing senses of self, as they had been denied the opportunity to 'live out' their ambitions. In addition, Gearing reinforced the importance of culture in relation to the formation of specific identities and the difficulties in transitioning away from a particular sense of self once participants had left the world of professional football. Here Gearing's research solidified the importance of examining identity construction and reconstruction with reference to social theory that addresses the cultural arrangements of a particular occupational environment, and how the presence of strong social norms and values may impact upon the ability to successfully negotiate a new sense of self upon entering retirement.

## What were the strengths of the research?

The strengths of the research were predominantly associated with the unique data set obtained. Through the use of biographical interviewing, the work provided a series of personalized accounts of the key challenges associated with post-football retirement and the processes of forging and renegotiating new identities upon exiting the sport. By addressing such concerns, Gearing's work also attempted to situate strong empirical evidence against a theoretical backdrop that considered both the importance of structure (that is, the institutional culture of the clubs) and the importance of capturing intimate expressions of self as constructed through particular narrative exchanges. Moreover, the difficulties that the former professional players expressed upon navigating their transition into retirement still resonate with contemporary examples. This highlights a further strength of the research, demonstrating the importance of such work when attempting to understand the challenges that current professional footballers encounter upon facing career termination, a relatively uncommon experience outside the realms of elite sport.

## Were there any weaknesses?

While the work provided a range of experiences surrounding retirement, highlighting the core values attached to footballing identities and the inevitable difficulties in transitioning from one occupational sphere to another, the research could be considered dated. Many, but not all, of the reflections surrounding player experiences were taken from those who had competed in the 1940s, 1950s and 1960s. With heavy investment from multi-national corporations and a growth in the global sports media, the modern professional game has altered markedly since the time that many of Gearing's interviewees were playing and, in this sense, contemporary experiences of retirement from professional football could be considered radically different to those described, especially in relation to the economic realities pre- and post-retirement. However, Gearing did acknowledge such weaknesses, highlighting the differences in the economic circumstances of his respondents compared to those of modern-day players.

# 8

# MEDIA

*Richard Haynes*

---

**Chapter highlights**

- The media is integral to football.
- Football provides an important form of content for the media.
- Innovations in technology and the internet, especially the rise of socially networked media, have transformed the traditional dominance of the mass media in football.
- Battles over the 'triple play' of telephony, broadband and television will continue to transform the nature of televised football for the foreseeable future.

---

## Introduction

It is difficult to imagine contemporary football without the media. Even youth and amateur football are mediated in some shape or form on a regular basis, whether it be via local news outlets or, more popularly, on websites and socially networked media such as Facebook, Twitter and YouTube. If we think about how our own knowledge of football is informed and shaped, it becomes clear that the media and associated forms of communication have an important role in this process too. The multiple ways in which football is covered by the media for its various audiences informs and frames how we understand what football means to us both as individuals and collectively. This includes our understanding of how the sport is played, owned, coached, managed, refereed, supported, marketed and generally consumed in different forms, spaces and moments. For most people, most of the time, to think about football, whether consciously or not, is informed as much by their mediated experience of the game as it is by playing or watching the sport.

This gives the media an important place in the culture of football, and therefore within the study of football too.

Of course what we call the media, and the audiences for it, are not monolithic. That is, there are different kinds of media with different technologies; with different kinds of organizational structures; with competing public or commercial interests; with local, national or global audiences; and with different regulatory and legal requirements. So when talking about what we might call the 'football–media nexus', we must be mindful that it is a concept that has many variables, some of which have important consequences for not only how the sport is communicated and consumed, but also in some cases how the very structure of the sport is governed, organized and played. ('Nexus' refers to the connection or series of connections linking two or more things, so 'football–media nexus' refers to the inter-relationships between football and the media.) Conversely, football as a form of content has an increasing influence on the shape of the media itself, including on market structure, new technologies and regulation. This chapter will unpack some of the various relationships between football and the media, and should provide you with a more rounded historically and globally contextualized understanding of media sport more generally. (The word 'media' comes from the Latin plural of 'medium', and while the traditional view is that it should be treated as a plural noun, it is now used as both singular and plural; television, radio and newspapers/magazines were once known collectively as 'the mass media', though the addition of social media has broadened the scope of the term.)

Before we start, it is helpful to think about the kind of questions that we should ask about football's relationship with the media. One commonly asked question is whether or not the media produces a fair representation of football. In other words, does the media distort our view of football? If so, how can we recognize and analyze such representations, and how has football attempted to manage this process? One view of the media is that it is a 'mirror on the world', merely reflecting back what is happening, but such a view itself misrepresents the processes of mass communication; the media that we consume have gone through a number of stages of production and distribution to reach us, and we need to understand how media practitioners – journalists, editors, broadcasters and producers – do their jobs with the objective of producing media for different readers, listeners, viewers and browsers of content. For example, what is the role of football journalists? How does the nature of their work and how they report on football vary depending upon the publication or broadcaster they work for? How has the rise of football stars and their management as popular celebrities by agents and publicists changed the nature of football journalism? Have the ways in which journalists gather information from football – what we call the 'news–source relationships' – been transformed by the media management of teams, managers and players? To what extent might this be due to: increased suspicion of the press by governing bodies, clubs and players; new technological methods of newsgathering such as information through the internet; or the demands of audiences for different kinds of information about the game? Finally, when football becomes newsworthy, perhaps because of a scandal of some kind, why might news journalists and sports journalists report the same events differently? This latter question also raises the issue of how football organizes its own communications. With regard to media relations and the impact that technology and globalization might have had on the flow of communications, how have developments in socially networked media and increased access to mobile media transformed the way in which we access and consume information about football?

While traditional football journalism in the press maintains its function in the football–media nexus, the dominant media form is television. Football was first televised in the UK by the BBC in 1937, and, for several decades, administrators of the sport worried that the televising of football would have a damaging effect on attendance at games. Today, football receives enormous sums of money from television for the right to televise games, which has led many to question whether television exerts exceptional power and influence in the sport. Has football metaphorically 'sold its jersey' to television? Does the money invested by television companies in football mean that television executives now dictate how football is organized? How might this affect how football is played and consumed? Has the money flowing through the game transformed the sport purely to suit the television spectacle or are there other beneficiaries? Finally, how has the rise in the globalization of televised football changed the nature of fandom itself and how we access and view the game? Have these processes changed the meaning of football and the identities associated with it?

We can, therefore, see that the football–media nexus raises a set of important questions that need to be addressed when trying to understand the relationships between football and the media. The key to answering such questions is to acknowledge that to understand one side of the relationship, we must also understand the consequences for the other. In this sense, we need to understand the football–media nexus as a symbiotic relationship – one with mutual interests and complex interconnections.

## Football journalism and its discontents

The sport historian Tony Mason (1980) first alerted us to the centrality of the sporting press at the very birth of what we call association football. The media environment of the mid-to-late nineteenth century was different to the media landscape of the late twentieth century and unrecognizable from the landscape today. In terms of sport, the major difference was the evolution of a distinct sporting press, published on a weekly or bi-weekly basis and dedicated to sporting matters. Periodicals such as the *Athletic News* (1875–1931) were primarily targeted at a burgeoning middle-class market, and the development of organized sport and sports clubs – including football – were key to the new leisure pursuits of the middle class. The main protagonists in writing about football were football administrators themselves, who were evangelical amateur sportsmen with typewriters looking to drum up interest in and support for their new sports organizations. The coupling of football and publicity therefore has a long history, and takes us back to the roots of the organized game in Britain.

Post-war Britain saw a blossoming of media consumerism around football, including publications such as *Charles Buchan's Football Weekly* (1951) and *Raich Carter's Soccer Star* (1952) in the 1950s, followed by *Goal* (1968) and *Shoot* (1969) in the 1960s, aimed at a younger market. For many years these publications celebrated the star players and leading teams of each era, and set the tone for the elevation of football players in British popular culture alongside cigarette and bubblegum cards and Panini stickers.

The coverage of football in the press steadily grew in the inter-war period, especially in popular newspapers such as the *Daily Mirror* and the *Daily Express,* which began to carry more sports photojournalism in their match reports. This trend continued in the post-war period, which saw the emergence of leading football correspondents with national reputations such as Geoffrey Green of the *Times*, Peter Wilson of the *Daily Mirror*, Patrick Collins of the *Sunday People*, Ian Wooldridge of the *Daily Mail* and Hugh McIlvanney of the *Observer.* Newspapers also became an important source of information for the football pools, which gained enormous popular appeal in the middle of the twentieth century.

At a more local level, the regional press have long covered football, and local clubs are the domain of sports journalists who foster close but independent associations with club chairmen, managers, coaches, players and supporters' groups. Where regional papers cover more than one local club, the pressure for editorial neutrality places great strain on the newspaper's ability to serve the needs of its readership, which might have intense rivalries within it. In Scotland, for example, the popular tabloid the *Daily Record* has consistently trodden a fine line in its coverage of Celtic and Rangers, and has frequently been the focus of complaint from one side or the other for publishing what some might consider to be unfavourable reports.

While national newspapers can regularly transcend regional rivalries and ignore the nuances of local football sensitivities, local football reporters have to remain careful not to bite the hand that feeds them for fear of damaging relations between their newspapers and the club. The football press has historically been dependent on free access into football grounds based on the mutual benefit that local reporting brings to the publicity of the club. In a more commercially driven era of elite football, this historical relationship has occasionally broken down, either because club owners fear that critical reportage will damage reputations and upset commercial partners, or because they have commercialized aspects of press access to the club, such as the licensing of images on match days. Clubs such as Port Vale, Nottingham Forest, Newcastle United and Southampton have all imposed bans and restrictions on local football journalists and photographers based on the perceived interests of the club. In July 2015, Newcastle United introduced a new policy of 'preferred media partners', which awarded contracts for media access to a select group of media organizations including Sky Sports and the *Daily Mirror*, but excluded all others, including the local press (Edwards, 2015). In a quote-driven news environment, preferred media partners can look forward to privileged access to players, managers and coaching staff and other club information, whereas other media stakeholders are left out in the cold. However, strategic communications policies of this nature can also be viewed as a deliberate attempt to deny open communication, which ultimately impoverishes and sanitizes the information consumed by fans and the wider public. A football club, like any organization, fears bad news for obvious commercial reasons, but unlike many organizations there is a wider public interest in its daily business, the performance and condition of its players and the acumen of its team manager. Press bans have led journalists to pay for entry among supporters or, in the case of the *Plymouth Herald*, to send a cartoonist to matches in order to circumvent Southampton's ban on external press photography (Sweney, 2010). Commercial exclusion of the press or vindictive bans on individual journalists constrain the purpose of journalism. Football, historically deeply embedded in local communities, remains a central feature of local news output and can be central to the credibility of local newspapers in the eyes of their readers.

## Newshounds and celebrity footballers

On 25 January 1995, Eric Cantona, the French star player of Manchester United, infamously kung-fu kicked supporter Matthew Simmons following provocation by the Crystal Palace fan. Cantona was found guilty of assault and initially sentenced to two weeks in jail, which was later reduced to 120 hours of community service. Although the image of Cantona's kick remains iconic, the whole episode is equally notorious for his comments at a subsequent news conference. Cantona sat in front of the massed bank of reporters – or 'newshounds' as they are informally known – and photographers and, in his charismatic French accent, slowly and simply delivered his cryptic message: 'When seagulls follow the trawler, it is because they think sardines will be thrown into the sea' (Midgley, 2011). For Cantona, the statement expressed a prophetic condemnation of incessant celebrity-driven media; he had had enough of the feeding frenzy.

As the fame, fortunes and public profile of footballers changed because of increasing television exposure in the 1990s, so too did the variety of newspaper coverage of the sport. Football stories have long appeared outside the confines of the sports pages, particularly those involving sex, violence, drugs or gambling scandals. From the partying playboy image of George Best in the late 1960s to the moral panics surrounding the so-called football hooliganism of the 1970s, football has generated soft and hard news stories in the traditional news sections of newspapers for many decades. News and sports journalists do, however, look at the events on and off the field with quite different lenses, for quite different purposes. While sports journalists are preoccupied with reporting on the closed 'world of football' with a focus on performance, news journalists focus on the human-interest stories, celebrity gossip and scandals involving football stars. Chapter 9 analyzes the rise of celebrity footballers.

One early example of this occurred during the 1978 World Cup in Argentina, when Scotland was the only UK national team represented in the tournament. Expectations of success were very high prior to the tournament but things started to go wrong when news of drug-taking by Scotland forward Willie Johnston created a news-media storm around the Scotland camp (Murray, 2008). Football journalists who had spent a couple of weeks attached to the team maintained their focus on the hype surrounding Scotland's hopes in the tournament, whereas news journalists who had recently arrived in Argentina sought salacious stories from inside the Scotland camp. Front-page headlines in the British tabloids about the Johnston scandal undermined the public perception of the team, whose ignominy was compounded by poor results and an early exit from the tournament. The episode represents an early example of the contrasting news values of sports journalists and news journalists (the 'hounds' after blood). However, as the commercial value of footballers grew in the 1990s, so too did their non-sporting media profiles. The World Cup in Italy in 1990, which gained the media sobriquet 'Italia '90', was something of a watershed in the proliferation of media stories related to all things football. The media celebration of the English national team's advance to the semi-finals and Paul Gascoigne's tears on exit were symbolic of the changing social and cultural profile of the sport, which was more upbeat than in the late 1980s when it had suffered reputational damage, not least following the tragedies at Bradford, Heysel and Hillsborough. The editors of this volume use the term 'inflection point' to describe the change of direction that football took at this time. Low-brow football culture fused with high-brow art as the BBC's World Cup coverage used 'Nessun Dorma' from Puccini's opera *Turandot* as its theme tune, and features on football fashions and the crossover of football, youth cultures and popular music proliferated in the soft news stories of national newspapers (Redhead, 1991).

Public attention on football, especially on star players, has intensified in the 24-hour rolling news environment of contemporary media culture. Like all other celebrities in the media gaze, footballers have been targeted and subjected to intense scrutiny by news media. High-profile scoops on footballers, such as the exposé of Ryan Giggs' infidelity by the *News of the World* in 2011, reflect the intrusive and morally judgemental undertone of many celebrity media narratives, which are actually produced for the titillation of their readers. The Giggs story was initially suppressed through a 'super-injunction' that prevented the newspaper naming the high-profile footballer. However, the legal intervention proved powerless to prevent the speculation on social media as to the identity of the player, and in a move calculated to circumvent the super-injunction, which had been awarded in an English court, the Scottish newspaper the *Sunday Herald* named and shamed Giggs, suggesting that the court's jurisdiction did not apply to the Glasgow-based title (*Sunday Herald*, 2011). A similar attempt by Chelsea and England player John Terry, to suppress revelations about his affair with the girlfriend of fellow player Wayne Bridge, also revealed the problems associated with trying to manage news media through the courts when the internet and especially social media appear to operate outside such jurisdictions. Whether or not the law applies to the online world, once a star player's scandal goes viral, there is no turning back. In the case of both Giggs and Terry, public contrition enabled them to ride out the media storm and humiliation, albeit leaving in their wake private hurt and family destruction.

Football fans, by and large, appear to be indifferent to scandalous stories of players, unless the scandals have a direct impact on their professional abilities to perform. When former Sheffield United player Ched Evans was released from prison in October 2014 after serving half of his sentence following his conviction for rape, the furore regarding the prospect of his return to the sport inflamed a broader public debate on whether or not a convicted rapist should be allowed to continue a professional career in football which has a high public profile and significant monetary rewards (Gibson, 2015). Some fans championed the player's claim of innocence and turned to pernicious 'rape-blaming' commentaries on social media, naming the victim, who had to move house continually to avoid further attention. Nevertheless, a broader popular media stance refused to condone the actions of Evans and his friends, and challenged his right to return to professional football. In 2015, Sheffield United, Hartlepool, Oldham and Grimsby Town were all linked with signing the player but each retracted their initial offers following local public pressure from fans. There are clearly some offences that are never forgiven in the media and public life. (For more on Ched Evans and other football-related transgressions, see Chapter 11.)

Some players have been able to manufacture more positive exposure in tabloid news media, the most notable being David Beckham. As Ellis Cashmore has suggested, Beckham, assisted by a heavily professionalized squad of publicity and legal partners, has created a public persona that operates like a 'tabula rasa' (blank slate) onto which media audiences can inscribe their own meanings (Cashmore, 2014). Following other global mega-stars such as Madonna, Beckham the brand is heavily commercialized and ultimately flexible enough to fit the desires of anyone who is interested in him. The successful media and brand management of Beckham has therefore been viewed as model commodification of a player, which transcends his undoubted footballing talents and is reliant on strategic use of his wider celebrity status and legal control of his image rights (Haynes, 2007).

One final point of interest on footballers and the news media concerns the instances of players writing in national newspapers. Ghostwritten pieces on football by players and managers have a long tradition in British football, and in some cases, like former Tottenham Hotspur captain of the 1960s, Danny Blanchflower, these players and managers have retired from football and become fully-fledged journalists in their own right. Perhaps because the world of football is shrouded in a certain amount of mystique, the voices of players have been sought to provide an insight into what happens and why behind the scenes. What players say is not necessarily revelatory, but it can occasionally shed some light on what life as a professional footballer is actually like. Of course, the reporting of player stories is not so simple. Footballers are not trained to be journalists or even good communicators. The stories they have to tell might not always be of interest to a wider audience, and it is important to recognize that the sourcing and selecting of football stories is subject to broader processes that include the needs of media organizations to attract readers and sell advertising.

In the 1960s, as competition grew among the British newspapers, having your own 'voice of football' delivering an inside track was an important means of distinguishing your newspaper from rival publications. The ghostwritten column therefore became a new addition to the sports pages. Player and manager columns are usually written by a staff journalist and based on an interview or telephone conversation with the player or manager, who also takes the by-line. A significant issue with such columns has been the general inability of players to criticize their clubs, other players, managers and the game itself. In 2012, such constraints on disclosure from within the changing room were exploded through anonymity and a new column in the *Guardian* written by a player using the pseudonym 'the Secret Footballer'. It was an old newspaper device turned to ingenious effect, enabling an unknown Premier League footballer to explode some of the myths about the game, clubs and leading players, and claiming to 'lift the lid on the world of football'. While many may view such opinion pieces as 'yellow journalism', existing to sensationalize and lacking professional rigour, the Secret Footballer column is a rare attempt to produce an insider's view on the economics, politics and social agents in the contemporary game, including on the actions of owners, managers, coaches, players, agents and even the media itself. As we shall discuss below regarding the impact of social media on the football–media nexus, the Secret Footballer column is not alone in providing insider information from within the game. However, it is a rare instance of a footballer, shielded by anonymity, breaking ranks to provide a more honest and reflexive impression of football at a time of immense transformation in the commercial success of the sport.

## Football, public relations and self-mass communication

While the Secret Footballer column is a rare intervention by a player into the mainstream print media, footballers, and the industry as a whole, mainly manage their media relations and news output through publicists and communications professionals. Often turning to former sports journalists, football organizations require the strategic advice and communications skills of public relations professionals to manage their public affairs and ensure reputations are kept intact. Commercial partners of football also have reputations and brands to consider, and so there is a trinity of interests between football, sponsors and advertisers, and the media that require constant and vigilant management by a range of business professionals, including communications or public relations managers, who ensure that the various commercial stakeholders in the sport have their interests accounted for. The interconnections within this trinity of interests have become increasingly complex with the evolution of the internet, something that Brett Hutchins and David Rowe (2012, p. 5) have labelled 'networked media sport'. When we add the interests of the consumers of football, the fans, into the mix, the variegated nature of relations through networks such as social media make understanding the differentiated flows of communication even harder to grasp. As previously noted by Raymond Boyle and myself:

> The plenitude of content created by networked media sport is so expansive that it is increasingly difficult to fully comprehend the multitude of ways in which sport relates to new communications technologies. This is not only an issue for academic researchers of the sport-media-nexus, but also for the sports industries, the media industries and consumers of sport alike.
>
> *(Boyle and Haynes, 2014, p. 134)*

One of the best ways to understand how complex the management of communications in football can be is to consider the case study of Fifa's corruption scandal in 2015. In May 2015, the arrest of 14 Fifa executives or former executives on charges of financial corruption and kickbacks by the FBI created one of the largest global news stories of the year. News agencies around the world focused their attention on Fifa's headquarters in Zurich, Switzerland, and especially on the organization's embattled president, Sepp Blatter. The allegations of corruption, money laundering and racketeering were not new. Public mistrust of the governance and transparency of the world governing body of football had long been expressed in various forums, particularly regarding the award of the 2022 World Cup to Qatar. Investigations by the Insight reporters at the *Sunday Times* and journalist Andrew Jennings for the BBC's *Panorama* programme over the course of nearly a decade raised public awareness that bribery among Fifa's elite had potentially influenced the awarding of the World Cup to South Africa, Russia and Qatar. The subsequent FBI-led arrests precipitated a new phase of scrutiny and suspicion of Fifa and its senior officials, which included the organization's handling of the crisis. (This and other cases of corruption are dealt with in detail in Chapter 12.)

On the day of the arrests, Fifa's only response to the unfolding events came from its director of public affairs, Walter De Gregorio. Appointed in September 2011, De Gregorio, a former sports writer, was integral to Sepp Blatter's re-election campaign in 2010 and was spearheading his bid for the fifth term as Fifa president in 2015. According to Jennings, De Gregorio had for many years been managing Blatter's media affairs, ensuring that many sports journalists, including those in the UK, were fed information that led to the suppression of Fifa corruption stories, usually based on 'spin' that exonerated the Fifa president from any wrongdoing (Turvill, 2015). On the day of the arrests, De Gregorio gave a news conference for the world's media, making proclamations that welcomed the arrests as a positive development for Fifa.

However, there was no mention of Blatter's position on the matter, or how the organization would be responding to the scandal. His public relations performance was roundly criticized by communications experts from around the world on Twitter, including leading trade magazines such as *PR Week*, who thought his performance was 'arrogant' and 'deflective' (Bradley, 2015). The media coverage had raised concerns among some of Fifa's top-ranking commercial partners, including Visa and Coca-Cola, but there was little concession to the impact that this would have on the organization's governance, transparency or accountability. (*Editors' note:* Four of Fifa's sponsors – Coca-Cola, McDonald's, Visa and Anheuser-Busch InBev – threatened to end their association with football's governing body if it failed to commit to an independent reform process.)

The Fifa corruption scandal and investigations can and will be analyzed for many years to come as one of the most disturbing episodes ever to have arisen in global sport. In the context of the media, it will also be remembered as one of the worst news stories in the history of football, which was managed appallingly by both Fifa executives and their communications professionals. Beyond football, it served notice that what Hutchins and Rowe (2012) have identified as 'information accidents' in sport are now impossible to fully control in the era of what sociologist Manuel Castells (2009) has called 'self-mass communication', such as Twitter. Scandal in football, as in other domains of public life, can emerge rapidly from both inside and outside a club or governing body. Because most self-mass communication is now conducted on mobile devices such as smart-phones, text, images and video can be quickly uploaded to the internet with relative ease. What may once have been considered private spaces can, via social media, become public. What may once have been private conversations or thoughts are now often shared in social media communications that are easily copied, forwarded and reused by the mainstream media. Some football clubs introduced stringent guidelines or regulations to curb errant communications from players, managers and officials on social media, but many of these, such as a ban imposed by Manchester United on its players in 2010, were soon repealed as it became clear that social media can be an important marketing communications tool. For a football club, as for any major business, surveillance of social media is important for maintaining reputation. In October 2014, the Football Association (FA) issued its most high-profile punishment for the abuse of social media when it fined and banned Queens Park Rangers player Rio Ferdinand for three matches following his publication of a tweet that was deemed sexist for using the derogatory Caribbean slang word 'sket', meaning a promiscuous woman. Such micro-management of social media is highly problematic, not least because of who decides where the boundaries of taste and decency exist, especially if the communications are within the law and not causing serious offence or harm. (See Chapter 5 for more on social media and discriminatory sentiments as expressed by fans.)

The employment of social media managers in football organizations has therefore become a significant area of investment in their broader communications operations and some in football have taken a more 'empowered' approach to the use of social media. For example, in 2012, in an attempt to boost the profile of the women's professional game, the English Women's Super League introduced a digital ambassador programme to engage supporters and raise awareness of the different aspects of the women's game. Developments of this kind emphasize a deeper understanding of the changing dynamics of mobile media communications that have emerged in the second decade of networked media sport, so that 'selfies', 'photo-bombing' and irreverent YouTube memes such as the 'ice bucket challenge' videos are now part and parcel of the contemporary language of young footballers. The caveat to the use of these technologies of self-mass communication is the need to understand how such messages can be taken out of context, misappropriated or misconstrued. For example, when the women's national team returned to England from the World Cup in Canada in 2015, the FA's Twitter feed @England commented: 'Our #Lionesses go back to being mothers, partners and daughters today, but they have taken on another title – heroes' (BBC Sport, 2015a). While the sentiment may have been genuine, the tweet was soon trending, with complaints that the players were being stereotyped in traditional female roles, undermining their achievements.

Social media 'information accidents' and conversations are now a firm part of the football media landscape. One further dynamic to note in this regard is to consider how social media, especially Twitter, are now used by media professionals, including journalists and broadcasters, to shape the news agenda on football. Research by Boyle and Haynes (2014) revealed that sports journalists engage with social media for a variety of reasons. For one, Twitter is clearly now considered to be a bona fide news source by other journalists and players. It is also used as a barometer of fan opinion on particular issues, as we have seen with the Evans and Fifa examples. To call these interactions 'conversations' is perhaps stretching the imagination, but they are certainly new forms of engagement between those who are in the news, those who write the news and those who read the news. Indeed, in the context of social media themselves, these distinctions are increasingly meaningless. Finally, Twitter is a platform to promote and raise user profiles and stories. Twitter increasingly shapes contemporary news stories, yet the manner by which these stories gain mainstream attention or traction is often through more traditional media outlets, suggesting a co-existence between media forms rather than some sort of dominance by any one platform. We should expect football news to be characterized by a polymedia environment, in which multiple sources of information, with multiple and flexible modes of delivery, will prevail for the foreseeable future. However, one media form continues to dominate the economics of football: television.

## When the tail wags the dog: television and football

In their study on the political economy of television sports rights around the world, Tom Evens and colleagues (2013) highlight the ways in which 'synergetic relationships' have emerged between professional sports organizations and television conglomerates. From the 1980s onward, a process that they term the 'marketization of broadcasting', by which they mean the rise of commercial, subscription-based television services, has eroded the importance of free-to-air public service broadcasting, especially in the coverage of sport. Football, in particular, has been at the cutting edge of these developments, and since the early

1990s there has been a profound transformation in the ways in which football is televised, distributed and consumed.

These changes have largely been due to two processes:

1.  the technological developments in television delivery systems, with satellite and cable networks increasingly prevalent around the world;
2.  the deregulation of communications and broadcasting to increase competition in television markets.

One consequence of these developments has been the increased competition for television rights in response to the evolution of niche multi-channel pay television such as Sky (formerly BSkyB). The rise of the Premier League in England has been the focus of a number of critical sociological and media studies, which have identified the social, economic and cultural dynamics of late modernity (King, 2002; Sandvoss, 2003; Boyle and Haynes, 2004; Millward, 2011). Football in its new configuration is characterized by increased consumerism, rationalization and globalization. All of these transformative processes have made football beholden to the commercial drivers of neo-liberal market economics and individualism – just witness the enormous salaries now enjoyed by the elite players in the major European leagues – at the same time as disenfranchising many supporters (i.e. disconnecting them from the traditions and social bonds that they have with a club), who have made their fandom the site of vigorous cultural politics and activism (for example, the anti-Glazer campaign by Manchester United fans in the early 2000s).

The two decades of the Premier League have been bankrolled by investment from television (Evens *et al.*, 2013). This has been further supplemented by sponsorship and commercial streams of income, and in some instances capital investment by wealthy, multi-millionaire owners (Millward, 2013). The consequences of investment in the English professional game have been quite profound and require brief summary. The Premier League was formed in 1992 after a period of social, economic and political crises in the sport, motivating the FA to prompt the then leading clubs in the old First Division to break away from the former governing structures of the Football League to form a far more selective, commercially aspirational competition that would place more power in the hands of the clubs and their chairmen. A crucial dynamic of the new league was a more expansive contract with television, specifically Sky, which handed over more control and commercial incentives to the satellite company.

One example of this control was the power of television companies to change the scheduling of matches to suit their needs. Successive rights deals have ratcheted up the value of television income to the top flight of domestic football, at times prompted by new competitors to Sky's dominance (which have included NTL, ITV Digital, Setanta, ESPN and BT) and an expansionist strategy to sell the Premier League brand and its TV rights on a global scale. Renewed deals for televised coverage of the three seasons from 2013–2014 to 2015–2016 were estimated to be worth a total of £5.5 billion when overseas rights were included.

Domestic rights alone for this period were worth £3 billion and in February 2015 the UK rights to the Premier League were sold to Sky and BT Sport again for £5.14 billion in a three-year contract from the 2016–2017 season (BBC Sport, 2015b). While the figure appears staggering, it is not out of line with other major sports contracts; for example, America's National Basketball Association (NBA) has a $24 billion (£15.28 billion) contract over nine years with Turner Broadcasting and Disney's ESPN, a company that also holds a $15 billion (£9.55 billion) contract with the National Football Association (NFL) to screen Monday Night Football.

The enormous influx of money into the sport has changed the value of being in England's elite league and transformed its financial and operational structures. These structural changes reflect broader processes in the globalization of international business, which sociologists such as Roland Robertson (2000) had begun to identify and analyze in the late twentieth century. The marriage of television and professional football interests has therefore seen increasing transnational flows of capital through international investment in football, the international migration of specialized labour in the form of players, coaches and managers, and increasing socio-cultural homogenization created by transnational media and communications; this has made the Premier League and its clubs a global brand, thereby intensifying a global consciousness of its existence. The heightened competition to maintain a position in the Premier League has increased the investment and financial risk that many clubs are prepared to engage in. Attracting increasing numbers of international players to England has been the hallmark of this process, transforming the profile of English football squads, which are increasingly bereft of domestic talent. The globalization of players was accompanied by similar transitions in the rising numbers of international owners, most notably Russian billionaire Roman Abramovich, as well as increasing numbers of international managers, coaches and ancillary staff operating in England.

As the television-led commercialization of English domestic football ensued through the 1990s and into the new century, the nature and form of ownership also underwent a significant shift. Many clubs sought investment through flotation as public limited companies, which in turn encouraged investment from media corporations, including satellite broadcaster Sky, cable and telecommunications company NTL and commercial television company Granada (now merged as part of ITV) (Boyle and Haynes, 2004). This period in the mid-1990s famously led to global media conglomerate News Corporation attempting to buy Manchester United, a transaction that was vehemently opposed by a section of supporters and was ultimately blocked by the then Conservative government on public interest grounds (Brown and Walsh, 1999). This temporary block on global interests owning a stake in English club football did not last long. From 2003, with the sale of Chelsea to Abramovich, the Premier League witnessed a flood of investment from wealthy private interests, which saw the shares of publicly floated clubs returned to private ownership. At the start of the 2015–2016 season, 11 of the 20 Premier League clubs had majority international owners.

Although the motivations of the international owners of Premier League clubs may vary, as too may the reactions of supporters to such investment, there is a unified objective to increase the capital gains from such investment, through increased season ticket sales, increased television and commercial revenue and the general enhancement of the club brand through association with the Premier League. Pre-season tours of South East Asia, the Middle East and elsewhere are testament to the global aspirations of clubs and their owners, the naturalized progression of which has led to the notion of the 39th game, whereby a final set of Premier League matches might be played outside England in one of the key markets for the brand, such as China, India or the Middle East (Rumsby, 2014). If such a scenario ever came to fruition, fans in the UK would no doubt be able to watch such games live on pay TV.

## Sky and the Premier League

Having initially beaten off competition from commercial terrestrial television channels when the Premier League began in 1992, Sky has enjoyed a hegemonic – that is, culturally dominant – position in televising the competition and, in part due to its sports coverage, has become the most successful commercial television company in Europe. Its majority shareholder is Rupert Murdoch's 21st Century Fox (previously part of News Corporation, which now focuses only on the publishing business), which holds 39 per cent of the shares in Sky. Sky has operations in the UK, Ireland, Italy, Germany and Austria and has over 20 million household subscribers. Attempts to compete with Sky Sports by cable television companies – the ill-fated digital terrestrial platform ITV Digital (originally branded OnDigital), the Irish-owned sports channel Setanta and finally the dominant American television sports franchise ESPN – were all seen off by Sky thanks to a succession of clever marketing and pricing policies that showed strategic awareness of the importance of the Premier League rights to the success of the company. Other sports, especially Test cricket and championship boxing, and first-run Hollywood movies have also helped Sky to maintain dominance in the UK domestic market, but football has been the key driver of premium profits for the company, which has managed to absorb each cycle of inflation in the cost of the rights to the Premier League.

Sky's ability to grow its number of subscribers and its profits has been due to its ability to transform the availability of packages to meet the needs of contemporary viewers, who now prefer to time-shift their viewing by recording programmes on digital television recorders or downloading programmes on demand. Although these new technologies and modes of access have transformed the viewing habits of many people, live televised sport, including football, is one of the key media forms that continues to bring people together to share a live viewing experience. Live sport is also available on multiple devices by use of applications (apps) on mobiles, laptops, tablets and gaming devices, and also to non-subscribers on a pay-per-view basis via its internet television service Now TV.

The broadening of Sky's customer base has enabled the company to maintain its strategic financial objective to increase what is called the Average Revenue Per User (ARPU), which in the first quarter of 2015 was £47 per month (Jackson, 2015). While this financial information may at first sight only be of interest to shareholders, it does provide an important clue to understanding why the rights to Premier League and Champions League football have been so cherished by Sky, a model copied across most subscription-based television services in Europe. Sky Sports packages have on average cost £20 per month over a decade or more, and live Premier League and Champions League football formed the key enticement for drawing in new customers. It has been a strategic approach that has served the company well for over two decades. However, the use of television football rights in pursuit of consumers for pay TV, broadband and telephony, known as the 'triple play' of televised football, entered a new phase of heightened competition in 2015 with the increase in the scale and scope of BT Sport in the British and European sports rights markets.

In November 2013, BT paid £897 million for the UK rights to televise the Champions League exclusively from the 2015–2016 season. The amount was double that previously paid jointly by Sky and ITV. The hyperinflation of the cost of rights is symbolic of how important media corporations and telecommunications companies now consider football to be in their competition to attract new households to their services. When this is combined with the shared television rights to the Premier League from 2016–2017, noted above, it is evident that BT Sport has taken a sizeable bite into Sky's hegemonic position in the coverage of live televised football in the UK. Why did BT, traditionally a telecommunications company, move into televising football? The answer, again, reveals much about the contemporary environment of converged communications and technology that now dominates many of our lives in the developed world. As our cultural experience of television, the internet and telephony have merged – experienced on mobile devices or on adaptable screens – so too have the corporations who dominate these sectors sought to commodify these services in combination with each other. Once Sky started to bundle telephone and broadband services with its television subscriptions, it was perhaps inevitable that BT, the UK's major supplier of telecommunications, would move into the television market to compete with its new rival for the broadband market.

BT's investment in BT Sport television services and the rights to premium televised football must, therefore, be viewed as an attempt to attract broadband customers, especially for its superfast fibre-optic service, and not to develop a rival platform to Sky television per se. Providing free access to BT Sport to its broadband customers was confirmation that BT saw the battleground with Sky as being the broadband market and was not aiming to grow profit directly from television services. The case suggests how what was once a sport has been changed into a portal to any number of products and services; Chapter 10 focuses on why consumption has become so central to a sophisticated understanding of modern football.

One final threat to the stability of the television football market is worth noting. The rise of broadband internet capacity has enabled the illegal streaming of television channels on the web to grow exponentially. The demand for watching football remains greater than many people's ability or willingness to pay for access to subscription-based televised sports services. The streaming of Premier League matches online infringes the copyright of broadcasters, and television companies invest significant resources in tracing and closing down such content. The problem for the Premier League is that rights to live games have been sold so widely around the world that the piracy of coverage is incredibly difficult, indeed almost impossible, to police. Football fans around the world, always resourceful and increasingly technologically literate, continue to find ways to evade detection by the specialist organizations now contracted by rights holders to close such services down.

Sky and the Premier League have also faced legal challenges to closing down access to live English football via the importation of television decoders from other territories inside the European Union. Sky charges a higher premium to commercial premises, such as pubs, for which subscriptions can cost up to £12,000 a year. When screening Premier League matches in such premises, the legitimate Sky service shows a small pint glass symbol in the corner of the screen. Sky's practice of charging differential rates to households and commercial premises has led to many pubs withdrawing from screening live football due to the cost or, in some cases, looking to alternative suppliers such as the Greek television service Nova, which charges considerably less for access to its football channel, which also carries the Premier League. This practice has led to a number of court cases against publicans, and one Portsmouth landlady, Karen Murphy, took her case with Sky and the Premier League on appeal to the European Court of Justice, claiming that the restraints on the importation of foreign decoders was contrary to the freedom of services in the European Economic Area. In February 2012, Murphy won her appeal to subscribe to Nova as the ECJ ruled that it was not an offence to subscribe to a non-UK EU satellite broadcaster and to use a foreign decoder card to receive broadcasts from that broadcaster (BBC News, 2012). However, the ECJ also recognized that although there is no copyright in the matches themselves, there is copyright in the 'branding' around the football: the Premier League graphics, music and highlights used in Sky's coverage. Any transmission of Premier League coverage that shows its logo therefore requires permission to do so in that territory. The result has been viewed as victory on both sides, and the consequences of the Murphy case will continue to reverberate through television football rights deals in Europe for the foreseeable future.

## Editors' conclusion

In October 2015, FC United of Manchester – a club formed in 2005 by Manchester United supporters opposed to the American businessman Malcolm Glazer's takeover, and owned and democratically run by its supporters – issued the most defiant challenge yet to the media's domination of football. The club refused to change its kick-off time for an FA Cup first-round tie against Chesterfield to accommodate television coverage. Since its inception, the club had campaigned on a number of issues affecting the sport and its fans, particularly kick-off times, which, it maintains, should be fixed to accommodate fans rather than the media. The FA responded by insisting that the club shift the kick-off to Monday evening. As the *Daily Mail*'s Mike Keegan reported, some fans announced their intention to protest by spending the first 45 minutes behind a stand listening to radio commentary 'attempting to embarrass the broadcaster' (Keegan, 2015). The club had earlier succeeded in resisting an attempt by the BBC to change a kick-off time to suit an app streaming arrangement, but it was powerless to resist the FA. It was a minor case, but one with major resonance: English football's governing organization effectively prioritized broadcasters' interests over those of fans.

As this chapter has revealed, the media in general, and television in particular, has grown to its present position of power and influence with the consent of governing organizations, both national and international. Since the 1960s, the mutual benefits are obvious: broadcasters have attracted viewing audiences and the revenues that these typically draw (from advertising and subscription – Sky's 2015 operating profit was £1.35 billion). Football's transition to a global culture industry wouldn't have been possible without the kind of coverage afforded it by television. Without the international exposure provided by television, commercial sponsors (or 'partners', as they are often called) would have been less motivated to align themselves with a sport that looked in the late 1980s to be doomed, as we saw in Chapter 2. In this sense, the media has been football's saviour. But it may also have become its master.

## Research in Action

**'"Truly a fan experience"? The cultural politics of the live site' by David Rowe and Stephanie Alice Baker (2012)**

### What were the goals of the research?

The primary focus of this research was the changing nature of mediated football fandom in the twenty-first century, especially at organized 'live sites' called Fan Fests created around the world by Fifa during its premier championship, the World Cup. Through participant observation of fan behaviour at one of the live sites in Sydney, Australia during the televising of the 2010 World Cup in South Africa, the researchers were able to test the organizers' claim that mass public viewing of football would produce a 'truly fan experience' that would replicate the experience of supporters actually inside the stadium. The study enabled the researchers to explore themes of globalization at local and global levels, and assess the extent to which localized national fan identities have been destabilized and transformed by the socio-cultural impact of the World Cup as a transnational mediated phenomenon.

## Why was the research relevant?

Rowe and Baker's research was a rare attempt to understand the socio-cultural complexities of mediated ways of 'being there' at a football event, beyond watching a game at home. The collective viewing of football is an increasingly common phenomenon, which has different ontological dimensions to home viewing because of the dynamics of the crowd. Their research therefore moved beyond a traditional sender–content–receiver model of mass communications to explore the dynamism of these emergent mediated forms of football fandom and suggest that both football organizations and news journalism should understand such phenomena in more complex ways, beyond traditional models of rival sets of supporters traditionally associated with football fandom in the stadium. The research had broader significance for understanding the cultural politics of fan identities and embodiment in mediated contexts. In other words, it posed the question whether it is any longer possible to distinguish the experiences of 'being there' and 'viewing from a distance'. Do we, in fact, need a more nuanced, synthesized understanding of both experiences? The research shed light on how live sites have the potential to mediate local, national and international audiences, compressing time and space and binding together diverse spectator cohorts around the world.

## What methods were used?

The research was based on the observations of four researchers on a selected sample of night-time live site events in Sydney, Australia, over the 31-day duration of the 2010 World Cup. The researchers visited the Fan Fest site at times when live World Cup matches were being televised on large screens, as well as moments when they were not. The observation team also focused on some distinct event, team and fan configurations that reflected different identities associated with the location of the World Cup (hosted in South Africa); the location of the mediated live event (hosted in Australia); the games of interest to large national migrant groups in Sydney (such as those from England, Italy and Greece); games of interest to smaller minority groups in Australia (including those from Uruguay and Ghana); and mediated contests that were of either high or low significance, which was contingent on the nations involved and their history and status in the World Cup (for example, matches involving Brazil would be deemed high-status contests, whereas games involving first-time World Cup finalists would be considered of minority interest). The research devised an instruction guide to address crowd positioning, interactions and flows, the structures and techniques of crowd-control and the modes of co-present and distant communication. Observers noted and recorded a range of actions by fans, and used public-space photography to capture the configuration of large groups of people at the live sites.

### What were the main arguments?

The researchers drew on some important sociological ideas on the role of reflexivity in modern social life proposed by Ulrich Beck, Anthony Giddens and Scott Lash. Referring back to oneself in a highly mediated world has, the authors argued, intensified this self-reflexive process. One might simply think of the 'selfie' as a prime example of how new media technologies are transforming the spatial configuration of public life. The media is key to the collapsing of distinctions between local events and the global public sphere, as mediating mega-events transports viewers beyond their immediate locale. The researchers therefore argued that being at a live site creates through mediation a 'double-embodied sport experience' in the sense that fans are 'being there from a distance'. Broadcasts of the World Cup make it possible for those at the live site to view the matches taking place without contributing to them, but social media, like Twitter or Instagram, do enable commentary and communication on the event to be shared from outside the stadium to be picked up by those inside, and similarly experiences of those inside the stadium to be shared with those outside. There are multiple dynamics to these modern mediated processes, some of which are orchestrated by the official organizers of the live sites and the media, which Rowe and Baker argued inform and encourage fans to be self-conscious and reflexive in their performances, which are then relayed to others as exaggerated displays of fandom.

Rowe and Baker examined the similarities and differences between being there and viewing from a distance but reiterated the need to avoid simple dichotomies between the mediated and embodied experiences of fans. For instance, the authors described how the construction and management of live sites replicated some of the viewing experiences of being inside the stadium, with 'scarcity of view' and highly commercialized operations for food, drink and merchandizing. There were, however, noticeable differences in fan experience, in that those at the live site had in general a static view of a large screen, whereas fans in the stadium had a more dynamic embodied experience and engagement with other supporters and the players. Nevertheless, the researchers were struck by the emotional dimension of public viewing, which became a major factor in constructing the embodied fan experience at the live sites. Therefore, they argued that distinguishing between 'real' and mediated emotions at live sites is erroneous and misrepresentative of collective fan viewing.

### And the conclusions or key findings?

The significant finding of the research was that mediation, the process performed by the mass media in communicating events, is integral to contemporary football fandom. For Rowe and Baker, the interrelationship between mediation and embodiment of an event like the World Cup creates multiple ways of 'seeing and being seen', of 'acting and being acted upon' and of 'performing and watching the performances of others'. The researchers were particularly struck by what they observed as the 'reflexive mediation' of fans both at the live site and at the event itself, which revealed a self-conscious awareness by fans that they were being 'imaged' around the globe. Fans, in the context of highly mediated global sports mega-events like the World Cup, are very aware of the media's dependency on their performance to create part of the mediated event itself. This led the researchers to conclude that the sport–media–globalization nexus has broadened its scope of interest in the event to include fans, which in turn has led to more focused media practices to capture this dynamic of sports mega-events. The researchers therefore managed to problematize the standard ways in which research on sports audiences, itself very limited, seeks to capture and explain the experiences of those involved in the mediatized contexts of sport, such as World Cup live sites. While the media coverage of football fan sites tended to replicate the standard fan posturing of rival fan groups, the researchers actually discovered more complex forms of fan sociality which were contingent on a number of forces, including crowd assembly, mediation, globalization, commercialization, governmentalization and embodiment. ('Governmentalize' means to bring under governmental or national control.)

### What were the strengths of the research?

The strength of the research was that it provided some empirical evidence to challenge normative conceptual ideas of the significant differences between the experiences of spectators at football matches and those of collective fan viewing at organized live sites. The research provided preliminary insights for further work on the cultural politics of football fandom and notions of cultural citizenship that centre on the televising of major sporting events such as the World Cup.

### Were there any weaknesses?

As Rowe and Baker pointed out, their research was a preliminary and limited study of fan experiences at live sites. The research was based purely on participant observation and did not include any interviews with participants. As the authors revealed in a methodological footnote, this was mainly due to the last-minute planning of the research, which meant that ethical clearance could not be given. Future research on the collective viewing of football could take a more in-depth approach to gathering empirical data from fans, which could be triangulated with official sources of data, observations and any quantitative methods, such as surveys, that could be carried out.

# 9

# CELEBRITY

*Ellis Cashmore*

---

## Chapter highlights

- David Beckham symbolized the new era of celebrity footballers.
- Some theories of the origins of celebrity culture start in the Bronze Age, others in the 1960s.
- Advertisers, especially Nike, use footballers to endorse products in the same way in which they use singers and actors.
- While celebrity footballers are often called role models, their influence is restricted to shopping habits.
- Celebrity footballers inspire emotions like love and hate because we feel we know them – intimately.

---

## Introduction

The fans loved him, the advertisers loved him, the media loved him – or, at least, they loved his newsworthiness. He was the perfect role model: a gifted footballer with Greek god looks, no known habits that involved toxic substances and a wholesome commitment to family life. Then, on 11 April 2004, a British tabloid ran a story that alleged that he'd been involved in an affair with a woman who was not his wife. In an instant, David Beckham, the distillation of respectability, became a villain, an opportunistic philanderer who'd taken advantage of his secondment in Spain (he was playing for Real Madrid) to jump into bed with an available woman. The media pronounced the end of Beckham; his decade of idolatry was at an end. No longer the untouchable, godlike being, 'Goldenballs' could be tempted just like any other man.

But the doomsayers who had predicted the ruination of Beckham's reputation and the end of his brand were wide of the mark. Ten years later, Beckham brought his two-decade playing career to an end and, in his first full year of retirement, posted the highest earnings of his career with £48.02 million ($75 million) in 2014 (his previous high was £32.65 million, i.e. $51 million, in 2012). He ranked second behind Michael Jordan in *Forbes*' assessment of the highest-paid retired athletes. Beckham's franchise included deals with Breitling, Sky Sports, Belstaff and adidas. A deal with Jaguar in China continued a trend of expanding his influence in the world's most populous country. The affair that many thought would bring disaster to Brand Beckham wasn't even a bump in the road; in fact, it probably enhanced it, adding a dash of devilry to the otherworldly image of a man who was beginning to look a bit of a goody two-shoes. All that was wrong with Beckham was that he was just too perfect – too perfect, that is, to be a celebrity. By the mid-noughties, fans didn't want their idols to have moral superiority; they wanted them to have the same faults and foibles as everyone else. Beckham remained a stylish, likeable and unthreatening expression of twenty-first-century celebrity culture.

The 2004 scandal wouldn't qualify as a milestone, though it reminds us how quickly culture changes. Seemingly damaged by a peccadillo, a relatively minor sin – what people would later call a 'transgression' – his halo slipped, only to be replaced with a designer crown. Contrary to accepted wisdom, a well-timed scandal, far from destroying a celebrity, can actually burnish them. The year after Beckham's scandal, a British tabloid featured pictures of über-model Kate Moss doing cocaine; the style icon lost contracts from Burberry, Chanel and H&M reportedly totalling close to $4 million (as Vicky Ward reported in 2005). However, in 2014, Moss was estimated to be worth $88 million, according to Ali Gray of *Marie Claire* (2014). Moss also had a bulging portfolio of endorsement contracts with Rimmel, St Tropez self-tan and David Yurman, the luxury jeweller. And, in case you're wondering why I compare a footballer with a supermodel, the celebrity paradigm doesn't discriminate on the basis of what celebrities actually do; it's what fans think they do that matters. I'll elaborate shortly. (A paradigm is a model or worldview that underlies the way in which we understand life.)

Celebrity culture, as we know it, didn't just pop out of a vacuum in the early 2000s, and its impact on football wasn't confined to Beckham's elevation to the A-list. But there is a sense in which his arrival, not just as a football player but as an all-round celebrity, symbolized a dramatic change in a sport that had previously been…well, a sport. It became entertainment. So, when Mark Turner (2014) analyzed what he called 'the cultural and commercial reinvention of English football since the late 1980s' and focused on 'the close relationship between the "new" football post 1992 and celebrity culture', it's surprising that he managed *not* to mention the man who not only epitomized both of these developments but also helped to catalyze them. Beckham exemplified the transformation of association football from a sport, with roots in nineteenth-century England, to a global entertainment industry with commercial operations practically everywhere. (In fact, Beckham himself practically became an industry; *Forbes*' Kurt Badenhausen reported turnover of $75 million in 2015.)

Historically, there had been players who transcended football, the most obvious being Pelé, who, in the 1960s and 1970s rivalled Muhammad Ali as the best-known sporting figure in the world. Diego Maradona, too, became an international personality. British players George Best, Kevin Keegan and Paul Gascoigne were well-known characters whose fame extended beyond football. Yet only Gascoigne collided with a culture obsessed with celebrity, fame and the commercial opportunities offered by these. The media loved him arguably more than they later loved Beckham; unlike Beckham, though, Gascoigne was like a lone swimmer trying to stay afloat in a whirlpool. While he didn't realize it, Gascoigne possessed gifts that he never asked for, the main one being his football skill, but another being the attention of the media on an unprecedented scale in the 1980s. By the time Beckham surfaced – he started dating Posh Spice, as Victoria Adams was then called, in 1997 – the commercial reinvention was in full swing and players were equipped with a support staff, including agents, managers, bodyguards and ancillary workers, to prevent the kind of interface that Gascoigne experienced.

It's a tribute to the wider complexity of contemporary football that we can look back less than three decades and find a world almost unrecognizable from the glamorous, inclusive, classless, showbusiness-like football culture of today, in which celebrities populate a landscape once dominated by honour-seeking men with solid working-class credentials and resplendent masculine pride. How did football become part of celebrity culture?

Few people seriously doubt that the cultural shift that has introduced what we recognize as the celebrity has affected practically every aspect of modern life, from politics to religion, education to the arts. But what exactly is it? Plainly defined, 'celebrity' is the status of being known, praised, exalted or attributed with importance. The provenance of the word is revealing; from the French '*célébrité*', which derives from the Latin '*celebritas*' meaning 'honoured' or 'renowned', the term has strayed into the English language dissociated from references to accomplishments or great deeds. In other words, while we tend to think that fame is a by-product ('so-and-so is well known for their acting, singing, etc.'), fame is actually just *fame* – the state of being well known by many people.

Celebrities don't typically ply their labour so much as their *presence*, usually in the form of a moving visual image that appears on television or computer screens or a stationary representation in a print advertisement. Either way, the effect is to implicate those looking at or reading about the celebrity in an act of consumption. As Egon Franck and Stephan Nüesch have pointed out, 'the well-knowness [sic] of celebrities has become a viable commodity all by itself'; it has become saleable 'independent of accomplishment, heroics, or talent' (2007, p. 225). Celebrities are, by definition, renowned, though not necessarily for anything they have done or said.

'Wait!' traditionalists will shout. 'Footballers are not like Amy Childs or the Kardashians, who are just known for their visibility in the media – their well-knownness; they're known for their gifts and achievements.' To an extent, this *is* right: football figures have typically risen to prominence through their accomplishments. But celebrity culture is inclusive and rewards anything that fans find gratifying, whether a series of electrifying performances on the field of play, a lifestyle of excess or even an amusing Twitter account. In celebrity culture, talent is very much in the mind of the consumer.

## Celebrity culture's Big Bang Theory

Some scholars argue that there is nothing new in celebrity culture and that there have been famous people throughout history. Leo Braudy has studied what he calls *The Frenzy of Renown* (1997), the word 'frenzy' suggesting the wild excitement that populations have generated about some key figures in history. Tom Payne (2009) plots the evolution of fame from the Bronze Age (i.e. the late fourth and early third millennia BC). Other writers, like Pete Ward (2010), believe that celebrity culture lies at the intersection of the sacred and the profane, the spiritual and the carnal; in other words, it is a kind of substitute religion, with today's celebrities the equivalent of gods. Still others consider celebrities as effectively being well-paid puppets who have their strings pulled by what Graeme Turner calls 'large internationalized media conglomerates' (2004, p. 84). In the view of P. David Marshall (2014), buying commodities associated with celebrities provides a sense of individualism and personality. There is a range of theories about the origins and purposes of celebrity culture, and a number of common themes – the media, consumption and commodification being three of the recurring ones. ('Commodification' means turning people and ideas, as well as goods and services, into buyable commodities.) The media has transformed football from a sport into a market in which everything is available for purchase. Celebrity players don't just play football; they also advertise whatever the market has to offer.

Celebrity culture's equivalent of the Big Bang Theory came in 1962, when a fireball of radiation exploded. Actually, it wasn't a fireball but a scandal involving the actors Elizabeth Taylor, then the world's most glamorous, extravagant, conspicuous consumer, and Richard Burton, a handsome, womanizing, hard-drinking thespian. They were in Rome filming *Cleopatra*. Both Taylor and Burton were married to other people, both had children and they were, remember, in a Roman Catholic country, in the same city as the Vatican in fact. Furthermore, it was the early 1960s, when what we now call cheating was known as adultery (as in 'Thou shalt not commit ...').

At the time, the word 'paparazzi' sounded to most non-Italians like a pasta dish or a make of scooter. In Italy, a legion of freelance photojournalists, armed with the then new zoom lens cameras and a willingness to annoy and upset the previously untouchable stars, were adept at capturing stories that their subjects preferred to remain untold. Gossip, rumour, hearsay and miscellaneous tittle-tattle were raw material for the paps.

Today, the idea of a private life is an anachronism – something that belongs to another period of time. In an age when social media combined with an inquisitive and often predatory mainstream media have made it practically impossible for anyone, especially those in the public eye, to conceal aspects of their life, privacy seems a thing of the past. Taylor has the ambiguous distinction of being the person who started the dismantling of privacy. Her life was turned inside out by the increasingly curious media, which became ever more conjectural in the 1970s (by which I mean that it became less reliant on facts and more prepared to speculate on events). 'Never before had celebrity scandal pushed so far into global consciousness', reflects David Kamp (1998).

It was no more than coincidence that in the year that the Taylor–Burton fireball exploded, the first of the active communications satellites (i.e. one capable of both receiving and retransmitting signals) was launched by the US. Known as Telstar, it was used for television broadcasting and telephone communication. (The prefix '*tele*' means 'at distance'.) Over the next several decades, thousands of similar satellites were shot into space, making it possible to relay messages around the world instantly (at the last count, there were 1,100 active satellites and about 2,600 that have come to the end of their service life and are just floating around in space). The 1962 World Cup was played in Chile in June, a month before Telstar went into orbit; as a result, viewers outside South America had to wait four days or more before they could watch the games on television. The 1966 World Cup was beamed via satellite and was the first tournament to be shown live in several countries. The Summer Olympics had been internationally broadcast live two years before. By the early 1980s, the proliferation of TV channels had created a new problem for broadcasters: how to fill them. Some channels specialized in 24-hour news, others offered music videos, while still others opted for old movies. Sport was another choice, and ESPN was the first all-sport channel.

The media didn't create celebrity culture, though it satisfied what philosophers call a *necessary condition*. For example, without water and oxygen, there would be no human life; hence, these things are necessary conditions for the existence of human beings. However, the media didn't constitute a *sufficient condition* (e.g. pouring rain is a sufficient condition to make the streets wet, but not a necessary condition – someone could have turned on fire hoses). So celebrities, at least in the way in which we understand them now, were not created by the media, but they couldn't exist without the media. What's missing is *voyeurism*. The word usually has sexual connotations; it generally describes the act of watching others and deriving sexual gratification from this. I'm broadening its scope to include taking any form of satisfaction not just from watching others but also from following their exploits, habits, company and practically any other part of their lives via the media. In the 1980s, Madonna exploited the expansion of media opportunities, inciting journalists with one scandal after another, so that she became almost impossible to ignore. Journalists were constantly on-guard. Madonna, more than any other public figure of the time, served as an exemplar – that is, a typical example of the new celebrity: prepared to disclose details, however intimate, about her life; willing to provoke controversy, no matter how outrageous; and eager to engage with her fans through any medium available, including music, film, books and, of course, TV. (The global computer network we now know as the internet didn't become popular for personal (rather than professional) use until the early 1990s.)

After Madonna, any aspiring singer or actor knew that they would have to surrender what used to be called a private life to their public. We – the public, audience, fans, consumers – became guiltless peeping Toms, and the media responded to our appetite for scandal, gossip and rumour. Stars in the old sense of the word were consigned to history. Fans didn't want their celebrities to be inaccessible godlike creatures; they wanted them to be just like them – human. Princess Diana was the distillation of this new kind of celebrity; a royal with a human touch, she entranced populations and inadvertently incited paparazzi to guerrilla tactics in their efforts to capture her image.

## Sport, sex and pop music

Hollywood actors had been the go-to figures for advertising endorsements since the 1930s. Pop stars, too, found ads a lucrative supplement to their earnings, especially after the rise of the video in the 1980s. Ad agencies not only featured pop artists in their campaigns, but also used their music in the advertisements. The problem, at least for advertisers, was that showbusiness entertainers were becoming unreliable. After Taylor's scandal, an ever more intrusive media had broken through the protective wall of the studio system. Rather than waiting for news to break, writers and paps went looking for stories, especially of stars' indiscretions. Well-publicized arrests, such as those of actors Rob Lowe in 1988, Christian Slater in 1989 and Paul Reubens (aka Pee-Wee Herman) in 1991, shook the confidence of advertisers. At first, pop stars looked a heaven-sent alternative. But Madonna's deliberate attempts to conjure scandals made her an unstable proposition, and even the biggest-selling artist in the world, Michael Jackson, was beginning to reveal idiosyncrasies in the late 1980s. Both artists had turbulent deals with Pepsi; Madonna was released from hers after a controversial video in 1989, while earlier, in 1984, Jackson's hair had caught fire while filming a Pepsi commercial and he was rushed to hospital.

Just when advertisers were wondering where they would find dependable, substantial and well-grounded endorsers with authenticity, a 6′ 6″ basketball player jumped into the picture. Prior to the 1980s, athletes were too pasteurized to be effective endorsers: safe but colourless. Every so often, a Muhammad Ali or a George Best would burst through, but athletes were generally a poor second to film or rock stars, who radiated glamour and in this respect were ideal for recommending products. In the US, Nike took a gamble in 1984, signing a promising but not yet proven Chicago Bulls player to a five-year contract worth $2.5 million. It maybe doesn't sound like a lot of money compared with Kevin Durant's £185 million ($285 million) deal with Under Armour or even Beckham's £103 million ($160 million) deal with adidas, but in the 1980s it was staggeringly risky. Nike's share of the market grew in direct proportion to Michael Jordan's presence in advertising campaigns, alerting advertisers to the benefits of featuring athletes as what Americans call 'shillers' (people who pretend to give impartial endorsements of things in which they have a vested interest; Jordan still earns about $100 million a year from endorsements). Even sceptics who thought that Jordan's influence would be restricted to sport-related products such as Nike's were won over by the next development: Jordan also appeared in ads for breakfast cereal, underwear, sunglasses, cologne and other products unrelated to sport. He somehow gave even the most mundane products a majestic sheen.

When you think about it, what do celebrities do most effectively? They make us buy stuff. Well, not exactly *make* – but they influence our purchasing decisions. Admission tickets, downloads, TV subscriptions, biographies and video games all have to be paid for. But celebrities affect our choice of shampoo, watch, car, mortgage, food and practically anything else that can be bought and sold. Even reality TV stars, many of whom stay on the public radar for only a few months, usually snag a few endorsement deals before they slide towards oblivion.

The inclusion of sportsmen and, later, sportswomen – Maria Sharapova moved to the US in 1994 and soon became the most prolific female endorser – in advertising and marketing was crucial to the absorption of football into celebrity culture. At the time of Jordan's ascent, football had no equivalents. Roberto Baggio, known by his Italian compatriots as '*Il Divin Codino*' ('The Divine Ponytail') was close, though England's Paul Gascoigne was a paparazzo's dream, especially after he moved to Italy in 1992. In the same year, Eric Cantona became a Manchester United player and later signed for Nike. But it wasn't until 1996, when Nike signed a $100 million contract with the Brazilian Football Confederation (CBF), that it found a footballer with comparable charisma to Jordan: Ronaldo (Luís Nazário de Lima). By the late 1990s, Nike was close to catching lightning in a bottle; it had worked out a method of turning ordinary mortals with above-average proficiency in sport into fully accessorized celebrities. Baggio and Gascoigne were antediluvian celebrities in the sense that they cultivated their own aura independently of global corporations. Cantona was a forerunner, his mercurial temperament making him one of the sport's most watchable characters in the early 1990s. When, in 1995, he leapt into the crowd and attacked an abusive fan, Nike was in a strong position to benefit from Cantona's notoriety. 'An advertisement featuring the footballer, cataloguing his misdemeanours … was played on TV news and documentaries to the point of exhaustion', wrote journalist Jim White (1995).

In his book on Nike, Donald Katz reflects that in the early 1990s, 'Sports had arguably surpassed popular music as the captivating medium most essential to being perceived as "young and alive"' (1994, p. 25). Katz goes further: 'Sports, as never before, had so completely permeated the logic of the marketplace in consumer goods that by 1992 the psychological content of selling was often more sports-oriented than it was sexual' (1994, p. 26).

As a 'captivating medium,' to use Katz's phrase, sport was able to exchange its power to draw followers for hard cash. If the American TV network NBC's $601 million contract with NBA for four years' coverage from 1990 seemed a bold move in its day, Rupert Murdoch's deals appeared ruinous. The owner of Fox, in 1993, bid a stunning $1.58 billion (£1 billion) to televise NFL games. This came a year after BSkyB (now Sky), in which Murdoch had a controlling interest, made a surprising £304 million bid for a five-year deal with England's then new Premier League; this was nearly seven times more than the previous TV deal and reflected Murdoch's confidence in football's capacity to draw audiences. (See Chapter 8 for more on Sky and the Premier League.) Since the early 1990s, the value of broadcasting deals with major sports has increased exponentially, underlining the magnetic power of sport and its integration into the mainstream entertainment industry. The status of its players reflected this integration; many elite performers shared rank with Hollywood A-listers, supermodels and rock stars.

In the 1990s, Nike's choice of athletes as endorsers was understandable, even logical. But why would advertisers hoping to sell products unrelated to sport want to hire sportsmen and sportswomen? Unnerved by the unreliability of rock and movie stars, yet heartened by the elevation of Jordan, advertisers found the combination of athleticism, health, wholesomeness and a dash of volatility perfect for purveying practically anything. Cantona retired suddenly in 1997, aged 30, but continued to appear in ads for Nike and multiple other brands, as well as in feature films. By this time, football was advertising's new rock 'n' roll. The global popularity of the sport, particularly with a young demographic, made its players as desirable to advertisers – and sometimes as iconic – as pop or film stars. (A demographic is a particular sector of a population.)

In 1999, the female footballer Brandi Chastain shot to fame. After scoring the winning penalty for the US in the Women's World Cup final, she 'ripped off her shirt to reveal a Nike sports bra in a memorable and controversial goal celebration' (Gee, 2014). She was the first of a number of female footballers, including Mia Hamm, Birgit Prinz and Marta, to rise to international prominence, though without acquiring comparable celebrity status to, for example, Serena Williams, NASCAR driver Danica Patrick or MMA fighter Ronda Rousey, all regular endorsers of products and services, from jeans to internet domain registrars. In fact, it could be argued that footballers' partners – or WAGS, as the British call them – achieve greater celebrity status by association than women footballers earn by playing the game.

As sure-footed as Nike was in its selection of athletes, it slipped up when, in 2003, it signed the then 14-year-old football prodigy Freddy Adu. Hailed as a new Pelé-in-the-making, Adu played for Major League Soccer's DC United, but then drifted to lower league clubs in Brazil and Finland before returning without fanfare to the US in 2015.

The reader might be wondering why I've devoted so much space in a chapter on celebrity to advertising. Every time we look at, read about, talk about, follow or otherwise engage with a celebrity, we are submitting to advertising. 'Submitting' is actually not quite the right verb, as it suggests yielding to a superior force; but think in terms of consenting to undergo a certain treatment, like submitting yourself to a body search or having your teeth drilled. We actively give our permission in these instances; in the same way, we actively engage with celebrities whose lives we find interesting. If we didn't find them interesting, there would be no celebrities. Exactly why we find them interesting I will come to shortly. But we're not needy, lacking emotional support or left insecure by the decline in the significance of religion in modern society (if you even believe its significance *has* declined). Celebrities were delivered to us by an industry ready to walk through open doors, push open those left ajar and break down those that were locked in their efforts to create new markets. When looking for origins, we shouldn't be dazzled by the sparkly celebrities who float across our screens and brief us about their lives in 140 characters. There is an unlovely, grinding, hard-nosed industrial enterprise that delivers them.

So John Vincent and colleagues were right when they wrote that '[David] Beckham's potent combination of sporting prowess, physical attractiveness, sex appeal, celebrity marriage, working-class roots, capacity for hard work, and multi-faceted masculinity make him a model endorsement prospect for many global companies' (2009, p. 176). But adidas, H&M, Haig whisky and the several other companies that trade with Brand Beckham and keep the multiple personalities of the former footballer in the public eye provide both the power and the apparatus that produces and then delivers the cultural phenomenon.

## What are role models for?

When Christopher Lasch wrote, 'Advertising serves not so much to advertise products as to promote consumption as a way of life' (1979, p. 72), he steered us towards understanding sport, and indeed all forms of popular entertainment, as advertising. Every time we watch a football game or a movie, or play a video game or even spend time online, we are exposing ourselves to advertising. The sheer ubiquity of ads validates the rightness of consumption 'as a way of life'. (Consumption is the focus of Chapter 10.)

The likes of Jordan and Beckham were, from one vantage point, exceptional; but, from another, they were typical. Several studies have confirmed that consumers, especially young consumers, are impressionable when in range of celebrities. For example, a 2004 study by Alan J. Bush and colleagues focused on the shopping habits of Generation Y (i.e. those born between 1977 and 1994) and how they responded to brands endorsed by famous athletes. The study concluded 'that celebrity sports athletes *are* important to adolescents when they make brand choices and talk about these brands positively' (2004, p. 113). This was American research, though similar findings came from elsewhere in the world. Heejoon Chung's South Korean study, conducted around the same time, assessed the impact of Chan Ho Park, who was playing in Major League Baseball in the US. Chung widened the scope of his research to suggest that '[an] intriguing aspect of late capitalism is, then, its ability not only to tame resistance but also to turn it into a whole new commodity' (2003, p. 101). (See Goscilo and Strukov (2011) for a similar Russian study.)

It seems self-reflexivity crept in; advertisers selected figures like Cantona and basketball's Dennis Rodman to counterpoint or emphasize their contrast with the likes of Jordan and Beckham, both apparently wholesome and radiating goodness. Football had a surfeit of players with reputations that barely needed defiling any further by advertisers. All the same, rule-defying players in the Maradona tradition were eminently exploitable. Implausible research, such as that of Jason P. Doyle and colleagues, found that 'respondent attitudes towards sponsors and event brands can be adversely impacted when negative publicity surrounding an associated celebrity endorser emerges' (2014, p. 319). This unsubtle conclusion fails to understand that the behaviour that incites the publicity dictates the response of consumers. Beckham was alleged to have had sex with someone other than his wife, a deed later duplicated by Tiger Woods; however, neither the men nor the brands they endorsed suffered. Lance Armstrong took drugs; so did Kate Moss. He crashed and burned; she rose phoenix-like. Drugs are okay for a supermodel, but not for an athlete. In most cases, though, athletes are rehabilitative. Luis Suárez was suspended and fined for racial abuse in 2011, but was featured in ads for, among others, adidas and Qatar Airways within three years. Michael Vick, the NFL quarterback who was dropped as an endorser by several companies when he was convicted and jailed for dog-fighting crimes in 2007, was later re-signed by Nike. Vick, like Woods, is a black athlete, while Suárez is Latin American, suggesting that ethnicity is not a crucial factor in the process.

A study into the effects of sport celebrities' transgressions by Anne-Marie Sassenberg highlighted how consumers reacted specifically to sex offences: 'Consumers indicated that when the off-field SCT (sport celebrity transgression) was rape, it negatively affected their perceptions' not only of the celebrity but also of the brands with which he was associated (2015, p. 87). (I write 'he' though the research dealt with rape abstractly; I am mindful that there are male victims of rape, though no known female celebrity athlete perpetrators.) The study explored how *perceptions* of transgressions vary according to age, gender and other variables. The dynamics (i.e. the forces that produce change) are more variegated than popularly imagined; consumers don't automatically turn against an athlete and the products he or she endorses because of a reported act that appears to go against a norm, law or code of conduct.

There is at least inferential evidence that celebrities have a kind of licence to break rules and go unpunished. Their commercial sponsors, as the companies whose products they endorse are usually called, are often prepared to capitalize on their trespasses. Straying from accepted standards of social or sexual behaviour can be commercially exploitable, as Ophir Sefiha points out: 'Our perceptions of deviance are often little more than a sophisticated commodity form whose consumption offers immediate pleasures without having to incur the very real social and individual costs of these behaviors' (2012, p. 596). In other words, bad behaviour brings its own rewards for both the player and the companies who use that player to promote their brands. This makes footballers (and athletes generally) very good role models. I'll explain.

Role models are people looked to by others as examples to be imitated. Reuben A. Buford May puts it this way: 'Young men think of a role model in much the same way as the idea is defined in the social learning literature – that is, a model that influences the observer's attitudes, behaviors, or aspirations' (2009, p. 450). The likes of Jordan, Beckham, Armstrong and Suárez and every other athlete mentioned so far in this chapter are frequently called role models, though there is no research to support the view that young people actually *copy* anything other than their athletic performance and perhaps their hairstyles (and sometimes their tattoos). This does not nullify their power to influence us, however.

Steve Dix and colleagues provide a slightly different understanding of a role model as 'anyone that the individual comes into contract with, directly or indirectly, [who] can potentially influence the consumers' consumption-related decisions and actions' (2010, p. 38). This was an Australian study and it was complemented by research by Canadian scholars Ann L. Pegoraro and colleagues, who discovered that '[a] new consumerism has emerged from the early 1980s, creating a different era of status consumption. People are now more likely to compare themselves with or aspire to the lifestyles of those far above them in the economic hierarchy' (2010, p. 1470). Role models are again conceptualized as being in the service of advertisers: 'In a consumerist culture, individuals' self-identities are almost exclusively formed and maintained by consumption. In a sense you become what you buy.' If, as many suggest, celebrity footballers, like other well-known athletes, are role models, their role is to consume commodities in a way that makes their fans try to copy (i.e. emulate) them.

What happens on the field of play is of little importance. An Indian study of cricketers by Yogesh Upadhyay and S. K. Singh found that: 'Poor performance … does not result in complete reversal of cricketers' status as role models' and their efficacy as endorsers is not diminished (2010, p. 74). ('Efficacy' refers to the ability to produce a desired result, in this case promoting sales.) Their behaviour during competition may be despicable, and off-field they could be vile egomaniacs with nothing but contempt for the fans who adore them. But, as long as people keep buying the products that they endorse, they are effective role models, at least in the way in which we are treating the term – which, in practice, is the only meaningful way we can treat it, as there is no credible evidence that the influence of celebrity footballers operates in any other way. So before we repeat without thinking that 'footballers are role models', we should remind ourselves exactly what this means: not that players are guiding lights of morality, or shining examples of honesty, goodness and uprightness, but that they are persuasive advertisers who shape the buying habits of aspirational young shoppers.

## The feeling of intimacy … at distance

So far, we have searched for the source of celebrity culture and found it in the media's changing orientation, scope and methods. The advertising industry was vital in both promoting and exploiting our interest in celebrities and, when established endorsers became unreliable, advertisers turned to athletes as a way of enhancing sales of products – even products that had no associations with sport. Playing the most popular game in the world, footballers were natural targets for advertisers.

Beckham was not only the most prominent celebrity endorser, but also, in several ways, the epitome, or perfect example, of the celebrity footballer: a serial endorser of countless products whose life was monitored closely by the media wherever he went, his appearance and feats keeping audiences interested, perhaps even captivated. His minor transgression had no impact on either his capacity to entrance his followers or his ability to sell merchandise. In fact, there is no credible proof that transgressions hurt celebrity athletes' appeal – if by appeal we mean the quality of being attractive or interesting, rather than liked. Armstrong was disgraced publicly, shamed by the media and widely disliked – but he remained a figure of immense interest long after his confession to doping in 2013. This prompts a question raised by Nicolás Salazar-Sutil: '*Why* we need celebrities is not the point in contention, but *how* we need them' (2008, p. 444).

Salazar-Sutil proposes that sport offers the kind of satisfactions once gained from traditional spheres: 'Football has an increasingly broad and influential cultural role insofar as it can substitute experiences that would have been attributed traditionally to religious, economic or political practices' (2008, p. 455). It's an imaginative claim; perhaps our confidence in traditional institutions, such as the church and mainstream politics, has eroded and the fulfilment that they used to provide has vanished, leaving us to turn to sport for emotional gratification.

Len Sherman supports this view: 'We have forsaken our traditional heroes and replaced them with actors and athletes' (1992, p. 26). ('Forsaken' is an old-fashioned word meaning 'abandoned'.) Players talk about winning a football game as if they've conquered Everest, and pop stars believe that their status entitles them to make pronouncements on how to save the planet, solve third world debt or bring peace on earth. This is the kind of influence that Salazar-Sutil has in mind. But, of course, advertisers are more pragmatic; they are interested in how influential sportsmen and women could be in affecting what consumers buy. Yet when Salazar-Sutil asks *how*, he invites an investigation of the ways in which we engage with celebrities. Intuitively, we know that this is more than a mechanical process.

'Love, affection, sympathy, gratitude, respect – these and other emotions help us maintain relationships, communities, and even nations', writes Scott R. Harris, adding that emotions 'give color and meaning to virtually all our experiences ... they sustain our most valued relationships and identities' (2015, p. 3). How many of us haven't been angry at, sympathized with or been disgusted by somebody we have never met, know purely through the media and have seen only in two dimensions – on paper or a screen? Unintentionally and perhaps fortuitously, celebrities give the kind of colour and meaning that Harris believes to be so important to our experiences. If they didn't enrich our experiences, they wouldn't be celebrities, at least not in the way in which we understand celebrities today. Admiring from afar and genuflecting to signal our respect might have worked in another era when people became famous for outstanding military deeds, bold political leadership or principled guidance on moral and spiritual questions. But the vast majority of today's celebrities are entertainers; as such, they do no more than amuse us. We don't defer to them; in fact, we think of them as very much like ourselves, except with more money and more media exposure.

In her analysis of Cristiano Ronaldo, Ana Jorge proposes that fans produce celebrities 'by creating and negotiating meaning' (2015). By this, she means that celebrity footballers like Ronaldo are flesh-and-blood human beings at one level, but creations of our imaginations at another. (I will cover Jorge's research in more detail in the Research in Action section at the end of this chapter.) Think for a moment: what do you actually know about celebrities? Obviously, the news and gossip we derive from media, both traditional and social, constitutes raw material. But we process that material in a way that suits us. There is one Ronaldo: Madeira's most famous native, the prodigiously skilled goal-scorer *par excellence*. And there is another Ronaldo who exists independently of time and space – simply because he is in our imaginations. We see and hear so much about Ronaldo that we feel we know him. Actually, we do – or, at least, we know the Ronaldo that we imagine. All celebrities inspire fans to believe that they know them. How otherwise would they elicit the kind of emotions that Harris argues are so pivotal in sustaining relationships and identities? Identities are explored more fully in Chapter 7; in the present context, I define them as the attribution of certain characteristics and qualities to ourselves.

When Sean Redmond writes, 'Celebrities are liquid figures ... They exist across numerous temporal and spatial dimensions' (2013, p. 5), he is making the same point. The media offer frames of reference, but we create our own celebrities. If we felt we knew Ronaldo or other globally famous footballers as anonymous, abstract, personality-less characters, we wouldn't experience the gamut of emotions from love to detestation (this is stronger than hate!). We're able to engage with them emotionally because our bond is what Donald Horton and R. Richard Wohl (1956) have called 'intimacy at a distance'. Like it or not, we do get the feeling that we 'know' celebrities and, according to Horton and Wohl, this is because we have *parasocial relations* with them. The two psychologists were writing in 1956 when television was still a new technology and viewers were forming unusual attachments: they were developing 'friendships' with television characters, some fictional and others real (like announcers or weather forecasters). They also 'hated' some characters. Familiarity led to a sense of intimacy. Viewers actually thought that they knew the figures whom they saw on their screens. The relationships were and still are strictly one-way. Horton and Wohl called them parasocial because 'para' means 'beyond', as in 'paranormal'.

The character Jess in Gurinder Chadha's film and musical *Bend It Like Beckham* has a parasocial relationship. Unable to confide in her parents or close friends, Jess has her feelings stirred every night by a poster of David Beckham on her bedroom ceiling and she spends time confessing her deepest desires to the inert image. The fictional Jess may have a lot in common with countless other worshipful fans. For her and maybe them, Beckham is a lifeline connecting them to resources that, at least in their eyes, aren't available to dilettantes or outsiders. Only they truly have access. To them, their relationships are singular, personal, and exclusive. But posters don't respect fans any more than dolls or any other kind of celebrity merchandise. They simply exist.

As in every relationship, there is an exchange: fans get gripping inside information on the so-called private lives of celebrities and celebrities themselves get influence. This sounds like a cynical interpretation. But take note of Dix and colleagues' observation: 'Young adults' perception of celebrity athlete endorsers has a positive influence on their product-switching intentions, complaint intentions, positive word-of-mouth and brand loyalty' (2010, p. 43). (By 'complaint intentions', Dix and colleagues presumably mean that consumers are less likely to find a product unsatisfactory or unacceptable if it is endorsed by someone whom they admire, respect or just like.)

Without parasocial relationships, there would be no celebrities. Just reading about famous personalities in newspapers and magazines wouldn't implicate us in relationships of enough shade, detail and nuance to create an affiliation or attachment of significance. The commercial implications of this are clear, as Dix and colleagues (2010) conclude: 'This confirms the assumption that athletes are important socialization agents for young adults, and that, as role models, they have significant impact on purchase intentions and consumer behaviour.'

Like parents, schoolteachers and peers, athletes help to shape us; in particular, they shape our spending habits and, if we follow the logic of Pegoraro and colleagues (2010), our identities. The difference is that we may never actually stand face to face with or talk to athletes. Thanks to Twitter, Instagram and other social media, physical proximity is irrelevant; online interactivity makes possible the kind of exchanges that enrich parasocial relations and enhance the influence of celebrities. Writing in the 1950s, Horton and Wohl couldn't have predicted how their concept would take on such significance after the rise of Web 2.0.

## Conclusion

If celebrity culture seems unstoppable, it's because the engine that drives it is consumerism – the preoccupation of society with the acquisition of products and commodities (i.e. consumer goods). Some celebrities beguile us, while others just interest us shallowly, but all engage us in a way that makes it more likely that we will spend money. Even if we don't buy the products that they endorse, we'll shop for products that keep us in step with their march. Football's seamless integration into celebrity culture started in the early 1990s, as advertisers realized that its star players could be effective 'brand ambassadors' (to use the term advertisers prefer) and media corporations realized the potential of sport to draw viewers to their screens. Michael Jordan was a trailblazing celebrity, thanks in part to his basketball ability but also to the imaginative marketing of Nike, a global corporation that has been a celebrity particle accelerator whereby footballers and other sports stars have collided with each other in dazzling commercials.

## CELEBRITY AND FOOTBALL: A TIMELINE

### 1960s

**1962** The Elizabeth Taylor–Richard Burton scandal unfolds.

Telstar 1 is the first of several communications satellites capable of sending signals to earth to go into orbit over the next several years; they provide the stimulus for the development of a global media.

**1964** The Summer Olympics in Tokyo are broadcast internationally 'live.'

**1966** The World Cup is broadcast internationally 'live' from England.

**1967** George Best's fame broadens as he features in Manchester United's win over Benfica in the European Cup Final.

### 1970s

**1971** Pelé makes his last international appearance for Brazil; in the 2000s, he will endorse the drug Viagra.

**1972** Computer scientists exhibit an early version of what is later to become the internet.

**1977** Kevin Keegan joins SV Hamburg; he will earn £250,000 a year, including endorsement deals.

**1979** Christopher Lasch's influential book *The Culture of Narcissism* is published; it depicts a culture increasingly reliant on the media to define its 'needs'.

### 1980s

**1980** ESPN starts transmission; by 1998, it will broadcast to 160 countries.

**1981** Diana Spencer marries Prince Charles; the Royal Wedding attracts 28 million British television viewers and 750 million worldwide.

**1983** Madonna releases her first album.

**1984** Michael Jordan leads the US national basketball team to Olympic gold; he later turns professional and signs a deal with Nike worth $2.5 million.

Rob Lowe's career is threatened by the release of a sex tape featuring him and two girls, one of whom is under 16.

**1989** The Sky satellite TV channel is launched.

### 1990s

**1991** Diego Maradona fails a dope test and is banned for 15 months.

**1992** Mike Tyson is sentenced to three years' imprisonment after being convicted of rape.

Paul Gascoigne moves to SS Lazio in Italy.

**1993** Paul Gascoigne has a violent dispute with Italian paparazzi.

**1994** After leading Italy to the World Cup final, scoring five goals in the process, Roberto Baggio misses the deciding penalty.

**1995** Eric Cantona is banned from English football for eight months for his kung-fu kick on a Crystal Palace supporter; Nike capitalizes on his reputation as an anti-hero in an ad campaign.

**1996** Nike signs a £67 million ($100 million) contract with the Brazilian Football Confederation (CBF); Ronaldo has a personal contract with Nike believed to be worth $1 million a year, a significant sum for a relatively unproven 19-year-old.

Tiger Woods makes his professional debut and signs a five-year deal with Nike valued at $40 million.

The Spice Girls' 'Wannabe' is released and launches a band that is later listed by *Forbes* as one of the top global 'brands'.

**1997** The *Daily Mirror* pays a reported £265,000 ($450,000) for the British rights to publish shots of Diana and Dodi Fayed on their vacation off Sardinia; the photographer Mario Brenna earns an estimated $7 million from global sales of the pictures.

Diana dies in a car accident in Paris; the paparazzi who chase her prior to the crash are later cleared of wrongdoing.

David Beckham meets Posh Spice aka Victoria Adams.

**1998** David Beckham announces his engagement to Victoria Adams.

**1999** David and Victoria Beckham marry.

## 2000s

**2000** The British and American versions of *Big Brother* start.

Venus Williams signs a $40 million promotional deal with Reebok; it is the most lucrative endorsement contract held by a woman.

**2001** The Spice Girls break up.

**2002** There are just nine dominant media corporations: AOL Time Warner, Disney, Bertelsmann, Viacom, TCI, General Electric, Rupert Murdoch's News Corporation, Sony and Seagram.

**2003** The 14-year-old Freddy Adu makes his debut for DC United in the MLS and signs a $1 million deal with Nike; Adu will move to 11 more clubs in Europe and South America before returning to the MLS in 2015.

Michael Jackson is interviewed on television and indicates that he has shared his bed with children.

LeBron James turns professional and signs a reported $90 million contract with Nike.

David Beckham moves from Manchester United to Real Madrid after globally reported transfer negotiations.

**2004** David Beckham is involved in an internationally publicized scandal after reports of an extra-marital affair.

Kate Moss loses several modelling contracts worth an estimated £6 million ($10 million) after being pictured by a British newspaper apparently using cocaine.

Facebook launches.

**2005** Kate Moss attracts several new modelling contracts worth an estimated £12 million ($20 million).

**2006** Victoria Beckham launches her own denim line, dVb Style, as well as an eyewear range and a fragrance, Intimately Beckham.

Twitter launches.

**2007** David Beckham transfers to LA Galaxy.

**2008** Madonna is romantically involved with New York Yankee Alex Rodriguez.

**2009** The Tiger Woods scandal results in his withdrawal from competition; Accenture, AT&T and Pepsi drop him, but he remains the highest-paid athlete in the world thanks to huge deals with Nike, Electronic Arts and Upper Deck.

## 2010s

**2010** Instagram launches.

**2011** Welsh football player Ryan Giggs is named on Twitter as having taken out a legal injunction over an alleged affair with a reality TV star; the case reveals that several other football celebrities have taken out injunctions to prevent the publication of information about their private lives.

**2012** Lionel Messi appears with Kobe Bryant in a Turkish Airways commercial; it gets 57 million views on YouTube in its first two weeks.

**2013** David Beckham retires from active football.

**2014** The now-retired David Beckham earns £27 million ($42 million) in endorsements.

**2015** Cristiano Ronaldo is the tenth highest-paid celebrity in the world, with annual earnings of £60 million ($79.5 million).

Try to picture a time when football wasn't entertainment; just 30 years ago, it would have been insulting to suggest a sport based on unsparing competition and played in a spirit of honest endeavour was merely entertainment, or that its players could be compared with frivolous performers like singers and actors.

Today we follow footballers with the same zeal that fans once reserved for Hollywood stars. Technology, and social media in particular, has made it possible not only to follow their exploits on a screen, as we did from the 1960s, but also to become intimate with them. Well, perhaps not become intimate, but at least feel intimate – having the perception that we are closely acquainted. Technology has also made celebrity footballers influential. Fans mimic footballers in multiple ways; spending money on products approved by their role models is one of them. Celebrity culture has transformed football into a high-gloss division of showbusiness, its players into living advertisements and its fans into idolatrous disciples whose loyalties are validated as much by their PayPal accounts as by their presence at the match.

## Research in Action

**'"Cristiano Ronaldo is cheap chic, *Twilight* actors are special": young audiences of celebrities, class and locality' by Ana Jorge (2015)**

### What were the goals of the research?

Using Cristiano Ronaldo, the world's most glamorous and revered footballer of his time, Ana Jorge, of Universidade Nova de Lisboa in Portugal, explored the ways in which young Portuguese people participate in what she calls 'the social construction of celebrity, their own identities and ultimately their country's place in global culture'.

### Why was the research relevant?

The research was relevant because it focused on how the relationships that young people establish with celebrities help them to project a social position and negotiate their ambitions. As such, it made clear that following a celebrity or several celebrities was not just a superficial practice with no lasting consequences, but an integral part of cultural life. The discussion surrounding Ronaldo, a local celebrity turned global megastar, showed that the meanings that young people attribute to celebrities 'link class and the semi-peripheral position that Portugal occupies in the global circuits of culture'. In other words, this was a minor study but with major implications.

### What methods were used?

#### Sample

Fieldwork was conducted with a total of 48 respondents, aged 12–17, all from Portugal. Jorge sought fans of the celebrities who were most popular among teenagers in the country at the time of the fieldwork: actors from *The Twilight Saga*, Miley Cyrus, Justin Bieber and members of Tokio Hotel (the German rock band). She recruited participants from a youth centre in a disadvantaged neighbourhood, one public and one private religious school in Lisbon, and a rural school. Jorge interviewed her participants individually, protecting their identities by using pseudonyms.

#### Interviews

The interviews were semi-structured and the young people were asked about their family, friends and life projects, attitudes and media habits, and opinions towards celebrity culture and their idols. Unlike structured interviews, in which the researcher asks a prescribed schedule of questions, semi-structured interviews have a loose schedule of questions but allow the interviewer to deviate to pursue in more detail issues that may arise during the course of the interview.

#### Focus groups

Jorge also assembled focus groups, in different combinations of gender and age. The researcher observed the groups after photo elicitation, a method of interview employed in visual sociology that uses visual images to elicit comments; in this instance, the images were of various celebrities, including Ronaldo, Robert Pattinson and Kristen Stewart. The material was audio-recorded and transcribed, and individual summaries of the participants were prepared in order to expand the profiles 'as revealed by the interview and focus group'. All of the data were then coded into previously constructed categories, using MaxQDA software developed for computer-assisted qualitative and mixed methods.

### What were the main arguments?

- 'Part of the popular fascination and cultural relevance of the celebrity has to do with the symbolic, cultural and economic power it entails', wrote Jorge. It is a strong argument and deserves closer scrutiny. She meant that our fascination with celebrities conceals an assumption that success is an individual enterprise and that anyone can potentially progress as far as their talent combined with ambition and hard work can take them. While we remain preoccupied with celebrities, we avoid discussing structured inequalities and the kind of poverty that is a permanent feature of Portuguese society. Effectively, celebrity culture promulgates (i.e. promotes) neo-liberal ideology. ('Neo-liberal' denotes a modified form of liberalism tending to favour free-market capitalism.) Jorge's research investigated how young people's fixation with the lives of celebrities shapes their understanding of society and their place in that society.

- 'National celebrity culture is more associated with an attributed status, whereas foreign and global celebrity is seen as achieved and thus more worthy', wrote Jorge. Portugal occupies the western part of the Iberian peninsular and has a population of less than 11 million, of whom 27 per cent live in the country's Metropolitan Lisbon area (by comparison, the population of London is 8.3 million). Jorge described Portugal as a 'semi-periphery': 'as a result of its colonial and dictatorial past, as well as its geopolitical situation, the country is neither in the centre nor at the development levels of central Europe, nor in the remote periphery of the world economy and culture'. That the country boasts arguably the world's most illustrious footballer (with apologies to Lionel Messi) means that some young people harbour an aspiration to become globally famous: 'For fans who showed a craving for fame, giving up their privacy would be an acceptable price to pay to attain visibility, although theirs is a concept of global fame.'

  With the exception of Ronaldo, local celebrities (those whose fame doesn't extend beyond Portugal) 'are too close to be seen with a superior cultural status'. Young people from different class backgrounds agree that authenticity 'seems more associated with the big global celebrities, connected with cultural industries'. This finding has faint echoes of what Australians call 'cultural cringe', which inclines them to dismiss their own culture as inferior to the cultures of other countries. This distorts the subtlety of Jorge's argument, though there is at least the inference that Portuguese youth value global celebrities rather than their own. Portugal's own A-list member Ronaldo elicited mixed responses, ranging from adoration to resentment at his showiness.

### And the conclusions or key findings?

There were several interesting findings, though one thread ran through all of them: *negotiation*: 'Portuguese fans have to negotiate not only their dreams to ascend to celebrity, particularly global ... they also have to negotiate their role in fan communities of global celebrities.' Jorge argued: 'Female celebrities from pop music tended to be appropriated by young girls as legitimation of the identities they had chosen for themselves, thus helping to negotiate their own authenticity.' The term 'negotiate' suggests finding a way around, through or towards something – perhaps a goal or a feeling. This project used methods designed to understand rather than explain how young people negotiate their relationships with celebrities and with other fans. These celebrities are not so much people as resources – people who are drawn on in order to function effectively. As Jorge wrote: 'Individuals are seen both as products of specific discourses and as discourse producers/subjects who can reproduce existing discourses but also contribute to change by creating and negotiating meaning.' When approached in this way, so-called celebrity adulation is actually a creative process in which young people use media images and texts for their own purposes.

### *What were the strengths of the research?*

Qualitative techniques invariably yield richer and more immersive or three-dimensional data than quantitative methods that are aimed at making cultural phenomena measurable. By using a semi-structured questionnaire schedule, the interviewer has the freedom to allow participants to express thoughts and opinions that she or he may not have anticipated. Qualitative approaches, therefore, allow for discovery. In this research Jorge used a kind of mashup of techniques and produced an interesting set of responses that lacked the neatness of quantitative research conclusions but provided credible insights that were sometimes contradictory and confusing – which is how much of cultural life is, of course.

### *Were there any weaknesses?*

The study laboured with the distinction between ascribed and achieved celebrity, assuming that some statuses are just foisted onto individuals, while others are honestly earned. ('Ascribed' means attributed to someone or something). Clearly, this is not the case: all celebrity status is ascribed in the sense that we, the fans, attribute figures whom we find interesting with special qualities, which we call charisma, aura or gifts. Celebrity is something we create; it isn't just a quality possessed by a select few. Equally, all celebrities achieve something, however menial – even if it's just an appearance on a reality or quiz show. So, while the empirical evidence presented demonstrated perfectly how fans endow or ascribe the celebrities that they follow with special attributes, Jorge contradicted her own findings by clinging to the spurious distinction. Some might argue that Ronaldo's CV earned him his status. But did it? He happens to live in a time and place where the ability to control and manipulate an air-filled sphere with a circumference of 68–70 cm is respected and rewarded. In another era, proficiency in kicking a football might be dismissed. Celebrity is a cultural production; as such, it is always ascribed.

# 10

# CONSUMPTION

*Kevin Dixon*

---

**Chapter highlights**

- Since the late nineteenth century, football has cultivated consumers.
- The almost universal adoption of neo-liberalism in the 1980s contributed towards the intensification of the consumer experience in football.
- While there is no single theory of consumption, there are a number of complementary, overlapping and sometimes contradictory theoretical explanations that can be applied to football.
- Some theories emphasize the position of capitalist exploitation in football, while others regard consumers as communicators and rational decision makers.

---

## Introduction

> I keep all that is related to Lens. I have jerseys ... like all supporters. I have the jersey of each season. I often go on the Lens website. All the anthems we sing ... our logo ... everybody identifies with Lens ... In addition we play with Lens equipment ... [We wear] jerseys, shorts, socks, sweat shirts, track-suits. We have everything ... We identify a lot actually. We sing Lens anthems like 'La Lensoise'. I have three CDs that have been issued. One jersey costs about €50; one tracksuit is about the same price. Yes, that's all it costs!
>
> *(Christophe, Lens fan, quoted in Derbaix and Decrop, 2011, p. 271)*

For Christophe and millions of others like him, consumption is inseparable from football culture; in fact, engaging in football culture means consuming. Let me explain: the purchasing of boots, shorts, socks, shirts, tickets, football paraphernalia, ephemera and related gifts; watching television shows; reading newspapers or books; listening to music; admiring art; playing computer games; travelling to the match; acquiring matchday food and drink; gambling; celebrating; commiserating; communicating with others (online or otherwise) and many other actions besides are all, in the end, acts of consumption.

Whether experiencing football as a player, coach or fan, consumption infiltrates every level of practice, so much so that affiliation to football is impossible without it. As such, it becomes clear that consumption is more than merely an economic transaction; it is a way of thinking or being that emerges within people as a consequence of subcultural immersion. In order to process how such a wide range of actions can be perceived as acts of consumption, the following definition from Alan Warde (2005, p. 137) is helpful:

> [Consumption is] … a process whereby agents engage in appropriation and appreciation, whether for utilitarian, expressive or contemplative purposes, of goods, services, performances, information or ambience, whether purchased or not, over which the agent has some degree of discretion.

Warde recognizes the place and importance of the experiential component as a defining constituent of consumption. Here, his intention is not to downgrade or downplay the economic element, but rather to acknowledge that consumption has become so ingrained into routine actions of everyday life that people are not always fully conscious of the acts of consumption (experiential or otherwise) in which they are engaged. This is because they are 'actually doing things like driving, eating, or playing' (Warde, 2005, p. 150). Thus, consumption speaks not only a tough economic language, but it also sings to the soft, intricate levels of human existence – particularly to our identity, as expressed through routine communications. There is no doubt that consumption has become an identifying feature of modern society; consuming is a central social activity – we all do it. Marketing, branding and advertising create interest, which turns to fascination and then demand, and so creates a market. In fact, the market is now global; everyone, everywhere is in some way involved in consuming products and services.

With this in mind, the following chapter addresses the topic of consumption in football from three main perspectives:

1. It briefly examines the history of football-related consumption from the rise of leisure-centred culture in the late nineteenth century until the 1980s.
2. It discusses the post-1980s almost universal emergence of a neo-liberal political economy and its implications for football consumers.
3. It gives consideration to complementary and competing theoretical explanations of football consumption.

Let's begin with a chronological discussion relating to 'the home of football', England, and the rise of leisure consumption.

## The home of football and the rise of leisure consumption

According to Zygmunt Bauman (2005, p. 82), all human beings are, and always have been, consumers. With this, he explains that the human concern with consumption certainly precedes the contemporary infatuation, and yet this position is not readily enforced in the literature on football. For instance, Ed Horton (1997), David Conn (1997), Stephen Morrow (1999) and Craig McGill (2001), amongst others, imply that consumption and the capitalist exploitation of football is a new phenomenon. Moreover, they write with nostalgia about an era when fans were not exploited as consumers. In this section, I argue that such logic is based on a popular misconception and that these authors have not fully understood the continuity that exists across time and space in relation to consumption. Thus, I argue below that since the late nineteenth century, football has cultivated consumers.

### Trade unions, legislation and the rise of leisure consumption

The trade union movement in early nineteenth-century Britain played an important role in the initial development of consumer culture. Indeed, Andy Bennett (2005) explains that representation and subsequent pressure of workers' unions led to the initiation of government statutes that were, in turn, crucial to the evolution of leisure in the UK. The statutes that would set in motion the conditions in which future generations of working people would develop a taste for consumption include:

• the Factories Act of 1847 (also known as the Ten Hours Act), which freed workers on Saturdays for the pursuit of leisure;
• the Reform Acts of 1867 and 1884, which extended the franchise to various classes of working men and women;
• the Union Chargeability Act of 1865, which allowed greater mobility of labour;
• the Education Act of 1870, which sought to extend the educational franchise to the lower classes (Wigglesworth, 1996; Taylor, 2008).

Alongside a generic pay increase for working people, perhaps the most important amendment to working conditions (from the perspective of the development of football cultures) was the establishment of a free Saturday afternoon (otherwise known as the Saturday half-holiday) for workers as a form of common practice in many trades by the 1870s (Cunningham, 1980; Holt, 1990; Brailsford, 1991). With disposable income and spare time to occupy, working people became willing consumers of the once-elite public-school game that began to diffuse into the wider population. (I will return to issues of social diffusion later in this chapter.) As football teams were established through old boys' networks (former public-school boys), within industry and armed forces regiments, and by churches and pubs, team identities were constructed to reflect the character and the imagined communities of their founding locality/group (Williams, 1997; Croll, 2000; Beaven, 2005; Taylor, 2008). According to Adam Brown (2008), identity was consumed, in turn, through club symbolism such as club nicknames, badges, songs and ground locations that were used to evoke a sense of passion and group unity within the lives of football supporters. (See Chapter 3 for a discussion of empire and the diffusion of football, and Chapter 7 for an exploration of the power of football in generating individual and group identity.)

Furthermore, local affiliations to specific teams helped to stimulate and nurture football rivalries, and subsequently this is thought to have had a direct effect on the size of crowds attending football matches. For instance, when discussing the first Tyne–Wear derby between Sunderland AFC and Newcastle United FC, Anton Rippon (1981, p. 52) reports that '30,000 supporters attended this match on Christmas Eve 1898'. The important point to note here is that the average attendance for Sunderland matches in the same season was 12,300 (Tabner, 2002, p. 96). Likewise, Nicholas Fishwick (1989, p. 52) has shown that local derbies between Wednesday and United in Sheffield would double the average gate. So, as matches played on public holidays were likely to attract a larger audience, they were often deliberately scheduled to be derby matches to add to the attractiveness, showcasing the commercial potential of spectator football.

## Professionalism, business and the nascent consumer market

Professionalism (being paid to play football) was prompted by local rivalries and, according to Stefan Szymanski and Tim Kuypers (1999, p. 4), the beginnings of commercialization and professionalism were 'two sides of the same coin'. After all, the best players attracted the biggest crowds, and gate money paid for the best players. Steven Tischler (1981) adds to this when he argues that football clubs could not afford to be complacent on this issue. He states that the entrepreneur could not assume that his customers would continue to contribute to the gate if the team lost – or the quality of the play was poor. As a consequence, he explains, those clubs that had embraced the commercial potential of football began to apply pressure on the Football Association (FA), established in 1863, in a galvanized movement to legalize professionalism. This was achieved in 1885.

The Football League was established in 1888 to ensure that competition was equally matched. This was thought to be important, not only to ensure a fair contest but also as a technique that would stimulate audience and demand (Wigglesworth, 1996, p. 35). However, despite this logic, the Football League and clubs within it were not purely profit maximizers. In fact, Peter Sloane (1971) points out that any profit made from football was strictly regulated. For instance, in 1889 the FA placed a 'limit of five per-cent of the paid up shared capital' as the maximum dividend that a member club could pay out (Holt, 1990, p. 283). So, while there is evidence to reject the idea that football clubs were purely profit maximizers, it is also true that maximizing income did become critical for maintaining clubs financially, and this led to the introduction of established business methods into the operations of football clubs. Szymanski and Kuypers (1999, p. 7) explain:

> The basic elements of football business ... have been [present] since the earliest days of the professional game: A product (entertainment of the game) supplied by workers (players and coaching staff) using land (grounds), buildings (stadiums) and equipment (ball, boots, kit) for a wage and sold to customers (supporters and other spectators) in competition and through co-operation with rivals.

Likewise, Tischler (1981, p. 69) argues that football resembled a microcosm of the larger business environment, dealing in sports in the same way that others traded in houses, food and pencils. 'The natural order of the workplace', he insists, 'found its extension in football'. Indeed, football and football cultures were supported by other stable and emergent forms of consumption. It is suggested that football's growing popularity was positively reinforced by communication technologies such as printing, the media and rising levels of literacy within the British population more generally (Wigglesworth, 1996). The rise of the Saturday night Sports Special (a type of newspaper popular from the late nineteenth century) cemented this relationship with the British public, revealing the commercial demand for football and its place within British culture – with spectator sport becoming part of a wider system of enter-tainment. Other technological advancements such as the nationwide introduction of the railway system also contributed to this process by making travel accessible and relatively inexpensive for spectators and for tourists more generally. By the late 1920s, 'football special' trains were common occurrences as supporters began to travel in order to watch their teams away from home, especially in cup competitions.

It is important to note, however, that the safety and comfort of fans was not a priority for event organizers. Taylor (1992, p. 11) points out that 'often the first improvements at football grounds were simply attempts to make sure spectators paid to watch'. Turnstiles, fencing, primitive stands and 'earth mounds and wagons for spectators to stand on' were all designed to control the movement of the crowd and 'to ensure that they paid for the privilege' (Mason, 1980, p. 140). Thus, as soon as football became a form of mass entertainment, facilities were required for supporters, and in turn those facilities demanded expenditure which had to be covered by entrance charges. In this respect, football was a business, with entrepreneurs responding to the economic stimuli underpinning the growth of nineteenth-century commercialized leisure (Vamplew, 1988; Szymanski and Kuypers, 1999; Taylor, 2008). Unlike other pursuits that today we recognize as sports, football, as a commercial activity, was not considered comparable with, say, cricket, rugby or athletics, all of which were amateur and thus 'pure' sports undefiled by the professionalism that association football had allowed since 1885.

Entrepreneurs in football were not exclusively club owners or board members. In fact, people from various walks of life were known to capitalize on the local football match. Taylor (1992, p. 11) notes that 'if hills overlooked the pitch', as they did for the cup replay between Bolton and Notts County in 1884, 'four or five thousand supporters might gather in the farmer's field ... though the farmer charged half price for admission'. Less surprisingly, industrialists too began to cater for the football audience. James Walvin (1994, pp. 64–66) notes that from the 1880s, football merchandise was produced by (for example) Lewis's of Manchester, who offered for sale 'knickerbockers' (knee-length trousers, used and marketed as sports clothing) at 6s 9d (approximately 34 pence), jerseys for 3s 11d (approximately 20 pence) and hand-sewn footballs for 10s 6d (approximately 53 pence). Walvin notes that there was a market for durable turf and even herbal and patient medicines (i.e. medicine available without a prescription but patented under a brand name) for players with knocks, bruises and strains. He writes:

> The economic spin-off from the game had, within thirty years of the establishment of the FA, become a sizable industry itself, and around football there developed a cocoon of ancillary trades and services all of which were made possible only by the increasing amount of money made available for leisure.
>
> (Walvin, 1994, p. 66)

It is clear, then, that catering for large urban populations of football fans could be reasonably lucrative, not only for football clubs but also for train companies, the media and manufacturers of football merchandise in the form of playing equipment, medicines, umbrellas, streamers, rattles, scarves and beer (Benson, 1994). While other sports prided themselves on their amateur status, football – like professional boxing – saw nothing wrong with making a profit from its activities. So with clear opportunities for money to be made, the evolution of spectator football was such that by the early decades of the twentieth century, its importance had grown to the extent that it was considered to be a dominant aspect of leisure. By 1937–1938, 14 million people watched First Division matches, producing an average crowd per match of approximately 30,000 (Jones, 1986, p. 38). Additionally, the weekly football results were vital to the gambling industry and in the 1930s, via the Football Pools alone, between 10 and 15 million people per week were 'sending off postal orders totaling £800,000 to the Football Pools company' (Clarke and Critcher, 1995, p. 75).

However, in spite of the early popularity and commercial potential of football, levels of support could not be guaranteed in light of a growing leisure market that would offer new and novel ways for working men and women to 'spend' their leisure time. Football audiences would also find themselves enticed by other attractions, such as cinema, music and dance cultures. In addition, the number of wireless licenses increased from 2,178,259 in 1926 to 9,082,666 in 1938, bringing a new form of leisure consumption into the home (Jones, 1986, p. 37). The 1960s brought the mass consumption of television, with the BBC and ITV channels in full operation by the mid-1950s (Horrie, 2002; Horne, 2006). Thus, in order to maintain its position as a dominant form of leisure consumption, football would require the implementation of a serious commercial strategy.

## Neo-liberalism and the football consumer

In his historical analysis of the football industry post-1940, Anthony King (1998) makes reference to Britain's gradual move to a post-Fordist leisure-centred state, highlighting the importance of a consumer-based economy. In the late twentieth century, this was propelled by an almost universal neo-liberal political movement that was beginning to gather momentum. To explain, neo-liberal economic philosophy is driven by policies (such as privatization, fiscal austerity, deregulation, free trade and reductions in government spending) that enhance the role of the private sector in the economy, on the premise that this is the best way to stimulate economic growth and, consequently, to benefit all citizens. ('Post-Fordism' is the theory that modern industrial production changed from large-scale mass production pioneered by the car manufacturer Henry Ford towards smaller, more flexible manufacturing units.)

It is worth noting here that some scholars do not agree that neo-liberalism is the best economic policy, but they can't help but be impressed with its ideological dominance. As social theorist Pierre Bourdieu (2000) explains, neo-liberal policies are presented in the language of mathematics and this, he asserts, is partially responsible for its meteoric rise and acceptance within public consciousness. When presented in this way (and while there are other alternatives), Bourdieu argues that neo-liberal philosophy becomes detached from real life to give the impression of scientific credibility along with the power to argue for the inevitability of its proposals and solutions (Bourdieu, 2003). ('Neo-liberal' relates to new forms of liberalism, the prefix 'neo' meaning 'new' or 'revived'; typically, liberalism involves respecting individual liberty, free trade and moderate political and social reform.)

In doing so, Bourdieu argues that neo-liberalism can present itself as progressive, when in fact it is conservative and allows for forms of economic regression to be passed off as reform and revolution. Consequently, then, despite the fact that this system greatly favours those who already own large amounts of economic capital (and associated symbolic capital), social agents are coerced into believing that the game is fair and that everyone profits from 'free markets'. Bourdieu uses this as an example of the power of 'misrecognition', whereby certain individuals (largely rich capitalists) benefit without appearing to do so in the eyes of the repressed. This results in what he calls 'symbolic violence', in which the dominated are complicit in their own subordination. Before providing an example of the potential negative consequences of neo-liberalism for consumers of football, it is first appropriate to point out how the free market has changed football.

### How the free market changed the game

Allen Guttmann (1986) points out that crowds for First Division football matches in England in the 1940s averaged 41,000 and three decades later only 12,000. Amongst the possible causes, lack of customer service and competition from alternative leisure genres were identified as potential contributory factors towards this trend (Smith and Stewart, 2007). Moreover, protectionism and agendas of self-preservation (relating to the leadership of English football) rather than forward-thinking business strategies that could grow and sustain the game were cast as potential millstones that would drag football towards financial ruin (King, 1998).

Gradually, then, the acknowledgement that football could no longer support itself solely through its traditional means of gate revenue was becoming widely accepted. In turn, it was this issue that stimulated debate about the potential merits of jersey sponsorship for Football League clubs. To recap slightly, in 1973 the German football club Eintracht Braunschweig was the first football team in the world to present a sponsor logo, Jägermeister, on its jersey; and in 1976 the English club Kettering Town FC followed suit by displaying the sponsor Kettering Tyres. At the time, both attempts were blocked by their respective football governing bodies and consequently both teams were forced to remove any signs of sponsorship (Unlucan, 2015).

In 1983, this decision was dramatically reversed in England when the Football League surrendered its position in response to an ultimatum from big-city teams who were beginning to realize the potential of their collective power. The ultimatum was as follows: if the Football League would not approve shirt advertisements, big-city clubs would band together to sign an independent television contract. With the Football League backed into a corner (based on the fact that its television revenue was dependent on the attraction of big-city clubs), jersey advertisements were now made permissible. Soon after, and as a consequence of government inquiries into the Bradford fire (1985) and the Hillsborough disaster (1989), neo-liberal policy was promoted as a possible saviour of the English game. The promoted idea (that was rapidly gathering momentum) was to enhance the experience of fans by treating them as customers of a safe, enjoyable, leisure pursuit and a viable business (Popplewell, 1986; Taylor, 1990). On the latter point, television deals would play a crucial role in football's transformation.

According to Raymond Boyle and Richard Haynes (2004, p. 20), media deregulation from the late 1980s onwards helped to accelerate the development of subscription-based, cable and digital televised networks, and freeview customers were transformed into entertainment customers paying premiums. In Germany, television money rose from DM20 million (€10.2 million) with free-to-air stations in 1987 to €429.5 million in 2006–2007. Likewise, in Spain, club revenues increased dramatically as a result of the contracts that the Professional Football League and individual clubs signed with various television companies in the 1990s (Conejo et al., 2007). The same can be said of Brazil, although Christopher Gaffney (2015, p. 159) points out that the expansion of pay-per-view and cable coverage has had a negative impact on stadium attendances, creating a situation in which profits have increased with fewer fans in the stadiums.

Television deals in England began to change in 1988 when added competition from global broadcasters introduced a largely domestic English football industry to the rigours of the world market. In this instance, ITV paid £44 million for a four-year deal, whereas a two-year contract had cost only £4.5 million in 1983 (Cashmore, 2010). Following the formation of the Premier League in 1992 (when teams in the First Division broke away from the rest of the Football League in order to ensure that England's most successful teams would retain most of their television revenue), the deal was renegotiated and Sky (a commercial television network) won the TV rights, paying £305 million for a five-year contract. Since 1992, Sky has secured exclusive rights to televise a proportion of Premier League matches, and in turn those matches have been sold to customers on a subscription and/or pay-per-view basis. In 2012, both Sky and British Telecom (BT) paid more than £3 billion between them for a three-year deal. (Sky and BT are covered in Chapter 8.)

Notwithstanding the fact that satellite television was the catalyst that injected finance into the top tier of English football and thus stimulated the market, football clubs and other capitalist organizations also began to exploit new areas of consumer spending on an unprecedented scale. So, while it is plausible to suggest that a small amount of football merchandise may have been sold to fans since the early part of the twentieth century, it was clear that by the century's end football-related merchandise was ubiquitous, as the journalist S. Winterburn (1998) describes:

> Christmas, a special time to gather among the Arsenal quilt sets and the Liverpool soap on a rope ... Someone somewhere might be generous enough to present you with a £179.99 Chelsea mobile phone, available in both home and away colours, as is Blackpool's more realistically priced mug. At £2.95 each ... they can afford to keep one at home and take another on their travels ... Before they have even grown out of their nappies they have already been targeted as potential spenders. The tiny Barnsley fan can opt for a suit bearing 'I'm a little Tyke' message for just £15.99, or a baby grow for £8.99. For those who have outgrown romper suits ... you may opt for the rather more subtle framed picture ... The Manchester United fan is well accommodated for with a signed print of the 1968 European Cup reunion, retailing at £270.

In order for the scope and depth of merchandising (as detailed above) to become a reality, football clubs initiated marketing, sales and customer service departments to dream up new and innovative ways to sell merchandise and new experiences to earnest football fans (Smith and Stewart, 2010). I will return to the consumption of merchandise later in this chapter, but first, by way of a case study, I draw attention to a collection of historical examples relating to neo-liberal leadership and customer service at the English football club Newcastle United (NUFC).

### Neo-liberalism, market demand and the diminution of customer power: the case of NUFC

In the post-war period, many English football clubs resembled family dynasties in that leadership was handed down through generations of a small group of men. For example, Gordon McKeag was appointed to the board of NUFC in 1972 upon the death of his father William McKeag. This situation was not unique to NUFC, nor indeed to English football; Moorehouse (1994), for instance, has previously noted a similar issue in relation to Celtic FC (CFC), where the White and Kelly families (former board members and major shareholders at CFC) were alleged to have referred to CFC as a precious heirloom to be handed down from generation to generation. Moreover, because of this inevitable association between families and board members, fans were sceptical about the motives of any given football club leadership (beyond maintaining power through generations). Consequently, football fans felt disconnected from the decision-making processes at football clubs.

At NUFC, the situation was as follows. After a period of stadium neglect in the 1970s and 1980s, NUFC was forced to revamp the stadium in connection with government white papers. The West Stand had been condemned in 1986 in the aftermath of the Bradford fire and was in the process of being rebuilt and paid for. The board had declared a shortage of money to improve the football ground, and consequently star players Chris Waddle, Peter Beardsley and Paul Gascoigne (all born in Newcastle-upon-Tyne) were sold to the highest bidder. Thus, when John Hall and the Magpie Group (a consortium of north-east businessmen) set out a proposal for new leadership at NUFC, fans reacted positively, not solely at the prospect of a change of personnel but also to welcome a neo-liberal, forward-thinking business strategy for the club. Hall (now Sir John Hall MBE) is a self-made millionaire who rose to prominence as the mastermind behind the Newcastle and Gateshead MetroCentre, a purpose-built shopping complex that at the time of construction was Britain's largest (Goldblatt, 2015). By 1988, Hall was able to sell his stake in this £270 million retail development for an estimated £50 million profit, freeing monies to invest in and potentially revolutionize NUFC (Williams, 1997).

The proposal put forward by Hall and the Magpie Group laid down the following conditions. The group would revitalize the board. They would raise money by implementing a share issue for fans. They would inject £5 million immediately, increase democracy by removing absolute power from a small minority of people, redevelop the ground and call a halt to selling players to rebalance the books (BBC North East News, 1988). Perhaps the most appealing aspect of this to fans was the 'share' issue: the opportunity to buy a stake in the club and to have a say in future decisions. Consequently, fans were willing to take their place as 'consumers' on the premise that they could use this as a position of power from which to campaign for inclusion in club matters. After all, the free market is dependent on consumers for successful trade, and thus fans were approaching interactions with cultural superiors (Hall and his board) not as passive subjects but rather as important players in the destiny of the club.

However, over the period of Hall's reign as chairman (1991–1998) and as a partial consequence of NUFC's relative success in the Premier League (finishing as one of the top three teams in 1993–1994, 1995–1996 and 1996–1997), demand for tickets increased. Supporters soon found themselves not as active policy drivers for the club (as they had hoped), but as reactive to the impulses of the neo-liberal leadership agenda. In relation to match tickets, the chairman was able to put in place numerous schemes in order to encourage fans to consume by reminding them that they were fortunate to have a ticket at all, given the length of the waiting list. For instance, the club introduced a bond scheme in 1994. This involved an option to pay £500 to secure first refusal on a specific seat for ten years. In addition, and to supplement executive boxes, in 1996 the club offered 300 season tickets for sale at £1,500 under the title 1892 Club (so called to signify the date of the club's genesis). This strategy allowed the club to bypass the lengthy season ticket waiting lists in order sell new tickets at a premium price.

While fans understood that increases in revenue were good for the neo-liberal objectives of the new order, they were beginning to understand that it was money and not loyalty that was valued by the neo-liberal leadership. In 1999, this strategy became more difficult to ignore when 4,000 fans with season tickets in the Milburn Stand and Leazes End of St James' Park received a letter from the club stating that unless they were willing to pay £1,350 or £995 respectively for the seats that they had occupied in previous seasons (making new tickets approximately £500 more expensive), they would be moved to alternative seats in the new upper tiers. This situation was made even more unpalatable for NUFC fans by the fact that half of those affected by this situation were bondholders who had paid £500 as recently as 1994 in order to give them an option on a specific seat for ten years (Conn, 1999). Affected fans attempted to exercise their consumer rights by joining the activist group Save Our Seats (SOS), with some members taking to the law courts to block the proposals of the club leadership. However, after two High Court cases, the club was allowed to move fans as they had proposed under an exceptional circumstances clause (BBC Sport, 2000). As a gesture of goodwill, the club did not pursue fans for legal costs awarded over their insured limit (Conn, 2006).

When multi-billionaire businessman Mike Ashley (owner of the company Sports Direct and, in 2015, the 22nd richest person in the UK) took over as owner of NUFC in 2007, similar patterns emerged. Business decisions were taken without fan consultation and those decisions often occurred at the expense of tradition. For instance, in 2009 Ashley announced future plans to sell the club's stadium naming rights. Ashley's aim was initially to showcase the sponsorship capabilities of the stadium, and in order to demonstrate how this might work for external businesses in future, he temporarily changed the stadium name to SportsDirect.com@St.James'Park. This change, it is worth noting, was official only. Fans, some media outlets and Newcastle City Council continued to refer to the stadium as St James' Park (BBC News, 2011).

On 10 November 2011, the name was changed again to the Sports Direct Arena, with no financial fee incurred by the named company. This was maintained until the 2012–2013 season, when Wonga took over the sponsorship deal, paying approximately £6 million per season for the privilege and investing an additional £1.5 million into youth football (*Metro*, 2013). In order to sweeten the blow dealt to fans upset at the club advertising a morally questionable short-term loan provider, Wonga agreed to reinstate St James' Park as the official stadium name.

Using NUFC as our example, the following becomes clear. The same business-minded strengths responsible for turning around the fortunes of the club have become associated with negative consequences for less affluent fans. Notwithstanding this, it is apparent that both the fans and the club epitomize the success of neo-liberal philosophy, but they do so in very different ways. Club owners invest material resources (on a grand scale) in the club, with the long-term aim of returning a profit; indeed, at NUFC the Hall and Shepherd families managed to extract £145 million (over their tenure), despite the club's miniscule profits and overall losses (Goldblatt, 2015). Conversely, fans invest emotionally in the team and consequently they become regular consumers of match tickets, club merchandise (inadvertently advertising commercial sponsors), television and other products – hence collectively upholding and reaffirming the ultimate triumph of neo-liberal leadership and consumer culture through their actions.

## Theoretical approaches to consumption

In this section, I take a closer look at the theoretical approaches that attempt to explain the relationship between emotion, identity and consumption (as expressed above). It is important to note that there is no single theory of consumption, but rather that there are a number of complimentary, overlapping and contradictory theoretical positions that characterize a continually developing field of scholarship (Cook, 2008). Some of these approaches are discussed below, starting with the idea that consumption is used primarily to emulate others.

### Consumption as emulation

In his 1899 book *The Theory of the Leisure Class* (reprinted in 1925), Thorstein Veblen provides an analysis of the spending patterns of the rich in the late nineteenth century and makes a number of observations that may help to explain historical events (and perhaps some contemporary developments too) relating to the consumption of football. Let's look at the main tenets of his argument. First, he argues that all societies across time and space have a leisure class; that is to say that within any society, there are a group of people who distance themselves from menial work (work that is lacking prestige). Of course, the definition of menial work can and does change across cultural contexts, but nonetheless Veblen argues that the leisure class always occupy the apex of the social system.

In the context of late-nineteenth-century America, he highlights the importance of conspicuous consumption as a means of demonstrating membership of the leisure class. By emphasizing that consumption must be conspicuous, Veblen explains that it is not good enough to simply have wealth; instead, one must be seen to be spending money – and the more frivolous the activity and its distance from menial labour, the more successful one is perceived to be. Indeed, it is important to remember that in the nineteenth century, amateur sport played its part as a form of conspicuous consumption because it was associated with wealthy people. Veblen explains how amateur forms of sporting practice are forms of conspicuous consumption through which those who occupy the apex of a system choose to express their social standing by distancing themselves completely from those activities that in any way resemble work.

Veblen adds to this by explaining that the trickle-down mechanism of emulation works in the following way. First, high-status goods are initially adopted by the wealthy and then eventually this adoption is mimicked by households further down the wealth distribution (Schor, 2007). This means that, as the income of manual workers improves over time and cultural conditions allow, then high-status luxuries or leisure pursuits become lower-status necessities due to a cultural desire for emulation. Indeed, in the case of football (explained earlier), we can see how a high-status game associated with the social elite (public-school boys) was eventually diffused into the mainstream of British society. Once this diffusion has occurred, Veblen explains that the social elite tend to distance themselves from this tainted form of consumption. Historically, we can see value in Veblen's theory when we examine the conflict between amateurs (often public-school boys of high social standing who wanted to maintain the moral code of football by refusing to play for money) and those who campaigned for professionalism (often working-class men who saw payment as a necessity for involvement). It is worth noting here that because amateurs did not require payment due to their financial position and social standing, the moral argument is universally thought to have been a smoke-screen for wider social contestation and an attempt to maintain class segregation (Dixon and Gibbons, 2014; Cleland, 2015).

From a Veblenian perspective, then, consumption is carried out purely for its social value (relying on a commonly recognized set of consensual status symbols) rather than for intrinsic benefits or personal reasons. It should be noted, however, that Veblen's thesis has been highly criticized in recent years for overstating the case and therefore ignoring reverse emulation of popular culture by the elite classes. For instance, one must not assume that the stable traditional structures observed by Veblen in 1899 remain the same across time. As such, contemporary scholarly work must take into account the ambiguity and instability that exists at every stage of late modern development. The commodification of social meanings, the break-up of traditional class groupings, the increasing mobility and globalization of communities, and the malleability of personal identities must all be considered when evaluating emulation through lifestyle consumption (Binkley, 2007).

For this reason, Veblen's theory is seldom used in late modern discussions of the sociology of football consumption; however, with modifications (to allow for inevitable social evolution), there may be grounds for adopting a Veblenian perspective with regard to contemporary football stars or celebrities. After all, football stars in the contemporary setting are (in the public perception, at least) set apart from the social processes of production. Moreover, as Matthias Varul (2007) argues, sports celebrities act as commodity culture innovators and serve as role models whose consumption, style and behaviour are emulated. They are indirectly financed by their audiences, who take vicarious pleasure in their leisure pursuits. Furthermore, because of the mixed social background of the members of this new leisure class (predominantly working- and middle-class), Varul implies that trickle-up effects are at least as important as trickle-down effects in the production of consumer trends to emulate. Chapter 9 considers the ways in which celebrity athletes are used for marketing, how they are turned into brands and whether those brands are damaged by transgressions.

## Consumption as distinction

No doubt influenced by Veblen, Pierre Bourdieu discusses consumption as a form of identity and status. He argues that we consume according to who we are; that is to say, our identity is signposted through our consumption of goods, services and practices. Thus, he explains that our expressions of 'taste' (types of associated consumption that project social stigma or reward according to the critical onlooker) will provide reliable clues about our social status, including social class. Writing about sport and social class in 1978 (p. 820), Bourdieu raised the following rhetorical question: '[A]ccording to what principles do agents choose between the different sports activities or entertainments which in any given time are offered to them as being possible?' He answers this question, in part, with reference to hidden entry requirements. In the following quotation (1978, p. 838), Bourdieu is making reference to what he considers to be bourgeoisie sports (that is, sports associated with upper-class people):

> [Entry requirements are derived from] family tradition and early training, and also the obligatory clothing, bearing and techniques of sociability which keep these sports closed to the working classes and to individuals rising from the lower-middle and even upper-middle classes; and secondly because economic constraints define the field of possibilities and impossibilities.

Here, Bourdieu pays attention to the ways in which lifestyles are enacted via everyday consumption choices and constraints. Moreover, he insists that those choices to act in one way or another occur semi-consciously, because all actions are learned and then naturalized within dispositions that reflect not only us as individuals but also our social positions. Using evidence collected in 1978 (the date is emphasized in order to stress that this example is frozen in time and its relevance should not be taken out of this context), he argues that middle- and upper-class people tend to avoid and express disdain for spectator football due to its mass popularization. He writes: '[T]he probability of watching one of the reputedly most popular sporting spectacles, such as football or rugby on television, declines markedly as one rises in the social hierarchy'. Here, Bourdieu insists that sport, like any other form of consumption, can be used as an expression of distinction (rather than attempting to emulate another group of higher social status, as Veblen conceives) to fulfil a sense of togetherness with one's in-group, and distinction from those thought to be different, for whatever reason.

While Bourdieu's theory is often criticized for being deterministic in the sense that individualistic actions are thought to conceal wider cultural norms (thus giving the impression of cultural stagnation), some scholars suggest that this aspect of his work has been misunderstood. ('Determinism' is the theory that all human action is ultimately determined by causes that are external to will. For some scholars, this implies that humans have no free will and are purely products rather than producers; the opposite viewpoint is called voluntarism, which holds that human free will is the dominant factor in social life.) Tony Rees and colleagues (2014) argue that on closer inspection it is clear that Bourdieu recognizes that cultural conditions are, in fact, dynamic. After all, he acknowledges that a range of practices can be produced, reproduced, altered and transformed across time by agents immersed in any given subcultural context (Bourdieu and Wacquant, 1992). So for instance, while social life is in part habitual (where dispositions and ways of thinking and acting are passed on in an active and reciprocal manner between succeeding generations), it is also true that when confronted with new technology or new information, or when contemporary conditions allow for agents to mix with others with diverse tastes and with different levels of affluence, then people have the capacity to 'reflect' on and change behaviours. In other words, as social life has evolved across time, reflexivity has become internalized by most people as part of their habitus (a set of semi-conscious rules and dispositions that are learned through teachings and life experience).

When investigating distinction in more recent times, Richard Peterson (2005, p. 259) was able to uphold and accentuate this logic when he revealed that, 'to our great surprise, those in high status occupations were ... more likely than others to report being involved in a wide range of lower status activities'. Peterson thus implies that agents holding high social status are not averse to participating in consumption practices associated with lower orders. In fact, he suggests that we are in an era of 'cultural omnivores' in the sense that people tend to have a taste for everything and that this has replaced the old arrangement where elite status was associated with snobbery. Thus, it is now widely conceived that people are reflexive beings and one outcome of this has been that diversity is now valued by most people. Consequently, the cultural omnivore appears to be more suited to the late modern world with fewer boundaries and a global inclusivity that is respectful of diversities (Peterson, 2005; Warde and Gayo-Cal, 2009; Widdop et al., 2014). (An omnivore is an animal, including humans, that consumes a variety of foods.)

Again, it is important to stress that this does not mean that people no longer affiliate themselves with social groups (socio-economic or otherwise); however, it does mean that contemporary conditions (economic, technological, social, political) have increased people's sense of reflexivity beyond traditional class groups and associated consumption. Moreover, it is important to note here that distinction functions within as well as between social groups, and in either instance it is perceptions of consumer activity that tend to be the platform from which distinction judgements are made (Richardson, 2004). I was able to evidence this in 2014 when football fans – all participants in a study who were interviewed about their life experiences as fans of the same team – identified a proportion of fellow fans whom they considered to be fake (Dixon, 2014b). Such judgements were made on the basis of consumption rituals that were duly disparaged. As William Miller (1997, p. 218) explains, distinction 'needs images of bad taste … to articulate the judgements that it asserts' and those judgements, in turn, rely on consumption and its lateral surveillance.

## Consumption and corporate values

Theories of consumption (like those expressed by Bourdieu and Veblen) can, of course, only ever tell half of the story. After all, it is important to remember (and I have highlighted this in earlier discussions of neo-liberalism) that objects and experiences of consumption will inevitably conceal corporate values. Thus, in what follows I draw attention to theoretical ideas that discuss the impact of global corporate values on the everyday life of football consumers.

Within the sociology of consumption, scholars frequently debate whether people consume with free will (sometimes referred to as agency) or as a consequence of tuition or corporate manipulation, or perhaps a combination of all of the above. So, while Theodor Adorno and Max Horkheimer (1972) describe hapless consumers, manipulated by producers, Stuart Hall (1980), Henry Jenkins (1992), Kathy Davis (1995) and others talk about the 'agentic' consumer. In terms of football, Steve Redhead (1997) provides examples of agentic consumers who tend to include fanzine producers, members of football fan organizations and more generally consumers who emphasize the importance of choice, control and power in their relationship with football clubs, advertisers and multinational corporations. This is a more voluntaristic approach than Bourdieu's, stressing the role of human agency (i.e. the power of the individual to bring about change). However, while Redhead and others are right to point out this development, it is important not to overstate the case for the agentic consumer. After all, the agency perspective downplays the power of producers and the relationship between individual choice and predictable market outcomes (Schor, 2007). In fact, it may be reasonable to suggest that agency (or the idea of agency, at least) is constructed by producers, rather than being deployed against them. In the example below, Umberto Eco (1986, p. 148) explains how branding developed in the 1970s has been used to sell dreams and lifestyles to consumers ever since:

> A firm produces polo shirts with an alligator logo. A generation begin to wear the polo shirts. Each consumer advertises via the alligator on his chest. A TV broadcast sees some young people wearing the alligator polo shirt. The young and the old buy the polo shirt because they have the young look.

So, while it is true that consumers have gained a form of power (the freedom to choose, an awareness of statutory rights, the ability to resist and to hold producers to account, etc.), they cannot reject consumption as a way of life, and, as such, it is reasonable to suggest that they are under the spell of commercial marketing strategists (Bauman, 2007; Edwards, 2014). On this point, Ann Pegoraro and colleagues (2010) make reference to the role of advertising on television and the internet in nurturing materialism and inventing consumer wants or even needs. For example, those who consume football via television are bombarded with advertisements, not only during the advertisement break but also on billboards, team shirts, advertisement hoardings and stands, not to mention in commentary from sports presenters who plug associate sponsors at every opportunity. Viewing via online streaming yields similar results, with the consumption of football broadcasts just one click away from a sponsor's website where purchases can be made.

Moreover, clubs send messages directly to fans in various other ways too: through matchday programmes, television and internet channels (e.g. MUTV, a channel dedicated to Manchester United FC), radio and television interviews, official and unofficial websites, newsletters, posters and any other means of promotion (Harris and Ogbonna, 2008, p. 388). The retro-fitting of football stadiums with wireless technologies is the latest technique being used to communicate with customers and to encourage match attendees to buy services during games (*Telegraph*, 2015). It is clear, then, that the business of football marketing is constantly evolving. In fact, such is the knowledge of marketing experts that they can actually encourage consumption even before a product has been brought to market. Here, by way of example, I am referring to the initiation of Japan's J-League in 1993. In this instance, even before a ball had been kicked, football teams and associated sponsors began to make money through aggressive marketing techniques. As a result, in its inaugural year the J-League made US$1.6 billion in sales, and the league's official sponsor Sony Creative Products opened 100 stores nationwide and sold over US$300 million dollars' worth of hats, jackets and other merchandise stamped with the J-League logo (Edwards, 2014, p. 437).

The success of J-League sponsor Sony is one instance of a wider issue that has implications for the way in which scholars might think about consumption within the sociology of football. To explain, it is likely that most of us are familiar with the term 'the football industry' – the inference being that there is a market in which products related to football can be traded. But while we might presume that football's market is its fans (or consumers), it might be worth pausing and reflecting for one moment. Think about the governing bodies of football's mega-events, Fifa or perhaps Uefa. What is it that they do? On reflection, it might be reasonable to suggest that they do not target fans directly (if at all), but rather that they make deals with global brands (Visa, adidas, Coca-Cola, Canon and so on) whose aim is to reach the global audience of football in order to consolidate or extend their consumer markets. In other words, football becomes the matchmaker for putting together supporters and advertisers. In fact, it wouldn't be a stretch to say that by entering into so many marketing arrangements, the football industry is now 'pimping' its fans to global corporations.

To explain the omnipresence of seemingly generic (but successful) marketing strategies, it is worth briefly drawing on the work of Alan Bryman (2004). As an example, he uses the template of Disney theme parks to demonstrate how a series of increasingly common marketing procedures are used (by every business throughout the world, not exclusively by Disney) to ensure the satisfaction of consumers, offering new strategies for selling in post-Fordist times (Horne, 2006, p. 38). Coining the word 'Disneyization', he discussed the importance of four components that encourage variety, choice and differentiation; in doing so, he insists that they provide the ingredients that encourage people to consume. Those four components are:

1.  *theming*: the creation of an experience with a distinct theme (such as a Mexican restaurant) or a brand and its expression;
2.  *hybrid consumption*: purposefully entangled forms of consumption associated with different institutional spheres;
3.  *emotional labour*: the fostering of emotion that satisfies the needs of consumers;
4.  *merchandizing*: the promotion of goods and services bearing copyright images and logos.

Each can be evidenced through football and each is briefly discussed below.

## Disneyization: theming and hybrid consumption

Theming and hybrid consumption are interlinked. The theme 'football' and its various permutations (the club, the cup competition, the league, etc.) is clear, but it is the presence of multiple forms of consumption (or hybrid consumption) that has transformed the experience for football consumers in late modern life. This is clearly expressed by Cornel Sandvoss (with particular reference to the Bayer Leverkusen football stadium) in the opening paragraphs of his 2003 book, *A Game of Two Halves: Football, Television and Globalization* (p. 1):

> In August 1998 I arrived at the BayArena, home of German first division side Bayer Leverkusen. The name of the ground had been changed at the beginning of the season to promote the team's sponsor and owner – the pharmaceutical multinational Bayer. I had bought a season ticket for the largest section of the redeveloped ground, namely 'Family Street' ... Fathers with their sons and daughters, mothers and their children slowly took up their seats and avidly followed the pre-entertainment on the newly installed giant video screens ... At half time, hordes of fans, often driven by their children, fought their way to a newly built onsite McDonalds restaurant.

As Bryman would conceive it, the themed 'Family Street' section and the multiple forms of consumption on display (in the example above) are thought to create an atmosphere conducive to consumption. Moreover, whether in Germany or anywhere else in the world, the refurbishment or relocation of football stadiums in or near city centres has become part of urban revitalization efforts. Public–private partnerships between cities and clubs help to position football stadiums as anchors or main attractions around which shops, restaurants, new transit hubs and entertainment districts can arise. The stadiums themselves have become sites of entertainment outside of providing seating to view a sports contest, with pubs, betting shops, food establishments, museums, club shops, ATM machines, pre-match entertainment, corporate experiences and much more all integrated into the matchday space. Moreover, it is also worth noting that on any regular day, football clubs maintain their status as service providers. They are known to offer for consumption stadium tours, consumer 'experience' packages to observe the day-to-day activities of the club and, more generally, facilities that can be booked for corporate events, birthdays or even weddings (Cook, 2007; Dixon, 2011).

Such options are now commonplace in many countries, though Ingar Mehus and Guy Osborn (2010) credit developments in England as the catalyst that began to alter the dynamics of world football. With specific reference to Norway, they insist that despite cultural differences (between Norway and England), football has become a product that is to be sold. Thus, there appears to be no limit to commercialization and hybrid forms of consumption entangled with football. Even art galleries are known to have become affiliated to football, particularly during international tournaments. For example, for Euro 96 in England, Manchester City Art Gallery opened *Offside! Contemporary Artists and Football*; the 2002 World Cup in Korea and Japan brought the *Football through Art* exhibition to the Chosun Ilbo Gallery; for the 2006 World Cup in Germany, Harald Szeemann (an international curator) prepared an exhibition on football and art entitled *Rundlederwelten* ('*Round Leather Worlds*'); and in 2010, the World Cup in South Africa inspired an exhibition named *Halakasha!* at the Standard Bank Gallery (Strozek, 2015, p. 1).

Moreover, while themed mega-events (such as World Cup tournaments) are the stimulus for forms of cultural consumption (such as art festivals), they also arouse major economic interest elsewhere. Writing in relation to South African and Brazilian societies, Barbara Schausteck de Almeida and colleagues (2015, p. 266) speak of the business opportunities that mega-events can provide. The World Cup, they suggest, is used to justify accelerated infrastructural investments and to offer valuable promotional opportunities in which Brazil, South Africa and other countries are showcased to global audiences, helping to attract tourism and outside investment.

## Disneyization: merchandizing and emotional labour

The latter two components of Disneyization, merchandizing and emotional labour, can be observed through the marketing and sales of merchandise and the emotional appropriation of these commodities. Take, for instance, the following quote from Lens fan Veronique:

> The scarf means everything. It is brandished during the *Lensoise,* the *Marseillaise* from Lens [i.e. the French national anthem adapted to Lens].

Believe me when I say that the one who doesn't have his scarf looks a bit silly hanging his arms [without it].

*(Veronique, Lens fan, quoted in Derbaix and Decrop, 2011 p. 277)*

Consumption (such as the purchasing of the scarf mentioned above) is sustained, it seems, through the perceived emotional congruence that exists between the fan, market products and the club. Consequently, corporate sponsors are able to use the emotional connection between the consumer and the football club to their advantage. As Hans Bauer and colleagues (2005) assert, familiarity with club sponsors tends to increase the likelihood that fans will purchase products and services associated with this sponsor. Moreover, it allows businesses to connect with millions of people around the world on a deep, emotional level and offers an opportunity to drive sales and make a lasting impression with the connected consumer through traditional routes or non-traditional means such as social media.

Consequently, companies that operate in different industries such as finance, gambling and betting, real estate, oil and gas, food and beverages, aviation and more besides are willing to sponsor football. With respect to the sponsorship of club shirts (or jerseys), Manchester United and General Motors agreed a deal to display Chevrolet on team shirts from the 2014–2015 season. The club will earn £51 million per year from this contract. FC Barcelona receives approximately £25 million per year from its association with the Qatar Foundation; Bayern Munich FC grosses £23.5 million per year from Deutsche Telekom, and AC Milan earns approximately £10 million annually through partnership with Emirates Airlines (Unlucan, 2015, p. 45).

Another advantage for businesses associated with football is that football fans, coaches and players are self-regulating consumers. By this, I mean that not only do they consume for themselves but they also use football-related gifts to reinforce friendships or to stimulate football consumption in a new generation of youths. So consumption is a source of solidarity and self-identity; how we spend our money and to what extent defines who we are and our membership of social groups. Grant McCracken (1986, p. 78) refers to the purchasing of gifts as a process of exchange rituals, where a gift is offered because it possesses meaningful properties (often bound by emotion) that the giver wishes to see transferred to the receiver. From bibs, cots and clothes, to wallpaper, posters and computer games, to match tickets, season tickets and away trips – fans punctuate all experiences with consumption. Thus, with a similar outcome to that described by Jean Baudrillard (1998) when he observes a system of obligatory consumption that ultimately fails to produce pleasure for the consumer, it seems that consumers of football are seduced by the creations of the market that cater for the supported team.

Speaking with reference to Spanish football club Real Madrid, Jesus Rodriguez-Pomeda and colleagues (2014, p. 4) bring to attention the deliberate attempts by the club to evoke emotion and pride in its fans. This manufactured process, they assert, plays on the knowledge that emotions bring communities together because it is those communities that support commercial markets. Indeed, even when fulfilling corporate social responsibility initiatives, football clubs (led by this logic) are focused on stimulating emotive tendencies in people. For instance, when investigating such initiatives in the German Bundesliga, Danyel Reiche (2014) draws attention to the social projects that focus on children. After all, positive association with various youth groups could ensure a lifelong commitment to the club as a consumer.

Of course, football clubs and commercial associates have known for a long time that football fans are not typical consumers. For instance, a report by the English Football Task Force (FTF), submitted to the Minister for Sport in 1999, states that 'football is not a normal customer business relationship, but an expression of loyalty to a football club … Fans of English clubs are not customers that will move to a different team if theirs is unsuccessful'. In a paper I co-authored with Jamie Cleland (2015, p. 547), this point was further emphasized by a football fan in the following way:

> It has got an emotional attachment, it's right in our souls, it's part of our identity, it's what we are … we are treated worse than consumers because the owner knows that we will never support anyone else.

Consequently, then, even when dissatisfied with the club or performances of the team, fans still have an overriding, compelling desire to consume based on an inelastic emotional commitment to the team. Furthermore, the purchasing of an item of merchandise is only the beginning of a utilitarian or emotional relationship with the commodified product. On appropriation, material goods (emblazoned with the club badge) become infused with meaning beyond their economic or use value. On this note, Christian Derbaix and Alain Decrop (2011) discuss instances in which French football fans travel to away matches and collect souvenirs, displaying them at home in a bespoke manner to 'make memories'. The authors also report instances in which an item (such as the scarf) was modified in order that its meaning was even more specific to an individual consumer. Such examples are illustrations of what Paul Willis (1990) has termed 'grounded aesthetics' in the sense that effective and innovative attachments are made to material goods. As he explains, capitalist culture has unwittingly provided the tools for further symbolic expression given that commodities have rapidly became a symbolic aspect of everyday life. Thus, when appropriated in creative ways, the emotional connection to commodities is accentuated and this further intensifies the cyclical relationship between emotion and sustained material consumption.

## Conclusion

Throughout this chapter, I have argued that consumption is more than economic exchange; it is a way of thinking or being that emerges within people as a consequence of subcultural immersion. The development of the consumer mindset has been evidenced via a chronological assessment of football and its relationship to consumption. This has revealed that, following the foundation of the FA in 1863, a nascent consumer market for football began to emerge. Workforce legislation (including the Saturday half-holiday), higher earnings, communities in search of identity, ticket sales and the development of football grounds, the legalization of professionalism, the expansion of the railways, the reporting of football in the popular press, connections with alcohol and gambling, the minimal equipment required to play the game, and merchandising to symbolize support and identity have all been highlighted as factors that have gradually combined to provide the conditions for football's consumer market to grow.

While football consumption has always been present, it was not until the 1980s that the widespread adoption of neo-liberal political philosophy began to evoke a more serious, long-term strategy for football as a business and industry. Consequently, football clubs have attracted sponsorship and lucrative television deals and initiated marketing, sales and customer service departments to find new and innovative ways to sell merchandise and experiences to the consumer. This trend has continued to advance in late modern life and theoretical perspectives are split about whether the advance of consumer culture is a good or a bad thing. On the one hand, consumption gives us the platform from which to communicate things about ourselves. We can consume to emulate a group that we would like to belong to; to affirm our identity as part of a group or as an individual; and to uphold distinction between 'us' and 'them'. On the other hand, we can be manipulated to consume. That is to say, we can be seduced into wanting the latest football strip, renewing season tickets and buying merchandise and other experiences when we don't really need any of it. After all, in football, the emotional connection to the game, the team and the club and the perceived loyalty to like-minded people past and present stimulate an unquenchable desire for continued consumption.

## Research in Action

'Examining the relationship between brand emotion and brand extension among supporters of professional football clubs' by Ibrahim Abosag, Stuart Roper and Daniel Hind (2010)

### What were the goals of the research?

This project set out to examine the relationship between supporters' emotional attachment to what they perceive as club tradition and their strength of support for brand extension in Norwegian football. Brand extension, in this instance, refers to the strategies that football clubs use to look for new sources of revenue, often through the introduction of new products or services.

## Why was the research relevant?

The research was relevant as it tested dominant arguments of consumption outside of the 'big five' most commonly researched countries (England, France, Germany, Italy and Spain), examining perceptions of branding in a smaller European market, Norway.

## What methods were used?

A mixed-methods approach was used (i.e. quantitative as well as qualitative methods), with the latter informing the former. The sample consisted of employees and fans of professional clubs in the Norwegian domestic league, otherwise known as the Tippeligaen. Two clubs were chosen (as recommended by Miles and Huberman (1994, p. 28)) to reflect two distinct cases – that is, two clubs with different on-field sporting success, geographical location, market size, competitive pressures, business format and structure. The two clubs were:

1.  Tromso Idrettslag, established in 1920 and located in the eighth largest city in Norway, Tromso; and
2.  Valerenga Idrettsforening, established in 1913 and located in the capital city of Norway, Oslo.

Prior to the development of the quantitative element, the authors conducted semi-structured interviews with managers, directors of marketing and directors of media relations at both clubs (N=3 per club). Those interviews were focused on experiences and perceptions of the club, its values, its relevance and the role of branding and brand management. They lasted between 55 and 80 minutes and were audio recorded and then later transcribed.

Following this, the research team then interviewed lower-level employees (N=6 per club), players (N=3 per club) and fans (N=6 per club), totalling 36 interviews for this project. Again, interviews were semi-structured and the topics remained the same, but this time the duration was shorter (between 10 and 30 minutes). A key objective at this stage (Stage 1) was to investigate whether or not participants perceived the club as a commercial brand and the extent to which branding had been recognized and accepted by supporters.

Content analysis was then performed on the interview transcripts using data software Nvivo (a computer system that systematically codes or organizes qualitative data, based on key words, phrases or passages). The outcome of the content analysis was then used to inform Stage 2 of the research strategy, the quantitative component.

Having been designed and then pre-tested on a small sample (N=8) to check validity, a questionnaire consisting of 19 statements (based on the detailed information gleaned at Stage 2 and measured on a five-point Likert scale) was used to focus on fans' attitudes towards the supported club as a commercial brand. The questionnaire was displayed and advertised by both of the professional football clubs, each providing a direct link from their websites. As a secondary technique, the web link for the questionnaire was emailed to a group of fans known to the authors and they were encouraged to forward this link to other fans. This technique is known as 'snowballing'. Approximately 900 questionnaires were returned.

### What were the main arguments?

Both quantitative and qualitative data complemented each other and conversely the findings stood in contrast to those of some of the other literature within the field. For instance:

- Chadwick and Beech (2007) and Chadwick and Holt (2006) warned that supporters do not like to think of their club being sullied by commercialism and that many are appalled by the thought of their club being reduced to a brand, due in part to the tight fit between the football club and individuals' identities. However, the results from this Norwegian sample demonstrated that the participants were prepared to accept their position as consumers given that they now understood and accepted the financial challenges faced by football clubs (to stay competitive) and recognized their social responsibility as supporters to consume for the sake of the club.
- The authors revealed that if fans are convinced that increased consumption and extended commercial strategies from the club lead to increased on-field success, this reinforces and actively encourages continued consumption.
- The authors pointed out that history and heritage is still important to fans (and the club can use its heritage and history to boost sales) but this seems to be outweighed by their concern for future success. After all, heritage and history are only kept alive as long as the club survives. Consequently, supporters appear to accept that greater 'professionalism' and commercialism is needed to extend and export the brand into Europe and beyond.

### And the conclusions or key findings?

This study challenged the received wisdom that supporters of football clubs are likely to disapprove of or reject the thought of their favourite club as a brand. In this instance, quite the opposite was found; that is to say, supporters were supportive of brand extension and, moreover, they were proud of the brand that they had helped to create. However, the authors did offer a word of caution: they argued that although most fans appear to support brand extension, it must be carefully designed by the club to ensure that the right blend is achieved between respect for tradition and heritage (for current consumers) and modifications to brand image that will help to attract new supporters without ostracizing others. Overall, though, they concluded that smaller clubs can apply brand-building strategies without sacrificing proximity to their existing supporters.

## *What were the strengths of the research?*

The methods of the work, while relatively uncommon, were a strength of this study. To explain, both quantitative and qualitative approaches have strengths and weaknesses, and yet a combination of methodologies (as used in this study) can focus on the strengths of both broad approaches. In this instance, the qualitative element was used to enable the researchers to develop an overall picture of the subject under investigation by guiding the initial phases of the research. This was important because it allowed the issues that were central to those people directly implicated (in this instance, employees and fans of football clubs) to be raised in the second phase without the need for presumption on behalf of the researcher. Consequently, it allowed for unexpected developments to present themselves, helping to create an authentic representation of the population under investigation.

However, while findings gleaned from qualitative research (Stage 1) had much value in unveiling in-depth explanation of the subject under study, the authors realized that those explanations were limited to the confines of a small sample. Consequently, at Stage 2, the authors created a survey instrument to quantify the pervasiveness of Stage 1 findings across a larger sample. In other words, quantitative research was used to confirm or disconfirm any apparently significant trends that emerged from the qualitative analysis.

## *Were there any weaknesses?*

The work offered a good assessment of the perceptions of brand extension from the perspective of a group of Norwegian fans and club employees. As such, it was extremely valuable, especially because its findings challenged existing trends. The parameters of the research could have been extended, however, to include a fuller engagement with social theory in order to help explain more fully the trends identified and the cross-cultural differences evident between this study and the those relating to Europe's 'big five' leagues.

The theoretical and empirical argument could also have been extended to ask and attempt to answer some more fundamental questions, such as:

- What exactly is 'brand emotion'?
- Are consumers actually emotionally engaged by commodities?
- If so, do they consume because of marketing techniques, or simply because products are available to buy?
- If marketing procedures are a crucial factor, then how do advertisers hook us in this way?
- If we consume irrespective of marketing techniques, why? Moreover, are companies wasting their money on marketing?

# 11

# TRANSGRESSION

*Andy Ruddock*

---

**Chapter highlights**

- 'Transgression' refers to the violation of a boundary established by law, rule or custom.
- The sports media play a crucial role in establishing the boundaries.
- Stories about footballers who break rules symbolize how media industries define important affairs in public culture.
- 'Cultural indicators' is a term coined by media scholar George Gerbner, who argued that since the 1950s, media audiences have been exposed to an unbroken flow of stories about male transgression, often in the form of violence, mostly directed at women.
- Gerbner's ideas help to explain why the transgressions of some players attract so much media and public attention.

---

## Introduction

Eamonn Carrabine *et al.* (2014, p. 1061) define transgression as '[t]he act of overstepping boundaries or limits established by rules, laws, principles, custom, convention or tradition'. As this definition indicates, the line between right and wrong is often difficult to see, because it is drawn by explicit and implicit 'rules'. As public figures, footballers often get caught in the confusion that results. For example, when England international Paul Gascoigne infamously told a whole country (Norway) to 'fuck off' on television, he crossed one set of lines (broadcast embargoes on swearing, the popular expectation that footballers should adopt ambassadorial roles, respect for supporters), while adhering to other standards (the informal rules of 'banter'). However you interpret this incident, it speaks to a larger truth: footballers who are seen to break the rules in the media become part of the process that determines how we make rules in the first place.

Footballing transgressions that become part of a social conversation about right and wrong often focus on matters of gender and violence. Gascoigne's 'clown prince' persona was tarnished by reports of spousal abuse. In 2015, three Leicester City players were sacked following the circulation of a video clip showing the men racially abusing, insulting and degrading Thai sex workers. The incident dramatized the relationship between 'formal' and 'informal' rules – from the explicit, legal issue of racial abuse to the implicit racism and sexism of sex tourism.

A vivid example of how media stories about footballers, gender and violence mobilize debates about transgression came in 2014, when Welsh professional footballer Ched Evans was released from prison on probation, having served half of a five-year rape sentence. Evans sought to resume his career first with Sheffield United and then with Oldham Athletic, both of whom were playing in the English League One. Both proposed moves imploded after protests from fans, club sponsors and public figures (BBC News, 2015a). Even politicians weighed in. The leader of the UK Labour Party, Ed Miliband, gave the following advice:

> I think that it's right Oldham are thinking again about whether Ched Evans should be hired by them because you are a role model, he's been convicted of a very serious crime. Personally, if I was in their shoes, he hasn't shown remorse and I wouldn't take him on.
>
> *(BBC News, 2015b)*

Miliband's intervention made Evans a character in a media event that powerfully dramatized grave questions about how society approaches justice, victim support and rehabilitation. As such, Evans embodied a defining feature of modern social life: the capacity of media industries to *create* social reality by *organizing* how we think about real social problems. Evans quickly discovered that it was impossible to separate his career from his existence as a symbol of transgression. He had become what media scholar George Gerbner (1969a) called a 'cultural indicator' – a sign of the changing symbolic environment and an emblem of players who transgress public conceptions about what is right and what is wrong. This happened independently of Evans' wishes.

Gerbner believed that media industries bombarded audiences with a staple menu of stories and characters that, together, affected how those audiences perceived social reality. The topic of male violence was a powerful exemplar of this process in action (Gerbner *et al.*, 1980). Understanding why male violence was such a persistent feature of media content promised to reveal much about how media became central players in drawing the boundaries of transgression. Through painstaking content analysis of years of prime-time television, Gerbner showed that television told stories in which certain kinds of men got away with violence time and time again. The key here was to understand that these stories were not really about violence per se, but about who had the power to transgress and who did not. The idea that Evans' return to the professional ranks, and television screens, would tell a similar story – as a man who might enjoy the glamour of professional sport despite having been convicted of a heinous crime – indicates that he represented a series of concerns about the impact of media that have been in play for decades.

This chapter outlines how Gerbner's ideas help to explain the social relevance of football and male football stars as media phenomena that map the boundaries of transgression. It also demonstrates the value of media theory in explaining why football is a key cultural player in the sociological experience of transgression. Evans is a relevant case study as a representation of how media have infiltrated social, legal and economic practices. Seeing his story through the lens of Gerbner's ideas allows the following insight: stories of player transgression inherit a history of male representation that charts the rise of media industries as primary definers of right and wrong.

The argument evolves through the following stages. First, it explores how Evans became a cultural indicator of the integration of media and everyday life. Next, the chapter considers how Gerbner's work on media and public culture contextualizes Evans within a history, where violence directed at women has consistently symbolized the political effects of living in media-saturated societies. Third, the case is made that Gerbner's ideas represent a useful strategy in connecting football and media theory. This is because sociologists have always seen individual players as indices of changes in British life – a trend encouraged by media sport. Finally, the chapter provides a case study in how ideas about the mediation of masculine transgression inform research on everyday supporter practices. This connects the explicit transgression of star players with the implicit policing of boundaries between right and wrong that occur in everyday life.

## Living in a media world

The outcry following Evans' efforts to return to professional football reflected not just the severity of his crime but also the growing influence of the media as primary definers of reality. Evans' actions became the focus of public concern because everyone involved in the story was newsworthy; even the woman, who was entitled to the anonymity legally afforded rape victims, was outed on social media (Wright, 2015). The speed with which Evans' release was transformed into a public drama demonstrated how media ubiquity creates management challenges for sport and society – for football clubs, the businesses that support them, and even the law.

Evans' offence dramatized a broader historical change, where an expanding media sphere intruded on the authority of institutions that have traditionally policed the line between the acceptable and the transgressive. Three days after the player's guilty verdict was delivered in 2012, ex-barrister Amanda Bancroft described how the intense social media reaction to the judgement had created a legal cacophony that threatened to drown out the most important truth to which the story spoke: the existence of a pervasive rape culture that made it difficult for the victims of sexual violence to win justice. Social media platform Twitter rapidly became a battleground between users who opposed the verdict and others who supported it. Some of the former reverted to familiar tactics of victim blaming, and some even named the alleged plaintiff. Others pointed out that such tweets were illegal, as rape survivors are entitled to anonymity. This raised a series of questions about the legality of tweeting. Bancroft pointed out that naming a victim 'in a written publication available to the public' was clearly illegal and that the author was subject to prosecution (Bancroft, 2012). She observed that the Evans story focused too much on changing modes of media communication and too little on how to manage violence against women. If basic sociological definitions of transgression emphasize the inherent confusion caused by the mix of formal and informal standards, the proliferation of media communication has become a key amplifier of this eternal cultural truth.

Bancroft's observations spoke to a changing understanding of media influence that scholars were developing at around the same time. Bancroft complained that actors in the Evans case spent too much time managing media and too little discussing how to act against rape culture. This idea – that organizations today have to think not only about acting but also about explaining their actions in the media – is the touchstone of a relatively new concept called 'mediatization'. This concept helps to explain how stories about the transgressions of footballers play an important cultural role in drawing the line between right and wrong.

Mediatization explains how the ordinary cultural work that people and organizations have always done must now adapt to the requirements of media industries (Hepp, 2013; Hjarvard, 2013). The thinking behind the concept is as follows. Humans have always created reality through communication. Societies function when they have rules and values that are widely understood, and those values have always been created and shared through symbols and stories – entities that teach us how the world works. Mobile, ubiquitous devices have magnified the capacity of media businesses to monopolize this process. Mobility has created a media omnipresence, such that it is difficult to find corners of the social world in which we cannot access media. If there was a time when media use generally belonged to defined spaces – the living room, the bedroom, the cinema – that time has long gone (Hjarvard, 2013). This is all common sense. What isn't so obvious is how these developments amplify the powers of media businesses when it comes to defining moral values.

The Evans story was relevant to this issue because it dramatized ubiquitous, media-shaped but apparently chaotic social occasions. Supporter protests had stopped clubs from signing players before (Ruddock, 2005). Also, many athletes had used digital resources to manufacture their own public image before Evans. Indeed, such actions are an obligatory feature of sporting careers (Hutchins and Rowe, 2012). But what was new in the Evans case was an intensification of the 'media practices' that have become a familiar part of sport. It's this amplification that lies at the heart of the concept of mediatization, which in turn explains how the media furore around the player actively created the boundaries of transgression.

All sides in the dispute used the media to get their point across as Evans attempted his comeback. Oldham conceded defeat in their efforts to sign him in the face of a 30,000-strong online fan protest poll, threats and sponsor concerns. In retaliation, Evans established a website from which he continued to protest his innocence and condemn the 'mob rule' blocking his rehabilitation. The only stable element in the tragic tale was the fact that it reflected how battle lines over right and wrong ran through efforts that courted popular consent through media. No one controlled the controversy – not the clubs who wanted to sign him, nor the club sponsors who worried what association with Evans would do to their businesses, nor the protestors who wanted a more informed public discussion about rape culture. The only consensus apparent was that this would be a media debate, choreographed by the commercial platforms that made participation possible. No one would win without 'doing' media. This is the essence of media power, as it is understood in the concept of mediatization – the idea that social life requires us to engage with the media even when we want to do something else.

This indeed created a new reality. Ched Evans was not the first footballer to attempt a comeback after being imprisoned for a serious crime; the protestors were not the first people to question whether players should be allowed to return to their profession after such offences, given that 'professional football player' is a job that carries with it unusual amounts of cash and kudos. But the difference here was that the actors in the drama were confronted with new questions. In particular, both Twitter users and Evans faced the possibility that their media actions were transgressive, because they were not just people voicing opinions but authors providing media content for the public on live legal issues. And the courts had to decide what to do about that.

This is why the Evans case was a story about violence that dramatized the complexities of living in a world in which people regularly 'live' the realities of right and wrong through the media. I have described this as intensification. The implication is that the Evans case condensed a set of media processes that were already in train. Developing that thought, it could be argued that the story showed how a familiar tale took on a new social relevance when it was told through a new 'message system'. The concept here is that this story about violence told us something about the general features of storytelling, as they play out in media sport. To understand where this idea comes from, there's no better place to start than with George Gerbner.

## Understanding Gerbner

Ched Evans became infamous partly because supporters, clubs and businesses all actively participated in determining the nature of his transgression, under conditions in which media content and social thought blended. Whatever their motivations and opinions, their actions combined to challenge the integrity of the legal system – an especially clear example of how the media actively make social reality. But how did we get here? In asking this question, it's worth noting that the topic of mediated male violence has been used to address the deepening global influence of media industries over the rules of social life before, and that brings us back to George Gerbner.

Understanding the impact of *this* tale of transgression means asking how systems of communication work. Media content expresses the arrangement of the technologies and organizations that provide that content. You have probably heard the phrase 'The medium is the message', credited to the Canadian media theorist Marshall McLuhan. McLuhan is the best known of a group of twentieth-century scholars (including economist Harold Lasswell, cultural historian James Carey and political economist Dallas Smyth) who argued that media content reflected the economic and political organization of media industries. Gerbner followed this line of thought to explain how media violence enacted by male characters provided a case study in how media industries shaped public values. Consequently, his ideas explain how Evans' notoriety expressed the general role that media play in creating moral realities.

Gerbner argued that media violence reflected fundamental principles in the nature of media power, and his thoughts on this reflected what some feared would happen if Evans resumed his playing career. Sky television presenter Charlie Webster threatened to resign her position as a patron for Sheffield United's Community Foundation if Evans returned to the club. She explained her reasons to *Telegraph* journalist Radhika Sanghani (Sanghani, 2014):

> I just think it's a really bad message to send out to our community and our next generation… that someone can be convicted of rape unanimously, and walk out of prison and walk straight into the same job. He's in a high profile job and with that celebrity and his position comes responsibility. It's basically sending a message that you do what you want really.

This was precisely the media violence problem Gerbner had identified 40 years before. After looking at decades of prime-time US television, Gerbner believed that the 'small screen' did indeed send its audiences the message that some men could do as they pleased, while women suffered the consequences (Gerbner, 1994). Webster worried that the spectacle of the Twitter abuse directed at her and Evans' victim would discourage other women from reporting cases of sexual violence. This is exactly the 'effect' that Gerbner described when looking at the political attitudes of people who consumed high levels of media violence; such people were more likely than light viewers to think that the world was a scary place that they could do little to affect (Gerbner, 1994). Comparing Gerbner's views with those of some of the characters in the Evans story, then, it seems that the rise of ubiquitous media only added to the power that the media enjoyed in defining social rules. To deepen our understanding of how this could be, it's necessary to look further at Gerbner's understanding of media power.

## Gender and violence

Gerbner's career as a media scholar started with an analysis of why post-war American culture seemed to take pleasure in terrorizing women. This question served a larger project on how the media enculturated audiences into the social arrangements of a new consumer society (Gerbner, 1960). In this regard, his research on violence and gender was intended to address how media entertainment established the rules of consumer society, and stories about people who transgressed legal or cultural boundaries became integral to this mission.

For example, Gerbner started his work by examining 'confession' magazines popular with female audiences in the 1950s. These titles featured lurid stories about ordinary women who broke social taboos. Each told of women who were attacked, frightened and shamed when they dared to step beyond the confines of marriage and domesticity. Gerbner associated the terrorization of women with the organization of media industries and consumer markets. He argued that the terror being directed at women had the ideological effect of encouraging them to stick to roles as homemakers and consumers, thereby enforcing an informal transgression boundary. Tales of the dangers that lurked when women did things like going on holiday on their own 'helped' them to understand what was appropriate in their new moral universe (Gerbner, 1958). This study also claimed that social arguments about moral boundaries were affected by the relationship between the media and consumer culture.

That trend continued with the advent of television. In the 1960s, the US government established a task force to examine the role of television in social violence. American society at that time seemed characterized by collective acts of transgression, particularly acts of mass civil disobedience. As part of this investigation, Gerbner was paid to investigate exactly how much violence American audiences were exposed to, and the extent to which this violence encouraged transgression (Gerbner, 1994; Morgan, 2012). Gerbner used this as an opportunity to test his thesis that television represented a profound change in how society drew moral boundaries. Eventually this idea was also expressed with reference to the media fate of women as victims of media violence.

Gerbner believed that society lived through storytelling; our values and place in the world have always been communicated to us in stories. For centuries, these stories came from churches, schools and families. But since the advent of television, more and more of the tales that we consume have come from media organizations. This represented a major change in the processes of socialization. Seen this way, it's pretty clear that Gerbner was addressing the process of 'mediatization' long before the phrase became common within scholarly parlance. Gerbner wanted to know what this change implied for creativity, diversity and participation. Could industrialized, centralized storytelling sustain democracy (Gerbner, 1960)? With this question in mind, Gerbner turned his attention to the matter of violence, and the onscreen violence directed at women became a key part of the answers he provided. The important thing about this research was that it used the theme of violence to analyze the broader role of media in making the rules of life.

Working with colleagues from the University of Pennsylvania, Gerbner developed methods for 'measuring' the amount of violence on television and then looked at how consuming this violence affected the worldview of 'heavy' viewers. Starting in 1967, his team began compiling annual 'violence profiles' – content analyses that literally counted the incidents of violence contained in a weekly sample of prime-time US broadcasts. By 1994, the team had coded 3,000 shows, containing over 39,000 characters (Gerbner, 1994).

Two major insights emerged. Violence was indeed a major, structural feature of television content. But more intriguingly, violence seemed to tell a particular story about gender. The characters most likely to get away with violence were white middle-class men. On the other hand, Gerbner noted that '[w]omen generally pay a higher price in victimization for their violent actions than men do, and the price rises as they age. Older men suffer 182 victims for 100 perpetrators; older women suffer 215 (Gerbner, 1995, p. 159). In other words, television told stories in which men could get away with breaking rules, but women couldn't.

But what did viewers make of this? To answer this question, Gerbner and his colleagues used surveys that compared television consumption and political attitudes. The outcome of this research was the development of what they termed the 'Mean World Syndrome', meaning that viewers (and, presumably, all other kinds of consumers) integrate and absorb a sense of danger, mistrust and meanness in the world and accept everyday violence as normal (Media Education Foundation, 2010). Heavy television viewers were significantly more likely to overestimate their chances of being a victim of violent crime and be suspicious of other people (Gerbner et al., 1980). But while this was true across the board, it was especially true for women: 'Viewers who see members of their own group have a higher calculus of risk than those of other groups, develop a greater sense of apprehension, mistrust, and alienation' (Gerbner, 1994, p. 160).

Thirty years of data showed the pattern noted in confession magazines was writ large across television. Magazines played on the anxieties of a new, relatively affluent female audience, and television maintained the global view that the world was an especially dangerous place for women. This situation was sustained by relations of production and distribution. Stories in which men broke rules as they pleased suited global ambitions. Production decisions were made to suit global markets, and especially the need to fill screen time with syndicated material. Stories driven by male violence travelled well in a global market that discouraged complex, culturally specific forms of storytelling.

Gerbner's bottom line was that the spectacle of media violence against women was a symbol of global media's lack of investment in sustaining public culture. It was nothing less that a calamitous icon of the failure of post-war democracy. The intimidation directed at women by men through media had, for half a century, represented how centrally-organized storytelling produced powerful public visions of an entrenched cultural pecking order whereby men prevailed over women, time and time again. This was expressed in repeated stories in which men broke rules without consequence, while women suffered for the transgressions of others. This was the most profound moral boundary that the media made.

Evans' story fit this narrative. Charlie Webster's concern over the potential effects of the Evans affair had the weight of history behind it. So this establishes a second question for interrogation: what did the Evans case reveal about the realities of political debate about sexual violence in digital cultures, as a vivid example of the role that media play in defining the border between right and wrong?

## Media and change

So far, this chapter has established two pessimistic questions that a Gerbnerian perspective asks of the Evans case. For all of the changed conditions brought about by social media and the like, here was just another example of a depressing tendency whereby the media teach lessons about social boundaries through stories about the suffering of women. However, Gerbner did not have a fatalistic view of media industries, and believed that understanding how message systems worked was a vital first step in demanding change.

He quickly dismissed the idea that mass culture simply described a situation in which a small number of powerful people transmitted messages to the masses. Industrialized storytelling involved a fine division of labour where thousands could be involved in the production and delivery of media content, having the potential to affect the developing message at each step of the way (Gerbner, 1958, 1960). Consequently, although structures made stories, alternative social arrangements built around the media made significant differences. Gerbner was interested in comparative analysis of different media systems. Looking at the portrayal of heroes in US, Western European and Eastern European films, Gerbner (1969b) found that although violence was globally prevalent, the *kinds* of violence that viewers saw varied (as the argument in Chapter 2 explains). Succinctly, in the US and Western Europe, when violence happened, it was presented as a matter of individual vice; Eastern European films were more likely to present the social causes of violence. So, although the prevalence of male heroes and violence was a cinematic *lingua franca*, the meanings of the stories changed from culture to culture. The lesson was that it was possible to house media industries in different social structures that made it easier to express multiple points of view with the same narrative elements. Regarding media violence, what this meant was that although violent men had featured in public stories for as long as public stories had existed, they did not all play the same role, to the same end. This establishes a third question to apply to the Evans case: how was this *not* just another story about women suffering at the hands of men? Was there anything about the fact that this happened within the sphere of media sport that made it different?

Gerbner wanted the data from his violence profiles to empower audiences and media professionals to maximize creativity and cultural participation by challenging dominant stories about right and wrong. The commonality of stories in which men were violent and women suffered represented an inability to provide a different set of public ideas about what women could be. One way to change this was to present the Screen Actors' Guild with the data to prove how limited the roles available to women actors were (Gerbner, 1995). Another was to encourage audience activism through the creation of the 'Cultural Environment Movement' (CEM). Towards the end of his life, Gerbner was more interested in media audiences than media industries. He tried to organize a CEM that would serve as a hub of activism for anyone who wished to see more diversity in popular culture (Gerbner, 1994). This was the least successful aspect of Gerbner's career (Morgan, 2012). However, there are reasons to think that this is because the CEM concept was ahead of its time, and that football fans now habitually use digital media to perform the sort of activism that he had envisaged. So the final question raised from a Gerbnerian perspective is this: did aspects of the Evans story show how the message systems around football have changed in ways that allow for more participation from a CEM that has developed around media sport? In other words, does today's media sphere create a space in which football fans can play a more active role in determining the bounds of transgression?

## Football players and football fans as cultural indicators and cultural activists

Gerbner's basic idea was that media stories about the violent abuse of women have long represented the idea that the industrialization of message systems affect the public stories that we consume, and, in the end, the way that we perceive social reality, especially around the boundaries of acceptable behaviour. However, these same 'lessons' – that it's a man's world in which life is scary for women – actually express different aspects of a message systems approach. In the confession magazine trade, it reflected the need to address female consumers in a way that was acceptable to consumer society. When it came to television, male violence was more about the growing importance of international syndication deals. In football, the Evans case could be taken as an index of how media industries and consumer logic had become a natural part of the lives of players and fans.

There are substantial reasons to believe that 'being' a player and 'being' a fan have both been substantially affected by the mediatization of football; here, the idea is that you have to 'do' media to be one or the other. This mediatization has complemented the synthesis between traditional fan practices and the needs of consumer culture. Everyday talk about football is commonplace and can take on a political character when subjects like the Evans case occupy public attention. Women, violence and the media are familiar themes; when they are incorporated into a football story, they are charged with new relevance and precipitate discussions not only about the changing status of footballers and how the media have, in large part, instigated those changes, but also about changes in the way in which we perceive women and violence.

The ideas that players are cultural indicators of changing social boundaries, and that the controversies surrounding the game are the progeny of message systems, is already recognized in existing work on the sociology of football and media sport. It's a general precept in the humanities that public figures should always be understood as the product of historical, social and cultural circumstances (Carr, 1963), and this is certainly an idea that football scholars have embraced. Sociologically speaking, Charles Critcher (1979) saw the English game's early 'superstars' of the 1960s and 1970s as symbols of a more general aspiration towards class mobility – representatives of the idea that the proper thing to do for working-class lads was to get a job that would pay for a nice suburban house. From a more media-centred point of view, by the 1990s Ellis Cashmore (1999) was defining David Beckham as a symbol of the synthesis between football, global entertainment and consumer culture. Cashmore's analysis of Beckham presaged work on the integration of sport and the media. David Rowe (2004) described the emergence of a 'media sport cultural complex', in which football was the vanguard of global media markets – the 'content key' that would unlock the vast commercial potential of global media audiences. In *Sport Beyond Television*, Brett Hutchins and David Rowe (2012) described how digital technologies made the image rights of professional athletes a primary economic consideration in the development of media sport. Beckham may have remained an atypical figure as the undisputed master of football celebrity, but the idea that control over image rights was a central bargaining chip in contract negotiations was commonplace. In their analysis of how this change had come about, the authors returned once again to violence and transgression.

Hutchins and Rowe noted that Joey Barton, an English player who had been disciplined and convicted for numerous acts of violence on and off the pitch, was paid £13,000 a week for image rights while playing for Newcastle United in the Premier League. This was notable for linking media sport to Gerbner's history of the media, violence, gender and transgression. Succinctly, in terms of commercial appeal and celebrity power, Barton's on- and off-field transgressions had done nothing to diminish his appeal; indeed, the reverse might have been true. Here was another example of how one transgression – the proclivity to violence – buttressed another cultural border: the idea that it's a man's world. Certainly, this was the 'lesson' of digital sport, according to Hutchins and Rowe. While digital media created the capacity to make a panoply of sports and athletes available to the public, in reality the new media environment had merely extended the dominance of traditional male sports. The ideas that football stars express social relations, that their public images are significant commodities in media-dependent sport economies and that these developments also express the longevity of patriarchy all strengthen the argument that Ched Evans stood for something other than himself, and part of this had something to do with the processing of his story through the media.

This makes sense from the perspective of fan experiences. Satellite television and the internet clearly changed how football is consumed (Gibbons and Dixon, 2010), but it's worth remembering that the emphasis on football as a consumer experience was, at one time, welcomed as a solution to problems that the game faced in becoming an inclusive experience. In the wake of the Hillsborough disaster, the reconstruction of stadiums as leisure sites recast football fans as people with rights, not hooligans who needed to be controlled (Taylor, 1990). This change sat neatly alongside the hope that the new stadiums would also be more welcoming places for female, black and Asian supporters (Nash, 2000). In combination, the redevelopment of football's physical and media infrastructure established new lines of 'conflict' in battles over what football represented, in terms of its cultural politics.

Gender became one of the telling battles in this fight. On the one hand, the new exposure of the game as a major source of media entertainment – something that caught the attention of more than just supporters – established football as one of the spheres in which societies thought about what sexism meant in everyday life. For example, when Sky Sports presenters Richard Keys and Andy Gray were captured on camera deriding a female match official because she was a woman, sexually harassing a female colleague and inquiring whether pundit and former player Jamie Redknapp had 'smashed' a female celebrity (a quote from Keys), the public furore led to the end of their long careers as two of the most recognized faces in televised football (Ruddock, 2012). But their professional transgression didn't altogether end their media careers. Virtual outcasts for a short while, Gray and Keys revived their media careers with a show on the British radio station talkSPORT and regular appearances on the Qatari satellite television network Al Jazeera's beIN Sports channel (Kelner, 2011). In this sense, they represented the way in which changing media landscapes supported a new sexism where women could be insulted or ignored with vigour.

When it comes to fans, scholars have also noted how the internet has created safe havens for unreconstructed sexism. Catherine Palmer (2009), for example, has noted that where aggressive displays of footballing masculinity used to be once-a-week affairs, acted out within stadiums for a couple of hours, internet communities let men indulge in the same pleasures as they please. The work of Rowe, Ruddock and Hutchins on the gratifications of online fandom found that the enjoyment of indulging in unreconstructed gendered abuse was a major factor. One online football fan put it like this: 'We swear a lot, we make jokes about people's mums, we particularly say the C word … it's cathartic'. As Jamie Cleland's (2014) work on online fans and racism has shown, the internet has aggravated conflict around sport by making people more willing to voice bigoted opinions – because it is so easy to do so – but at the same time has multiplied the opportunities to confront these anti-social attitudes.

Taking all of this together, it becomes possible to see how a situation in which so many people spoke out against the return of a not especially well-known player to the professional ranks made perfect sense in a sport message system in which individual players and ordinary fans are significantly involved in the production of media content – and with it, the communication processes through which we decide what is right and what is wrong. The argument is not that the story was caused by the media; it is that its unfolding as a public event can be explained with reference to how football's changing message system provided a variation on a theme, where the media's occupation of social imaginations has often been represented by stories of violence against women, and this in turn reflects the role that media sport plays in defining transgression. The return of a convicted rapist to the professional ranks would probably have been controversial in earlier decades, but the scale of the story reflected the transformation of football into a media narrative that affects all who produce and consume the game – and that even draws in audiences who are not especially interested in sport. The debate over how to manage the transgression of a law accessed a deeper history of how commercial media, and media sport, drive debates on the less formal rules of what it means to be women and men.

## Conclusion

When players transgress, and when their actions become the subject of intense public scrutiny, they dramatize the integration of football, media and politics. Media stories affect how we make sense of social life. Footballers are media characters, 'assembled' through media work. They 'function' in much the same way as any media figure – even fictional ones. This is especially true when they come to represent important social values, such as formal and informal distinctions between right and wrong. Sociological definitions of transgression underline that the boundaries of acceptability are fluid; they change with time, and are drawn through the intersection of formal and informal rules. When footballers become subjects of media scandals, they often find themselves living out these tensions.

To grasp these ideas, it helps to see football as a form of media entertainment. Gerbner's concept of cultural indicators provides a useful way of connecting sociological studies on footballers as symbols of social issues with the recognition that the game is a globally significant form of commercial popular culture. In this sense, football is part of a history of thought, focusing on how the media define acceptable behaviour. The media practices of players, clubs, sponsors and the public invest footballers with cultural values. (See Gerbner (1998) for an overview of his approach to the whole subject of cultural values.) Consequently, we can attribute the magnitude of media attention devoted to the transgression of players like Ched Evans to their status as media figures, or avatars of established conventions where media storytelling becomes integral to how society defines right from wrong. Ultimately, stories about football and transgression reflect the media's role in orchestrating public thought on moral values.

## Editors' postscript

After his attempt to appeal against his conviction was rejected, Evans took his case to the Criminal Cases Review Commission (CCRC), which investigates possible miscarriages of justice and, in October 2015, after a ten-month investigation, the CCRC decided to refer the case to the court of appeal. The chair of the CCRC declared: 'The decision of the commission is not a judgment on guilt or innocence in relation to Ched Evans, nor is it a judgment about the honesty or integrity of the victim or any other person involved in the case' (quoted in Grierson, 2015). Essentially, this meant that new information – not raised at trial – had been brought to light. The decision raised the possibility of the court of appeal quashing the conviction.

## Research in Action

**'"Born on Swan Street, next to the Yarra": social media and inventing commitment' by Andy Ruddock (2013)**

### What were the goals of the research?

The central goal of this research was to analyze the overlapping and intersecting issues of technological change, corporate power and cultural practices that shape the contemporary sports media landscape. Its inductive method was to use Melbourne Heart's fans' social media practices as a case study and draw general conclusions from particular instances.

### Why was the research relevant?

This research examined online communities to assess the role that fans played in launching a new Australian A-League Club, the Melbourne Heart (now Melbourne City FC). It is relevant to this chapter because the theme was how supporters who adopted masculine styles of fandom modelled on European traditions eagerly collaborated with an organization that embraced a gamut of commercial, media-based strategies to create a niche in a crowded Melburnian sports market.

This chapter has argued that society is fascinated with football and transgression due to the logic of commercial storytelling. Gerbner wasn't in the least bit interested in the question of whether media violence made audiences violent; he was far more concerned with the role that it played in a bigger media effect – persuading audiences that consumption is the only true path to happiness. The lesson from confession magazines was that the only thing that women could do about the world was to stay at home and buy things. Television violence encouraged similarly passive attitudes. But the bigger point was that commercial storytelling naturalized consumption as the path towards the satisfaction of personal and cultural needs.

Bearing all of this in mind, this study set out to show how Melbourne Heart supporters found ways to reconcile fan traditions with an organization that used a range of media and commercial appeals to create a meaningful presence in a city in which nine Australian Football League teams and an existing A-League franchise, the Melbourne Victory, could lay better claim to the notions of authenticity and tradition that are usually central to the fan experience. Included here was the question of how a particular form of behaviour that stood on the border of transgression – raucous fan practices – could complement the smooth operation of a commercial, media-directed enterprise.

## What methods were used?

### Online

The study analyzed posts to a thread on the Australian football fan site bigfooty.com, which asked who intended to support the club and why people were attracted to the new venture. The thread started in 2009, and the study analyzed the 591 posts that were made up until September 2011, when the Heart kicked off their second season. This sampling method was chosen because it offered a valid snapshot of a unique event: the conspicuous invention of a fan tradition where supporters were openly asked to reflect on their supporting choices – something rare in a world where fandom is often explained in terms of duties rather than choices (Brown *et al.*, 2008; Millward, 2011).

### Coding

Analytically, each post was coded using Nvivo 9 software, using categories developed to mirror key variables that sociological studies have identified as being significant factors in the formation of fan practices. In execution, the coding identified instances where supporters discussed the commercial operations of the club (the methods for deciding the name and the design of the strip by popular vote), but also larger topics such as the mediatization of sport. It paid particular attention to the way in which posters made sense of how the new club fit within supporting traditions. This method, then, was a simple descriptive one that aimed to map the parameters of the cultural logic that Melbourne's sporting audience applied to a novel experience. The purpose was to map the process through which a member of that audience would become a supporter, and what that transition meant within the topic of media and sport.

## What were the main arguments?

The main argument to emerge was that people who voiced the decision to support the Heart were perfectly comfortable with the commercial and media operations that were set in motion to create the new venture, and indeed appreciated the opportunities that commerce and media provided to fill a cultural space in their lives. Commercial considerations such as liking the kit ranked far ahead of more 'traditional' compulsions, such as antipathy towards the Melbourne Victory.

But perhaps more interesting was the way in which certain supporters, who valued the live experiences that the club would afford, also embraced the capacity of digital media to enhance matchday pleasures. The thread saw the announcement of the 'Yarraside', an active supporter group founded by an English ex-pat, who were committed to creating a vocal, rowdy stadium presence that (so the argument went) any real football team needs. For the Yarraside, online media tools were a vital way of achieving three goals:

1.  aligning the group with European fan models, based through online discussions and the sharing of media clips;
2.  negotiating a space within the ground by articulating its intentions to the club and other supporters; and
3.  and generally enjoying the online 'banter' that has become a part of the supporter experience.

In this sense, the data supported the arguments made by other authors that discussing the commercial and media-related aspects of the sport has become a major site of pleasure for football supporters (Crawford, 2004). Hence, where traditional accounts of supporters have emphasized themes of tradition and that the live fan experience is the only one that counts (Ruddock, 2005; Brown et al., 2008), Melbourne Heart supporters saw no contradiction in embracing commerce and the media to create an experience that felt authentic.

## And the conclusions or key findings?

The bottom line was this: traditional, masculine forms of 'rowdy' fandom, to which the commercialization and mediatization of football had been anathema, had learned to work with and thrive within the game as a convergent media message system. Behaviours that broke formal rules – such as standing in stadiums – were re-articulated as participatory methods for enhancing the appeal of the club as an authentic brand.

## What were the strengths of the research?

I have selected this study in order to spark a methodological debate that is relevant to researchers who want to say something interesting about football culture, but have limited research resources.

### *Were there any weaknesses?*

As Gibbons and Dixon (2010) point out, the study of online football communities has become increasingly possible, and much of this is down to the easy accessibility of data. This 'ease', however, disguises a range of research challenges. Aside from ethical concerns about whether a post to a message board should be considered as public or private (Lipinski, 2008; Markham and Buchanan, 2012; Neuhaus and Webmoor, 2012), there's the added problem of whether pithy posts say anything about the complexity of fan lives that blend the online and offline worlds. 'Snapshots' like those offered in the Melbourne Heart study don't say very much about what being a fan is like or how this existence affects cultural politics (Gibbons and Dixon, 2010).

However, the degree to which this criticism is itself valid depends on the nature of the research question. Additionally, there are ontological issues to consider. Take the idea that it's better to combine online research with face-to-face research, or at least that one should immerse oneself in an online community over a long period of time. There are certainly situations in which this would be preferable. However, adopting this approach *tout court* masks the materiality of sporting audiences. Most audiences never meet, and people's sense of being an audience, an important condition of modern life, is based on anecdotal evidence of what other people in that collective are like. Additionally, while some fans might immerse themselves in online communities, others don't, and it's a mistake to assume that only the former matter. For most people, most of the time, engaging with media is a fairly casual affair (Bird, 2011).

Consequently, the study argued that the online discussion about the Heart was a valid source of data, because it represented a moment when people were given the rare chance to focus on the commercialization and mediatization of football. In particular, it showed how supporters think about the malleability of transgression boundaries. Some fans found a way to sell their transgression as a valuable commodity to a sport business. These findings were also significant in relation to questions that we might ask about the media and football, in terms of concepts and methods. Would a more immersive approach have been better?

# 12

# CORRUPTION

*Ellis Cashmore and Kevin Dixon*

---

**Chapter highlights**

- Corruption has been a feature of professional football's history.
- Bungs and match fixing are two of the various forms corruption can take.
- Fifa's global expansion made it one of the largest and richest organizations in sport.
- Why Isn't there more rule breaking in football?
- We can never know the true extent of corruption in football.

---

## Introduction

There are two types of corruption in professional football: the type we hear about and the type we don't hear about. Cynics suspect there is much more of the latter. And, in recent years, we have heard an awful lot about the former. The Fifa scandal that started in 2010 was football's equivalent of turning over a rock that had stood solidly and reliably in place for decades to reveal hitherto unseen insect life beneath. If football's rock-like foundational institution concealed corruption, who could be confident that any area of football was free from some form of venality?

Before opening our argument, we should define our central concept. 'Corruption' is a generic term describing dishonest and fraudulent conduct by those in positions of power or influence; it typically involves bribery (i.e. cash in return for favours). The term has connotations of decay; for example, the decline of the Roman Empire was characterized by widespread corruption. And it involves moral depravation; it is never a good thing.

So, is association football a sport that has lost its moral compass? Or did it ever truly have certain knowledge of right and wrong? After all, unlike many of the other sporting activities that also formed governing organizations in the late nineteenth century, including athletics (1880), rugby (1871) and tennis (1888), football was never predicated on the muscular Christian idea that the moral behaviour learned on the sports field was transferable to the world beyond and that competition should be based on the principle of fair play.

While other sports remained studiously amateur, resisting the pressure of professionalism, at least until later in the twentieth century (in rugby's case, 1995), football became an industry. The original covenant of the British Amateur Athletic Association, drafted in 1866, excluded mechanics, artisans and labourers from its definition of an amateur, its fear being that working–class competitors would be susceptible to cash incentives. But football's players were exactly these types of artisans – the term means workers in trades that involve making things by hand. They played for wages.

In this sense, football was closer to the US's baseball, a sport that was professional at its outset and developed as a commercial enterprise, giving players the chance to make a living from the sport. If baseball had any residual pretensions to fair play, they were destroyed by the 1919 World Series, which was corrupted by gambling syndicates. In a sense, this was sport's most momentous scandal to date. When the nineteenth-century historian John Dalberg Acton wrote 'Power corrupts', he obviously didn't foresee how, after his death in 1869, money would become as effective a force as power.

We will discover that, far from being a new phenomenon, corruption has been a feature of football for practically its entire history. We will also learn that, while the early cases of football corruption were in England, as the sport's popularity spread across the world, corruption appeared in several other countries where the game is played, suggesting that it was – and is – endemic.

While it's misleading to assume that the international scandal occasioned by Fifa officials from 2010 was unique, its scale and level was certainly unprecedented. Corruption has been barely acknowledged for most of football's history, at least its history as a professional sport (from 1883 onwards), though it became a recognizable feature as recently as this century. This is because, in the 1990s, football reached what's called an *inflection point*, this being a stage when a significant change occurred. The change was driven by explosive growth in the global media and the incorporation of football into the entertainment industry. The sport had always been allegiance-rich, fanaticism-rich, exultancy-rich and even faith-rich. After the inflection point, it became cash-rich too.

Some readers might question the prevalence of corruption in football: are we considering isolated episodes or a rampant theme that runs through the history of the sport? To answer this question, we will, in this chapter, navigate our way through the evidence of 'match fixing' (arranging to predetermine, or 'fix', the results of games for the purpose of gambling), 'bungs' (illicit payments made to and by agents and to managers to facilitate the transfer of players) and 'kickbacks' (bribes received and administered by officials with the power to influence the destination of international football tournaments, media rights and official sponsorships).

# A history of corruption

## *Early twentieth century*

Corruption in sport can be traced back to the ancient Olympics (and, in all likelihood, before), when it was suspected that athletes would accept bribes to 'throw' the outcome – that is, deliberately to lose competitions (De Muinck and Quatacker, 2013, p. 7). In more recent history, it's thought that the first modern sports to involve corruption were baseball and boxing – a well-known case being the 1919 baseball scandal in which the Chicago White Sox were judged to have thrown the World Series, deliberately losing to the Cincinnati Reds. A fix of this scale was unheard of (or at least this was the first major incident where working-class sporting heroes had been caught cheating in such a way) and consequently it was unpalatable for most people who invested emotionally in the romantic pretence that underpinned myths of sportsmanship, heroism and virtue. To think that eight baseball superstars (including the hero Shoeless Joe Jackson) would deliberately play to lose (prioritizing financial gain ahead of talent and the moral integrity of sporting competition) was unthinkable to baseball fans. Yet the US legal system found them guilty of nine accounts of fraud. Each of the defendants was served with lifetime banning orders for bringing baseball into disrepute.

Given its scale, this incident is often reported as the first major occurrence of corruption in sport, and yet in the same year in England, corruption featured in a trial at London's Bow Street Police Court. The defendant, Henry Thatcher (a man known to be engaged in betting on football and horse racing), was sentenced to three months' imprisonment for his attempt to bribe football players. According to the *Times* (1919, p. 6), Thatcher's proposition was:

> If Chelsea loses this Saturday and the holiday match, and Millwall wins, Millwall will be a good card for the punters. I should like to get hold of four players. I've got you and Griffiths. How would the captain and the goalkeeper do? If you lose or draw you will get £15 each, so if you get the other three there will be £60 to cut up between you. [£15 represented about four weeks' footballers' wages in 1919.]

The tactics of the match fixer (i.e. Thatcher) have not altered form much since 1919. As Richard McLaren (2008) explains, all match fixes are instigated by a 'runner' (a person who sets up the fix via communication with the athlete or official). In this instance the runner was Thatcher, but in contemporary football runners are often ex-players who are able to mingle freely with current football players without causing suspicion. The popularity of spread betting, in which a bettor wins or loses money according to the margin by which the value of a particular outcome varies from the range (i.e. spread) of expected values quoted by a bookmaker, has made it easier to predetermine outcomes. Bettors can gamble on a range of outcomes – for example, when and who will get a booking, the number of throw-ins, the time of the first free kick, etc. But in the early twentieth century, gambling was illegal in Britain and many other parts of the world anyway, so even the act of placing a bet was outlawed.

The Thatcher case of 1919 was the most prominent to date, but not the first reported case in Britain. There were others, including a 1904 case involving Manchester City captain Billy Meredith, who offered Aston Villa captain Alec Leake £10 to ensure that City won a match; and the lesser-known trial of Pascoe Bioletti in 1913. Bioletti, a known gambler, was charged under the Prevention of Corruption Act 1906, having offered £55 to Jesse Pennington (the captain of West Bromwich Albion) as an incentive to draw or lose a match against Everton. Thinking on his feet (in an attempt to collect evidence against Bioletti), Pennington asked Bioletti to put this proposition into writing, and when Bioletti obliged, Pennington communicated this to the chairman of his club, who in turn informed the police.

While Albion played no part in match fixing, the game ended in a draw and Bioletti, under the impression that a match fix had taken place, handed over the money as agreed – only to be arrested as a consequence. When searched, Bioletti was found to possess a book of football coupons for a £5,000 sweepstake from a company called White Fisher and Co. Police investigations later revealed that Pascoe Bioletti's son, William Alfred Bioletti, owned a betting business in Geneva under the name of White Fisher and Co. (*Times*, 1913a). More evidence came to light in the same month of that year, with Bioletti answering a similar charge for offering £55 to Francis Womack, the captain of Birmingham City FC, to throw a game (*Times*, 1913b). The sums appear modest, but footballers' wages were capped at £4 per week until 1920, when the maximum wage was raised to £9 and then lowered to £8, so their situation was not unlike that of baseball players, whose wages were also restricted.

An infamous game between Manchester United and Liverpool in 1915 highlighted how deeply illegal gambling had become entrenched in football culture (Sharpe, 2015). In the lead-up to the game, the players (and their associates) were aware that illegal bookmakers had priced a 2–0 victory for United at 8/1; armed with this knowledge, players from both teams agreed to fix the match in order to serve two objectives. The first was to help to secure United's top-flight status (the club was close to relegation). This is a potential outcome of asymmetry (when the league system creates a situation in which one team has everything to lose while the other has nothing to gain). The second objective (as we might expect) was to make money in the process. While both objectives are linked, the former has long been associated with corruption in football and is thought to be a by-product of the organization of league systems. Here, we refer specifically to the annual promotion and relegation function that operates as an outcome of the league system in professional football. The idea, while based on meritocracy and fair play, has created a lucrative market for gambling, and this in turn has stimulated the conditions for corruption to thrive – often with the help of officials, managers or, as in this instance, players.

Nine months after this match, seven players – including one Liverpool player memorably named Tom Fairfoul – were given lifetime bans for their roles. But one further complication remained. Despite proving beyond reasonable doubt that match fixing had taken place and that this had had a direct impact on relegation, no points were deducted from Manchester United and the club finished the season one point clear of Chelsea, a club that subsequently looked destined for relegation. Consequently, Chelsea successfully appealed this decision and the club was not relegated. Instead, the First Division (as the top flight was then called) was extended to 22 teams – and remained that way until it was replaced by the Premier League in 1992. In June 1919, the four Liverpool players previously banned for life were allowed to return to football on account of their army service during the First World War (1914–1918).

Early examples of bribes and bungs were also evident in Scotland. For instance, at the Glasgow Sheriff court in 1924, John Browning and Archibald Kyle pleaded guilty to offering a gift of £30 to the captain of Bo'ness United FC as an inducement to lose their match against Lochgelly United on 8 March (Bo'ness is about 27 miles east of Glasgow; Lochgelly is in the east of Scotland). Both defendants were sentenced to 60 days' imprisonment, with 'hard labour' (heavy manual work) as a punishment (*Times*, 1924, p. 11). While the Bo'ness captain maintained his integrity as a law-abiding role model, other Scottish football players did not fit this bill. For example, in 1932, the captain of Montrose, Gavin Hamilton, was imprisoned for 60 days for attempting to bribe David Mooney to lose a match against Edinburgh City. Mooney was offered £50 for his part in the scam and he told the court about his visit from Hamilton: 'Hamilton stated that he was working with a bookmaker. It was suggested that if goals did not come quick enough, a penalty was to be given away' (*Times*, 1932, p. 4). When confronted, Hamilton denied making the offer and stated that, since he wasn't playing in the game, he thought that it would be proper to bet on Edinburgh City to win the match.

## The Kay case

'It is clear that over a long period of three years from one end of this kingdom to another you have befouled professional soccer and corrupted your friends and acquaintances.' The presiding judge, Mr Justice Lawton, was addressing Jimmy Gauld as he sentenced him to four years' imprisonment. He was, said Lawton, 'responsible for the ruin of footballers of distinction' (quoted in Cashmore and Cleland, 2014, p. 14; see also Baker, 2011). Gauld was a former professional player for Charlton Athletic, Everton and other clubs. After retiring in 1962, he used his contacts to fix matches. For almost his entire active playing career, Gauld earned a wage indexed to the national average. In 1960, his wage was £20 per week, while the average wage was £15. The maximum wage limit had been established in 1904 (then at £4 per week), meaning that all players' earnings were linked to national wage scales. So Gauld, in common with most other professionals, didn't leave football with enough wealth to retire in comfort. The wage ceiling remained in place till 1961, after which some players negotiated higher salaries. The England captain Johnny Haynes secured a 500 per cent increase from his club Fulham, making him the first £100 per week player. Most players benefited from the rule change but few earned close to Haynes, who was regarded as one of the leading players, if not *the* leading player, of his generation.

In 1962, the best-paid players at Sheffield Wednesday earned between £30 and £35 weekly and travelled to training on public transport. Among them were Peter Swan and Tony Kay. Their teammate David 'Bronco' Layne had once played with Gauld, who was by that time contemplating making a living off the playing field. The proposition was simple: Gauld would bet on Ipswich to win a game against Sheffield Wednesday in December and pay Layne £100 to make sure the result favoured him. Realizing he couldn't single-handedly manipulate the result, Layne recruited Swan and Kay as his accomplices. As Kay later reflected, 'Layne approached me before the Ipswich game and said, "What do you reckon today?" I said, "Well, we've never won down here [Portman Road]." He said: "Give me £50 and I'll get you twice your money." I thought that was a good deal' (quoted in Jackson, 2004). He and Swan agreed to place their own bets, effectively betting against themselves. Ipswich won 2–0. Kay won £150. Shortly after the game, Kay became the most expensive player in Britain, transferring to Everton for a record fee of £60,000. He played 44 games. Everton won the league title in 1963. Kay earned £80 per week – not as much as Haynes, but enough to place him among the league's elite earners.

In a sport in which players' earnings were limited and their contracts weighted in favour of employers, who could trade them like merchandise to other clubs, the temptation to supplement income by throwing games would have been near irresistible. Were it not for an improbable conversation, no one outside the four conspirators would have ever known about the fix. Gauld had acted through Layne, so Kay never met him until 1964 when he turned up unannounced and asked to speak to Kay. Unbeknown to Kay, Gauld had been prompted by a journalist, Michael Gabbert, who had been investigating irregular patterns of betting on football. Gabbert had identified Gauld as the fixer and threatened to expose him. Gauld approached Kay and surreptitiously recorded a conversation in which he talked about the Ipswich game. Gauld then sold the story to the *People*, a Sunday newspaper, for £7,000. It was a suicidal deal that landed Gauld in jail for four years. The three players were imprisoned for four months and banned from football for life, although Swan was allowed back to play in his late thirties. It also dragged Kay and the others into a scandal that, in its way, ended whatever innocence football had previously held. While Kay, Swan and Layne were the most prominent figures on trial in 1965, a total of ten current or former players were indicted and Gauld was named as the 'central figure'.

## Bungs, the 'black toto' and other frauds

Association football originated and professionalized in Britain. As the sport expanded, the corruption evidenced in Britain manifested itself internationally. In 1974, for example, a player and an official of the Greek football club Olympiakos of Savalion were jailed for four months as punishment for bribing the goalkeeper of an opposing team to help them to win a game (*Times*, 1974). In 1983, in Budapest, Hungary, 43 members of a crime syndicate went on trial for rigging the national football pools (a legitimate betting pool based on predicting the outcomes of domestic football matches). The latter case was thought to have unveiled the largest corruption racket(s) in Eastern Europe (at this time), implicating in excess of 200 people. Roger Boyes, correspondent for the *Times*, revealed that 196 football players and a number of referees, ex-players and car dealers were implicated as part of one of two syndicates, both of which were conspiring to fix matches by bribing players and officials – although the syndicates were not synchronized in their efforts. Boyes (1983, p. 20) writes:

> A typically Hungarian complication was that the two syndicates were not in collusion. So some teams found themselves bribed twice over. Fans can remember ... scenes with players throwing themselves down in agony when through on goal or referees declaring an offside violation if a goal was scored accidentally.

Boyes explains how the Hungarian fans with whom he had spoken were incensed by this scandal, and yet the match fixers' fellow players held more lenient views.

Match-fixing cases have affected every major European football nation, most memorably in Italy, where the *Totonero* case of 1980 culminated in a collective total of 50 years of bans, a combined 25-points deduction and the three-year suspension of Paoli Rossi, which was later reduced to two years. In July 2006, the BBC's Dan Warren described this as 'the worst scandal of them all', but, of course, this was just before the Fifa scandal broke (Warren, 2006). Rossi scored six goals as Italy won the World Cup in 1982, and '*Totonero*' literally means 'black toto', a reference to *Totocalcio*, an Italian football betting game. As we will discover shortly, this was the first of two major corruption scandals to affect Italian football.

In 1985, the chairman of the Bulgarian Football Federation, Dymitrl Nikolev, was convicted of using international matches to maximize personal financial gain from football. He received $600 for agreeing to send the Bulgarian national team to play in Spain. He was also paid $500 for sending the Bulgarian team to Argentina; 3,000 Deutschmarks for sending the team to Athens; and 2,500 levas (approximately £2,000) for staging a football match in Bulgaria. For these and other offences, Nikolev was sentenced to 18 years' imprisonment (*Times*, 1985).

The Uefa Champions League began in 1992, replacing the European Cup, which had been held annually since 1955 (the European Cup was a straight knockout tournament, whereas the Champions League has a group stage, enabling more teams to enter); it became the premier event in European competition. In France in 1993, Olympique Marseille became the focal point of what was, up until then, the most audacious incident of match fixing in history. Marseille president (and then owner of adidas) Bernard Tapie bribed Valenciennes to throw a game, which effectively handed Marseille the Ligue 1 title. Already a powerful force in European football, Marseille went on to win the first Uefa Champions League trophy, beating AC Milan. In 1995, Tapie was sentenced to two years in prison, including eight months non-suspended, and was later implicated in a tax fraud investigation, while Marseille was stripped of the Ligue 1 title and then relegated (Warren, 2006).

In the same year as Tapie's conviction, George Graham, a former player and the then manager of English club Arsenal, was found guilty of misconduct and suspended from all football activity for his involvement in a bung scandal (White, 2006). In football, a 'bung' refers to a payment made to someone to persuade them to do something dishonestly when negotiating the transfer of a player from one club to another. Hypothetically speaking, the manager of club Alpha is interested in signing Player X, who plays for club Omega. He consults with Player X's agent and learns that the player's present salary is £2.5 million per year. He enquires whether Player X would be interested in transferring from Omega to Alpha if he can secure an annual salary of £4 million plus bonuses, which will include £750,000 upfront payment on signing. The agent confirms interest. The manager of Alpha knows the manager of Omega and approaches him with a tentative deal. They agree that the player is worth about £5 million on the transfer market. The manager of Alpha presents a proposition: 'If I can persuade my club's owner to pay £8 million, would your club's owner make it worth my while? Let's say he paid £500,000 into a bank account in the Cayman Islands.' The manager of Omega discreetly suggests the deal to his club's owner and raises the possibility that he too would appreciate £500,000 in another bank account, this time in Switzerland. The owner of Omega agrees. The manager of Alpha then returns to the agent, who earns a commission of 7 per cent of all of Player X's earnings: 'I'm going to persuade my club's owner to pay £8 million for a player worth no more than £5 million, double your man's salary and sweeten the deal with £500,000. That means you stand to earn a £52,500 lump sum (i.e. 7 per cent of the £750,000 upfront payment for signing), then £280,000 every year off Player X's salary. So I'd now like you to incentivize me with £50,000 to be paid into a bank account in the Cayman Islands.' All parties agree and the transfer is completed. Result: the manager of Alpha sees the balance of his private bank account rise by £550,000; the manager of Omega sees the balance of his account go up by £500,000; Player X's agent pays out £35,000, but offsets this against the extra commission that he will earn after the transfer; Player X doubles his wages to £5 million, with bonuses; the owner of Omega receives £8 million for a player valued at only £5 million on the transfer market and pays out a total of £1 million to the two managers. None of these beneficiaries is inclined to report the arrangement or they would incriminate themselves. The only loser is the owner of Alpha, who has paid £8 million; but he and Player X are oblivious to the machinations, so they remain blissfully ignorant but contented. No one is ever likely to tell. This is why enquiries into bungs rarely lead to convictions, the only exception being the Graham case (BBC Sport, 2006).

Graham was an acquaintance of Rune Hauge, a football agent who handled the affairs of players John Jensen and Pål Lydersen, whom Graham wished to sign for Arsenal. Hauge encouraged the double transfer as he stood to increase his commission from the enhanced salaries offered to both players. While Graham insisted he did not ask for an incentive, it later became clear that Hauge had paid him £425,000. Hauge was banned from operating as an agent for life by Fifa, although this was later reduced to two years. How did the Graham–Hauge arrangement come to light? This remains obscure; somehow, an unnamed 'whistleblower' must have suspected an illicit compact.

## The other global game

As well as familiar or recurrent forms of corruption, it's important to note that criminal ingenuity is such that new forms continue to come to light. For instance, in 2006, Kasper Lindberg wrote an article covering a scandal in the illegal trading of football players. This article celebrated the work of Belgian senator Jean-Marie Dedecker and his investigation of 442 cases involving Nigerian players in Belgium. Dedecker was able to highlight that a disproportionate ratio of legal to illegal football agents (30:170 respectively) were operating in Belgium, linking African youth talent to major European clubs. He explained that the illegal movement of players works as follows. First, agents (that is ex-football stars, now working as agents) use their celebrity status to recruit boys with potential. The boys are tempted with stories of success, glory, fame and associated wealth. Once hooked on this idea, they are encouraged to travel to Europe. When they leave Africa for 'career progression' purposes, the academy connected with the boys receives a transfer fee, but the boys themselves do not benefit financially at all. They are simply lured by a fairytale, which for most of the youngsters does not come true or materialize into a long-term professional career. Players are treated like cattle, with only food and shelter guaranteed in Belgium. The feeder club and the illegal agent are rewarded for their work, while the players are left to prove themselves worthy once more in a gladiatorial fight for financial freedom (Lindberg, 2006, p. 3).

2005 saw the unveiling of a corruption scandal when Vietnam lost the final of the South East Asian Games to Thailand by a score of 3–0. After this match, Vietnam midfielder Quoc Vuong met with a bookie in a Ho Chi Minh City hotel and accepted $6,300 for his role in throwing the game. As rumours began to spread and the police initiated criminal investigations, Quoc Vuong was arrested in December 2005. Other arrests followed: Bat Hieu, Hia Lam, Van Truong, Quoc Anh, Phuoc Vinh and team captain Tai Em. As the police closed in on Hanoi goalkeeper Do Thanh Ton, he committed suicide. The police investigation revealed large-scale betting rings within Vietnam's professional football league (Quinn, 2006).

The global prevalence of corruption is undeniable, but it appears that some countries hold a more relaxed approach to its policing. Scholars have argued that cultures of corruption are sustained when corruption is, to an extent, normalized. Tone Sissener (2001) suggests that this tends to occur where cultural conditions cultivate a laissez-faire attitude, allowing people to convince themselves that corruption is a way of life and that if they were not benefiting from it, then someone else would be. This in turn affects the way in which people perceive illegal acts. So, while it is fair to say that everyone has a moral compass, it is important to recognize that it is set at different reference points as a consequence of that person's perceived necessity to act (often for financial gain), that person's cultural teachings and values (passed down to succeeding generations) and routines of action (behaviour enacted semi-automatically). By way of example, Eugenio Paradiso (2014, p. 5) writes of the cultural conditions that allow corruption to thrive in Argentinian football:

> Among the structural conditions that lead to corruption in football we find clientelist networks that involve politicians, club officials, police and groups of organized fans. Other factors include the inaction of the judicial system, the organization of the AFA (Argentine FA) and its member clubs and an overall lack of transparency. In this context corruption is exacerbated by a culture of impunity, which in turn is a consequence of those structural factors mentioned.

Paradiso's reference to 'clientelist networks' raises an important point. 'Clientelism' is described by Natalia Roudakova (2008, p. 42) as 'a form of social and political organization where access to public resources is controlled by powerful patrons and delivered to less powerful clients in exchange for defence and other forms of service'. In addition, Christopher Gaffney (2009) points out that those involved in systems of clientelism do not want to give up the benefits that corruption can forge. Thus, he holds that corruption in Argentine football is a self-sustaining mechanism whereby those who do not take advantage are often labelled *giles* (idiots).

But while it's true that some cultures might be willing to turn a blind eye to forms of corrupt practice and others are committed to exposing it, there are always people willing to risk exposure and all of the consequences that come with it in the pursuit of money and power. And as we have explained earlier, referees have shown a willingness to accept bribes. In Germany, a shock 4–2 cup win for Paderborn over Hamburg in 2006 brought the refereeing performance of Robert Hoyzer into question. His favourable treatment of Paderborn saw complaints filed to the German Football Association (DFB), who conducted an inquiry alongside a criminal investigation (by the police) that uncovered links to a Croatian gambling syndicate. Hoyzer confessed to trying to fix matches in the German Cup and eventually received a 29-month prison sentence, while Ante Sapina (the Croatian named as the match-fixing orchestrator) was jailed for 35 months (Warren, 2006).

Also in 2006, the case known as the *Calciopoli* involved claims of systematic rigging at boardroom level, with a number of teams and their directors found guilty (although many continue to contest the verdicts) of having contrived to weight the whole footballing infrastructure in their favour. Serie A clubs Juventus, Lazio and Fiorentina were all demoted to Serie B, and Milan and Reggina were docked points. All were barred from playing in Europe – Juventus, Milan and Fiorentina in the Champions League, Lazio in the Uefa Cup. During the investigation, 50 arrests were made. Five years later, a separate case confirmed the suspicion that corruption was part of the very nature of Italian football rather than the practice of a few rogue players or opportunistic fixers.

As well as the usual embarrassment that corruption causes for the host nation, this scandal instigated a wider debate that Richard Giulianotti (1999) had previously referred to as the effect of the increasing complexity of institutional relations that are bound together in football's expanding economy. Giulianotti points to a growing trend whereby owners or major shareholders in some football clubs are also key actors in the media. For example, in the case of the *Calciopoli*, scholars Tito Boeri and Battista Severgnini (2008) explain that all of the clubs except Reggina had some form of direct or indirect control over the media and held a significant share of broadcasting rights. The problem here is that in situations like this, the impartiality of the media is compromised in favour of the associated football club. For instance, it was revealed retrospectively that during *Calciopoli*, Juventus manager Luciano Moggi was able to influence the television show *Il Processo di Biscardi* by manipulating the results of viewer polls and influencing the selection of matches to be analyzed, the guests to be interviewed and any criticisms made (Numerato, 2009, p. 264). So, while it is not always the case, Dino Numerato continues, it is important to note that the media can facilitate or provide an effective smokescreen that will allow corruption to flourish.

The involvement of organized crime in football corruption was revealed once more in 2010 by police investigating drug and prostitution rings in Germany. During the course of these investigations, police stumbled upon evidence of a network of Croatian criminals (resident in Germany) who were manipulating football results across Europe and then making profits in Asian gambling markets. As the evidence mounted, German prosecutors began what has become known as the Bochum Trial, unveiling about 270 fixed matches in twelve countries; Germany, Switzerland and Turkey hosted the largest number of fixed matches (Magnay, 2010). The games under suspicion were mostly lower-league games across nine countries, and not in the major leagues in England, Spain or Italy, but 12 Europa League and three Champions League games were involved.

This trial revealed that the once small-scale, petty criminal activity of a few lone wolf criminals has changed into a lucrative black market business for organized crime. Liquidity in Asian betting markets makes this possible, allowing high-stakes wagers to be placed without drawing attention in a way that changed betting trends and altered odds (Forrest, 2012a, 2012b). In turn, this situation allows criminals to offer substantial bribes (relative to wages) to players. Investigative journalist Declan Hill (2008) points out that the illegal Asian gambling industry continues to thrive. He indicates that prominent businessmen and politicians sit at the top of this gambling structure; while they are not involved in the mechanics of this illegal industry, they use influence in the high offices of power to protect organized crime groups and bookies, and this in turn enables matches to be fixed.

In 2013, the president of the South African Football Association Kirsten Nematandani and officials Dennis Mumble, Lindile Kika, Adeel Carelse and Barney Kujane were asked to take a voluntary leave of absence. This motion was proposed in response to allegations of match fixing organized by the convicted fixer Wilson Raj Perumal and his company Football4U (Riddell and Knight, 2014). The method used was to bribe referees to manipulate games in order to meet the requirements of organized gambling rings – and in the build-up to the 2010 World Cup, a number of matches were alleged to have been fixed.

A similar situation was uncovered in 2015 when the Greek courts were in the process of investigating allegations of organized criminality within the Hellenic Football Federation (HFF). Accusations of illegal betting, the selection of referees due to their willingness to fix matches, rigged HFF elections and the maintenance of order on threat of violence/intimidation were all lines of enquiry under investigation. In an interview with Matt Scott (2015), an investigator for *Inside World Football*, Panathinaikos owner Yiannis Alafouzos spoke about 'The System', a name given to describe an underworld cartel believed to have been influencing the outcomes of games, leagues and cup competitions for a prolonged period:

> The System today is a group of people who are either high-ranking employees or officials of HFF. Together with one specific team and its owner, they are controlling and conducting which teams go up or down, disciplinary decisions, who will be punished, who will be prosecuted by the football authorities, which referee will be appointed to a game … In addition there is illegal betting. Teams exchange players between themselves on loan. They fix games to relegate certain clubs and save others and for betting purposes … They go after teams that are not in The System or favour a team in The System.

The 'one specific team' and owner that Alafouzos refers to above are Greek champions Olympiakos Piraeus and owner Vangelis Marinakis. On 18 June 2015, he was banned from football as an investigation continued into allegations that a criminal organization is controlling the domestic game. It was alleged that Marinakis and others were responsible for directing a criminal organization since 2011 with the aim of 'absolute control of Greek football's fate by the methods of blackmailing and fraud' (Korreas quoted in Wood, 2015).

The litany of cases described here is not exhaustive, but offers evidence that, since 1900, corruption has run like a thread through football's history. Match fixing and bungs are cross stitches of football's fabric. Football has charged its governing organizations with responsibility for controlling and running the sport; as such, they have been obliged to police football and, where possible, extirpate corruption. The most powerful and encompassing governing organization has failed to do this, as we will now learn. (For more on other forms of transgressive behaviours, including violence and sexual violence, see Chapters 2 and 11.)

## Fifa and institutional corruption

As football has grown to its current high point of global popularity and the value of staging prestigious tournaments has risen, the sport's governors have become influential figures. (The rise of Fifa is charted in Chapter 3.) A single vote can change the destination of a Fifa World Cup, a tournament that brings with it sizeable munificence. Evidence in recent years has uncovered endemic corruption, reaching all parts of the Fifa organization, all across the globe (Jennings, 2011). Senior officials of the ruling executive committee have been exposed: João Havelange, the former Fifa president, who made his successor, Sepp Blatter, his assistant; his fellow Brazilian and former son-in-law Ricardo Teixeira; the Paraguayan Nicolás Leoz; the Trinidadian Jack Warner; the Qatari Mohamed bin Hammam; and the American Chuck Blazer. In 2013, a Swiss court concluded that Havelange had taken millions of dollars in illicit payments (kickbacks).

In 1974, Havelange became Fifa's president. One of his initiatives was to set up a partnership with International Sport and Leisure (ISL), an organization founded in 1982 by Horst Dassler, the owner of adidas (who died in 1987), Patrick Nally of the West Nally sports marketing agency, and Al Killeen, vice-president of Coca-Cola. In 1975, the soft drinks corporation had agreed to fund a scheme to produce more coaches, referees and sports doctors. The World Development programme (later renamed the Fifa/Coca-Cola International Academy) became the flagship of Coca-Cola's involvement in association football. It was to all intents and purposes a marketing instrument, but it was crucial for Fifa's promotion (West Nally, n.d.). Andrew Jennings (2006, p. 20) regards the Coke deal as particularly significant: 'Once Coca-Cola had signed up, everyone wanted a piece of the action. Sponsors competed for the right to use Fifa's badge and slap the words "World Cup" on their products.'

Coca-Cola wasn't the only company to see the commercial potential offered by Fifa. According to Jennings (2006, p. 13), Dassler 'wanted sports federations to sign contracts that committed their teams to wear Adidas [sic – 'adidas' is properly spelt in all lower case] kit. He wanted individual stars to wear the three stripes. And he wanted the world to watch on television'. Jennings traces how Dassler became a key figure in the post-1974 development of Fifa. When it came to the election of officials, '[h]e surveyed the likely candidates, did his private deals, and helped them to victory with Adidas [sic] money'. Dassler was effectively the kingmaker: 'He made them presidents and let them remember – charmingly of course – that he could keep them in power, or push them out' (Jennings, 2006, p. 13). In Jennings' account, Dassler effectively controlled Fifa during this period.

ISL was awarded the television and marketing rights to the World Cups; these included stadium advertising, merchandising and, most importantly, the television contracts. ISL's task was then to divide up the territorial rights and negotiate separately with nearly 100 broadcasters around the world. (Chapter 8 focuses on the media's impact on football generally.) The exact sum that ISL paid Fifa for the package of global rights is still not known, but essentially ISL needed to recoup £1.4 billion (approximately €2.3 billion or $2.5 billion) to break even. The company went broke in 2001, owing millions of pounds to creditors. Fifa repaid more than £1.6 billion to the creditors of ISL in 2004. 'Amid the financial wreckage, investigators found evidence that commissions – known to you and me as bribes – had been paid to senior Fifa officials in return for their help in securing lucrative TV deals, most visibly in South American territories', writes David Bond (2013). The president of the South American football confederation CONMEBOL, Nicolás Leoz, also resigned, ostensibly on 'health and personal grounds'. He claimed that he had received money from ISL for a school project. The exact machinations of the ISL case will, in all probability, never be known. But kickbacks were, it seems, paid by ISL to individuals within Fifa with enough influence to help the organization to procure media rights in particular territories. So there was a triangular arrangement between Fifa, ISL and television companies. Clearly, the broadcast rights to World Cups, which are of course in four-yearly cycles, are valuable. The values change over time and according to the territories, making a precise evaluation impossible; however, as an illustration, ESPN paid £100 million in 2005 for the English-language rights to screen the 2010 tournament in the US, while Univision paid $325 million for the Spanish rights. These amounts rose to about $1 billion for the 2014 World Cup. This is for a single territory, remember; and, while the US offers a lucrative market for advertisers, it is not known for its love of association football. The global broadcast rights are spread over 200 territories, not all as lucrative as the US, but worth comfortably in excess of the $4 billion (£2.44 billion) accrued from the 2010 World Cup in South Africa. With these figures in mind, it is easy to understand how an errant million or two could find their way into an unnamed bank account owned by a Fifa official without being missed.

Giulianotti and Robertson (2009, p. 124) speculate that the flow of corruption is top-down: 'International governing bodies have exacerbated cultures of corruption in some developing nations by bribing football delegates in return for compliant voting.' Since the 1970s, Fifa has recruited large memberships from relatively small nations with modest Gross Domestic Products (GDPs) – the market value of all officially recognized final goods and services produced within a country. This has been justified as part of the organization's globalizing mission and, in the view of many, it is a laudable project: to democratize participation. It also confers voting power on small nations.

Up until the election of Havelange, the method of choosing host nations was a vote taken by all 209 members; this was changed to 22 voting members. So when countries bid for the right to host World Cups, a clear line of potential corruption opens up. Theoretically, a member of Fifa's voting Executive Committee (ExCo) could receive a kickback from one of the bidders and use a portion of this to secure the votes of several other nations. No matter how technically excellent a bid may be or how persuasive the lobbying becomes, hard cash can buy crucial votes.

The spectre of this kind of corruption loomed after the oil-rich Gulf nation Qatar was awarded the 2022 tournament, despite being unsuitable in almost every respect, bar one – it sits on the world's third largest natural gas reserves. Two members of the Executive Committee were suspended in 2010 after the *Sunday Times* newspaper reported that they took $1.5 million each in bribes from Qatar's World Cup bid committee. The following year, Lord Triesman, who was the English FA's chairman from 2008 to 2010, told a UK parliament committee that while lobbying for an English bid, four Fifa officials asked him for 'certain favours' in exchange for their votes. We cover the Fifa case event by event in the timeline towards the end of the chapter and we profile the investigation that initiated the scandal in this chapter's Research in Action section.

In 2015, Sepp Blatter's reign as Fifa president came to an end, but only after he was re-elected and then, within days, resigned the post. It was a dramatic twist in the long-running scandal and one that permitted candidates for the presidency the opportunity to promise rigorous reforms. All of Blatter's potential successors acknowledged the need for a radical overhaul of an organization that had grown in size and prosperity in the previous four decades, but whose officers had shown a willingness to behave dishonestly in return for money and personal gain. Suspensions for several prominent Fifa and former Fifa officials, including ex-players Michel Platini and Franz Beckenbauer, followed, suggesting that no one, no matter how well respected, was above suspicion. The popular view was 'one bad apple…'; in other words, unscrupulous individuals were to blame for the rottenness that had spread to all spheres of Fifa's influence. This offered a solution: identify the individuals, throw them out and restore the entire organization to its former freshness. It was a convenient explanation, but was it a plausible one?

## Why? … Why not?

When we ask why there is corruption, the answer seems so obvious that it's hardly worth asking. As rational creatures, humans, when presented with the opportunity to enrich themselves, weigh up the possible costs against the potential benefits; if they decide that the latter outweigh the former, they proceed. The key variables are the degree of risk and the scale of reward. It's an answer, but it's hardly informative. Perhaps we need a fresh set of questions. A starter might be: why isn't there *more* corruption? Think about this: if we calculated risks and rewards, we'd probably take more chances. Something makes us conform to popular notions of rightness and abide by the rules. Perhaps this is what we should be trying to explain.

The English philosopher Thomas Hobbes (1588–1679) is often credited with being the first thinker to attempt a systematic answer. He claimed that human action is motivated entirely by selfish concerns. Strong government backed up by external constraint is needed to keep human behaviour within acceptable limits, although this can never be 100 per cent effective and there will always be rule-breakers (i.e. transgressors).

The French sociologist Emile Durkheim (1858–1917) regarded crime and other forms of transgression as constituents of any society; their function is to identify the boundaries of legitimate behaviour and remind us what happens to those who violate them (Durkheim, 1982 [1895]). Every society needs rules and the means to enforce those rules; without them, there would be no order. Thus, we're all potential transgressors. For Durkheim, this was quite normal.

Taking his cue from these observations, the US scholar Travis Hirschi (1969) reversed the usual criminological problem and wondered not why people break laws but why they stay on the right side of them. His response was that most of us are bonded to society. Imagine a semi-professional player with a club in the Evo-Stik Premier League, who believes he should properly be playing with the pros. When someone offers him £2,000 to get a yellow card within the first 15 minutes of a certain game, he knows it would be easy. A reckless tackle or a petulant gesture to the referee is all it takes. No one would be aware of his motives. The person proposing the arrangement intends to place a bet on the card being shown. How the player reacts, according to Hirschi, would depend on his:

- *Attachment*: By this, Hirschi meant how sensitive people are to the opinions of others. If the player is not at all sensitive, then he won't mind behaving in a way that's contrary to their expectations. If he has internalized their attitudes (i.e. made them part of his own), then he's likely to conform. The player would weigh the responses of his wife, children and peers against the £2,000 reward.
- *Commitment*: The more obligated or devoted we become to social institutions, including family and job, the more we fear the consequences of breaking rules. Our footballer might feel frustrated, but understand the impact of his action on others should he be found out.
- *Involvement*: The more heavily we are involved in conventional day-to-day activity, the less time we have to spend on transgressive behaviour.
- *Beliefs*: The more we buy into the values, goals, morality and legitimacy of a society, the less likely we are to deviate. So, if our player has lost faith in the

legitimacy of the sport and is convinced he has been unfairly overlooked, he may well be tempted to take the money.

The case of the player is fictional, although we base it on a Glossop North End player who led a Premier League lifestyle thanks to the extra income he made not from bribes but from a drugs ring and who was jailed for eleven years in 2012 (*Manchester Evening News*, 2012). The parallels are far from exact, but the point is clear: everyone is potentially a transgressor; what stops us, for the most part, is our investment in society. When the likelihood of detection is as low as it would be in the above example, the chances of being caught are almost nil. Neither of the parties involved (the player and the briber) has any interest in disclosure, and the bookie who takes the bet knows nothing about it.

Of course, this doesn't answer the question why well-paid officials with respon-sible positions and prestigious standing in society would take chances. After all, they are typically affluent individuals, well taken care of with pension plans and, in some cases, generous expense accounts. Their attachments and commitments are undoubtedly strong; their involvement occupies much of their time; and their beliefs in the values embodied by their society, we might surmise, are firm. And yet they break rules.

'Facilitation payments' – cash or goods paid to a foreign government official to perform or speed up the performance of their duties – are not illegal, according to US anti-bribery law. Ambiguity about what constitutes improper hospitality allows bribery to go relatively unchecked in international trade. Even the most stringent laws against corruption have limited effect. In 2015, the anti-corruption campaign organization Transparency International reported that that no one has ever been prosecuted for facilitation payments in the UK and that there is a low risk of prosecution (Connett, 2015). It would be unworldly to assume that deals are not habitually 'facilitated'. (Is it a coincidence that the word 'facilitation' derives from the same Latin root as 'facile', which means ignoring the true complexities of an issue?)

Think about any organization you know, large or small, anywhere in the world, from the World Trade Organization to your local football club. If Robert Michels (1876–1936) is to be believed, there will be a small cluster of people calling the shots. Such groups are *elites* that have disproportionate access to scarce resources, however a particular culture defines them. All large-scale operations or organizations – whether political, corporate, voluntary or any other kind – have a tendency to become *oligarchies*. No matter how democrati-cally assembled and fairly regulated an operation or organization is, elites, like cream, rise to the top. This happens with such consistency over time and place that Michels called the tendency an 'iron law', suggesting its resistance to change (2009 [1911]).

Often in complex organizations, decisions are needed quickly and there is no time for consultation, so the decision-makers take the initiative. Fifa is no different. Despite its democratic origins and its libertarian credo, it is a huge global organization that governs a sport played by 209 nations, all affiliated. Let's assume Michels is right and Fifa is an oligarchy.

Another writer of Michels' era, Vilfredo Pareto (1848–1923), theorized that in any congregation of people, some will be best equipped to rule, by virtue of their intellect, courage, leadership skills, etc. But once they get to the top, they sense that there are challengers trying to oust them and so devote their energies to protecting their own interests, usually by justifying their positions. Today, this would mean influencing the media. They become so preoccupied with maintaining their grip that they neglect their main purpose, which is running their operations smoothly and fairly. Pareto argued that as one elite is challenged and replaced, so the next generation follows its example and attempts to perpetuate itself rather than running the organization effectively. Pareto called this the 'circulation of elites' (Pareto quoted in Finer, 1966).

Complementing this mistrustful pair was a third writer, Gaetano Mosca (1858–1941), who claimed that elites will form and dictate according to their own needs, no matter if the economy is capitalist, communist, socialist or any variety of these. In any kind of political system, whether democratic, autocratic, theocratic, monarchic or communist, elites will govern. The composition of elites will vary; they may be military, religious, plutocratic (i.e. those having the most wealth) or democratically elected, but they will always cluster into a small power-holding group (Mosca, 1939 [1884]).

While these writers were viewing society in the late nineteenth and early twentieth centuries, it could be argued that their observations are more relevant today than ever. Globalization has weakened traditional authority and control in particular countries, giving rise to corporate elites that exert influence in many parts of the world. Global organizations tend to float across national boundaries, making them difficult, if not impossible, to police.

Maybe this doesn't make the international corruption of Fifa any more palatable, but it helps to make it more comprehensible: many officials in positions of authority soon become accustomed to life as 'fat cats' and start mixing in the right company, schmoozing with the right people and perhaps even greasing a few palms in an effort to stay comfortably in power. Vigilance is the first casualty; breaches of rules are conveniently ignored if favours are returned. While Fifa exists to run world football, its officials are often motivated by the effort to stay in their jobs. This may not exactly commission corruption, but nor does it deter it. Remember also: Fifa is accountable to no one. As a voluntarily elected body, it is self-appointed, does not depend on any particular nation for support and defines its own conditions of existence.

## Football's dark figure

Criminologists often refer to the 'dark figure of crime' to describe undiscovered, unreported crime. There is an unknown amount of crime going on at any one moment, much of it committed by the agents charged with the responsibility of preventing and solving it. We might argue that there is a dark figure of corruption in football. Towards the end of this chapter, we present a timeline of the best-known cases of corruption in football; even when summarized, it is a formidable roll. We have no conception of how much corruption has *actually* taken place over the period in question, which begins in 1904, but we can state with some certainty that it will never be eliminated from football. Corruption is a permanent fixture in a professional sport in which favours are sought and offered and the chances of detection are slight. Gambling has been globalized by online bookmakers and the rise in the popularity of spread betting practically invites surreptitious arrangements that will never reach public visibility, if only because all of the parties involved have an interest in keeping them private.

Hirschi's theory encourages us to ask why people do not break rules. Many professional players are too well paid to be tempted by bribes, but less affluent players are more susceptible to 'backhanders', as secret and illegal payments are known in football. The theory also forces us to consider whether the bungs that have, on rare occasions, become major cases in the past are representative of a larger pattern of corruption that is likely to remain undisclosed, if only because the victims never realize that they are victims; the beneficiaries of bungs are agents and managers and the victims are club owners, to whom the odd million or so may not be a significant loss, even if they knew about it (which they rarely do). Only the naïve would assume that the number of bung cases we know of represents anything but the tiniest fraction of the actual number of bungs.

In the mid-twentieth century, the world acknowledged the accomplishment of Fifa. It had created a sporting tournament to rival the Olympic Games and, with the onset of television, a spectacle that would make it the wealthiest and most powerful sport federation in history. The organization's capital (i.e. available funds held in reserve) is $1.52 billion (about £1 billion). Fifa's revenue for 2015 was $2 billion (£1.28 billion), with $337 million (£216 million) in profits, according to Associated Press (2015). From 1974, when Havelange became president, Fifa globalized not just football but the consumption it entailed. The cost of the splendour and magnificence of the World Cup didn't become clear until the next century.

Now, the world is more ambivalent towards Fifa; intrigued by the clandestine deals that perverted the governance of football and appalled by the grotesque abuses of power and privilege, the world has become aware that the organization has outgrown itself. With global expansion came weakened central authority and a disintegration of integrity. Could it ever extirpate the rottenness or restore public confidence in its ability to run football? If Michels *et al.* are to be believed, the second question is easier to answer: yes, cosmetic changes, such as electing new officials with reform programmes, can be persuasive, especially when they're supported by the media. The public can be coaxed into believing that the organization is prepared to turn over a new leaf. But purging a complex organization of key individuals is insufficient to prevent the operation of the iron law of oligarchy, and rulers who are prepared to put their own interests before those of the sport are bound to re-emerge. This is simply an effect of scale and power. Replacing office-holders creates the illusion of change, but, if elite theory is to be accepted, the pattern will reassert itself.

Earlier, we modified the historian John Dalberg Acton's maxim, making money rather than power the precursor of corruption. Much of the evidence presented in this chapter supports this; every instance of corruption involves the exchange of hard cash. Even so, there are other forms of capital. For example, at the 1976 Summer Olympics in Montreal, which was an amateur tournament, Boris Onischenko, a pentathlete from Ukraine, was discovered to have used an ingeniously wired épée that allowed him to register hits at will (Henderson, 2001). Some might argue that this was straightforward cheating rather than corruption, but it was dishonest and fraudulent, and it seems unlikely that Onischenko acted without the knowledge and assistance of several others. For what? Not money – he stood to gain none. In any case, Ukraine was, at the time, in the Soviet Union and thus a communist state. There are other instances in amateur sport when collective fraudulence seems to have been motivated by purposes other than financial gain. Tom Brady had a five-year contract with the NFL's New England Patriots worth $57 million (£36.5 million), and yet, in 2015, was given a four-game suspension for his role in the deliberate deflation of balls used in a game, designed to give his team an unfair advantage. A federal judge later nullified the suspension. Again, this would not qualify as corruption in the accepted sense, but it underlines how money is not always the only motivation to break rules in sport.

In times of scarcity – of food or fuel, for example – some items take on greater value than money and become usable as barter. Success in sport might also qualify as barter. But in football, the overwhelming number of cases of corruption spring from the desire to make money. Horst Dassler, one of the founders of adidas in the 1960s, worked assiduously to place friends and allies in positions of power. What did he want in return? Andrew Jennings (2006, p. 391) answers: 'Exclusive contracts for ISL, the sports marketing company he founded, and world domination for his sports kit company Adidas [sic].' In other words, to earn more money. adidas was again entangled in scandal when, in 2015, it was alleged that its one-time CEO Robert Louis-Dreyfus deployed a slush fund (i.e. a reserve of money used for illicit purposes) and made £5 million of it available to Germany's World Cup bidding committee, of which Franz Beckenbauer was the head.

Of course, the desire to earn more money is the product of a particular kind of culture in which money has value, can be used in exchange for goods and services and usually confers prestige and influence on its possessor. In some circumstances, it is a means to power and authority. US politics is populated by individuals rich enough to fund expensive presidential campaigns. In 2012, for instance, Mitt Romney, Barack Obama's Republican rival, raised $2 billion to fund his unsuccessful campaign. Donald Trump, whose personal wealth was estimated by *Forbes* at $4 billion, ran for the US presidency in 2015, suggesting that those who have serious money are prepared to use it to gain power. Sepp Blatter, who was also implicated in the ISL scandal, presents a comparable figure in football: for a long time the head of the most lucrative and powerful organization in sport, the recipient of a six-figure salary plus generous bonuses, he flew by private plane and enjoyed an opulent and sybaritic lifestyle. Why, then, at 79 (his age in 2015) did he cling to his position as president of Fifa while being assailed from all directions, persecuted by the media and condemned by football fans? Power for some people is like a dependency-inducing drug: the more they have, the more they crave.

Like any other form of popular entertainment, football presents only part of itself to its audience. Few people are privy to deals that are struck behind the scenes in Hollywood or the bargaining that goes on when negotiating a record deal. For all anyone knows, underhand, unscrupulous and dishonest activities go on every day. Audiences are interested only in what they see on the screen, on stage or, in football's case, on the pitch. Guilty secrets are rarely shared. But, in football, they are shared often enough. Knowing fans are rarely surprised. In 2015, the year of the Fifa presidential elections, no one seriously doubted that Blatter would somehow secure enough votes to earn him re-election, despite his widespread unpopularity. The only surprise was that he resigned within days of winning re-election for the fifth consecutive time and after 17 years in power.

## Conclusion

There will be more cases of corruption, bribery, bungs, match fixing and miscellaneous skulduggery in football, and they will surprise only children and the unwary. Football lost its innocence even before it officially allowed professionalism; for as long as the game has been played, there have been those who have tried to profit from the inestimable appetite that fans have for watching 11 men face another 11. When Gjalt De Graaf (2007, p. 76) admits 'We know little of what corruption control works best and most efficiently', he implicitly accepts that there is no such thing as freedom from corruption. Corruption can be reduced and policed more effectively. But it is no more possible to eliminate it from football than it is from any other sphere of social life.

This may sound a depressing way to conclude, but students of football, as opposed merely to football fans, must be prepared for uncomfortable truths. Remember: the human body's process of cell division, which is responsible for growth and development, is also responsible for the out-of-control replication known as tumours, which can metastasize and become cancer. Football's growth and expansion has been bountiful, but the money and power that it's produced are not unqualified benefits.

## CORRUPTION AND FOOTBALL: A TIMELINE

**FIFA** Cases in the long-running Fifa scandal that began in 2010.

*Unless otherwise stated, cases originated in the UK, the exception being Fifa-related cases, which are effectively global.*

### Pre-First World War

**1885** The English FA officially sanctions professionalism.

**1900** Burnley goalkeeper Jack Hillman is banned for one year for trying to bribe Nottingham Forest to lose.

**1904** Billy Meredith, Manchester City's captain, offers Aston Villa captain Alec Leake £10 to throw a game towards the end of the 1904–1905 season when City are making a challenge for the championship. Meredith is banned for one season. At the time, players earn 30–35 shillings per week, about £1.50 ($3 at the 1904 exchange rate).

France: The Fédération Internationale de Football Association (Fifa) is created and headquartered in Paris.

**1906** The Prevention of Corruption Act becomes law in the UK.

**1911** Middlesbrough's manager Andy Walker and chairman Thomas Gibson Poole are banned from football for trying to fix a home game against local rivals Sunderland.

**1913** Gambler Pascoe Bioletti offers the captain of West Bromwich Albion £55 as an inducement to draw or lose a match. In a sting operation involving the consent of the West Bromwich player, police arrest Bioletti when he hands over the money as agreed. Bioletti is found to possess a book of betting coupons amounting to £5,000.

### First World War

**1915** A total of seven players – three from Manchester United and four from Liverpool – are banned after gambling on the result of a match between the two sides, won 2–0 by United.

Henry Norris, the chairman of Arsenal, who is also an elected politician, argues that there has been so much match fixing during the 1914–1915 season that league positions should be disregarded; he makes the argument in the context of a debate over increasing the number of First Division clubs.

### Inter-war period

**1919** Henry Thatcher is sentenced to three months' imprisonment for his attempt to bribe two Millwall FC players to ensure a win or draw. The bribe is £4.

US: The Chicago Black Sox scandal in baseball becomes the most notorious case of corruption in sport to date.

**1924** John Browning and Archibald Kyle plead guilty to offering a gift of £30 to the captain of Scotland's Bo'ness United FC to ensure defeat. Both defendants are sentenced to 60 days' imprisonment.

**1925** Arsenal chairman Henry Norris, who had speculated on the prevalence of match fixing in 1914–1915, is accused by the *Daily Mail* of making illicit payments to Sunderland player Charlie Buchan as an inducement to join Arsenal. A subsequent FA investigation finds that Norris has also appropriated club funds for his personal use. Norris sues both the newspaper and the FA, but loses his cases and is banned from football for life.

**1926** France: Fifa sets up a commission to look into arranging a world championship for both professional and amateur players. The UK has openly professional football, while many nations prefer amateur versions; the Olympic Games permits only amateur football players to compete.

**1927** Italy: Torino wins Serie A but the club is later stripped of the title when a Torino official is found guilty of bribing Juventus defender Luigi Allemandi in a key match.

**1930** Uruguay: The first Fifa World Cup is held.

**1932** Fifa moves its headquarters to Switzerland; while it has been ostensibly an amateur organization to date, it resolves to develop a professional managerial structure and commercial purpose.

Gavin Hamilton of Scottish club Montrose is imprisoned for 60 days for offering £50 to player David Mooney to fix a match against Edinburgh City.

## Post-Second World War

**1960** The Betting and Gaming Act legalizes betting shops.

**1961** The maximum wage ceiling for footballers is removed.

**1963** Bristol Rovers' Esmond Million is found guilty of plotting to fix a match and is banned for life.

**1965** Tony Kay, Peter Swan and David Layne are jailed for four months in football's most sensational case of corruption to date. A total of ten league players are found guilty of match fixing, the 'fixer' being Jimmy Gauld, a former player, who is part of a betting syndicate.

**1974** Greece: One player and an official of Olympiakos of Savallon are jailed for four months as punishment for bribing the goalkeeper of an opposing team.

Italy: Juventus escape punishment after accusations that they used a go-between, Deszo Solti, to try to bribe Portuguese referee Francisco Marques Lobo before a European Cup semi-final against Derby County in 1973.

Germany: Polish players accuse Italians of offering them bribes to lose a World Cup match in Stuttgart; Italy needed a draw to stay in the competition.

**1978** Italy: Scottish referee John Gordon and fellow official Rollo Kyle are suspended by the Scottish FA after admitting that they accepted presents worth £1,000 from AC Milan before a Uefa Cup match with Levski Spartak. Milan is fined £8,000 by Uefa.

**1980** Italy: In the *Totonero* case, a collective total of 50 years of bans is issued for widespread match fixing in Serie A and Serie B. It is the biggest corruption case in the history of football to date. Paolo Rossi is suspended for three years (reduced to two on appeal) and returns to lead Italy to the 1982 World Cup final win.

International Sport and Leisure (ISL) is established. In 2001, it will collapse, owing millions of pounds to creditors. Fifa will repay more than £1.6 billion to creditors in 2004.

**1983** Hungary: Full-back Sandor Sallai and former national team manager Kalman Meszoly are among 43 members of a crime syndicate who go on trial for rigging the football pools. This case is thought to unveil the largest corruption racket in Eastern Europe (at this time), implicating in excess of 200 people.

**1985** Bulgaria: The chairman of the Bulgarian Football Federation, Dymitri Nikolev, is sentenced to 18 years in jail for accepting bribes to send the Bulgarian football team to play matches in Spain, Argentina and Greece.

## Inflection point

**1993** France: Olympique Marseille player Jean-Jacques Eydelie is arrested for trying to bribe three Valenciennes players to lose a league match six days before the French champions beat AC Milan to win the first Uefa Champions League. General manager Jean-Pierre Bernes is also charged, and an envelope containing £30,000 is dug up in the garden of the mother-in-law of Valenciennes player Christophe Robert. Uefa bars Marseille from defending the title. Marseille president Bernard Tapie will later be charged with corruption and sentenced to two years in jail, with one suspended, for match fixing.

**1994** Italy: Torino is placed under investigation by the Italian fraud squad after being accused of providing prostitutes for match officials in an attempt to win the 1992 Uefa Cup. The club is also alleged to have siphoned off under-the-counter cash from transfers, including £465,000 for the 'phantom transfer' of Alessandro Palestro, the son of a club secretary, who was not registered with the club but studying at university.

**1995** John Fashanu, Hans Segers and Bruce Grobbelaar are cleared of match fixing.

George Graham, a former player and manager of Arsenal, is found guilty of misconduct and suspended from all football activity for his involvement in a bung scandal.

Malaysia: Australian-born Singapore international Abbas Saad is the first of several players to be convicted after revelations of bribery.

**1997** Malaysia: Floodlight failures at Premier League stadiums are traced to a Malaysia-based betting syndicate, agents of which will be caught two years later.

**1998** Switzerland: Sepp Blatter is elected as Fifa president; he will preside for 17 years.

## Twenty-first century

**2004** The English FA begins work with betting exchange Betfair to prevent match fixing and illegal betting.

South Africa: 33 people, including referees and club officials, are arrested on match-fixing charges.

Greece: The Public Prosecutions Office investigates allegations of match fixing surrounding a Uefa Cup tie between Panionios and Dinamo Tblisi.

**2005** Germany: Referee Robert Hoyzer is jailed for 29 months for taking bribes. His chief accomplice, a Croat bar owner, is jailed for 35 months.

Vietnam: Large-scale betting rings are revealed in the country's professional football league.

Brazil: Fifa referee Elson Pereira de Carvalho and his colleague Paulo Jose Danelon are found to have accepted bribes to fix matches in the Brazilian championship. The replay of 11 matches is ordered, and Elson is banned for life.

Portugal: In the 'Golden Whistle' inquiry, 26 officials (including nine referees) are charged with match fixing.

Germany: The Deutscher Fussball-Bund (DFB) makes a payment of £4.7 million (€6.7 million) to Fifa; the money is ostensibly for a 'cultural programme' but, later, it is alleged that the actual purpose of the payment is to use Fifa accounts to repay a loan to former adidas CEO Robert Louis-Dreyfus (who dies in 2009). Louis-Dreyfus allegedly deploys a slush fund to buy key votes in the bidding process for the World Cup. adidas (a Fifa 'partner') insists it had nothing to do with the payment (see below, 2015). **FIFA**

**2006** Slovakia: Two former Slovak top-division referees are fined for offering and accepting a bribe to ensure that Dukla Banska Bystrica beat Puchov in 2003.

Belgium: Lierse, La Louviere and one other club are investigated for match fixing. A Finnish club, Alianssi, is also linked.

Italy: Serie A clubs Juventus, Lazio and Fiorentina are demoted to Serie B as a result of the *Calciopoli*, the biggest corruption scandal in football's history to date.

**2007** Harry Redknapp, the manager of several English clubs during his career, is arrested, along with other personnel from Portsmouth, and accused of tax evasion. He is later cleared, but during his trial jurors hear that he has received two transfer-related bonus payments totalling £189,000 into an account in Monaco.

**2010** Fifa receives nine official bids for the 2018 and 2022 World Cups. This starts the most turbulent period in the organization's history. Russia and Qatar will ultimately be named as winning bidders. **FIFA**

The English FA's bid leader is recorded making comments about alleged attempts by Spain and Russia to bribe referees at the then forthcoming 2010 World Cup. **FIFA**

Three Fifa officials are named in a BBC programme that alleges that they took bribes from ISL (see above). In 2013, an internal investigation concludes that two of the identified officials accepted illegal payments from ISL. **FIFA**

Fifa's Ethics Committee confirms the suspension of six Fifa officials after claims by a British newspaper that they offered to sell their World Cup votes. **FIFA**

**2011** Germany: The Bochum Trial takes place, concerning about 270 games across Europe and Asia.

Finland: Tampere United are indefinitely suspended from Finnish football for accepting payments from a person known for match fixing.

Turkey: A match-fixing investigation begins; 60 suspects are detained by the Istanbul Police Department.

Brazil: Two referees conspire to rig 11 games.

Lord Triesman testifies at a UK parliamentary enquiry into England's failed bids for the 2018 World Cup and accuses Fifa Executive Committee members of trying to secure cash and privileges in return for their votes. **FIFA**

Sepp Blatter is re-elected for a fourth term as president of Fifa and promises to pursue a reform agenda. **FIFA**

Mohamed Bin Hammam is banned for life by Fifa after a hearing into bribery allegations. This ban is annulled in 2012 due to lack of evidence. **FIFA**

Fifa commissions a report into allegations of corruption in world football which is led by former US attorney and newly appointed head of Fifa's ethics committee Michael Garcia. The 430-page report will be completed in 2014 (see below). **FIFA**

Uefa president Michel Platini receives £1.55 million from Fifa president Blatter for 'consultancy work' completed nine years earlier; this will become the focus of investigation in 2015. **FIFA**

**2012** Norway: Match-fixing investigations result in arrests of Norwegian and Swedish citizens, including players of Follo FK and Asker Fotball.

Poland: 11 players are fined and given suspended prison sentences for fixing a match to ensure that Zaglebie Lubin qualify for the Uefa Cup.

**2013** El Salvador: Fesfut, the national football federation, imposes lifetime bans on 14 members of the national team for match fixing.

England: Six people, including Blackburn Rovers forward DJ Campbell, are arrested for allegedly fixing football games.

Spain: League president Javier Tebas claims 'eight to ten' matches in La Liga are fixed every season.

Australia: Ten players in Victoria's Premier League are involved in an illegal betting syndicate.

Singapore: A betting syndicate is reported by Europol (the EU's intelligence-sharing agency) to have made €8 million from rigged games.

Korea: 41 players are given worldwide lifetime bans from football after match fixing.

South Africa: The president of the South African FA Kirsten Nematandani and officials Dennis Mumble, Lindile Kika, Adeel Carelse and Barney Kujane are asked to take a voluntary leave of absence in response to allegations of match fixing organized by the convicted fixer Wilson Raj Perumal and his company Football4U.

A Swiss court concludes that João Havelange, the Fifa president between 1974 and 1998, had taken millions of dollars in illicit payments. Havelange and former Executive Committee members Ricardo Teixeira and Nicolás Leoz are found to have accepted illegal payments from ISL between 1992 and 2000. Havelange resigns as honorary president. **FIFA**

Fifa suspends outgoing Executive Committee member Chuck Blazer for 90 days, citing breaches of the Code of Ethics. **FIFA**

**2014** Former German international player Franz Beckenbauer is provisionally suspended for 90 days for failing to cooperate with a Fifa corruption investigation. **FIFA**

Michael Garcia's report, commissioned two years earlier, is summarized and published in a 42-page document, prompting Garcia to resign in protest at the expurgated version, which he is widely reported as calling 'incomplete and erroneous'. **FIFA**

**2015** Greece: A magistrate accuses Olympiakos president Vangelis Marinakis of involvement in a match-fixing 'crime ring' and imposes sanctions, including an interim ban from all football activities.

Italy: National coach Antonio Conte faces a hearing over match-fixing links. He is accused of committing sports fraud, and players also have cases heard; Conte served a four-month ban in 2012–2013.

Seven Fifa officials are arrested in dawn raids at a hotel in Zurich. They are later charged by the US authorities along with two other Fifa officials and five corporate executives over allegations of racketeering, wire fraud and money-laundering conspiracies spanning 24 years. They are accused of breeding decades of 'rampant, systemic and deep-rooted' corruption within Fifa by the US Department of Justice. **FIFA**

Sepp Blatter is re-elected as Fifa president for a fifth term after his challenger, Prince Ali bin al-Hussein, withdraws during a second round of voting. Blatter will resign within days. **FIFA**

A letter seen by Press Association Sport reveals that the South African FA asked Fifa secretary-general Jerome Valcke to authorise a $10 million payment to Jack Warner to support football in the Caribbean. **FIFA**

Uefa president Michel Platini is suspended from duties for 90 days and former Fifa president Blatter, is given a provisional 90-day suspension, whilst investigations into a £1.55 million payment made in 2011 proceed (see above). **FIFA**

Fifa suspends Franz Beckenbauer, who was a member of the executive committee that in 2010 cast secret votes for the World Cup destinations; Fifa alleges that he has failed to co-operate with the ongoing Garcia inquiry into Fifa's vote to award the 2018 and 2022 World Cups to Russia and Qatar. **FIFA**

Germany: Prosecutors raid the headquarters of the DFB and the homes of its former treasurer Horst Schmidt, its former president Theo Zwanziger and its current president Wolfgang Niersbach, who was also deputy head of the committee that led the bid for the 2006 World Cup. The focus of investigation is a suspect payment of £4.7 million (€6.7 million) in 2005 (see above) that never made it onto the DFB's tax declarations. **FIFA**

Brazil: The former head of Brazilian football Jose Maria Marin is extradited to the US on bribery charges; he is amongst seven officials from Fifa who are re-arrested. **FIFA**

Nepal: Ganesh Thapa, president of the All-Nepal FA, is banned for 10 years for bribery by Fifa's Ethics committee.

Uruguay: Former Fifa vice president Eugenio Figueredo spends Christmas Day in jail and prepares to go to trial for corruption charges, accused of taking millions of US dollars in bribes.

Blatter implies that there was an agreement in place for Russia to host the 2018 World Cup before the vote took place. **FIFA**

Fifa's general secretary Jerome Valcke is suspended by Fifa's ethics committee while there is an investigation into whether he was involved in a ticket-touting operation at the 2014 World Cup in Brazil. **FIFA**

**2016** Fifa's Ethics committee suspends Blatter and Platini for eight years. **FIFA**

Nigeria: Sports minister Solomon Dalung has blamed the underdevelopment of Nigerian football on corruption, saying that exposing corrupt practices in Nigeria won't stop foreign investors.

Paraguay: CONMEBOL headquarters are raided by Paraguayan state prosecutors in connection with the US Justice Department's ongoing probe into former head Nicolás Leoz.

Honduras: Alfredo Hawit, president of CONCACAF and vice president of Fifa, is extradited to the USA, where he is accused of corruption; the Honduran lawyer was arrested in Switzerland in 2015, charged with accepting millions of dollars' worth of bribes from companies in connection with the sale of broadcast rights for football matches in Latin America.

Spain: Spanish prosecutors reportedly request that Brazilian player Neymar be charged on two counts of fraud and corruption relating to his move to Barcelona in 2013; prosecutors act on legal proceedings brought by a Brazilian investment that claims it should have received 40 per cent of the €83 million (£62 million) that Barcelona paid Neymar's former club, Santos (of Brazil), for the player.

Jérôme Valcke, Fifa's former secretary general who served as Blatter's right-hand man for nearly a decade, is dismissed by the organization following long-running allegations of corruption. Valcke had been under suspension since September 2015. **FIFA**

Bryan Jiminez, former head of the Guatemalan Football Federation (Fedefut), is arrested; he had been on the run for the previous month. He is the 40th individual or organization charged in connection with the Fifa investigation. **FIFA**

Disclosure of corruption in cricket (in South Africa and India, especially), tennis (16 top-50 players are alleged to have thrown matches) and athletics (widespread cover-ups of doping in Russia are revealed) suggest that football's corrupt practices are not uncommon in professional sport.

## Research in Action

**World Cup 'votes for sale' scandal by *Sunday Times* Insight team (2010)**

### *What were the goals of the research?*

A team of investigative journalists from the British newspaper the *Sunday Times* pursued allegations of bribery among members of Fifa's executive committee. The allegations originated in the aftermath of the collapse of International Sport and Leisure (ISL) in 2001. Fifa had granted ISL exclusive rights to market World Cup tournaments, meaning that the organization was able to negotiate deals with global corporations that wished to have their brands associated with the prestigious competition and to broadcasters that were prepared to pay handsomely for the right to screen the games. There were suspicions that bribes were paid for the lucrative Fifa contract. The BBC obtained a confidential ISL document, which listed 175 secret payments. Three members of Fifa's executive committee were identified. So when, in autumn 2010, the announcement of the hosts of the World Cup tournaments in 2018 and

2022 approached, Fifa was under suspicion. 'Football's world governing body is not an organization known for its transparency, before or since the election of Sepp Blatter as its autocratic president 12 years ago,' wrote Matt Dickinson of the *Times* (the *Sunday Times*' sister paper) on 18 October 2010. He was commenting on Fifa's typically incurious response to allegations of malpractice. 'The World Cup bidding process has also become all about inducements,' he argued. The announcement was due in seven weeks and Dickinson's paper urged Fifa to suspend bidding, given the circumstances. The *Sunday Times* Insight team investigated the allegations. Unlike other research projects featured in the Research in Action sections in this book, this project was not academic; it was undertaken by a team of journalists guided by the goal of uncovering the truth or falsity of the claims that the World Cup bidding process was flawed.

## Why was the research relevant?

The investigation catalyzed the scandal that eventually engulfed Fifa. There were other probes into Fifa, one of the most significant being that of Andrew Jennings, who worked with the BBC. The Insight team's investigation provided important evidence. There were several resignations and dismissals directly attributable to the research team's findings.

## What methods were used?

### Covert interviews

The Insight team identified key individuals, interviewed them and recorded conversations surreptitiously, sometimes posing as representatives of a US business consortium that wanted the World Cup to take place in the US. Typically, scholarly organizations deter this kind of undercover interviewing in their codes of ethics, although there are exceptional circumstances in which it is allowed. For example, the British Sociological Association stipulates: 'In some cases, where the public interest dictates otherwise and particularly where power is being abused, obligations of trust and protection may weigh less heavily' (point 15, Statement of Ethical Practice for the British Sociological Association, 2002). But more usually, academic research protects the identity of interviewees and provides a shield of confidentiality. This research used covert methods and explicitly named the individuals concerned in an effort to expose them. Michel Zen-Ruffinen, for example, was a former Fifa general secretary ('a former right-hand man' of Sepp Blatter) with whom the team set up a meeting. He asked for £210,000 as his fee. The newspapers called this 'cash for votes', meaning that Zen-Ruffinen said that he could deliver votes in favour of a particular nation bidding to host a World Cup tournament. Remember that the voting is intended to be a democratic process.

## Middleman

Zen-Ruffinen explained that he was against bribery but could make 'introductions' to people who were able to influence votes in exchange for bribes. In ethnographic research, finding a 'middleman' who provides leads to other potential contacts is a well-established strategy. The process of accumulating contacts is known as 'snowballing'; it enables the researcher to increase the size of a sample and so enhance its validity. The Insight team anonymized Zen-Ruffinen's contacts' names as 'X' in early stages of the research while the team built up evidence.

## What were the main arguments?

There were two main arguments:

1. The bidding process to determine the destination of the World Cup competition, far from being fair, democratic and transparent, was preferential, unrepresentative and concealed.
2. Several high-ranking officials in Fifa were taking bribes and thus undermining the integrity of the organization and, by implication, football itself.

## And the conclusions or key findings?

The team concluded that it was time 'to overhaul a rotten system lacking in credibility'. The corruption was widespread and not limited to any individual or territory. Fifa's lack of any adequate methods of policing itself had allowed corruption to flourish. The World Cup tournaments in 2018 and 2022 were awarded to Russia and Qatar respectively. At the time of the vote, Qatar's member of the Fifa executive was Mohamed bin Hammam, who had paid bribes totalling over $5 million to the leaders of 30 football federations around the world in the years leading up to the vote. He was subsequently banned from Fifa for life, though the decision was reversed by the Court of Arbitration for Sport due to insufficient evidence (Blake and Calvert, 2015).

## *What were the strengths of the research?*

Had the Insight team adopted a more conventional academic approach to the research, they would have provided assurances of confidentiality and afforded their interviewees anonymity. They may have published similar findings, but would have been obliged to use pseudonyms and not to identify the figures involved. In this case, the potency of the research would have been greatly reduced and may not have led to the exposé that followed. By naming the people implicated, the research prompted further enquiries and, over the next several years, Fifa's corruption was disclosed through further interviews, the painstaking analysis of correspondence including email messages and the forensic examination of international bank accounts.

## *Were there any weaknesses?*

As in any enquiry of this type, there is always the possibility that interviewees can lie. This is minimized in conventional academic research by the provision of anonymity. The initial Insight interviews were conducted undercover, meaning that the researchers used subterfuge – in this instance, posing as other people. This makes verification virtually impossible, so the chances of discovering fresh information are counterbalanced by the prospect of some of that information being false. In this case, the enquiry produced verifiable evidence that there were gross abuses of power and that the methods used were fully justified in the public interest. (See *Sunday Times* Insight team, 2010a, 2010b, 2010c.)

# BIBLIOGRAPHY

Abosag, Ibrahim, Roper, Stuart and Hind, Daniel. (2012). Examining the relationship between brand emotion and brand extension among supporters of professional football clubs. *European Journal of Marketing*, 46, 1233–1251.

Ackroyd, Stephen and Thompson, Paul. (1999). *Organizational Misbehaviour.* London: Sage.

Adams, Adi. (2011). Josh wears pink cleats: inclusive masculinity on the soccer field. *Journal of Homosexuality*, 58, 579–596.

Adams, Adi, Anderson, Eric and McCormack, Mark. (2010). Establishing and challenging masculinity: the influence of gendered discourses in organized sport. *Journal of Language and Social Psychology*, 29, 278–300.

Adams, Catherine, Ashton, Matthew, Lupton, Hannah and Pollack, Hanne. (2014). Sport is king: an investigation into local media coverage of women's sport in the UK East Midlands. *Journal of Gender Studies*, 23, 422–439.

Adkins, Lisa. (2002). *Revisions: Gender and Sexuality in Late Modernity.* Buckingham: Open University Press.

Adorno, Theodor and Horkheimer, Max. (1972). *Dialectic of Enlightenment.* New York: Herder & Herder.

Agergaard, Sine and Botelho, Vera Lucia. (2014). The way out? African players' migration to Scandinavian women's football. *Sport in Society: Cultures, Commerce, Media, Politics*, 17, 523–536.

Agergaard, Sine, Botelho, Vera Lucia and Tiesler, Nina Clara. (2014). The typology of athletic migrants revisited: transnational settlers, sojourner and mobiles. In Agergaard, Sine and Tiesler, Nina Clara (eds). *Women, Soccer and Transnational Migration.* London: Routledge, pp. 191–214.

Alegi, Peter. (2004). *Laduma! Soccer, Politics and Society in South Africa.* Scottsville: University of KwaZulu-Natal Press.

Alegi, Peter. (2010). *African Soccerscapes: How a Continent Changed the World's Game.* London: Hurst & Company.

Anderson, Eric. (2011). Inclusive masculinities of university soccer players in the American Midwest. *Gender and Education*, 23, 729–744.

Arms, Robert L., Russell, Gordon W. and Sandilands, Mark L. (1979). Effects of viewing aggressive sports on the hostility of spectators. *Social Psychology Quarterly*, 42, 275–279.

Armstrong, Gary and Giulianotti, Richard. (2002). Avenues of contestation: football hooligans running and ruling urban spaces. *Social Anthropology*, 10, 211–238.

Armstrong, Gary and Giulianotti, Richard (eds). (2004). *Football in Africa: Conflict, Conciliation, and Community*. Basingstoke: Palgrave Macmillan.

Armstrong, Gary and Young, Malcolm. (1999). Fanatical football chants: creating and controlling the carnival. In Finn, Gerry and Giulianotti, Richard (eds). *Football Culture: Local Contests, Global Visions*. London: Frank Cass, pp. 73–211.

Associated Press. (2015). FIFA sees record $2 billion revenue after World Cup in Brazil. *Huffington Post*, 20 March. Available at: http://huff.to/1JVf6e2 (accessed July 2015).

Back, Les, Crabbe, Tim and Solomos, John. (2001). *The Changing Face of Football: Racism, Multiculturalism and Identity in the English Game*. Oxford: Berg.

Badenhausen, Kurt. (2015). David Beckham banks his biggest year ever with earnings of $75 million. *Forbes*, 11 March. Available at: http://onforb.es/1f43Ynq (accessed July 2015).

Bairner, Alan. (1999). Soccer, masculinity, and violence in Northern Ireland: between hooliganism and terrorism. *Men and Masculinities*, 1, 284–301.

Bairner, Alan. (2006). The Leicester School and the study of football hooliganism. *Sport in Society*, 9, 583–598.

Baker, Andrew. (2011). Heroes trapped in time. *Independent*, 23 October. Available at: http://ind.pn/1kkHJwb (accessed November 2015).

Baldwin, Leigh and Panja, Tariq. (2011). FIFA says South Africa World Cup had sales of $3.7 billion. *BloombergBusiness*, 3 March. Available at: http://bloom.bg/1VH4QMI (accessed October 2015).

Bale, John. (1994). *Landscapes of Modern Sport*. London: Leicester University Press.

Bancroft, Amanda. (2012). Twitter reaction to Ched Evans case shows rape culture is alive and kicking. *Guardian*, 23 April. Available at: http://bit.ly/1LgP0Fm (accessed August 2015).

Bascombe, Chris. (2011). Luis Suárez found guilty: eight match ban and £40,000 fine for race abuse row with Patrice Evra angers Liverpool. *Telegraph*, 21 December. Available at: http://bit.ly/1NsONls (accessed November 2015).

Baudrillard, Jean. (1998). *The Consumer Society: Myths and Structures*. London: Sage.

Bauer, Hans, Sauer, Nichola and Schmitt, Philipp. (2005). Customer-based brand equity in the team sport industry: operationalization and impact on the economic success of sports teams. *European Journal of Marketing*, 39, 496–513.

Bauman, Zygmunt. (1995). *Life in Fragments: Essays in Postmodern Morality*, Oxford: Blackwell.

Bauman, Zygmunt. (2002). *Society under Siege*. Cambridge: Polity Press.

Bauman, Zygmunt. (2005). *Liquid Life*. Cambridge: Polity Press.

Bauman, Zygmunt. (2007). *Consuming Life*. Cambridge: Polity Press.

BBC News. (2011). Newcastle City Council condemns St James' Park name change. 10 November. Available at: http://bbc.in/1SazGMW (accessed November 2015).

BBC News. (2012). Pub landlady Karen Murphy wins TV football court case. 24 February. Available at: http://bbc.in/1Sag9My (accessed November 2015).

BBC News. (2013a). Brazil referee decapitated after stabbing player. 7 July. Available at: http://bbc.in/1L7GkBe (accessed June 2015).

BBC News. (2013b). Online football abuse targeted by police. 23 August. Available at: http://bbc.in/1MtpIp2 (accessed August 2015).

BBC News. (2015a). Ched Evans timeline: key events since player's release. 10 January. Available at: http://bbc.in/1Kmm2Fy (accessed August 2015).

BBC News. (2015b). Ched Evans: 'I wouldn't take footballer on', Miliband says. 5 January. Available at: http://bbc.in/1hgUzJL (accessed August 2015).

BBC News. (2015c). Egypt football riot death sentences upheld by court. 9 June. Available at: http://bbc.in/1Mtq5jB (accessed June 2015).

BBC North East News. (1988). John Hall's 'Magpie Group' pledge Newcastle United's future. Available at: http://bit.ly/1eUPCVw (accessed August 2015).

BBC Sport. (2000). United waive fans' court costs. 24 November. Available at: http://bbc.in/1LOwJm6 (accessed November 2015).

BBC Sport. (2005). Wenger backs non-English line-up. 15 February. Available at: http://bbc.in/1NJdzgG (accessed August 2015).

BBC Sport. (2006). Football's original bung scandal. 20 September. Available at: http://bbc.in/1MNSmlt (accessed August 2015).

BBC Sport. (2011). Sepp Blatter says on-pitch racism can be resolved with handshake. 16 November. Available at: http://bbc.in/1o8HnZv (accessed August 2015).

BBC Sport. (2015a). England women's team: FA deletes 'unfortunate' tweet. 6 July. Available at: http://bbc.in/1fhaUhh (accessed November 2015).

BBC Sport. (2015b). Premier League TV rights: Sky and BT pay £5.1bn for live games. 10 February. Available at: http://bbc.in/1IMj8dJ (accessed November 2015).

Beaven, Brad. (2005). *Leisure, Citizenship and Working-Class Men in Britain, 1850–1945*. Manchester: Manchester University Press.

Bennett, Andy. (2005). *Culture and Everyday Life*. London: Sage.

Ben-Porat, Amir. (2009). Not just for men: Israeli women who fancy football. *Soccer & Society*, 10, 883–896.

Benson, John. (1994). *The Rise of Consumer Society in Britain, 1880–1980*. London: Longman.

Best, Shaun. (2013). Liquid fandom: neo-tribes and fandom in the context of liquid modernity. *Soccer & Society*, 14, 80–92.

Binkley, Sam. (2007). Lifestyle consumption. *Blackwell Encyclopedia of Sociology*. Oxford: Blackwell Reference Online.

Bird, Elizabeth. (2011). Are we all producers now? *Cultural Studies*, 25, 502–516.

Birley, Derek. (1993). *Sport and the Making of Britain*. Manchester: Manchester University Press.

Blackshaw, Tony. (2008). Politics, theory and practice: contemporary theory and football. *Soccer & Society*, 9, 325–345.

Blake, Heidi and Calvert, Jonathan. (2015). *The Ugly Game: The Qatari Plot to Buy the World Cup*. London: Simon & Schuster.

Boeri, Tito and Severgnini, Battista. (2008). *The Italian Job: Match Rigging, Career Concerns and Media Concentration in Serie A*. IZA discussion paper n. 3745. Available at: http://ftp.iza.org/dp3745.pdf (accessed August 2015).

Bolsmann, Chris. (2010). South African football tours at the turn of the twentieth century: amateurs, pioneers and profits. *African Historical Review*, 42, 91–112.

Bolsmann, Chris. (2011). The 1899 Orange Free State Football Team of Europe: 'race', imperial loyalty and sports spectacle. *International Journal of the History of Sport*, 28, 81–97.

Bolsmann, Chris. (2013a). Professional football in apartheid South Africa: leisure, consumption and identity in the National Football League, 1959–1977. *International Journal of the History of Sport*, 30, 1947–1961.

Bolsmann, Chris. (2013b). To sing or not to sing? National anthems, football obsessions and Bafana Bafana's World Cup. In Bolsmann, Chris and Alegi, Peter (eds). *Africa's Soccer*

*World Cup: Critical Reflections on Play, Patriotism, Spectatorship, and Space.* Ann Arbor, MI: University of Michigan Press, pp. 109–118.

Bolsmann, Chris. (2014). The 2010 World Cup in South Africa: a continental spectacle? In Rinke, Stefan and Schiller, Kay (eds). *The Fifa World Cup 1930–2010: Politics, Commerce, Spectacle and Identities.* Göttingen: Wallstein Verlag, pp. 372–388.

Bond, David. (2013). Fifa's report into ISL scandal is just window dressing. *BBC Sport*, 30 April. Available at: http://bbc.in/1IjmEam (accessed August 2015).

Bond, Patrick and Cottle, Eddie. (2011). Economic promises and pitfalls of South Africa's World Cup. In Cottle, Eddie (ed.). *South Africa's World Cup: A Legacy for Whom?* Scottsville: University of KwaZulu-Natal Press, pp. 39–72.

Bonilla-Silva, Eduardo. (2003). *Racism without Racists: Color-Blind Racism and the Persistence of Racial Inequality in the United States.* Lanham, MD: Rowman & Littlefield.

Bonilla-Silva, Eduardo. (2006). *Racism without Racists: Color-Blind Racism and the Persistence of Racial Inequality* (2nd edition). Boulder, CO: Lynne Rienner.

Bonilla-Silva, Eduardo, Goar, Carla and Embrick, David. (2006). When whites flock together: the social psychology of white habitus. *Critical Sociology*, 32, 229–253.

Bourdieu, Pierre. (1977). *Outline of a Theory of Practice.* Cambridge: Cambridge University Press.

Bourdieu, Pierre. (1978). Sport and social class. *Social Science Information*, 12, 819–840.

Bourdieu, Pierre. (1984). *Distinction: A Social Critique of the Judgement of Taste.* London: Routledge & Kegan Paul.

Bourdieu, Pierre. (1993). *The Field of Cultural Production.* Cambridge: Polity Press.

Bourdieu, Pierre. (2000). *Pascalian Meditations.* Cambridge: Polity Press.

Bourdieu, Pierre. (2003). *Firing Back against the Tyranny of the Market.* London: Verso.

Bourdieu, Pierre and Wacquant, Loic. (1992). *Invitation to a Reflexive Sociology.* Cambridge: Polity Press.

Boyes, Roger. (1983). Blowing the whistle on a football scandal. *Times*, 6 August, p. 20.

Boyle, Raymond and Haynes, Richard. (2004). *Football in the New Media Age.* Edinburgh: Edinburgh University Press.

Boyle, Raymond and Haynes, Richard. (2014). Sport, public relations and social media. In Billings, Andrew and Hardin, Marie (eds). *Routledge Handbook of Sport and New Media.* New York: Routledge, pp. 133–142.

Brackenridge, Celia, Bringer, Joy D., Cockburn, Claudi, Nutt, Gareth, Pitchford, Andy, Russell, Kate and Pawlaczek, Zofia. (2004). The Football Association's Child Protection in Football Research Project 2002–2006: rationale, design and first year results. *Managing Leisure*, 9, 30–46.

Bradley, Diana. (2015). Crisis PR pros don't buy FIFA spokesman's positive take on arrests. *PR Week*, 27 May. Available at: http://bit.ly/1MvrPsu (accessed August 2015).

Brailsford, Dennis. (1991). *Sport, Time and Society: The British at Play.* London: Routledge.

Braudy, Leo. (1997). *The Frenzy of Renown: Fame and Its History*, New York: Vintage.

Brown, Adam. (2008). 'Our club, our rules': fan communities at FC United of Manchester. *Soccer & Society*, 9, 346–358.

Brown, Adam and Walsh, Andy. (1999). *Not for Sale! Manchester United, Murdoch and the Defeat of BSkyB.* Edinburgh and London: Mainstream.

Brown, Adam, Crabbe, Tim and Mellor, Gavin. (2006). English football and its communities. *International Review of Modern Sociology*, 32, 159–179.

Brown, Adam, Crabbe, Tim and Mellor, Gavin. (2008). Introduction: football and community – practical and theoretical considerations. *Soccer & Society*, 9, 303–312.

Brown, Matthew. (2014). *From Frontiers to Football: An Alternative History of Latin America since 1800.* London: Reaktion.

Brus, Anne and Trangbaek, Else. (2003). Asserting the right to play: women's football in Denmark. *Soccer & Society*, 4, 95–111.

Bryman, Alan. (2004). *The Disneyization of Society*. London: Sage.

Buckley, Will. (2009). The forgotten story of … the Dick, Kerr's Ladies football team. *Guardian*, 9 September. Available at: http://bit.ly/1icnEap (accessed September 2015).

Buford May, Reuben A. (2009). The good and bad of it all: professional black male basketball players as role models for young black male basketball players. *Sociology of Sport Journal*, 26, 443–461.

Burdsey, Daniel. (2004). 'One of the lads'? Dual ethnicity and assimilated ethnicities in the careers of British Asian professional footballers. *Ethnic and Racial Studies*, 27, 757–779.

Burdsey, Daniel. (2007). *British Asians and Football: Culture, Identity, Exclusion*. London: Routledge.

Burdsey, Daniel. (2009). Forgotten fields? Centralizing the experiences of minority ethnic men's football clubs in England. *Soccer & Society*, 10, 704–721.

Burdsey, Daniel. (2011). *Race, Ethnicity and Football: Persisting Debates and Emergent Issues*. London: Routledge.

Burns, Tom. (1992). *Erving Goffman*. London: Routledge.

Bush, Alan J., Martin, Craig A. and Bush, Victoria D. (2004). Sports celebrity influence on the behavioral intentions of Generation Y. *Journal of Advertising Research*, 44, 108–118.

Butler, Judith. (1997). *Excitable Speech: A Politics of the Performative*. London: Routledge.

Carnibella, Giovanni, Fox, Anne, Fox, Kate, McCann, Joe, Marsh, James and Marsh, Peter. (1996). *Football Violence in Europe*. Unpublished report to the Amsterdam Group. Oxford: Social Issues Research Centre. Available at: http://bit.ly/1iDKiYo (accessed November 2015).

Carr, Edward Hallett. (1963). *What Is History?* London: Penguin.

Carrabine, Eamonn, Cox, Pamela, Fussey, Pete, Hobbs, Dick, South, Nigel, Thiel, Darren and Turton, Jackie. (2014). *Criminology: A Sociological Introduction* (3rd edition). London: Routledge.

Cashmore, Ellis. (1999). *Beckham*. Cambridge: Polity Press.

Cashmore, Ellis. (2008). *Sport and Exercise Psychology: The Key Concepts*. London: Routledge.

Cashmore, Ellis. (2010). *Making Sense of Sports*. London: Routledge.

Cashmore, Ellis. (2014). *Celebrity Culture* (2nd edition). London: Routledge.

Cashmore, Ellis and Cleland, Jamie. (2011). Why aren't there more black football managers? *Ethnic and Racial Studies*, 34, 1594–1607.

Cashmore, Ellis and Cleland, Jamie. (2012). Fans, homophobia and masculinities in association football: evidence of a more inclusive environment. *The British Journal of Sociology*, 63, 370–387.

Cashmore, Ellis and Cleland, Jamie. (2014). *Football's Dark Side: Corruption, Homophobia, Violence and Racism in the Beautiful Game*. Basingstoke: Palgrave Pivot.

Cashmore, Ellis and Parker, Andrew. (2003). One David Beckham? Celebrity, masculinity and the soccerati. *Sociology of Sport Journal*, 20, 214–231.

Castells, Manuel. (2009). *Communications Power*. Cambridge: Cambridge University Press.

Caudwell, Jayne. (1999). Women's football in the United Kingdom: theorizing gender and unpacking the butch lesbian image. *Journal of Sport & Social Issues*, 23, 390–402.

Caudwell, Jayne. (2011). Gender, feminism and football studies. *Soccer & Society*, 12, 330–344.

Cawthorne, Nigel. (2012). *Football Hooligans*. London: Hachette.

Chadwick, Simon and Beech, John. (2007). Introduction: the marketing of sport. In Beech, John and Chadwick, Simon (eds). *The Marketing of Sport*. Harlow: Pearson Education, pp. 3–22.

Chadwick, Simon and Holt, Michael. (2006). Building global sports brands: key success factors in the marketing of the UEFA Champions League. In Desbordes, Michael (ed.). *Marketing and Football: An International Perspective*. Oxford: Butterworth-Heinemann, pp. 22–50.

Chester, Daniel Norman. (1968). *Report of the Committee on Football*. London: HM Stationery Office.

Chisari, Fabio. (2004). 'The cursed cup': Italian responses to the 1985 Heysel disaster. *Soccer & Society*, 5, 201–218.

Christensen, Mette Krogh and Sørensen, Jan Kahr. (2009). Sport or school: dreams and dilemmas for talented young Danish football players. *European Physical Education Review*, 15, 115–133.

Christensen, Mette Krogh, Laursen, Dan Norgaard and Sørensen, Jan Kahr. (2011). Situated learning in youth elite football: a Danish case study among talented male under-18 football players. *Physical Education and Sport Pedagogy*, 16, 163–178.

Christenson, Marcus and Kelso, Paul. (2004) Soccer chief's plan to boost women's game? Hotpants, *Guardian*, 16 January. Available at: http://bit.ly/1JJSSy9 (accessed September 2015).

Chung, Heejoon. (2003). Sport star vs rock star in globalizing popular culture: similarities, difference and paradox in discussion of celebrities. *International Review for the Sociology of Sport*, 38, 99–108.

Clark, Sheryl and Paechter, Carrie. (2007). Why can't girls play football? Gender dynamics and the playground. *Sport, Education and Society*, 12, 261–276.

Clark, Tom. (2006). 'I'm Scunthorpe 'til I die': constructing and (re)negotiating identity through the terrace chant. *Soccer & Society*, 7, 494–507.

Clarke, John. (1973). *Football Hooliganism and the Skinheads*. Sub and Popular Culture Series. Birmingham: Centre for Contemporary Cultural Studies, University of Birmingham.

Clarke, John. (1976). The skinheads and the magical recovery of community. In Hall, Stuart and Jefferson, Tony (eds). *Resistance Through Rituals: Youth Subcultures in Post-War Britain*. London: Hutchinson, pp. 99–102.

Clarke, John and Critcher, Charles. (1995). *The Devil Makes Work: Leisure in Capitalist Britain*. London: Macmillan.

Cleland, Jamie. (2009). The changing organizational structure of football clubs and their relationship with the external media. *International Journal of Sport Communication*, 2, 417–431.

Cleland, Jamie. (2011). The media and football supporters: a changing relationship. *Media, Culture & Society*, 33, 299–315.

Cleland, Jamie. (2014). Racism, football fans and online message boards: how social media has added a new dimension to racist discourse in English football. *Journal of Sport & Social Issues*, 38, 415–431.

Cleland, Jamie. (2015). *A Sociology of Football in a Global Context*. London: Routledge.

Cleland, Jamie and Cashmore, Ellis. (2013). Football fans' views of racism in British football. *International Review for the Sociology of Sport*. Available at: http://bit.ly/1IXYCBZ (accessed August 2015).

Cleland, Jamie and Cashmore, Ellis. (2014). Fans, racism and British football in the twenty-first century: the existence of a colour-blind ideology. *Journal of Ethnic and Migration Studies*, 40, 638–654.

Cleland, Jamie and Dixon, Kevin. (2015). 'Black and whiters': the relative powerlessness of 'active' supporter organization mobility at English Premier League football clubs. *Soccer & Society*, 16, 540–554.

Coakley, Jay. (2009). Violence in sports: how does it affect our lives? In Coakley, Jay and Pike, Elizabeth (eds). *Sports in Society: Issues and Controversies*. London: McGraw-Hill, pp. 194–228.

Coddington, Anne. (1997). *One of the Lads: Women that Follow Football*. London: HarperCollins.

Cohen, Ira. (2008). Anthony Giddens. In Stones, Rob (ed.). *Key Sociological Thinkers* (2nd edition). Basingstoke: Palgrave Macmillan, pp. 323–338.

Collins, Tony and Vamplew, Wray. (2002). *Mud, Sweat and Beers: A Cultural History of Sport and Alcohol*. Oxford: Berg.

Collinson, David. (1988). Engineering humour: masculinity, joking and conflict in shopfloor relations. *Organization Studies*, 9, 181–199.

Collinson, David. (1992). *Managing the Shopfloor: Subjectivity, Masculinity and Workplace Culture*. Berlin: de Gruyter.

Collinson, David. (1994). Strategies of resistance: power, knowledge and subjectivity in the workplace. In Jermier, John M., Knights, David and Nord, Walter (eds). *Resistance and Power in Organizations*. London: Routledge, pp. 25–68.

Conejo, Rosa Aza, Banos-Pinto, Jose, Dominguez, Juan Francisco Canal and Guerrero, Placido Rodriguez. (2007). The economic impact of football on the regional economy. *International Journal of Sports Management and Marketing*, 2, 459–474.

Conn, David. (1997). *The Football Business*. Edinburgh and London: Mainstream.

Conn, David. (1999). Newcastle's bond holders sacrificed on altar of profit. *Independent*, 21 October. Available at: http://ind.pn/1NDgo1y (accessed October 2015).

Conn, David. (2006). How the Geordie Nation turned into a cash cow. *Guardian*, 8 February. Available at: http://bit.ly/1IP5vZJ (accessed August 2015).

Conn, David. (2015a). Football Association welcomes a 70% rise in reporting racist abuse. *Guardian*, 2 March. Available at: http://bit.ly/1ExjLAX (accessed August 2015).

Conn, David. (2015b). Social media cauldron of hate to players a sad reflection of modern life. *Guardian*, 16 April. Available at: http://bit.ly/1TM49kd (accessed August 2015).

Connell, Raewyn. (2002). *Gender*. Malden: Blackwell.

Connell, Raewyn. (2005). *Masculinities*. Cambridge: Polity Press.

Connett, David. (2015). Anti-corruption campaigners furious as Government considers softening Bribery Act. *Independent*, 29 July. Available at: http://ind.pn/1IsoG72 (accessed July 2015).

Conway, Richard. (2014). Gordon Taylor: 'hidden resistance' to hiring black managers. BBC Sport, 23 September. Available at: http://bbc.in/1uVXASE (accessed August 2015).

Cook, Daniel. (2007). Consumption, urban / city as consumerspace. *Blackwell Encyclopedia of Sociology*. Oxford: Blackwell Reference Online.

Cook, Daniel. (2008). The missing child in consumption theory. *Journal of Consumer Culture*, 8, 219–242.

Couppis, Maria. (2008). *Dopamine and the Positively Reinforcing Properties of Aggression*. Unpublished PhD thesis, Nashville, TN: Vanderbilt University.

Crabbe, Tim. (2008). Postmodern community and future directions: fishing for community: England fans at the 2006 FIFA World Cup. *Soccer & Society*, 9, 428–438.

Crawford, Garry. (2004). *Consuming Sport: Fans, Sport and Culture*. London: Routledge.

Creek, Frederick Norman Smith. (1933). *A History of the Corinthian Football Club*. London: Longmans, Green & Co.

Critcher, Charles. (1979). *Football since the War in Working Class Culture: Studies in History and Theory*. London: Hutchinson.

Croll, Andy. (2000). *Civilizing the Urban: Popular Culture and Public Space in Merthyr, c. 1870–1914*. Cardiff: University of Wales Press.

Croydon, Emily. (2013). Women's Euros 2013: women's football's forgotten heroines, *BBC Sport*. Available at: http://bbc.in/1LRHpiG (accessed October 2015).

Cunningham, Hugh. (1980). *Leisure in the Industrial Revolution, 1780–1880*. London: Croom Helm.

Cushion, Christopher and Jones, Robyn L. (2006). Power, discourse, and symbolic violence in professional youth soccer: the case of Albion football club. *Sociology of Sport Journal*, 23, 142–161.

Cushion, Christopher and Jones, Robyn L. (2014). A Bourdieusian analysis of cultural reproduction: socialisation and the 'hidden curriculum' in professional football. *Sport, Education and Society*, 19, 276–298.

Daniel, Paul. (2004). Football for children or children for football? A contemporary boys' league and the politics of childhood. In Wagg, Steve (ed.). *British Football and Social Exclusion: Sport in the Global Society*. London: Routledge, pp. 205–223.

Darby, Paul. (2002). *Africa, Football and Fifa: Politics, Colonialism and Resistance*. London: Frank Cass.

Darby, Paul. (2008). Stanley Rous's 'own goal': football politics, South Africa and the Fifa presidency. *Soccer & Society*, 9, 259–272.

Dart, Jon. (2008). Confessional tales from former football hooligans: a nostalgic, narcissistic wallow in football violence. *Soccer & Society*, 9, 42–55.

Dart, Jon. (2009). Blogging the 2006 Fifa World Cup Finals. *Sociology of Sport Journal*, 26, 107–126.

Davis, Kathy. (1995). *Reshaping the Female Body*. New York: Routledge.

Davis, Leon. (2014). Football fandom and authenticity: a critical discussion of historical and contemporary perspectives. *Soccer & Society*, 16, 422–436.

Davis, Margaret. (2014). Charges dropped against Tottenham fans facing prosecution for 'Yid' chant. *Independent*, 7 March. Available at: http://ind.pn/1kapDHR (accessed October 2015).

DBU. (n.d.). *Vision 2020*. Available at: http://bit.ly/1icqgVK (accessed September 2015).

De Graaf, Gjalt. (2007). Causes of corruption: towards a contextual theory of corruption. *Public Administration Quarterly*, 31, 39–84.

Degun, Tom. (2013). The future of football is feminine, says Blatter. *Inside the Games*, 2 January. Available at: http://bit.ly/1OxLF5A (accessed September 2015).

De Haan, Willem. (2008). Violence as an essentially contested concept. In Body-Gendrot, Sophie and Spierenburg, Pieter (eds). *Violence in Europe*. New York: Springer, pp. 27–40.

De Muinck, Pieterjan and Quatacker, Joachim. (2013). *Detecting Corruption in Soccer through the Inefficiency of Bookmakers*. Masters Thesis, Science and Business Administration, Gent, Belgium: Universiteit Gent. Available at: http://bit.ly/1DtIOtH (accessed August 2015).

Derbaix, Christian and Decrop, Alain. (2011). Colours and scarves: an ethnographic account of football fans and their paraphernalia. *Leisure Studies*, 30, 271–291.

DFB. (2015). Mitglieder-Statistik. Available at: http://bit.ly/1UAHIE8 (accessed September 2015).

Dickinson, Matt. (2010). Chance to overhaul rotten system lacking in credibility. *Times*, 18 October, p. 3.

Dix, Steve, Phau, Ian and Pougnet, Sonia (2010). *Bend It Like Beckham*: the influence of sports celebrities on young adult consumers. *Young Consumers*, 11, 36–46.

Dixon, Kevin. (2011). A third way for football fandom research: Anthony Giddens and structuration theory. *Soccer & Society*, 12, 279–298.

Dixon, Kevin. (2012). Learning the game: football fandom culture and the origins of practice. *International Review for the Sociology of Sport*, 48, 334–348.

Dixon, Kevin. (2013). *Consuming Football in Late Modern Life*. Farnham: Ashgate.

Dixon, Kevin. (2014a). The football fan and the pub: an enduring relationship. *International Review for the Sociology of Sport*, 49, 382–399.

Dixon, Kevin. (2014b). The role of lateral surveillance in the construction of authentic football fandom practice. *Surveillance & Society*, 11, 466–480.

Dixon, Kevin. (2014c). A woman's place recurring: structuration, football fandom and sub-cultural subservience. *Sport in Society, Cultures, Commerce, Media, Politics*, 18, 636–651.

Dixon, Kevin. (2014d). Football fandom and Disneyization in late-modern life. *Leisure Studies*, 33, 1–21.

Dixon, Kevin. (2015). Sports fans. In Houlihan, Barrie and Malcolm, Dominic (eds). *Sport and Society: A Student Introduction* (3rd edition). London: Sage, pp. 438–460.

Dixon, Kevin and Gibbons, Tom. (2014). Introduction. In Dixon, Kevin and Gibbons, Tom (eds). *The Impact of the 2012 Olympic and Paralympic Games: Diminishing Contrasts, Increasing Varieties*. London: Palgrave Pivot, pp. 1–14.

Dixon, Kevin, Lowes, Jacqueline and Gibbons, Tom. (2014). Show Racism the Red Card: potential barriers to the effective implementation of the anti-racist message. *Soccer & Society*. Available at: http://bit.ly/1PuX07h (accessed August 2015).

Doherty, Killian. (2013). Cape Town, the city without and within the white lines. In Bolsmann, Chris and Alegi, Peter (eds). *Africa's Soccer World Cup: Critical Reflections on Play, Patriotism, Spectatorship, and Space*. Ann Arbor, MI: University of Michigan Press, pp. 52–60.

Doidge, Mark. (2015). 'If you jump up and down, Balotelli dies': racism and player abuse in Italian football. *International Review for the Sociology of Sport*, 50, 249–264.

Domeneghetti, Roger. (2014). *From the Back Page to the Front Room: Football's Journey through the English Media*. Huddersfield: Ockley Books.

Dorling, Daniel. (2011). *Injustice: Why Social Inequality Persists*. Bristol: Policy Press.

Dougan, Derek. (1980). *Doog*. Newton Abbot: Readers Union.

Doyle, Jason P., Pentecost, Robin D. and Funk, Daniel C. (2014). The effect of familiarity on associated sponsor and event brand attitudes following negative celebrity endorser publicity. *Sport Management Review*, 17, 310–323.

Dunn, Carrie. (2014). *Female Football Fans: Community, Identity and Sexism*. Basingstoke: Palgrave Pivot.

Dunning, Eric. (1967). The concept of development: two illustrative case studies. In Rose, Peter (ed.). *The Study of Society: An Integrated Anthology*. New York: Random House, pp. 879–893.

Dunning, Eric. (2000). Towards a sociological understanding of football hooliganism as a world phenomenon. *European Journal on Criminal Policy and Research*, 8, 141–162.

Dunning, Eric, Malcolm, Dominic and Waddington, Ivan. (2004). *Sport Histories: Figurational Studies in the Development of Modern Sports*. London: Routledge.

Dunning, Eric, Murphy, Patrick and Williams, John. (2014 [1988]). *The Roots of Football Hooliganism: An Historical and Sociological Study*. London: Routledge.

Durkheim, Emile. (1982 [1895]). *The Rules of Sociological Method*. London: Macmillan.

ECA. (2014). *Women's Club Football Analysis*. Available at: http://bit.ly/1on3v0r (accessed October 2015).

Eco, Umberto. (1986). *Travels in Hyperreality*. San Diego, CA: Harcourt Brace Jovanovich.

Edwards, Elsie. (2014). Fields of individuals and neoliberal logics: Japanese soccer ideals and the 1990s economic crisis. *Journal of Sport & Social Issues*, 38, 432–464.

Edwards, Luke. (2015). Newcastle owner Mike Ashley's 'preferred media partners' strategy threatens objective and independent press. *Telegraph*, 31 July. Available at: http://bit.ly/1If6e2D (accessed November 2015).

Edwards, Piers. (2014). Lima 1964: The world's worst stadium disaster. *BBC News*, 23 May, Available at: http://bbc.in/1Mx7dBV (accessed June 2015).

Elias, Norbert. (1978 [1939]). *The Civilising Process*. Oxford: Blackwell.

Elias, Norbert and Dunning, Eric. (1986). *The Quest for Excitement: Sport and Leisure in the Civilizing Process*. Oxford: Blackwell.

Elias, Norbert and Scotson, John. (1994). *The Established and the Outsiders* (2nd edition). London: Sage.

Embrey, C. (1986). The nature of dissent: a study of school and junior club soccer. In Evans, J. (ed.). *Physical Education, Sport and Schooling: Studies in the Sociology of Physical Education*. London: Falmer, pp. 133–151.

Evens, Tom, Iosifidis, Petros and Smith, Paul. (2013). *The Political Economy of Television Sports Rights*. Basingstoke: Palgrave Macmillan.

Fairhurst, Gail T. and Sarr, Robert A. (1996). *The Art of Framing: Managing the Language of Leadership*. San Francisco, CA: Jossey-Bass.

Fawbert, Jack. (2011). 'Wot, no Asians?' West Ham United fandom, the cockney diaspora and the 'New' East Enders. In Burdsey, Daniel (ed.). *Race, Ethnicity and Football: Persisting Debates and Emergent Issues*. London: Routledge, pp. 175–190.

Fenton, Natalie. (2000). Mass media. In Taylor, Steve (ed.). *Sociology: Issues and Debates*. New York: Palgrave Macmillan, pp. 297–321.

Fifa. (1909). Minutes of the 6th Annual Fifa Congress, Budapest, 30–31 May.

Fifa. (2015). Canada set for biggest ever TV production in women's football. 17 April. Available at: http://fifa.to/1hKNvW2 (accessed October 2015).

Finer, Samuel. (1966). *Vilfredo Pareto: Sociological Writings*. London: Pall Mall Press.

Fishwick, Nicholas. (1989). *English Football and Society: 1910–1950*. Manchester: Manchester University Press.

Fleming, Peter and Sewell, Graham. (2002). Looking for the good soldier, Švejk: alternative modalities of resistance in the contemporary workplace. *Sociology*, 36, 857–872.

Fleming, Peter and Spicer, Andre. (2003). Working at a cynical distance: implications for power, subjectivity and resistance. *Organization*, 10, 157–179.

Forrest, David. (2012a). Corruption of football by match-fixers. *Football Perspectives* (University of Salford blog), 13 August. Available at: http://bit.ly/1Ip3qA2 (accessed August 2015).

Forrest, David. (2012b). The threat to football from betting-related corruption. *International Journal of Sport Finance*, 7, 99–116.

Foucault, Michel. (1977). *Discipline and Punish: The Birth of the Prison*. New York: Vintage.

Fournier, Valerie. (1999). The appeal to 'professionalism' as a disciplinary mechanism. *The Sociological Review*, 47, 280–307.

Franck, Egon and Nüesch, Stephan. (2007). Avoiding *Star Wars*: celebrity creation as media strategy. *Kyklos*, 60, 211–230.

FREE. (2015). *We're in the Final: Findings, Insights, Recommendations from the FREE Project*. Report on the FREE Concluding Conference, Brussels, Committee of the Regions, 17 March. Available at: http://bit.ly/1HdXnU2 (accessed November 2015).

Frosdick, Steve and Marsh, Peter (2005). *Football Hooliganism*. Cullompton: Willian.

Gaffney, Christopher. (2008). *Temples of the Earthbound Gods: Stadiums in the Cultural Landscapes of Rio de Janeiro and Buenos Aires*. Austin, TX: University of Texas Press.

Gaffney, Christopher. (2009). Stadiums and society in twenty-first century Buenos Aires. *Soccer & Society*, 10, 160–182.

Gaffney, Christopher. (2015). Virando o jogo: the challenges and possibilities for social mobilization in Brazilian football. *Journal of Sport & Social Issues*, 39, 155–174.

Galeano, Eduardo. (2003). *Soccer in Sun and Shadow*. London: Verso.

Gardiner, Simon and Welch, Roger. (2011). Football, racism and the limits of 'colour-blind' law?: revisited. In Burdsey, Daniel (ed.). *Race, Ethnicity and Football: Persisting Debates and Emergent Issues*. London: Routledge, pp. 222–236.

Gearing, Brian. (1999). Narratives of identity among former professional footballers in the United Kingdom. *Journal of Aging Studies*, 13, 43–58.

Gee, Alison. (2014). Why Women's World Cup champion Brandi Chastain bared her bra. BBC News, 13 July. Available at: http://bbc.in/1W57ADK (accessed October 2015).

George, Rosalyn and Brown, Naima. (2000). Are you in or out? An exploration of girl friendship groups in the primary phase of schooling. *International Journal of Inclusive Education*, 4, 289–300.

Gerbner, George. (1958). The social anatomy of the romance-confession cover girl. *Journalism and Mass Communication Quarterly*, 35, 299–306.

Gerbner, George. (1960). The individual in a mass culture. *Saturday Review*, 18 June, 11–37.

Gerbner, George. (1969a). Toward 'cultural indicators': the analysis of mass mediated public message. *AV Communication Review*, 17, 137–148.

Gerbner, George. (1969b). The film hero: a cross-cultural study. *Journalism Monographs*, 13, 1–54.

Gerbner, George. (1994). The politics of media violence: some reflections. In Hamelink, Cees J. and Linne, Olga (eds). *Mass Communication Research: On Problems and Policies*. Norwood, NJ: Ablex, pp. 133–146.

Gerbner, George. (1995). The cultural frontier: repression, violence and the liberating alternative. In Lee, Philip (ed.). *The Democratization of Communication*. Cardiff: University of Wales Press, pp. 153–172.

Gerbner, George. (1998). Cultivation analysis: an overview. *Mass Communication and Society*, 1, 175–195.

Gerbner, George, Gross, Larry, Morgan, Michael and Signorelli, Nancy. (1980). The mainstreaming of America: Violence profile No. 11. *Journal of Communication*, 30, 10–29.

Gethard, Gregg. (2006). How soccer explains post-war Germany. *Soccer & Society*, 7, 51–61.

Gibbons, Tom. (2014). *English National Identity and Football Fan Culture: Who Are Ya?* Farnham: Ashgate.

Gibbons, Tom and Dixon, Kevin. (2010). 'Surf's up!': a call to take English soccer fan interactions on the internet more seriously. *Soccer & Society*, 11, 599–613.

Gibbons, Tom and Nuttall, Danny. (2012). Using e-surveys to assess the views of football fans within online communities. *Sport in Society: Cultures, Commerce, Media and Politics*, 15, 1228–1241.

Gibbons, Tom and Nuttall, Danny. (2014). True fan = watch match? In search of the authentic soccer fan. *Soccer & Society*. Available at: http://bit.ly/1gQ9w5i (accessed May 2015).

Gibson, Owen. (2015). Ched Evans furore shows a sport out of step with the modern world. *Guardian*, 7 January. Available at: http://bit.ly/1Pf4fTW (accessed June 2015).

Giddens, Anthony. (1984). *The Constitution of Society*. Cambridge: Polity Press.

Giulianotti, Richard. (1995). Participant observation and research into football hooliganism: reflections on the problems of entree and everyday risks. *Sociology of Sport Journal*, 12, 1–20.

Giulianotti, Richard. (1999). *Football: A Sociology of the Global Game*. Cambridge: Polity Press.

Giulianotti, Richard. (2001). A different kind of carnival. In Perryman, Mark (ed.). *Hooligan Wars: Causes and Effects of Football Violence*. Edinburgh and London: Mainstream. pp. 141–154.

Giulianotti, Richard. (2002). Supporters, followers, fans, and flaneurs: a taxonomy of spectator identities in football. *Journal of Sport & Social Issues*, 26, 25–46.

Giulianotti, Richard. (2004). Civilizing games: Norbert Elias and the sociology of sport. In Giulianotti, Richard (ed.). *Sport and Modern Social Theorists*. Basingstoke: Palgrave Macmillan, pp.145–160.

Giulianotti, Richard and Robertson, Roland. (2009). *Globalization and Football*. London: Sage.

Goffman, Erving. (1959). *The Presentation of Self in Everyday Life*. Harmondsworth: Penguin.

Goffman, Erving. (1961). *Asylums*. New York: Doubleday.

Goffman, Erving. (1983). The interaction order. American Sociological Association, 1982 Presidential address. *American Sociological Association*, 48, 1–17.

Goldblatt, David. (2006). *The Ball Is Round: A Global History of Football*. London: Viking.

Goldblatt, David. (2014a). Another kind of history: globalization, global history and the World Cup. In Rinke, Stefan and Schiller, Kay (eds). *The Fifa World Cup 1930–2010: Politics, Commerce, Spectacle and Identities*. Göttingen: Wallstein Verlag, pp. 15–29.

Goldblatt, David. (2014b). *Futebol Nation: A Footballing History of Brazil*. New York: Penguin.

Goldblatt, David. (2015). *The Game of Our Lives: The Meaning and Making of English Football*. London: Penguin.

Goode, Erich and Ben-Yehuda, Nachman. (2006). *Moral Panics: The Social Construction of Deviance* (2nd edition). Oxford: Blackwell.

Goscilo, Helena and Strukov, Vlad. (2011). Russian celebrities home and abroad: united under Putin. *Celebrity Studies*, 2, 209–213.

Gray, Ali. (2014). Go ahead, just take a guess at how much money Kate Moss is worth... *Marie Claire*, 20 May. Available at: http://bit.ly/1f8dPZi (accessed July 2015).

Grierson, Simon. (2015). Ched Evans rape conviction referred to court of appeal. *Guardian*, 5 October. Available at: http://bit.ly/1NOFGdf (accessed November 2015).

*Guardian*. (2015). Juventus' Max Allegri: 'only a madman would take kids to stadiums in Italy'. Available at: http://bit.ly/1MtQkWZ (accessed June 2015).

Guttmann, Allen. (1986). *Sport Spectators*. New York: Columbia University Press.

Hague, Euan and Mercer, John. (1998). Geographical memory and urban identity in Scotland: Raith Rovers FC and Kirkcaldy. *Geography*, 83, 105–116.

Hain, Peter. (2012). *Outside In*. London: Biteback Publishing.

Hall, Stuart. (1980). Encoding/decoding. In Hall, Stuart, Hobson, Dorothy, Lowe, Andrew and Willis, Paul (eds). *Culture, Media, Language*. London: Hutchinson, pp. 128–138.

Hamilton, Adrian. (1998). *An Entirely Different Game: The British Influence on Brazilian Football*. Edinburgh and London: Mainstream.

Hare, Robert. (2002). Psychopathy and risk for recidivism and violence. In Gray, Nicola, Laing, Judith and Noaks, Leslie (eds). *Criminal Justice, Mental Health, and the Politics of Risk*. London: Cavendish, pp. 27–47.

Harris, John and Parker, Andrew (eds). (2009). *Sport and Social Identities*. Basingstoke: Palgrave Macmillan.

Harris, John. (2005). The image problem in women's football. *Journal of Sport & Social Issues*, 29, 184–197.

Harris, Lloyd and Ogbonna, Emmanuel. (2008). The dynamics underlying service firm–customer relationships: insights from a study of English Premier League soccer fans. *Journal of Service Research*, 10, 382–399.

Harris, Scott R. (2015). *An Invitation to the Sociology of Emotions*. London: Routledge.

Harwell, Drew. (2015). Why hardly anyone sponsored the most-watched soccer match in U.S. history. *Washington Post*, 6 July. Available at: http://wapo.st/1Uqq2aZ (accessed September 2015).

Haynes, Richard. (2007). Footballers' image rights in the new media age. *European Sports Management Quarterly*, 7, 361–374.

Henderson, Jon. (2001). The 10 greatest cheats in sporting history. *Observer Sport Monthly*, 8 July. Available at: http://bit.ly/1Mk6jYq (accessed November 2015).

Hepp, Andreas. (2013). *Cultures of Mediatization*. Cambridge: Polity Press.

Hern, Alex. (2015). Twitter CEO: we suck at dealing with trolls and abuse. *Guardian*, 5 February. Available at: http://bit.ly/1zbx1XT (accessed August 2015).

Highfield, Tim, Harrington, Stephen and Bruns, Alex. (2013). Twitter as a technology for audiences and fandom. *Information, Communication & Society*, 16, 315–339.

Hill, Declan. (2008). *Calcio mafia [The Fix]*. Milan: Rizzoli.

Hirschi, Travis. (1969). *The Causes of Delinquency*. Berkeley, CA: University of California Press.

Hjarvard, Stig. (2013). *The Mediatization of Culture and Society*. London: Routledge.

Hobsbawm, Eric. (1989). *The Age of Empire: 1875–1914*. New York: Vintage.

Holland, Brian. (1997). Surviving leisure time racism: the burden of racial harassment on Britain's black footballers. *Leisure Studies*, 16, 261–277.

Holt, Richard. (1990). *Sport and the British: A Modern History*. Oxford: Clarendon Press.

Home Office. (2013). Statistics on football-related arrests and football banning orders: season 2012–13. Available at: http://bit.ly/1nYSFLx (accessed August 2015).

Home Office. (2014). Statistics on football-related arrests and football banning orders: season 2013–14. Available at: http://bit.ly/1MtiO3c (accessed August 2015).

Hopkins, Matt and Treadwell, James (eds). (2014). *Football Hooliganism, Fan Behaviour and Crime: Contemporary Issues*. London: Palgrave Macmillan.

Horne, John. (2006). *Sport in Consumer Culture*. Basingstoke: Palgrave Macmillan.

Horne, John. (2007). The four 'knowns' of sports mega-events. *Leisure Studies*, 26, 81–96.

Horne, John and Manzenreiter, Wolfram. (2002). *Japan, Korea and the 2002 World Cup*. London: Routledge.

Horne, John, Tomlinson, Alan, Whannel, Garry and Woodward, Kath. (2013). *Understanding Sport: A Socio-Cultural Analysis*. London: Routledge.

Horrie, C. (2002). *Premiership: Lifting the Lid on a Natural Obsession*. London: Pocket.

Horton, Donald and Wohl, R. Richard. (1956). Mass communication and parasocial interaction. *Psychiatry*, 19, 215–229.

Horton, Ed. (1997). *Moving the Goalposts: Football's Exploitation*. Edinburgh and London: Mainstream.

Hughson, John and Free, Marcus. (2006). Paul Willis, cultural commodities, and collective sport fandom. *Sociology of Sport Journal*, 23, 72–85.

Hutchins, Brett and Rowe, David. (2012) *Sport Beyond Television: The Internet, Digital Media and the Rise of Networked Media Sport*. London: Routledge.

Hylton, Kevin. (2005). 'Race', sport and leisure: lessons from Critical Race theory. *Leisure Studies*, 24, 81–98.

Hylton, Kevin. (2009). *'Race' and Sport: Critical Race Theory*. London: Routledge.

Hylton, Kevin and Lawrence, Stefan. (2015). Reading Ronaldo: contingent whiteness in the football media. *Soccer & Society*, 16, 765–782.

Ilan, Jonathan. (2015). *Understanding Street Culture: Poverty, Crime, Youth and Cool*. London: Palgrave Macmillan.

*Independent*. (2015). Fifa corruption timeline: the events that led up to the resignation of president Sepp Blatter. 3 June. Available at: http://ind.pn/1MBmX1d (accessed November 2015).

Jackman, Mary. (2002). Violence in social life. *Annual Review of Sociology*, 28, 387–415.

Jackson, Jamie. (2004). Triumph and despair, *Observer*, 4 July. Available at: http://bit.ly/1Mxe3Ht (accessed November 2013).

Jackson, Mark. (2015). Sky UK sees stable growth to reach 5.53 million broadband subscribers. *ISP Review*, 21 April. Available at: http://bit.ly/1WHm1Ue (accessed November 2015).

Jeanes, Ruth. (2011). 'I'm into high-heels and makeup but I still love football': exploring gender identity and football participation with preadolescent girls. *Soccer & Society*, 12, 402–420.

Jenkins, Henry. (1992). *Textual Poachers: Television Fans and Participatory Culture*. New York: Routledge.

Jenkins, Richard. (2008). *Social Identity* (3rd edition). London: Routledge.

Jennings, Andrew. (2006). *Foul! The Secret World of Fifa: Bribes, Vote Riggings and Ticket Scandals*. London: HarperSport.

Jennings, Andrew. (2011). Investigating corruption in corporate sport: the IOC and FIFA. *International Review for the Sociology of Sport*, 46, 387–398.

Johns, David P. and Johns, Jennifer S. (2000). Surveillance, subjectivism and technologies of power: an analysis of the discursive practice of high-performance sport. *International Review for the Sociology of Sport*, 35, 219–234.

Jones, Ian, Brown, Lorraine and Richards, Steven. (2012). Watching the FIFA World Cup in 2010 in England: the sojourner perspective. *Leisure Studies*, 33, 48–61.

Jones, Katharine. (2008). Female fandom: identity, sexism and men's professional football in England. *Sociology of Sport Journal*, 25, 516–537.

Jones, Les. (2013). *Soccer: Canada's National Sport*. Toronto, ON: Covershots Inc.

Jones, R., Glintmeyer, N. and McKenzie, A. (2005). Slim bodies, eating disorders and the coach–athlete relationship: a tale of identity creation and disruption. *International Review for the Sociology of Sport*, 40, 377–391.

Jones, Stephen. (1986). *Workers at Play: A Social and Economic History of Leisure, 1918–1939*. London: Routledge.

Jorge, Ana. (2015). 'Cristiano Ronaldo is cheap chic, *Twilight* actors are special': young audiences of celebrities, class and locality. *Celebrity Studies*, 6, 39–53.

Kamp, David. (1998). When Liz met Dick. *Vanity Fair*, March. Available at: http://vnty.fr/1xwMZP9 (accessed July 2015).

Katz, Donald. (1994). *Just Do It: The Nike Spirit in the Corporate World*. Holbrook, MA: Adams Media.

Kech, Clemens. (2015). Heysel and its symbolic value in Europe's collective memory. In Pyta, Wolfram and Havemann, Nils (eds). *European Football and Collective Memory*. New York: Palgrave Macmillan, pp. 152–170.

Keegan, Mike. (2015). FC United supporters to boycott first half of FA Cup clash with Chesterfield in protest against match being switched to Monday. 30 October. Available at: http://dailym.ai/1MFHou5 (accessed November 2015).

Kelly, Seamus and Waddington, Ivan. (2006). Abuse, intimidation and violence as aspects of managerial control in professional soccer in Britain and Ireland. *International Review for the Sociology of Sport*, 41, 147–164.

Kelner, Martin. (2011). Richard Keys and Andy Gray's talkSPORT debut: what did you think? *Guardian*, 14 February. Available at: http://bit.ly/1RRZSeX (accessed November 2015).

Kelso, Paul. (2012). John Terry found guilty of racially abusing QPR's Anton Ferdinand in FA hearing and handed four match ban. *Telegraph*, 27 September. Available at: http://bit.ly/1hiDLT9 (accessed August 2015).

Kerr, John. (1994). *Understanding Soccer Hooliganism*. Maidenhead: McGraw-Hill.

Kerr, John. H. and de Kock, Hilde. (2002). Aggression, violence, and the death of a Dutch soccer hooligan: a reversal theory explanation. *Aggressive Behavior*, 28, 1–10.

Kick It Out (2014). 200 current Premier League and Football League stars undertake Kick

It Out consultation. 18 March. Available at: http://bit.ly/1DXRusN (accessed August 2015).

King, Anthony. (1997). The lads: masculinity and the new consumption of football. *Sociology*, 3, 329–346.

King, Anthony. (1998). *The End of the Terraces: The Transformation of English Football in the 1990s*. London: Leicester University Press.

King, Anthony. (2002). *The End of the Terraces: The Transformation of English Football in the 1990s* (revised edition). London: Bloomsbury 3PL.

King, Colin. (2004). *Offside Racism: Playing the White Man*. Oxford: Berg.

Kollewe, Julia. (2014). Adidas looks to outrun Nike with its biggest advertising campaign ever. *Guardian*, 7 August. Available at: http://bit.ly/1KW3J5g (accessed November 2015).

Kraszewski, Jon. (2008). Pittsburgh in Fort Worth: football bars, sports television, sport fandom and the management of home. *Journal of Sport & Social Issues*, 32, 139–157.

Kuper, Simon. (1994). *Football Against the Enemy*. London: Orion.

Lanfranchi, Pierre and Taylor, Matthew. (2001). *Moving with the Ball: The Migration of Professional Footballers*. Oxford: Berg.

Lanfranchi, Pierre, Eisenberg, Christiane, Mason, Tony and Wahl, Alfred. (2004). *100 Years of Football: The Fifa Centennial Book*. London: Weidenfeld & Nicolson.

Lapchick, Richard. (1975). *The Politics of Race and International Sport: The Case of South Africa*. Westport, CT: Greenwood Press.

Lasch, Christopher. (1979). *The Culture of Narcissism: American Life in an Age of Diminishing Expectations*. London: Abacus.

Lawrence, Stefan. (2014). Racialising the 'great man': a Critical Race study of idealised male athletic bodies in *Men's Health* magazine. *International Review for the Sociology of Sport*. Available at: http://bit.ly/1IYk4GV (accessed August 2015).

Lawrence, Stefan. (forthcoming). 'We are the boys from the Black Country!' (Re)imagining local, regional and spectator identities through fandom at Walsall Football Club. *Social and Cultural Geography*.

legislation.gov.uk. (n.d.). Public Order Act 1986. Available at: http://bit.ly/1j96fzC (accessed October 2015).

Lever, Janet. (1969). *Soccer:* opium of the Brazilian people. *Transaction*, 7, 36–43.

Levi, Michael, Maguire, Mike and Brookman, Fiona. (2002). Violent crime. *The Oxford Handbook of Criminology*. Oxford: Oxford University Press, pp. 796–843.

Lewinson, Ryan T. and Palma, Oscar E. (2012). The morality of fighting in ice hockey: should it be banned? *Journal of Sport & Social Issues*, 36, 106–112.

Lindberg, Kasper. (2006). The man who traced 442 soccer slaves. *Play the Game: The Fourth World Communications Conference on Sport and Society*, 6–10 November, Copenhagen, p. 3. Available at: http://bit.ly/1hiGITX (accessed August 2015).

Lipinski, Tomas. (2008). Emerging legal issues in the collection and dissemination of internet-sourced research data: Part I, basic tort law issues and negligence. *International Journal of Internet Research Ethics*, 1, 92–114. Available at: http://bit.ly/1kgwHHI (accessed October 2015).

Llopis-Goig, Ramon. (2007). The recent evolution of football violence in Spain. In Itkonen, Hannu, Salmikangas, Anna-Katriina and McEvoy, Eileen (eds). *The Changing Role of Public, Civic and Private Sector in Sport Culture*. Jyväskylä: University of Jyväskylä, pp. 155–162.

Lock, Daniel, Taylor, Tracy and Darcy, Simon. (2008). Soccer and social capital in Australia: social networks in transition. In Nicholson, Matthew and Hoye, Russell (eds). *Sport and Social Capital*. Oxford: Elsevier, pp. 317–338.

Lok, Jaco and de Rond, Mark. (2013). On the plasticity of institutions: containing and restoring practice breakdowns at the Cambridge University boat club. *Academy of Management Journal*, 56, 185–207.

Lösel, Friedrich and Bliesener, Thomas. (2003). Hooligan violence: a study on its prevalence, origins, and prevention. In Dünkel, Frieder and Drenkhahn, Kirstin (eds). *Youth Violence: New Patterns and Local Responses*. Mönchengladbach: Forum, pp. 245–264.

Luther, Jessica. (2015). US soccer has failed over Hope Solo – but it shouldn't just ape the NFL. *Guardian*, 15 June. Available at: http://bit.ly/1LaFgii (accessed June 2015).

Mac an Ghaill, Mairtin and Haywood, Chris. (2007). *Gender, Culture and Society: Contemporary Femininities and Masculinities*. Basingstoke: Palgrave Macmillan.

MacClancy, Jeremy (ed.). (1996). *Sport, Identity and Ethnicity*. London: Berg.

McCracken, Grant. (1986). Culture and consumption: a theoretical account of the structure and movement of the cultural meaning of consumer goods. *Journal of Consumer Research*, 13, 71–84.

McDonald, Mary. (2009). Dialogues on whiteness, leisure, and (anti)racism. *Journal of Leisure Research*, 41, 5–21.

McDowell, Matthew L. (2013). *Cultural History of Association Football in Scotland, 1865–1902: Understanding Sports as a Way of Understanding Society*. Lampeter: Edwin Mellen Press.

McGill, Craig. (2001). *Football Inc.: How Soccer Fans Are Losing the Game*. London: Vision.

McGillivray, David. (2006). Facilitating change in the educational experiences of professional footballers: the case of Scottish football. *Managing Leisure*, 11, 22–38.

McGillivray, David and McIntosh, Aaron. (2006). 'Football is my life': theorizing social practice in the Scottish professional football field. *Sport in Society*, 9, 371–387.

McGillivray, David, Fearn, Richard and McIntosh, Aaron. (2005). Caught up in and by the beautiful game: a case study of Scottish professional footballers. *Journal of Sport & Social Issues*, 29, 102–123.

McLaren, Richard. (2008). Corruption and its impact on fair play. *Marquette Sports Law Review*, 19, 15–38.

Maffesoli, Michel. (1996). *The Time of the Tribes: The Decline of Individualism in Mass Society* (trans. Don Smith). London: Sage.

Magnay, Diana. (2010). Soccer match-fixing trial begins in Germany. *CNN Online*, 6 October. Available at: http://cnn.it/1Nrr59b (accessed November 2015).

Maguire, Joseph. (1986). The emergence of football spectating as a social problem 1880–1985: a figurational and developmental perspective. *Sociology of Sport Journal*, 3, 217–244.

Maguire, Joseph. (2011). The emergence of football spectating as a social problem. *Sport in Society*, 14, 883–897.

Maguire, Joseph, Jarvie, Grant, Mansfield, Louise and Bradley, Joe. (2002). *Sports Worlds: A Sociological Perspective*. Champaign, IL: Human Kinetics.

Maguire, M. (2007). Crime data and statistics. In Maguire, M., Reiner, R. and Morgan, R. (eds). *The Oxford Handbook of Criminology* (4th edition). Oxford: Oxford University Press, pp. 241–301.

*Manchester Evening News*. (2012). Footballer behind £1m Hyde drug ring. 5 July. Available at: http://bit.ly/20u5ZMN (accessed November 2015).

Mangan, James A. (2001). Soccer as moral training: missionary intentions and imperial legacies. In Dimeo, Paul and Mills, James (eds). *Soccer in Asia: Empire, Nation and Diaspora*. London: Frank Cass, pp. 41–56.

Manley, Andrew, Palmer, Catherine and Roderick, Martin. (2012). Disciplinary power, the oligopticon and rhizomatic surveillance in elite sports academies. *Surveillance & Society*, 10, 303–319.

Manning, Peter K. (2008). Goffman on organizations. *Organization Studies*, 29, 677–699.

Margaret Thatcher Foundation. (2015). *Remarks Visiting Milton Keynes (Luton FC)*. Available at: http://bit.ly/1fkDP2M (accessed June 2015).

Markham, Annette and Buchanan, Elizabeth. (2012). *Ethical Decision-Making and Internet Research*. Association of Internet Researchers. Available at: http://bit.ly/1eu0Dwa (accessed November 2015).

Marsh, Peter E. (1977). Football hooliganism: fact or fiction? *British Journal of Law and Society*, 4, 256–259.

Marsh, Peter E. (1982a). Social order on the British soccer terraces. *International Social Science Journal*, 34, 247–256.

Marsh, Peter E. (1982b). *Aggro: The Illusion of Violence*. Oxford: Blackwell.

Marshall, P. David. (2014). *Celebrity and Power: Fame in Contemporary Culture*. Minneapolis, MN: University of Minnesota Press.

Mason, Tony. (1980). *Association Football and English Society 1863–1915*. Brighton: Harvester.

Mason, Tony. (1995). *Passion for the People*. London: Verso.

Mead, George Herbert. (1934). *Mind, Self, and Society from the Standpoint of a Social Behaviorist*. Chicago, IL: University of Chicago Press.

Media Education Foundation. (2010). *The Mean World Syndrome: Desensitization and Acceleration*. Available at: http://bit.ly/1fEoaZV (accessed November 2015).

Mehus, Ingar and Osborn, Guy. (2010). Consuming football: the Norwegian experience, the English Impact, and the possibilities of interdisciplinary research. *Scandinavian Sports Studies Forum*, 1, 89–113.

Mennesson, Christine. (2010). Gender regimes and habitus: an avenue for analysing gender building in sports contexts. *Sociology of Sport Journal*, 29, 4–21.

Messner, Michael. (1992). *Power at Play: Sports and the Problem of Masculinity*. Boston, MA: Beacon Press.

*Metro*. (2013). Is Wonga really Newcastle United's greatest ever sponsor after only five weeks? 23 August. Available at: http://bit.ly/1P84axX (accessed August 2015).

Mewett, Peter and Toffoletti, Kim. (2011). Finding footy: female fan socialization and Australian rules football. *Sport in Society*, 14, 670–684.

Michallat, Wendy. (2005). Droit au but: Violette Morris and women's football in 'les années folles'. *French Studies Bulletin*, 97, 13–17.

Michels, Robert. (2009 [1911]). *Political Parties: A Sociological Study of the Oligarchical Tendencies of Modern Democracy*. Truro: Dodo Press.

Midgley, Simon. (2011). 'When the seagulls follow the trawler, it is because they think sardines will be thrown into the sea'. *Independent*, 23 October. Available at: http://ind.pn/1IJY7PS (accessed October 2015).

Miles, Matthew and Huberman, Michael. (1994). *Qualitative Data Analysis: An Expanded Sourcebook*. London: Sage.

Miller, William. (1997). *The Anatomy of Disgust*. Cambridge, MA: Harvard University Press.

Millward, Peter. (2008). Rivalries and racisms: 'closed' and 'open' Islamophobic dispositions amongst football supporters. *Sociological Research Online*, 13. Available at: http://bit.ly/1JcUb9Z (accessed August 2015).

Millward, Peter. (2011). *The Global Football League: Transnational Networks, Social Movements and Sport in the New Media Age*. Basingstoke: Palgrave Macmillan.

Millward, Peter. (2013). New football directors in the twenty-first century: profit and revenue in the English Premier League's transnational age. *Leisure Studies*, 32, 399–414.

Modood, Tariq. (2007). *Multiculturalism*. Cambridge: Polity Press.

Monk, Des. (2000). Modern apprenticeships in football: success or failure? *Industrial and Commercial Training*, 32, 52–60.

Monk, Des and Russell, Dave. (2000). Training apprentices: tradition versus modernity in the football industry. *Soccer & Society*, 1, 62–79.

Moorehouse, Herbert F. (1994). From zines like these? Fanzines, tradition and identity in Scottish football. In Jarvie, Grant and Walker, Graham (eds). *Scottish Sport and the Making of the Nation: Ninety Minute Patriots*. Leicester: University of Leicester Press, pp. 173–194.

Moran, Richie. (2000). Racism in football: a victim's perspective. *Soccer & Society*, 1, 190–200.

Morgan, Michael. (2012). *George Gerbner: A Critical Introduction to Media and Communication Theory*. New York: Peter Lang.

Morrison, Elizabeth Wolfe and Milliken, Frances J. (2000). Organizational silence: a barrier to change and development in a pluralistic world. *The Academy of Management Review*, 25, 706–725.

Morrow, Stephen. (1999). *The New Business of Football: Accountability and Finance in Football*. Basingstoke: Palgrave Macmillan.

Mosca, Gaetano. (1939 [1884]). *Ruling Class*. New York: McGraw-Hill.

Murphy, Patrick, Sheard, Kenneth and Waddington, Ivan. (2000). Figurational sociology and its application to sport. In Coakley, Jay and Dunning, Eric. (eds) *Handbook of Sports Studies*. London: Sage. pp. 92–105.

Murphy, Patrick, Williams, John and Dunning, Eric. (1990). *Football on Trial: Spectator Violence and Development in the Football World*. London: Routledge.

Murray, Scott. (2008). The forgotten story of…Willie Johnston. *Guardian*, 23 December. Available at: http://bit.ly/1J0UCka (accessed August 2015).

Nagle, John, Dodd, Andrew, Ellis, Ralph and Downer, Jon. (2010). *The Football League Supporters Survey 2010*. Preston: The Football League. Available at: http://bit.ly/1Q7w9Bl (accessed November 2015).

Nash, Rex. (2000). The sociology of English football in the 1990s: fandom, business and future research. *Football Studies*, 3, 49–62.

Nash, Rex. (2001). English football fan groups in the 1990s: class, representation and fan power. *Soccer & Society*, 2, 39–58.

Natali, Marcos. (2007). The realm of the possible: remembering Brazilian *Futebol*. *Soccer & Society*, 8, 267–282.

Nayak, Anoop and Kehily, Mary Jane. (2013). *Gender, Youth and Culture: Young Masculinities and Femininities*. Basingstoke: Palgrave Macmillan.

Neuhaus, Fabian and Webmoor, Timothy. (2012). Agile ethics for massified research and visualization. *Information, Communication and Society*, 15, 43–65.

Newsham, Gail J. (1994). *In a League of Their Own! The Dick, Kerr Ladies 1917–1965*, Chorley: Pride of Place.

Numerato, Dino. (2009). The media and sports corruption: an outline of sociological understanding. *International Journal of Sport Communication*, 2, 261–273.

Obel, Camilla. (2012). Fantasy, fun and identity construction among female fans of rugby union. In Toffoletti, Kim and Mewett, Peter (eds). *Sport and Its Female Fans*. New York: Routledge, pp. 115–134.

Orwell, George. (1970). The sporting spirit. In Orwell, George. *In Front of Your Nose: The Collected Essays, Journalism*. Harmondsworth: Penguin, pp. 40–44.

Palmer, Catherine. (2009). The 'grog squad': an ethnography of beer consumption at Australian rules football. In Wenner, Lawrence and Jackson, Steven (eds). *Sport, Beer and Gender: Promotional Culture and Contemporary Social Life*. New York: Peter Lang, pp. 225–241.

Paradiso, Eugenio. (2009). The social, political, and economic causes of violence in Argentine soccer. *Nexus: The Canadian Student Journal of Anthropology*, 21, 65–79.

Paradiso, Eugenio. (2014). Football, clientelism and corruption in Argentina: an anthropological inquiry. *Soccer & Society*, I-First. Available at: http://bit.ly/1T2KagN (accessed August 2015).

Parker, Andrew. (1995). Great expectations: grimness or glamour? The football apprentice in the 1990s. *The Sports Historian*, 15, 107–126.

Parker, Andrew. (1996a). *Chasing the 'Big Time': Football Apprenticeship in the 1990s*. Unpublished PhD manuscript. Department of Sociology, University of Warwick.

Parker, Andrew. (1996b). Professional football club culture: Goffman, asylums and occupational socialization. Scottish Centre Research Papers in Sport, Leisure and Society 1. Moray House Institute of Education, Heriot-Watt University, Edinburgh, pp. 123–130.

Parker, Andrew. (2000a). Training for 'glory', schooling for 'failure'?: English professional football, traineeship and educational provision. *Journal of Education and Work*, 13, 61–76.

Parker, Andrew. (2000b). Masculinities and English professional football: youth traineeship, sub-cultural expectation and gender identity. In Walford, Geoffrey and Hudson, Caroline (eds). *Studies in Educational Ethnography (Genders and Sexualities in Educational Ethnography, Volume 3)*. Oxford: Emerald Group Publishing Limited, pp. 41–65.

Parker, Andrew. (2001). Soccer, servitude and sub-cultural identity: football traineeship and masculine construction. *Soccer & Society*, 2, 59–80.

Parker, Andrew. (2006). Lifelong learning to labour: apprenticeship, masculinity and communities of practice. *British Educational Research Journal*, 32, 687–701.

Parker, Andrew and Harris, John. (2009). Introduction: sport and social identities. In Harris, John and Parker, Andrew (eds). *Sport and Social Identities*. Basingstoke: Palgrave Macmillan, pp. 1–14.

Payne, Tom. (2009). *Fame: From the Bronze Age to Britney*. London: Vintage.

Pearson, Roberta. (2010). Fandom in the digital era. *Popular Communication*, 8, 84–95.

Peeters, Rens and Elling, Agnes. (2015). The coming of age of women's football in the Dutch sports media, 1995–2013. *Soccer & Society*, 16, 620–638.

Pegoraro, Ann, Ayer, Steven and O'Reilly, Norman. (2010). Consumer consumption and advertising through sport. *American Behavioural Scientist*, 53, 1454–1475.

Perry, Samuel. (2012). Racial habitus, moral conflict, and white moral hegemony within interracial evangelical organizations. *Qualitative Sociology*, 35, 89–108.

Perryman, Mark. (2001). Hooligan wars. In Perryman, Mark (ed.). *Hooligan Wars: Causes and Effects of Football Violence*. Edinburgh and London: Mainstream, pp. 13–33.

Peterson, Richard. (2005). Problems in comparative research: the example of omnivorousness. *Poetics*, 3, 257–282.

Pfister, Gertrud. (2012). It is never too late to win: sporting activities and performances of ageing women. *Sport in Society*, 3, 369–384.

Pfister, Gertrud, Fasting, Kari, Scraton, Sheila and Vázquez, Benilde. (2002). Women and football – a contradiction? The beginnings of women's football in four European countries. In Scraton, Sheila and Flintoff, Anne (eds). *Gender and Sport: A Reader*. London: Routledge, pp. 66–77.

Piderit, Sandy Kristin and Ashford, Susan J. (2003). Breaking silence: tactical choices women managers make in speaking up about gender-equity issues. *Journal of Management Studies*, 40, 1477–1502.

Pilz, Gunter A. (1996). Social factors influencing sport and violence: on the 'problem' of football hooliganism in Germany. *International Review for the Sociology of Sport*, 31, 49–66.

Pingue, Frank. (2015). Women's World Cup final draws record audience for football in

America as US beat Japan to seal third title in Canada. *Daily Mail*, 7 July. Available at: http://dailym.ai/1VMX9GH (accessed September 2015).

Piquero, Alex R., Jennings, Wesley G. and Farrington, David P. (2015). The life-course offending trajectories of football hooligans. *European Journal of Criminology*, 12, 113–125.

Pitchford, Andy, Brackenridge, Celia, Bringer, Joy D., Cockburn, Claudi, Nutt, Gareth, Pawlaczek, Zofia and Russell, Kate. (2004). Children in football: seen but not heard. *Soccer & Society*, 5, 43–60.

Platts, Chris and Smith, Andy. (2009). The education, rights and welfare of young people in professional football in England: some implications of the white paper in sport. *International Journal of Sport Policy*, 1, 323–339.

Podaliri, Carlo and Balestri, Carlo. (1998). The Ultràs, racism and football culture in Italy. In Brown, Adam (ed.). *Fanatics! Power, Identity and Fandom in Football*. London: Routledge, pp. 88–100.

Ponting, Ivan. (1996). Obituary: Neil Franklin. *Independent*, 10 February. Available at: http://ind.pn/1ORDjru (accessed September 2015).

Pope, Stacey and Kirk, David. (2014). The role of physical education and other formative experiences of three generations of female football fans. *Sport, Education and Society*, 19, 223–240.

Popplewell, Oliver Burry. (1986). *Committee of Inquiry into Crowd Safety and Control at Sports Grounds: Final Report*. London: HMSO. Available at: http://bit.ly/1Ht4st6 (accessed August 2015).

Potrac, Paul and Jones, Robyn L. (2011). Power in coaching. In Jones, Robyn L., Potrac, Paul, Cushion, Chris and Ronglan, Lars Tore (eds). *The Sociology of Sports Coaching*. London: Routledge, pp. 135–150.

Poulton, Emma. (2007). 'Fantasy football hooliganism' in popular media. *Media, Culture & Society*, 29, 151–164.

Poulton, Emma. (2012). 'If you had balls, you'd be one of us!' Doing gendered research: methodological reflections on being a female academic researcher in the hyper-masculine subculture of 'football hooliganism'. *Sociological Research Online* [Online], 17. Available at: http://bit.ly/1DZY16b (accessed August 2015).

Poulton, Emma. (2013). The culture of production behind the (re)production of football hooligan culture. *Continuum*, 27, 770–784.

Poulton, Emma. (2014). The hooligan film factory: football violence in high definition. In Hopkins, Matt and Treadwell, James (eds). *Football Hooliganism, Fan Behaviour and Crime: Contemporary Issues*. London: Palgrave Macmillan, pp. 154–175.

Poulton, Emma and Durell, Oliver. (2014). Uses and meanings of 'Yid' in English football fandom: a case study of Tottenham Hotspur Football Club. *International Review for the Sociology of Sport*. Available at: http://bit.ly/1NdJEhw (accessed August 2015).

Premier League. (2006). *2005/06 National Fan Survey Report*. London: Premier League. Available at: http://bit.ly/1RZPi5J (accessed November 2015).

Price, John, Farrington, Neil and Hall, Lee. (2013). Changing the game? The impact of Twitter on relationships between football clubs, supporters and the sports media. *Soccer & Society*, 14, 446–461.

Pullen, Alison and Rhodes, Carl. (2014). Corporeal ethics and the politics of resistance in organizations. *Organization*, 21, 782–796.

Purdy, Laura, Jones, Robyn L. and Cassidy, Tania. (2009). Negotiation and capital: athletes' use of power in an elite men's rowing program. *Sport, Education and Society*, 14, 321–338.

Purdy, Laura, Potrac, Paul and Jones, Robyn L. (2008). Power, consent and resistance: an autoethnography of competitive rowing. *Sport, Education and Society*, 13, 319–336.

Quinn, Brian. (2006). Soccer, glitter and corruption. *The Winston Lord Roundtable on*

*Asia, the Rule of Law and U.S. Foreign Policy.* New York: Council on Foreign Relations. Available at: http://bit.ly/1NRrpMS (accessed November 2015).

Randhawa, Kuljit. (2011). Marrying passion and professionalism: examining the future of British Asian football. In Burdsey, Daniel (ed.). *Race, Ethnicity and Football: Persisting Debates and Emergent Issues.* London: Routledge, pp. 237–250.

Redhead, Steve. (1991). *Football with Attitude.* Manchester: Wordsmith.

Redhead, Steve. (1997). *Post-Fandom and the Millennial Blues: The Transformation of Soccer Culture.* London: Routledge.

Redhead, Steve. (2004a). *The Paul Virilio Reader.* Edinburgh: Edinburgh University Press.

Redhead, Steve. (2004b). *Paul Virilio: Theorist for an Accelerated Culture.* Edinburgh: Edinburgh University Press.

Redhead, Steve. (2006). This sporting life: the realism of *The Football Factory. Soccer & Society,* 8, 90–108.

Redhead, Steve. (2007). Those absent from the stadium are always right: accelerated culture, sport media and theory at the speed of light. *Journal of Sport & Social Issues,* 31, 226–241.

Redhead, Steve. (2008). Firms, crews and soccer thugs: the slight return of football hooligan subcultures. In Atkinson, Michael and Young, Kevin (eds). *Tribal Play: Subcultural Journeys Through Sport.* Bingley: JAI Press, pp. 67–81.

Redhead, Steve. (2014). The firm: towards a study of 400 football gangs. *Sport in Society,* 18, 329–346.

Redmond, Sean. (2013). *Celebrity and the Media.* Basingstoke: Palgrave Macmillan.

Rees, Tony, Gibbons, Tom and Dixon, Kevin. (2014). The surveillance of racing cyclists in training: a Bourdieusian perspective. *Surveillance & Society,* 11, 466–480.

Rehling, Nichola. (2011). 'It's about belonging': masculinity, collectivity, and community in British hooligan films. *Journal of Popular Film & Television,* 39, 162–173.

Reiche, Danyel. (2014). Drivers behind corporate social responsibility in the professional football sector: a case study of the German Bundesliga. *Soccer & Society,* 15, 472–502.

Rein, Irving, Kotler, Philip and Shields, Ben. (2006). *The Elusive Fan.* New York: McGraw-Hill.

Relvas, Hugo, Littlewood, Martin, Nesti, Mark, Gilbourne, David and Richardson, David. (2010). Organizational structures and working practices in elite European professional football clubs: understanding the relationship between youth and professional domains. *European Sport Management Quarterly,* 10, 165–187.

Richards, Alex. (2014). Paris Saint-Germain sack two chefs as Zlatan Ibrahimovic 'complains about quality of food'. *Mirror,* 16 March. Available at: http://bit.ly/1hiT3Ya (accessed June 2015).

Richardson, Brendan. (2004). New consumers and football fandom: the role of social habitus in consumer behaviour. *The Irish Journal of Management,* 25, 88–100.

Riddell, Don and Knight, Matthew. (2014). Wilson Raj Perumal: the man who fixed football. *CNN Online,* 26 August. Available at: http://cnn.it/1Qck9O3 (accessed November 2015).

Rinke, Stefan. (2014). Globalizing football in times of crisis: the first World Cup in Uruguay in 1930. In Rinke, Stefan and Schiller, Kay (eds) *The Fifa World Cup 1930–2010: Politics, Commerce, Spectacle and Identities.* Göttingen: Wallstein Verlag, pp. 49–65.

Rinke, Stefan and Schiller, Kay. (2014). Introduction. In Rinke, Stefan and Schiller, Kay (eds). *The Fifa World Cup 1930–2010: Politics, Commerce, Spectacle and Identities.* Göttingen: Wallstein Verlag, pp. 9–14.

Rippon, Anton. (1981). *Great Soccer Clubs of the North East.* Nottingham: Moorland Publishing.

Robertson, Roland. (2000). *Globalization: Social Theory and Global Culture*. London: Sage.

Robins, David. (1984). *We Hate Humans*. London: Penguin.

Robinson, Jessica S. R. (2008). Tackling the anxieties of the English: searching for the nation through football. *Soccer & Society*, 9, 215–230.

Robson, Garry. (2000). *No One Likes Us, We Don't Care: The Myth and Reality of Millwall*. Oxford: Berg.

Roche, Maurice. (2000). *Mega-Events and Modernity*. London: Routledge.

Roderick, Martin. (2003). *Work, Self and the Transformation of Identity: A Sociological Study of the Careers of Professional Footballers*. Unpublished PhD thesis, University of Leicester.

Roderick, Martin. (2006a). *The Work of Professional Football: A Labour of Love?* London: Routledge.

Roderick, Martin. (2006b). Adding insult to injury: workplace injury in English professional football. *Sociology of Health and Illness*, 28, 76–97.

Roderick, Martin. (2006c). A very precarious profession: uncertainty in the working lives of professional footballers. *Work, Employment and Society*, 20, 245–265.

Roderick, Martin. (2012). An unpaid labour of love: professional footballers, family life and the problem of job relocation. *Journal of Sport & Social Issues*, 36, 317–338.

Roderick, Martin. (2014). From identification to dis-identification: case studies of job loss in professional football. *Qualitative Research in Sport, Exercise and Health*, 6, 143–160.

Roderick, Martin, Waddington, Ivan and Parker, Garry. (2000). Playing hurt: managing injuries in English professional football. *International Review for the Sociology of Sport*, 35, 165–180.

Rodriguez-Pomeda, Jesus, Casani, Fernando and Alonso-Almeida, Mar. (2014). Emotions' management within the Real Madrid football club business model. *Soccer & Society*, I-First, 1–14. Available at: http://bit.ly/1JNIur1 (accessed August 2015).

Ronay, Barney. (2015). Arrigo Sacchi: 'I'm not racist … but there are too many blacks in youth teams'. *Guardian*, 17 February. Available at: http://bit.ly/1EjWanW (accessed August 2015).

Rose, Nikolas. (1997). Identity, genealogy, history. In Hall, Stuart and du Gay, Paul (eds). *Questions of Cultural Identity*. London: Sage, pp. 128–150.

Roudakova, Natalia. (2008). Media-political clientelism: lessons from anthropology. *Media, Culture & Society*, 30, 41–59.

Roversi, Antonio. (1991). Football violence in Italy. *International Review for the Sociology of Sport*, 26, 311–331.

Rowe, David. (2004). *Sport, Culture and the Media: The Unruly Trinity*. Maidenhead: Open University Press.

Rowe, David and Baker, Stephanie Alice. (2012). 'Truly a fan experience'? The cultural politics of the live site. In Krøvel, Roy and Roksvold, Thore (eds). *We Love To Hate Each Other: Mediated Football Fan Culture*. Gothenburg: Nordicom, pp. 301–318.

Ruddock, Andy. (2005). Let's kick racism out of football – and the lefties too! Responses to Lee Bowyer on a West Ham web site. *Journal of Sport & Social Issues*, 9, 369–385.

Ruddock, Andy. (2012). Cultivation analysis and ritual theory. In Shanahan, James, Morgan, Michael and Signorelli, Nancy (eds). *Living with Television Now: Advances in Culturation Theory and Research*. New York: Peter Lang, pp. 366–385.

Ruddock, Andy. (2013). 'Born on Swan Street, next to the Yarra': online opinion leaders and inventing commitment. In Hutchins, Brett and Rowe, David (eds). *Digital Media Sport: Technology, Power and Culture in the Network Society*. London: Routledge, pp. 153–165.

Rumsby, Ben. (2014). Why threat of the Premier League's globetrotting 39th game refuses to go away. *Telegraph*, 29 October. Available at: http://bit.ly/1Qnp2Eb (accessed November 2015).

Russell, David. (1997). *Football and the English*. Preston: Carnegie Publications.

Saeed, Amir and Kilvington, Daniel. (2011). British Asians and racism within contemporary English football. *Soccer & Society*, 12, 600–610.

Sage, George H. and Eitzen, Stanley. (2013). *Sociology of North American Sport*. New York: Oxford University Press.

Salazar-Sutil, Nicolás. (2008). Maradona Inc.: performance politics off the pitch. *International Journal of Cultural Studies*, 11, 441–458.

Sallaz, Jeffrey. (2010). Talking race, marketing culture: the racial habitus in and out of apartheid. *Social Problems*, 57, 294–314.

Sandvoss, Cornel. (2003). *A Game of Two Halves: Football, Television and Globalization*. London: Routledge.

Sanghani, Radhika. (2014). Charlie Webster: 'I don't want kids to cheer on rapist footballer Ched Evans as a hero'. *Telegraph*, 21 October. Available at: http://bit.ly/1NGhbAb (accessed October 2015).

Sassenberg, Anne-Marie. (2015). Effects of sport celebrity transgressions: an exploratory study. *Sport Marketing Quarterly*, 24, 78–90.

Schausteck de Almeida, Barbara, Bolsmann, Chris, Marchi Junior, Wanderley and de Souza, Juliano. (2015). Rationales, rhetoric and realities: FIFA's World Cup in South Africa 2010 and Brazil 2014. *International Review for the Sociology of Sport*, 50, 265–282.

Schor, Juliet. (2007). Conspicuous consumption. *Blackwell Encyclopedia of Sociology*. Oxford: Blackwell Reference Online.

Scott, Matt. (2015). Special report: Greek corruption 'cancer' reaches the heart of 'The System'. *Inside World Football*, 30 April. Available at: http://bit.ly/1DEssYq (accessed August 2015).

Scraton, Phil. (2004). Death on the terraces: the contexts and injustices of the 1989 Hillsborough disaster. *Soccer & Society*, 5, 183–200.

Sefiha, Ophir. (2012). Bad sports: explaining sport related deviance. *Sociology Compass*, 6, 949–961.

Settimi, Christina. (2014). The world's highest-paid soccer players. *Forbes*, 7 May. Available at: http://onforb.es/1JcguhS (accessed August 2015).

Sharpe, Graham. (2015). Football's first major match fixing scandal. *Daily Express*, 1 April. Available at: http://bit.ly/1NtQZJs (accessed August 2015).

Sheringham, Sam. (2015). Genovena Anonma: 'I had to strip naked to prove I was a woman'. BBC Sport, 14 January. Available at: http://bbc.in/14yrWkv (accessed October 2015).

Sherman, Len. (1992). *Big League, Big Time: The Birth of the Arizona Diamondbacks, the Billion-Dollar Business of Sports, and the Power of the Media in America*. New York: Basic Books.

Shogan, Debra. (1999). *The Making of High-Performance Athletes: Discipline, Diversity, and Ethics*. Toronto, ON: University of Toronto Press.

Sissener, Tone. (2001). Anthropological perspectives on corruption. Michelsen Institute: Development Studies and Human Rights. Available at: http://bit.ly/1kcnSiD (accessed November 2015).

Skinner, James, Zakus, Dwight and Edwards, Allan. (2008). Coming in from the margins: ethnicity, community support and the rebranding of Australian soccer. *Soccer & Society*, 9, 394–404.

Sloane, Peter J. (1971). The economics of professional football: the football club as a utility maximiser. *Scottish Journal of Political Economy*, 17, 121–146.

Smit, Barbara. (2006). *Pitch Invasion: Adidas, Puma and the Making of Modern Sport*. London: Allen Lane.

Smith, Aaron and Stewart, Bob. (2007). The travelling fan: understanding the mechanisms of sport fan consumption in a sport tourism setting. *Journal of Sport and Tourism*, 12, 155–181.

Smith, Aaron and Stewart, Bob. (2010). The special features of sports: a critical re-visit. *Sport Management Review*, 13, 1–13.

Smith, Chris. (2014) The biggest sponsors of Brazil's 2014 World Cup spend big to engage with fans. *Forbes*, 12 June. Available at: http://onforb.es/1NoIfV0 (accessed November 2015).

Smith, Michael D. (1983). *Violence and Sport*. Toronto, ON: Butterworth.

Snowball, Ben. (2015). Fuming female fan almost blinds referee after 'throwing hot tea in his face'. *Eurosport UK*, 6 April. Available at: http://yhoo.it/1IX1rWd (accessed June 2015).

Solomos, John and Back, Les. (1996). *Racism and Society*. London: Macmillan.

Spaaij, Ramon. (2006). *Understanding Football Hooliganism: A Comparison of Six Western European Football Clubs*. Amsterdam: Amsterdam University Press.

Spaaij, Ramon. (2007a). Football hooliganism as a transnational phenomenon: past and present analysis: a critique – more specificity and less generality. *The International Journal of the History of Sport*, 24, 411–431.

Spaaij, Ramon. (2007b). Football hooliganism in the Netherlands: patterns of continuity and change. *Soccer & Society*, 8, 316–334.

Spaaij, Ramon. (2008). Men like us, boys like them: violence, masculinity, and collective identity in football hooliganism. *Journal of Sport & Social Issues*, 32, 369–392.

Spaaij, Ramon. (2011). Mindless thugs running riot? Mainstream, alternative and online media representations of football crowd violence. *Media International Australia, Incorporating Culture & Policy*, 3, 126–136.

Spaaij, Ramon and Viñas, Carles. (2005). Passion, politics and violence: a socio-historical analysis of Spanish ultras. *Soccer & Society*, 6, 79–96.

Stanko, Elizabeth A. (2003). Introduction: conceptualising the meanings of violence. In Stanko, Elizabeth A. (ed.). *The Meanings of Violence*. London: Routledge, pp. 1–13.

Stone, Chris. (2007). The role of football in everyday life. *Soccer & Society*, 8, 169–184.

Strozek, Przenyslaw. (2015). Off-field spectacle: Polish contemporary art and the national game (1921–2012). *Soccer & Society*, I-First, 1–21. Available at: http://bit.ly/1SSY6zb (accessed August 2015).

Sugden, John and Tomlinson, Alan. (1998). *Fifa and the Contest of World Football: Who Rules the People's Game*. Cambridge: Polity Press.

Sugden, John and Tomlinson, Alan. (1999). *Great Balls of Fire: How Big Money Is Hijacking World Football*. Edinburgh and London: Mainstream.

Sugden, John and Tomlinson, Alan. (2003). *Badfellas: Fifa Family at War*. Edinburgh and London: Mainstream.

*Sunday Herald*. (2011). The insanity of this ban had to be exposed. 24 May. Available at: http://bit.ly/1Pf3TfV (accessed June 2015).

*Sunday Times* Insight team (Claire Newell, Jonathan Calvert, Solvej Krause and Cecile Schoon). (2010a). World Cup 'votes for sale' scandal escalates. *Sunday Times*, 24 October, p. 1; World Cup fixer reveals network of corruption, p. 1.; What a timid way to tackle corruption, p. 22.

*Sunday Times* Insight team (Claire Newell, Jonathan Calvert, Solvej Krause and Cecile Schoon). (2010b). Fifa boss digs in heels over corruption: Sepp Blatter has little support as he cries foul over the cash for votes affair. *Sunday Times*, 31 October, p. 9.

*Sunday Times* Insight team (Claire Newell, Jonathan Calvert, Solvej Krause and Cecile Schoon). (2010c). Fifa in new bribes claim. *Sunday Times*, 5 December, pp. 1 and 2.

Sweetman, Paul. (2003). Twenty-first century dis-ease? Habitual reflexivity or the reflexive habitus. *Sociological Review*, 51, 528–549.

Sweney, Mark. (2010). Southampton FC continues photography ban. *Guardian*, 10 August. Available at: http://bit.ly/1WF66jP (accessed June 2015).

Szymanski, Stefan and Kuypers, Tim. (1999). *Winners and Losers: The Business Strategy of Football*. London: Penguin.

Tabner, Brian. (2002). *Football through the Turnstiles … Again*. Bath: Bookcraft.

Taylor, Ian. (1971a). Soccer consciousness and soccer hooliganism. In Cohen, Stanley (ed.). *Images of Deviance*. London: Pelican, pp. 135–164.

Taylor, Ian. (1971b). Football mad: a speculative sociology of football hooliganism. *The Sociology of Sport*, 4, 357–377.

Taylor, Ian. (1976). Spectator violence around football: the rise and fall of the 'working-class weekend'. *Research Papers in Physical Education*, 4, 4–9.

Taylor, Matthew. (2008). *The Association Game: A History of British Football*. London: Pearson Longman.

Taylor, Peter. (1990). *The Hillsborough Stadium Disaster, 15 April 1989: Final Report*. London: HMSO. Available at: http://bit.ly/1McDNJ1 (accessed August 2015).

Taylor, Rogan. (1992). *Football and Its Fans: Supporters and Their Relationship with the Game, 1885–1985*. Leicester: Leicester University Press.

*Telegraph* (2015). Cutting-edge technology moves sport into the digital age. 13 May. Available at: http://bit.ly/1A31e2w (accessed August 2015).

Testa, Alberto and Armstrong, Gary. (2010). *Football, Fascism and Fandom: The Ultras of Italian Football*. London: A & C Black Publishers Ltd.

Thompson, Andrew, Potrac, Paul and Jones, Robyn L. (2015). 'I found out the hard way': micro-political workings in professional football. *Sport, Education and Society*, 20, 976–994.

Thorne, Barrie. (1993). *Gender Play: Girls and Boys in School*. Buckingham: Open University Press.

Thorpe, Holly. (2010). Bourdieu, gender reflexivity, and physical culture: a case of masculinities in the snowboarding field. *Journal of Sport & Social Issues*, 34, 176–214.

Thorpe, Simon. (2004). Pick the best, forget the rest? Training field dilemmas and children's football at the turn of the century. In Wagg, Steve (ed.). *British Football and Social Exclusion: Sport in the Global Society*. London: Routledge, pp. 224–241.

*Times*. (1913a). Alleged attempt to bribe football captain. 12 December, p. 5.

*Times*. (1913b). Alleged attempts to bribe football captains. 31 December, p. 56.

*Times*. (1919). Alleged attempt to bribe football player. 25 January, p. 6.

*Times*. (1924). Attempt to bribe football team. 25 June, p. 11.

*Times*. (1932). Attempt to bribe a football player. 24 February, p. 4.

*Times*. (1974). News in brief. 9 February, p. 5.

*Times*. (1985). Bulgarian football cheats get long prison sentences. 14 December, p. 7.

Tischler, Steven. (1981). *Footballers and Businessmen: The Origins of Professional Soccer in England*. New York: Holmes & Meier.

Tomlinson, Alan. (1983). Tuck up tight lads: structures of control within football culture. In Tomlinson, Alan (ed.). *Explorations in Football Culture*. Eastbourne: Leisure Studies Association Publications, pp. 149–174.

Tomlinson, Alan. (2014a). Fifa: beginnings, tensions and trajectories. In Rinke, Stefan and Schiller, Kay (eds). *The Fifa World Cup 1930–2010: Politics, Commerce, Spectacle and Identities*. Göttingen: Wallstein Verlag, pp. 30–49.

Tomlinson, Alan. (2014b). *Fifa: The Men, The Myths and the Money.* London: Routledge.

Tomlinson, Alan and Young, Christopher (eds). (2006). *National Identity and Global Sports Events: Culture, Politics and Spectacle in the Olympics and the Football World Cup.* Albany, NY: State University of New York Press.

Turner, Graeme. (2004). *Understanding Celebrity.* London: Sage.

Turner, Mark. (2014). From local heroism to global celebrity stardom: a critical reflection of the social cultural and political changes in British football culture from the 1950s to the formation of the Premier League. *Soccer & Society*, 15, 751–760.

Turvill, William. (2015). Andrew Jennings: apart from *Panorama* and *Sunday Times*, UK coverage of wrongdoing at FIFA has been 'appalling'. *Press Gazette*, 5 June. Available at: http://bit.ly/1HPChoR (accessed October 2015).

Uefa. (2014). *Women's Football across the Nations 2013/14.* Available at: http://uefa.to/1Np5T4r (accessed September 2015).

Uefa. (2015). *Women's Football across the Nations 2014/15.* Available at: http://uefa.to/193eYel (accessed September 2015).

Unlucan, Dogan. (2015). Jersey sponsor in football/soccer: the industry classification of main jersey sponsors of 1147 football/soccer clubs in top leagues of 79 countries. *Soccer & Society*, 16, 42–62.

Upadhyay, Yogesh and Singh, Shiv Kumar. (2010). When sports celebrity doesn't perform: how consumers react to celebrity endorsement. *Vision: The Journal of Business Perspective*, 14, 67–78.

Vamplew, Wray. (1988). *Pay Up and Play the Game: Professional Sport in Britain, 1875–1914.* Cambridge: Cambridge University Press.

Van der Brug, H. (1994). Football hooliganism in the Netherlands. In Giulianotti, Richard, Bonney, Norman and Hepworth, Mike (eds). *Football, Violence and Social Identity.* London: Routledge, pp. 174–195.

Van Dijk, Teun. (2004). Racist discourse. In Cashmore, Ellis (ed.). *Encyclopedia of Race and Ethnic Studies.* London: Routledge, pp. 351–355.

Van Wijk, Jim. (2015) Football League 'Rooney Rule': Kick It Out praises decision to look at ways to increase Black, Asian and Minority Ethnic managers. *Independent*, 5 June. Available at: http://ind.pn/1E0Og7t (accessed August 2015).

Varul, Matthias. (2007). Leisure class. *Blackwell Encyclopedia of Sociology.* Oxford: Blackwell Reference Online.

Veblen, Thorstein. (1925 [1899]). *The Theory of the Leisure Class: An Economic Study of Institutions.* New York: Mentor.

Viñas, Carles. (2005). *El mundo ultra: Los radicales del fútbol español.* Madrid: Temas de hoy.

Vincent, John and Harris, John. (2014). 'They think it's all Dover!' Popular newspaper narratives and images about the English football team and (re)presentations of national identity during Euro 2012. *Soccer & Society*, 15, 222–240.

Vincent, John and Hill, John. (2011). Flying the flag for the En-ger-land: the *Sun's* (re)construction of English identity during the 2010 World Cup. *Journal of Sport & Tourism*, 16, 187–209.

Vincent, John, Hill, John S. and Lee, Jason W. (2009). The multiple brand personalities of David Beckham: a case study of the Beckham brand. *Sport Marketing Quarterly*, 18, 173–180.

Wacquant, Loïc. (2004). *Body and Soul.* Oxford: Oxford University Press.

Wade, Peter. (2010). *Race and Ethnicity in Latin America* (2nd edition). London: Pluto Press.

Walvin, James. (1994). *The People's Game: The History of Football Revisited.* Edinburgh and London: Mainstream.

Wann, Daniel, Melnick, Merrill J., Russell, Gordon W. and Pease, Dale G. (2001). *Sports Fans: The Psychology and Social Impact of Spectators.* New York: Routledge.

Ward, Pete. (2010). *Gods Behaving Badly: Media, Religion, and Celebrity Culture*. London: SCM Press.

Ward, Vicky. (2005). The beautiful and the damned. *Vanity Fair*, 30 November. Available at: http://bit.ly/1YxVEgL

Warde, Alan. (2005). Consumption and theories of practice. *Journal of Consumer Culture*, 5, 131–153.

Warde, Alan and Gayo-Cal, Modesto. (2009). The anatomy of cultural omnivorousness: the case of the United Kingdom. *Poetics*, 37, 119–145.

Warren, Dan. (2006). The worst scandal of them all. *BBC Sport*, 14 July. Available at: http://bbc.in/1Hq2ZDG (accessed August 2015).

Waterfield, Bruno. (2013). Dutch teenagers and father jailed for kicking linesman to death. *Telegraph*, 17 June. Available at: http://bit.ly/1hjingO (accessed June 2015).

Weed, Mike. (2006). The story of an ethnography: the experience of watching the 2002 World Cup in the pub. *Soccer & Society*, 7, 76–95.

Weed, Mike. (2007). The pub as a virtual football fandom venue: an alternative to 'being there'? *Soccer & Society*, 8, 399–414.

Weed, Mike. (2008). Exploring the sport spectator experience: virtual sport spectatorship in the pub. *Soccer & Society*, 9, 189–197.

Weinberg, Ben. (2015). *Asia and the Future of Football: The Role of the Asian Football Confederation*. London: Routledge.

West Nally (n.d.). The Coca-Cola football story. Available at: http://bit.ly/1XPsucP (accessed November 2015).

White, Jim. (1995). The most lucrative kick of his life. *Independent*, 8 April. Available at: http://ind.pn/1O5JypO (accessed July 2015).

White, Jim. (2006). Undercover bungs sting was almost rumbled before it began. *Telegraph*, 16 September. Available at: http://bit.ly/1Q5lreA (accessed November 2015).

Widdop, Paul, Cutts, David and Jarvie, Grant. (2014). Omnivorousness in sport: the importance of social capital and networks. *International Review for the Sociology of Sport*, I-First, 1–24. Available at: http://bit.ly/1MRHFyi (accessed August 2015).

Wigglesworth, Neil. (1996). *The Evolution of English Sport*. London: Frank Cass.

Williams, Jean. (2007). *A Beautiful Game: International Perspectives on Women's Football*. Oxford: Berg.

Williams, Jean. (2011). *Women's Football, Europe and Professionalization 1971–2011*. Uefa Research Report. Available at: http://bit.ly/1hWkyX4 (accessed September 2015).

Williams, John. (1997). The 'New Football' in England and Sir John Hall's new 'Geordie Nation'. In Gehrmann, Siegfried (ed.). *Football and Regional Identity in Europe*. Munster: Lit Verlag, pp. 243–278.

Williams, John. (2003). The fastest growing sport? Women and football in England. *Soccer & Society*, 4, 112–127.

Williams, John. (2007). Rethinking sports fandom: the case of European soccer. *Leisure Studies*, 26, 127–146.

Williams, John, Dunning, Eric and Murphy, Patrick. (1984). *Hooligans Abroad: The Behaviour and Control of English Fans in Continental Europe*. London: Routledge.

Williams, John, Dunning, Eric and Murphy, Patrick. (1989). *Hooligans Abroad: The Behaviour and Control of English Fans in Continental Europe* (2nd edition). London: Routledge.

Williams, Shaun and Manley, Andrew. (2014). Elite coaching and the technocratic engineer: thanking the boys at Microsoft! *Sport, Education and Society*, DOI: 10.1080/13573322.2014.958116.

Willis, Paul. (1977). *Learning to Labour: How Working Class Kids Get Working Class Jobs*. Westmead: Saxon House.

Willis, Paul. (1990). *Common Culture: Symbolic Work at Play in the Everyday Cultures of the Young.* Milton Keynes: Open University Press.

Willsher, Kim and Martin, Marie-Helene. (2014). Helena Costa: I walked from Clermont Foot 63 after being sidelined by men. *Guardian*, 25 June. Available at: http://bit.ly/1lYE1GZ (accessed August 2015).

Wilson, Paul. (2011). Barcelona play by Fifa's new rules and English clubs must wise up. *Guardian*, 5 June. Available at: http://bit.ly/1NBeMV7 (accessed June 2015).

Winterburn, S. (1998). Geared up for a festive season. *Guardian*, 19 December, p. 11.

Wood, Graham. (2015). Owner of Greek champions banned over corruption probe. *Reuters*, 18 June. Available at: http://reut.rs/1eqtiDY (accessed November 2015).

Wright, Simon. (2015). Ched Evans rape victim 'outed' online again as foreign news website posts her picture. *Mirror*, 31 January. Available at: http://bit.ly/1Ww8yJi (accessed November 2015).

Yallop, David. (1999). *How They Stole the Game.* London: Poetic Publishing.

Zaitch, Damian and de Leeuw, Tom. (2010). Fighting with images: the production and consumption of violence among online football supporters. In Hayward, Keith and Presdee, Mike (eds). *Framing Crime: Cultural Criminology and the Image.* London: Routledge, pp. 172–188.

# INDEX